AWKWARD DOMINION

AWKWARD DOMINION

American Political, Economic, and Cultural
Relations with Europe, 1919–1933

FRANK COSTIGLIOLA

CORNELL UNIVERSITY PRESS

ITHACA AND LONDON

First published 1984 by Cornell University Press.
Published in the United Kingdom by
Cornell University Press Ltd., London.
International Standard Book Number 0-8014-1679-5
Library of Congress Catalog Card Number 84-45150
Printed in the United States of America
Librarians: Library of Congress cataloging information
appears on the last page of the book.

The paper in this book is acid-free and meets the guidelines
for permanence and durability of the Committee on Production
Guidelines for Book Longevity of the Council on Library Resources.

The picture on the dust jacket is the cover of a petition sent by Hungarian postal workers to President Herbert Hoover in 1932.

For my parents,
Umberto Costigliola and Nancy Costigliola,
who made it possible.
And for Jennifer, who makes it worthwhile.

Contents

Preface

The Depression and Second World War, which demolished the 1920s dream of peace and prosperity, also discredited the decade's foreign policy. In 1941 Henry Luce, publisher of *Time* and *Life* and prophet of an American century, dismissed 1920s diplomacy as "bungled." The winners write the history. Post–World War II advocates of global American involvement proudly contrasted their worldliness with the naiveté of 1919–33. Unlike leaders of the interwar years, policymakers after 1945 believed an American solution, often a military one, existed for most international problems. Most historians applauded post–World War II foreign policy as the mature assumption of global responsibility.

For many of us that easy confidence—along with much else—was lost in Vietnam. Developments in the 1960s and 1970s undermined the assumptions and the reality of the American Century. The winners of post-1945 were at least partly discredited. Along with other historians, I became interested in an earlier era, when the American dominion was more restrained and less militaristic. A wealth of new manuscript sources that made for exciting research also attracted scholars to the 1919–33 period. For me, the era was especially intriguing because of its cultural efflorescence and the network of links between culture, economics, and politics.

The product of these developments and interests is a multidimensional work, based on manuscript sources and secondary literature, that examines America's political, economic, and cultural relations with Europe from 1919 to 1933. The protagonists of the story include Ernest Hemingway and Henry Ford along with Herbert Hoover and Charles Hughes. The plot reveals the flawed genius in a policy that promoted American interests in Europe while protecting against unwanted entanglements.

Proud of the nation's economic might, societal success, and demon-

9

strated military potential, American leaders were nonetheless cautious in their exercise of power overseas. Although sophisticated in their understanding of the limits of power, policymakers were simplistic in their conviction that private enterprise and minimal government intervention could safeguard world prosperity. They responded to the explosive issues of the Versailles treaty, economic recovery, and cultural modernization with moderate solutions compatible, they believed, with both American interests and international stability. Chapters 1, 3, and 4 analyze these efforts to build a stable world order. The second chapter examines the domestic roots of foreign policy, and the fifth and sixth describe the business and cultural relations that flowered in the 1920s.

As Chapters 7 and 8 demonstrate, the American-dominated order proved inadequate to deal with the Depression and the rise of Nazism. But failure to contain the revolutionary upheavals of their time does not especially distinguish these leaders from other American foreign-policymakers in the twentieth century. Nor were policymakers of the 1920s unique in their overconfidence that private international loans could support the world economy. What does set them apart is the sensitivity they displayed to the dangers of overweening power, a sensitivity that guaranteed against perilous crusades. Ironically, their caution also ensured that American predominance would be limited and at times ineffectual, what Reinhold Niebuhr in 1930 called "awkward" dominion.

This book had a long gestation, and through the years I have received help and encouragement from many people. My analysis builds on the work of many excellent historians, especially William Appleman Williams, N. Gordon Levin, Werner Link, Carl Parrini, Robert Van Meter, Warren Susman, Michael Hogan, Charles Maier, Stephen Schuker, Sally Marks, Joan Hoff Wilson, Ellis Hawley, and Robert F. Smith. Friends and colleagues who offered valuable criticism include Melvyn Leffler, Lloyd Gardner, Robert Seidel, Dave Millar, James Findlay, Maury Klein, Gino Silvestri, Luther Spoehr, and Frederick Adams. Barbara Oertel helped with the early research. Heywood Fleisig inducted me into the mysteries of international finance. I am also indebted to a diverse group of people who inspired me to become a scholar or who supported me in their individual ways: Belle Rhodes, John W. Bristow, Nell Strippoli, Lorraine Postal, David Ellis, Richard Polenberg, Mack Walker, Carrol and Lovira Stedman, Joel Cohen, Barry Marks, Helen Norton Schabowsky, Charles Costigliola, and especially Margaret Ann Menzies. Judith Sealander has sustained me in many ways.

Many archivists and librarians cheerfully responded to what must have appeared interminable requests. Carl Backlund at the Federal Reserve

Bank of New York, Sven Welander at the United Nations Library, Nancy Bressler at Princeton, and Robert Wood at the Herbert Hoover Presidential Library were particularly helpful. The University of Rhode Island Library's interlibrary loan staff, Vicki Burnett, Sylvia Krausse, and Roberta Doran, performed far beyond the call of duty, as did Stephen Rollins, Marie Rudd, and Mimi Keefe at circulation. Especially gracious and hospitable were Everett N. Case and Josephine Young Case, custodians of the Owen D. Young papers. I am similarly grateful to Amory Houghton, Sr., and Amory Houghton, Jr., for access to the Alanson B. Houghton papers. The research for this book was facilitated by generous financial support from Cornell University, the University of Rhode Island, and the National Endowment for the Humanities. A battery of typists devoted significant portions of their careers to typing the manuscript: Althea Smith, Rachel Doctor, Louise Hilliard, Gail Cunningham, and Nancy Alling. I owe special thanks to Anne Lunt for superb copy editing and to Lawrence Malley and Kay Scheuer for skillfully shepherding the manuscript toward publication.

My greatest debt, however, is to Walter LaFeber. It is difficult to categorize the many things he has done for me and for the book. His scholarship, teaching, and personality have been the major inspiration of my career. Professor LaFeber is that rare person who combines the highest professional standards with personal warmth and concern for others. He oversaw this project's development from a seminar paper to a doctoral dissertation to—after many revisions—its present form. Although its faults are assuredly mine, its value owes much to him.

FRANK COSTIGLIOLA

Hopkinton City, Rhode Island

AWKWARD DOMINION

Introduction

The United States emerged from the Great War as the world's leading nation. With its economic superiority, cultural vigor, and demonstrated military potential, America enjoyed influence in virtually every European corner, in the Old World's chancelleries, countinghouses, and even coffeehouses. This influence gave the United States important, but not unlimited, power in Europe. This book examines the subtle texture of a time when many Europeans tailored their production consumption, entertainment, art, and thought on American models. It looks too at the more easily discernible pattern of relations among diplomats and businessmen. While recognizing the tactical differences among U.S. leaders, it focuses on the working American consensus which confronted Europeans.

The intent of this book is to examine United States-European relations in their broadest context. Such multidimensional analysis offers a fresh perspective on the traditional political and economic issues of the 1919-33 era. It reveals the cultural as well as political and economic aspects of the European response to American power, and highlights the cultural influence that, in transmuted form, persisted after that power withered during the Great Depression. America's cultural prestige was a key element in the atmosphere of political and economic relations. This inclusive analysis is essential to understanding the achievement and failures of the post–World War I years.

In the quarter-century following the Great Crash, many historians wrote the 1920s off as a decade of amusing antics, precarious prosperity, and isolationist diplomacy.[1] One example of such an approach is Frederick Lewis Allen's *Only Yesterday*,[2] published in the midst of the Depression, which poked fun at a silly decade of flat-chested flappers, narrow-minded businessmen, and tight-fisted diplomats. All this, Allen suggested, especially when mixed with bathtub gin, had to end in a crash. Though his focus was broad, Allen denigrated the achievements of the 1920s.

However historians evaluate the years 1919–33, they must come to grips with the period's central force: political, economic, and cultural upheaval. That systemic instability has often blinded historians to the real accomplishments of the era. Much of the recent historical literature performs a valuable corrective by considering the decade on its own terms, as a period of relative peace and prosperity. These works remind us that most Americans and Europeans of the 1920s believed they could avoid the catastrophes of war and depression. To disparage the 1920s as a period of "false" prosperity and peace because those happy conditions did not endure is to distort history. Certainly the economic and political collapse in the Great Depression evidenced a terrible failure. Yet it is impossible to show how the disaster could have been avoided. By 1929 it was probably beyond the power of the United States to save the international order short of massive intervention—something neither Americans nor Europeans would have tolerated. Moreover, the dissolution of post–World War II prosperity should make us more humble and sympathetic in our criticism of those who were unable to preserve post–World War I prosperity.

And yet we cannot forget how short the post–World War I economic expansion was, lasting only from 1924 to 1929. In Europe the pinch began in 1928. Basic economic conditions change from era to era, but certainly this prosperity was fleeting when compared to the pre–World War I or the post–World War II years. Similarly, the relative international political stability achieved in 1924–25 collapsed by 1931–32, as compared to much longer eras of relative political constancy in Europe before 1914 and after 1948. Finally, there was cultural turbulence in Europe and America during the 1919–33 period. This change was sometimes more subtle than that in the political and economic realms and did not fall neatly within specific dates, but it affected how people—leaders and lesser folk—worked, played, created, thought, and spoke.

Thus, in the areas of politics, economics, and culture the period 1919–33 exhibited dramatic upheaval. Although change is endemic to all historical eras, 1919–33 was a particularly unstable period in American-European affairs.

In the political realm, instability emerged from the Versailles, St. Germain, and Trianon treaties which made up the 1919 peace settlement. The key point was that these treaties *were* an international issue, an object of debate and struggle that ended only with the outbreak of war in 1939. The treaties imposed a settlement that the defeated nations—Germany, Austria, and Hungary—did not accept and that three of the four main victors—the United States, Great Britain, and Italy—soon saw as at least partially unwise and unsatisfactory. In opposition to the defeated nations, which wanted to overthrow the treaties, France and its eastern allies—Poland, Czechoslovakia, and Rumania—sought to preserve the 1919 settlement.

American pressures and sympathies, both official and unofficial, lay toward moderate treaty revision. Most Americans opposed a total overthrow of Versailles. They did not want to see Germany free of all fetters, nor did they appreciate any change, political, economic or social, that was drastic and destabilizing. Yet the peace treaties were too harsh, many Americans believed, and hampered integration of the defeated powers, particularly Germany, into a stable, prosperous, and peaceful Europe. Although the United States refused to form political alliances with Europeans after 1919, it consistently favored slow, moderate peace treaty revision that would ease the burdens on Germany. In the reparations conferences of 1924 and 1929, the unofficial American representatives who dominated the proceedings substantially transformed reparations from a club with which to beat Germany to a contractual debt owed by Germany. In 1924, at American and British insistence, France reluctantly relinquished its right under Versailles to march into Germany in case of reparations default. Americans encouraged Europeans to accept Germany into the Locarno Pacts and the League of Nations. In 1931, President Herbert Hoover and Secretary of State Henry L. Stimson went so far as to urge the French to pressure their Polish ally to revise the Polish corridor in Germany's favor.

Americans strongly favored European disarmament. Hence in the 1920s they sympathized with a largely disarmed Germany and suspected highly armed France. But when in 1932 the Germans pressed for the right to rearm, in violation of Versailles, America backed French opposition.

This American solution of peaceful change, of moderate Versailles revision, fit with the Progressive reform tradition such policymakers as Herbert Hoover and Charles E. Hughes carried with them into the postwar years. Like the Progressives of the previous decade, makers of American foreign policy in the 1920s sought stability and order through slow reform that would give repressed groups (workers in the 1910s, Germans in the 1920s) a stake in the improved, fairer system.

American leaders opposed sudden overthrow of the peace treaties just as they opposed socialist revolution at home or anywhere else. Taken in its widest context, the policy of peaceful change was part of America's effort throughout the twentieth century to combat revolutionary upheaval with moderate reform. Pacifying and rebuilding Germany was integral to containing the Bolshevik revolution. Bolshevik Russia presented both a symbolic and a substantive threat to the peaceful change alternative. Most American leaders viewed the Soviet Union as revolution incarnate, despite Moscow's caution and conservatism. If Germany's political and economic structure collapsed, its people, Americans feared, might in desperation forge a Russian alliance to overthrow both Versailles and capitalism. Their very opposition to revolution led Hoover, Hughes, and other American leaders to combat the French policy of rigidly enforcing Versailles, which would only build up pressures for change until they exploded in revolutionary upheaval.

This emphasis on stability meant, however, that when presented with the stark choice of rigid order or drastic change, Americans generally chose the former. For example, when confronted in 1932 with Germany's more insistent revisionary demands, Washington officials tilted from Berlin to Paris. This conservative bias in the peaceful change policy paralleled Americans' reaction to European domestic upheavals. Here again Americans preferred the middle road of democratic capitalism. Yet when faced with the options of revolutionary socialism or fascist order, Americans consistently picked the latter. The United States maintained cordial relations with Benito Mussolini, funding Italy's war debt on favorable terms, allowing private bankers to make large loans, and cooperating closely in 1931 on disarmament and political issues. Similarly, United States representatives welcomed a right-wing takeover in Bulgaria in 1923. In contrast to the good relations with Fascist Italy, the United States refused to recognize Soviet Russia, forbade long-term loans, and awaited the Communists' fall. Until Adolf Hitler came to power in January 1933, the United States government feared the Nazis as a revolutionary force, finding parallels between Hitler and Lenin rather than between Hitler and Mussolini. Nevertheless, despite this readiness to swing to the right, Americans preferred the middle solution of orderly moderation, as the Progressives defined their position, whether in Europe's domestic or foreign policy matters.

Confronted with disorder in the European and world economies, the United States responded with a solution parallel to the political answer of peaceful change. Orderly growth in the international capitalist economy, Americans believed, would reduce political tensions and the threat of revolution while expanding markets and investment opportunities for United States business. Although the United States carefully measured its political entanglements in Europe, its economic involvement was broad and deep. In the 1920s, moreover, economics and business enjoyed enormous popular prestige in both America and Europe. For reasons of conviction and of expedience, the United States government approached basically political questions such as reparations from an economic or business perspective. This economic emphasis was particularly suited to American policy's decentralized implementation and to its goal of a prosperous Europe. By 1923–24, government officials, central bankers, and top private businessmen forged a loose alliance. Although tactical differences often separated these leaders, they usually cooperated enough to present Europeans with a united front on war debt, loan, and other issues.

Before the crash, Americans pressed the Europeans to adopt the international gold standard, reduce government expenditures, and fund war debts and reparations. This financial program, the Yankees believed, would lay the foundation for Europe's recovery and reestablish an orderly flow of goods and capital. Responding to American and internal pressures, most European governments adopted the gold standard in the 1920s. This move boosted both international business and the power of America's huge gold reserve, but also burdened the world economy with a rigid monetary system that probably depressed prices. Similar consequences followed from American efforts to impose order upon the chaos of war debts and reparations. Under U.S. prodding, by 1929 the Allies and Germany settled these political debts on a fixed, reduced basis. This helped stabilize the world credit system, but the rigid debt settlements, like the rigid gold standard, proved brittle in the Depression.

Unfortunately America's formulas for orderly change proved unable in the early 1920s to cope with the accelerated pace of German revisionism or the decelerated pace of the world economy. Indeed United States policy may have contributed somewhat to the debacles by reviving Germany and rigidifying the financial structure.

These political and economic relations can only be understood in their cultural context. The term *culture* is here comprehensively defined to include high culture such as literature, painting, and formal music; popular entertainment forms such as jazz, dancing, film, and sports; mundane matters such as household appliances, foods, and gadgets; more abstract concerns such as religion, philosophy, and language; attitudes toward work, play, money, and war; and finally technological innovations that had sociological implications, such as increased emphasis on machines, statistics, and mass assembly-line production.

Europeans interpreted virtually every manifestation of American culture, whether it was music, films, or automobiles, as the product of a society dominated by technology and the machine. America's technological superiority, moreover, made other aspects of its culture more attractive to Europeans. And it was this technological influence that persisted in Europe after the fad for Americana faded in the Great Depression. In virtually every cultural aspect, there was significant interchange between

America and Europe during the 1919–33 period, with most, but not all, of the influence flowing eastward.

To war-weary Europe, struggling to cope with the problems of modern mass society, the United States, emerging from the war rich and buoyant, seemed to have the answers. Since the machine civilization was most advanced and apparently most successful in the United States, many European artists, businessmen, and politicians alike looked westward for models. To help Europe deal with the turbulence of modernization, America offered its own institutions and values, or what contemporaries termed *Americanism.*

Americanism meant a pragmatic, optimistic outlook on life; a peaceful, rational compromise of political differences; an efficient, modern way of organizing work that emphasized machines and mass assembly production; rising standards of living with declining class antagonisms; scientific use of statistics and other information; and the predominance of mass society (this meant democratic politics, widespread consumption, and popular entertainment). Many Europeans welcomed Americanism; others railed against it or were ambivalent, but nearly all believed it was in Europe's future.

In 1630, Governor John Winthrop predicted that America would become a model for the world—"a Citty Upon a Hill" with "the eies of all people" upon it.³ Three hundred years later Paul Claudel, ambassador from France and himself a man of letters, told Americans: "Your movies and talkies have soaked the French mind in American life, methods, and manners. American gasoline and American ideas have circulated throughout France, bringing a new vision of power and a new tempo of life. The place in French life and culture formerly held by Spain and Italy, in the nineteenth century by England, now belongs to America. More and more we are following America."⁴ Hans Joachim, a German writer, recalled the powerful influence in the 1920s of the United States as a land and as a symbol: "America was a good idea; it was the land of the future. It was at home in its age . . . we loved it. Long enough had . . . technology appeared only in the forms of tank, mine, shell-gas. . . . In America, it [technology] was at the service of human life. Our interest in elevators, radio towers, and jazz was . . . expressive of the wish to beat the sword into a plowshare. It was against cavalry but for horsepower. . . . It was an attitude that wanted to convert the flame thrower into a vacuum cleaner. . . . Our belief in America demonstrated where we stood."⁵ Europeans in the 1920s were entranced by the image of that city upon the hill.

America's cultural influence was both a product of and a contributor to the United States' economic, political, and (in 1917-19) military power in Europe. In 1917–18 the American economy's size and technological superiority made a psychological as well as military impact on Europe. Exhausted Europeans watched as the Americans quickly raised, equipped, and transported across the Atlantic a two-million-man army. Allies and Germans alike marveled at the Yankees' modern, efficient modes of transportation and organization.

The U.S. Committee on Public Information directed propaganda campaigns at war-weary Europeans eager for new, better answers. Other agencies, such as Herbert Hoover's American Relief Administration, made promotion of America and its way of life an integral part of their operation. Hoover made sure that relief recipients understood their food was coming from a beneficent America. When labor-management strife threatened to stop coal production in central Europe, Hoover's men introduced more liberal labor practices coupled with emphasis on increased labor productivity. President Woodrow Wilson was an enormously effective propagandist, even though—like his chief rival, Vladimir Lenin—he excited European expectations which he could not fulfill.

Indeed, the propaganda war between the United States' liberal capitalism and Russia's revolutionary socialism contained not only antagonistic but complementary aspects that prepared the ground for Europe's Americanization in the 1920s. Wilson and Lenin had both told the European masses that the old imperialist regimes with their balance-of-power politics had produced the war and had to be replaced. Both proclaimed a new era of popular sovereignty, mass society, economic growth, and technological improvement. By the early 1920s, most Europeans were disillusioned with both Wilson's and Lenin's millennial visions. Yet America's enormous economic power and apparent success as a society ensured that many Europeans looking for social solutions, including some of those who had been inspired by Lenin, would turn to the United States for models. Even the Russian Bolsheviks, despite continued hostility toward capitalism, tried to adopt many of America's technological wonders. The United States government ceased propaganda efforts in 1919, but in the ensuing decade private Americans advertised their ideas, institutions, and products in Europe.

Yankee merchandise, films, aviators, artists, entertainers, and above all dollars flooded the Old World, bringing Europeans direct evidence of the United States' position as the leader of Western civilization. Economic and cultural factors intertwined in various ways. In the early twenties, many European currencies depreciated rapidly, in part because of the United States' debt, tariff, and loan policies. This made living in Europe cheap for those with dollars. Alienated by the ascendant business civilization at home, many American artists fled to Europe, seeking high culture and low prices. Some had already acquired a taste for Europe while in the American army. These artists then discovered that many European writers, painters, and architects looked to America's machine- and business-dominated civilization for esthetic themes and inspiration. To the Americans' surprise, many Europeans took such creations as jazz and skyscrapers seriously. Many expatriate artists found in Europe the basis for an American art of which they could be proud. Some of these expatriates, such as Harold Loeb and Matthew Josephson, wrote enthu- siastically of Europe's Americanization. Others were more ambivalent about America's cultural influence. But as Malcolm Cowley, chronicler of the generation, explained, consciously or unconsciously they became purveyors in Europe of American products, life-styles, and ideas.

Hollywood films, a world box-office hit, had a more widespread im- pact. Europeans picked up the mannerisms they saw in Charlie Chaplin or Clara Bow movies and bought the American goods they ogled in the films. Yankee tourists enjoyed less popularity than Hollywood films, but the annual pilgrimage of hundreds of thousands boosted Europe's balance of payments while their demands created an American economy in Paris and other cities. Sometimes the link between culture and economics was a simple exchange, as when Secretary of the Treasury Andrew Mellon and other wealthy Americans made multimillion-dollar purchases of Rus- sian painting masterpieces, sold by the Soviets to pay for desperately needed machinery imports. Both sides ignored their political antagonism to forge one of the economic/cultural bonds that characterized American relations with Europe in the 1920s.

Two elements lay at the source of these cultural interactions: the United States' economic power, which captured European markets and imagi- nations while financing a flood of tourists and expatriate artists and giving Americans the money to buy what they wanted; and the process of Americanization. Contemporaries used *Americanization* to refer to both the United States' cultural penetration of Europe and the overlapping process of Europe's indigenous modernization. That America became a metaphor and a symbol for modernization testified to the nation's leading position in Western civilization.

In subtle yet important ways, this cultural influence and prestige en- hanced the ability of the United States to conduct its political and eco- nomic policies in Europe with minimal cost and entanglement. This was especially important after 1919, when the United States government, under both Democratic and Republican administrations, shifted away from direct, official involvement in European politics. The new diplomacy was unofficial rather than official, economic rather than political, limited rather than open-ended, cautious rather than crusading. The respect that many Europeans held for American ideas and methods made such diplomacy easier to implement. At the 1924 Dawes reparations conference, for example, the unofficial American representatives conducted a successful publicity campaign in Europe that presented their plan as a pragmatic and businesslike—that is, an American—solution. Recognizing the importance of prestige (or what they termed moral power), American leaders tried to limit their intervention to instances where it would be successful, thereby enhancing their reputation for effectiveness.

Although Europeans looked to the United States for dollars and for answers, they often resented America and defied its wishes. France, for example, consistently ignored American pleas and pressure for land disarmament and maintained its large army in readiness against Germany. Yet Paris officials never succeeded in obtaining what they most needed for security against Germany, a commitment from Washington. Comprehensive or lasting solutions were not possible without American approval and assistance; French security remained at an impasse.

Just as America's prestige flowered with its impressive performance in World War I and in the 1920s, so did its cultural influence, economic power, and political leverage wilt with the Depression and the dissolution of its economy. European artists became disillusioned with their Americanist dream of permanent prosperity and progress and, with the flow of checks and tourists drying up, most American artists went home. The Depression also revealed flaws in the American reconstruction of the world economy. The United States had stabilized trade and financial relations in ways that both protected American interests and enabled Europe to recover, and Americans confidently believed that the beneficent change of economic growth would make the system work. The gold standard, the political debt settlements, the private loans, and the high U.S. tariff were burdens Europe probably could have borne had prosperity continued. But in hard times the economic structure proved too rigid and too tilted toward American interests. It collapsed.

The economic collapse also crippled the policy of peaceful change. The Depression hit Germany hard, aggravated by Berlin's pursuit of a deflationary policy in the hope of convincing America and the Allies that reparation payments had become impossible. With surging strength, radical parties on the German right and left loudly demanded immediate and wholesale Versailles revision. The right-centrist government of Heinrich Brüning pointed to these pressures and demanded more rapid revision than the French would grant or the Americans thought proper. In late 1931, Hoover and Stimson hoped to satisfy German ambitions with revision of the Polish corridor, but the effort met determined Polish and French resistance. When Brüning was replaced in June 1932 with governments further to the right, the United States moved closer to the French position of Versailles enforcement. In the storm of depression, the American middle road of peaceful change proved impassable.

The Depression exposed the fatal flaws in the American-dominated political, economic, and cultural order. The system depended on continued international prosperity—a precarious prosperity that by the late 1920s required a continuous flow of Wall Street loans. Most American banking and government officials shied away from regulating this vital capital movement, relying instead on the collective wisdom of individual investors. The international economic structure was also weakened by American insistence on rebuilding with policies that stacked most burdens on the eastern shore of the North Atlantic and most benefits on its own.

American policymakers like Hoover, Hughes, Stimson, and Young had a sophisticated understanding of the uses and limits of national power. They understood that an American answer did *not* exist for every foreign problem, and that although the United States was the most powerful nation in the world, it was not all-powerful and could easily dissipate its strength through fruitless and unnecessary foreign entanglements. Excessive foreign intervention would generate further resentment overseas and division at home. The informal division of policy implementation among governmental officials, semiprivate central bankers, and private businessmen, moreover, provided checks and balance. Yet ironically, this division of power and restraint in its use made impossible the wholesale U.S. intervention in Europe that might have prevented world depression and world war.

The rise of Nazi Germany and Soviet Russia during this turbulent period of a revolutionary century made mock of American attempts to implement policies of peaceful, moderate political reform and orderly, capitalist economic growth. By 1933, only the cultural leg of the triad was left standing at all, and here too both the Nazis and the Soviets demonstrated that technological modernization was easily separated from the rest of the Americanization process. America could not control the chaos unloosed in 1914 after all.

[1]

The Flawed Peace,
1919–1921

The Great War destroyed centuries-old empires, decimated a generation of Europe's youth, and ended that continent's easy domination of
the world. It unleashed political, economic, and social turbulence that
persists today. Memory of the terrible carnage shaped later generations'
very conception of war.[1]

The greatest international political issue in Europe and America during
the two decades after the war was whether and how to enforce the
Versailles peace treaty. The chief economic problem was how, in a changed
world, to reestablish and maintain world prosperity. The main cultural
challenge was how to cope with modernization, accelerated by the impact
of the war and American influence. And the common denominator of
these political, economic, and cultural issues was the pace and nature of
change.

To Americans, as befitted their Progressive tradition of moderate reform, the proper path lay in slow, peaceful change in the Versailles peace
and in European domestic politics, orderly capitalist economic growth
to rebuild European prosperity and American markets, and the evolution
in Europe of American institutions, methods, and values. "The whole
world is in revolt all the time," declared Isaiah Bowman, an expert adviser
to Woodrow Wilson at the Versailles peace conference; "all that we care
about is that it be a thoughtful revolt and a *gradual* one."[2] The contradictions, both semantic and substantive, with this concept of revolution
summed up both American policy and its difficulties.

Although Americans clung to the policies of healing change for most
of the 1919–33 period, the flaws and limits of this approach began to
show up in 1919–21. Frightened by the threat of revolutionary upheaval
and unable to shake French preoccupation with security, Woodrow Wil-

25

son seriously compromised his original conception of the League of Nations as a tool for peaceful change as well as stability. The league emerged from the Versailles conference as an instrument for preserving the status quo rather than a vehicle for peaceful change. If Germany, or another power, wanted in the future to revise the 1919 settlement, it would have to do so largely outside the world organization. Wilson and other administration officials wanted to help rebuild the European economy, but not at the expense of U.S. economic interests, and certainly not by sacrificing their goal of a world economy open to the trade and investment of all nations. Thus began conflicts over debts, loans, trade, and gold that persisted into the 1930s. America's performance during the war, its financial strength, and its capture of popular imagination endowed American society with enormous prestige in Europe. Absorbing American culture from doughboys, publicity campaigns, Herbert Hoover's relief teams, or private aid groups, many Europeans interpreted America's social success as a challenge and an opportunity for their own continent. Yet even as Europe was influenced by American society, it defied the American government on many matters. This led to an impasse on issues such as military security, reparations, war debts, and further loans. Neither the American Congress or public nor, by 1920, the embittered president was willing to undertake the massive political and economic intervention in Europe necessary—if indeed then possible—to resolve these issues. In January 1919, however, at the opening of the Paris Peace Conference, Woodrow Wilson was confident that he could make Europe and the world safe for peace and democracy. Then he encountered the dilemmas that dashed most of his dreams.

The Peace Treaties

The president needed a quick peace to establish the League of Nations, stabilize Europe, and stop the epidemic of revolution that threatened to spread from Russia to the Atlantic. He could not risk long discussions or a prolonged break with the Allies. The war had hardened Wilson. Though he aimed at eventual integration of the German republic into a community of liberal capitalist industrial states, he thought Berlin deserved some punishment.[3] By early 1919, Wilson was hemmed in on all sides: by his yearning for the league and an open world economy, by challenges from Republicans at home and revolutionaries in Europe, by the insecurity of France and the grasping of Italy and Japan, by the emerging nations' squabbles for territory.

In addition to these troubles, many conference delegates suffered from the "Paris cold," the worldwide influenza pandemic that killed more people than the war. Wilson and most of his top advisers suffered from the disease, and three members of the American delegation died before the conference was over. "It is the most depressing atmosphere I have ever been in," reported one aide. "Everyone around seems to have something the matter with him."[4]

From this disorder, both physiological and political, emerged the treaties of Versailles with Germany, of Neuilly with Bulgaria, of St. Germain with Austria, and of Trianon with Hungary. The Versailles peace slashed the size of the German army and navy, prohibiting such weapons as tanks, aircraft, and submarines altogether—the first step, the treaty promised, to universal disarmament. The Germans gave back Alsace-Lorraine to France and for fifteen years yielded the coal-rich Saar Valley. This last provision was a compromise worked out by Americans and British to block French annexation, but still allow temporary ownership so as to compensate for wartime destruction. The treaty placed the Saar under political control of the league with a customs union with France and a plebiscite after fifteen years. Wilson also defeated a French bid for annexation of the Rhineland. After bitter controversy, the French accepted the alternative of inter-Allied occupation for fifteen years, demilitarization for fifty kilometers east of the Rhine, and most important, a treaty with Britain and the United States promising military aid if Germany attacked. With far less controversy, the victors provided for a plebiscite in Schleswig which ultimately returned half of the region to Denmark, and the retrocession to Belgium of the regions of Eupen, Malmedy, and Moresnet, which Prussia had annexed in 1815.[5] In the west and north, then, Germany lost little territory other than Alsace-Lorraine. The Germans grumbled, but accepted these boundaries for most of the interwar period.

The settlement in the east was far different. As the Polish expert of the American peace delegation admitted, "No other part of the territorial arrangements . . . has caused so much anger in Germany."[6] The victors insisted that Germany cede to the new Poland the mixed-population areas of Posen and West Prussia. This Polish "corridor" fulfilled one of Wilson's Fourteen Points of a united Poland with secure access to the sea. The Allies and Americans made German-speaking Danzig a free city under league protection so that Poland could use the port. The treaty provided for a plebiscite to divide mineral-rich upper Silesia.[7] To Germans, the Polish corridor between East Prussia and the rest of the Reich provided a highly visible and irritating reminder of defeat. Germany's determination to overthrow this border unsettled Europe throughout the postwar era.

Nor did the Germans accept reparations. During the terrible economic strain of the war, both sides had dreamed of recouping all with a huge indemnity from the defeated enemy. After the Armistice, the British and French bandied about figures of $120 to $200 billion. Aghast, Americans knew the Allies could never collect such sums. To attempt to would, Washington observers were convinced, wreck Germany's economy and drive the country to bolshevism. American economic experts pressed for a $30 billion bill, of which the Germans might pay half in their own currency. David Lloyd George of Britain and Georges Clemenceau of France protested, however, that if they accepted a fixed sum, no matter how large, disappointed voters would throw them out of office. That would mean, they warned, different delegations and a peace conference forced to start from scratch. A quick peace was essential to stabilize Europe, Wilson realized. He accepted the Allied demand for inclusion of military pensions in the reparations obligation. The Versailles treaty created a permanent Reparations Commission to tally Germany's bill. In May 1921 the commission set reparations at $33 billion. Whatever the amount, Germany was reluctant to pay, and in fact paid only $5 billion by 1932, when the reparations issue died but was not buried.[8] In postwar years reparations became tangled with inter-Allied war debts and the whole issue clouded with vehement emotion. In sum, the Versailles treaty humiliated and embittered Germany but did not destroy it. The Germans never accepted Versailles, and schemed incessantly to change it. Since Germany had the greatest power potential in Western Europe and neither Britain nor America after 1919 was willing to enforce Versailles, the treaty was, from the first, more a political issue than a political settlement.

The other losers shared Germany's ambition to overthrow the peace treaties. The Neuilly peace clipped Bulgaria of territory on all frontiers, limited its army, and levied heavy reparations.[9] In Paris, American delegates wanted to allow rump Austria to join Germany, but the French refused.[10] The treaty of St. Germain reduced Austria to an imperial-sized capital city with drastically shrunken hinterland. Perhaps Hungary lost the most: two-thirds of its historic territory and one-third of the Magyar people.[11] The peace treaties adhered scrupulously to self-determination as long as the people involved had not been on the losing side. Although a victor in the war, Italy, largely because of Wilson's insistence, had not satisfied its appetite for territory. This was another charter member of the revisionist group.[12]

The Flawed League

Fearing that the peace treaties would create this kind of bitterness and disappointment, Wilson had engineered the League of Nations so that it could facilitate peaceful change. En route to Paris, the president emphasized to advisers that the league would do more than guarantee "territorial integrity." The international organization would also "alter ... boundaries" in the event of "injustice" or if "conditions had changed." Harsh peace terms were probably inevitable now, but the league could ease them "as *passions subsided*." The world organization was vital, then, for "both *elasticity* and security," for both change and order.[13]

This dual role appeared in early versions of the Convenant drafted by Edward M. House and approved by Wilson. Article 10, the focus of furious controversy between Wilson and his critics, originally balanced order and change: "The Contracting Powers unite in several guarantees to each other of their *territorial integrity* and political independence *subject, however, to such territorial modifications, if any, as may become necessary in the future*."[14] Thus, Article 10, the heart of the League of Nations Covenant, would sanction both stability and reform in the international political structure. Dissatisfied nations such as Germany, once allowed to join the league, could press for change in the 1919 peace treaties within the context of that settlement and without having to overthrow it. This balanced original version of Article 10 did not eliminate the basic power equation that inevitably underlies international relations. Yet it might have proven to be a vehicle for institutionalized peaceful change and just might have relieved the tensions that eventually led to the rise of Adolf Hitler and then to World War II.

Yet because of their preoccupation with stability, the Americans at Versailles abandoned the balanced version of Article 10. Wilson's influential legal adviser, David Hunter Miller, warned that such an article would make "dissatisfaction permanent" and "legalize irredentist agitation in at least all of Eastern Europe."[15] The French also opposed this provision for legalized change. At first Wilson stuck by his original plan, but by February 2 he dropped the qualifying clause, thereby robbing the Covenant of much of its flexibility.[16] The president "could see no other way," explained a close adviser, "to stabilize a turbulent and too swiftly changing world" and reassure "terror-stricken France."[17] Wilson had to mollify France if he wanted any league at all. He also needed French cooperation for a quick, moderate peace that would stabilize Europe.

Alarmed, British representative Robert Cecil urged an additional article to redress the balance: "The Body of Delegates shall make provision for the periodic revision of treaties which have become obsolete."[18] Backed by the French, Wilson and Miller defeated it with the argument that it would give the league too much power and was "unconstitutional."[19] Yet Article 10 endowed the league with a similar mandate to preserve the status quo. In the end Wilson proposed what became the innocuous Article 19: "It shall be the right of the Body of Delegates from time to time to advise the reconsideration by the States, members of the League, of treaties which have become inapplicable, and of international conditions, the continuance of which may endanger the peace of the world."[20]

Frightened by disorder, Wilson crafted a postwar legal order committed to the status quo. Despite the inclusion of Articles 11, 13, and 19, which slightly tempered Article 10, the league Covenant did not, as Wilson had promised, institutionalize the process of change. Although anxious to pursue every possible avenue of revision, Germany, even after it joined the league in 1926, regarded Article 19 as a dead letter and did not even try to invoke it. Revisionists could alter the status quo only by overthrowing it.[21] Wilson was unwilling or unable to admit to himself the implications of his abandonment of a balanced league Covenant. After presenting the league plan to the plenary conference, he reportedly told his wife: "This is our first real step forward, for . . . once established the League can arbitrate and correct mistakes which are inevitable in the Treaty."[22] That was his argument in the fierce political fight over American adoption of the Covenant.

For all the gnashing of teeth over the league issue, most American political leaders, Democrat and Republican, agreed that some association of nations was necessary to contain revolution and facilitate peaceful change. Wilson and his closest followers insisted that the Covenant was fine as it stood.[23] After his stroke in September 1919, the president became even more rigid in his opposition to any modification of the league.

A key to understanding American foreign relations from 1921 to 1933 is that the Republicans who made foreign policy during those years— Herbert Hoover, Charles Evans Hughes, Warren G. Harding, Frank B. Kellogg, Henry L. Stimson, Calvin Coolidge—and elder statesmen such as Elihu Root and William H. Taft, all appreciated the value of a league in preserving order. Yet they rejected Wilson's league with Article 10 because it restricted the United States' freedom of action and the likelihood of modifying the peace treaties.

Herbert Hoover, probably the most significant figure, sat at the seat of power or close to it from 1917 to 1933. At Paris he advised Wilson and ran a massive relief program to stabilize Europe with food and technical assistance. Unlike other Wilson advisers who quit in frustration, Hoover stayed on (in a sense through 1958, with the publication of his measured tribute *The Ordeal of Woodrow Wilson*) because for him the only alternative to the treaty was "chaos over the whole earth." Privately he protested to Wilson against Article 10, but publicly he defended the

Treasury officials, who resented the Allies' eagerness to "milk" America.[47] Although Washington's opposition defeated the Keynes plan, the British did not abandon hope of redressing the economic imbalance with America. From 1919 to 1933, they repeatedly tried to reduce or cancel war debts, tap the United States money market, shut Americans out of the Empire, or force them into inflation.

Americans were generally successful in staving off these attacks. In 1919 a group of treasury officials led by Russell Leffingwell drew up the blueprint for financial reconstruction, a plan that guided American policy down to 1933. They wanted the government to get out of the foreign loan business quickly. They championed private enterprise as more efficient and in accord with capitalist doctrine. The public "is in no mood," Assistant Secretary Leffingwell cabled the peace delegation, "to tolerate the assumption by government of further financial burdens in aid to Europe." Public awareness of government loans to Europe after the Armistice caused "gravest difficulties" in selling United States government bonds.[48] Nevertheless, the treasury recognized the necessity of some public loans during the transition period, especially with the dangers posed by revolution in Europe and surpluses at home. The administration therefore pushed through Congress legislation for $1.5 billion of further credits to the Allies, $1 billion for financing exports through the War Finance Corporation (WFC), and $100 million for Hoover's American Relief Administration.[49] In addition, the Wilson administration funneled money into the reconstruction of war-torn northeast France under cover of demobilization and relief, and supplemented Hoover's funds with various indirect subsidies. Despite these substantial credits, by the fall of 1919 the treasury had largely phased out government lending.[50]

To take up the slack, the treasury was "doing whatever it can," Leffingwell assured Wilson, to encourage the movement of private capital. This was difficult, he explained, for "timid" capital preferred to "remain inert at home" than venture into Europe "on the verge of breakdown." Wilson needed no reminding that the league could restore confidence and "stability."[51] With Wilson locked in a death fight over his version of the league, leaders in and outside the administration tried to work up a scheme public enough to win the confidence of investors and private enough to win the support of the treasury.

They seemed to find an answer with the Edge Act, passed by Congress in December 1919. Drawn up by Federal Reserve Board lawyers, the act provided for private investment trusts incorporated under and regulated by the federal government. The trusts would receive payment for United States exports in foreign securities and reimburse the exporters with dollars. The capital of these risk-taking corporations would come from private investors and—this was the crucial point—from the U.S. Government's WFC. The new banks could tap the private money market because, Edge explained, they had "the moral backing and material support" of the government.[52]

The financial problems and policies that surfaced here foreshadowed those of the following decade. Both Democratic and Republican administrations were publicly committed to private financing of Europe's reconstruction. To provide the stability needed for private investment, the U.S. government in the 1920s pressed Europeans to reduce armaments, settle reparations through the Dawes Plan, and adopt the Locarno security pacts. To encourage investors, the government, acting through its chief financial agent, the Federal Reserve Bank of New York, made loans to central banks in Europe. Finally, the failure of the Edge banks to attract long-term capital, despite extensive publicity,[53] signaled that for all their advertising hoopla, business and governmental leaders could not turn private capital flows on and off like a spigot. This last was a crucial lesson not learned until the Great Depression.

Like loan policy, the American position on Allied war debts was shaped by domestic politics, international rivalry, and desire to mold Europe's reconstruction. Before leaving the treasury in November 1918, Secretary William McAdoo sketched the principles that, with few exceptions, informed war debt policy for the following fifteen years. McAdoo rejected the ideas of canceling the debts or using them as bargaining chips at the peace conference. Instead, the United States should insist on bilateral debt negotiations in Washington. This would head off a debtors' bloc, while enabling the United States to exert pressure on individual debtors. Although they disagreed as to interest and terms of repayment, few top political or business officials wanted outright cancellation with no quid pro quo.[54] In a revolutionary age, it was vital that nations fulfill contracts, even if only nominally. Moreover, Congress and the public firmly opposed cancellation and higher taxes. Administration officials feared that if they wrote off the debts, Congress would retaliate by cutting all credits to Europe and hardening opposition to the league treaty. As Davis put it, "Woodrow Wilson would have been charged with giving ten billion dollars for the League of Nations."[55] Unless the United States was willing to undertake active political and military involvement in Europe, war debts remained one of the few weapons in its arsenal.

Such leverage seemed vital if the United States hoped to establish a world economic order open to the trade and investment of all nations on an equal basis. The dispute over the open door went back to the Paris Economic Conference of 1916. The Allies had agreed to set up after the war a closed-door system of trade preferences, discriminating against enemy and neutral nations. The Allied governments would subsidize industries at home while financing and directing penetration of foreign markets. This scheme was anathema to Americans who, even after being invited to join in 1917, wanted no part of a postwar mercantilist trade war that would lead only to further wars and thwart ambitions to expand America's trade and investment worldwide.[56]

At the end of the war, Britain and France tried to implement their plan by proposing that wartime inter-Allied economic agencies continue in the postwar era to regulate shipping, trade, and finance. Wilson and his advisers rejected both Allied government control of American resources and the idea of discriminatory economic regulation by any government. With its economic might, the United States easily won this round, but the Allies threatened a rematch by scrambling for economic concessions after the peace.[57] In this struggle the war debts were a powerful club. "If Great Britain did not have to pay $4.5 billion to the United States," Davis recalled, it felt it "could win out against us."[58] In response to repeated requests for a lenient settlement of war debts, Treasury Secretary David Houston handed the British a list of prerequisites. American war debt concessions would come only after Britain and other Allies raised taxes, cut expenditures (especially on social welfare and armaments), reduced the money supply, cleared the way for private initiative and the open door, and disgorged excessive war booty.[59] Along with these belt-tightening, deflationary measures, Americans sought reestablishment of the gold standard on which depended, Davis declared, "the future stability of the world."[60]

Basically, American reconstruction policy operated, as Hoover explained it, as "a lever to force those European countries to . . . get down to work."[61] Promoting the work ethic was part of American policy toward Europe. Americans believed hard work was redeeming for political, social, and economic reasons. Work was the antithesis, Americans assumed, of both imperialist military waste and revolutionary socialist chaos. The unemployed were easy victims of radicalism on the right or left. Americans feared that exorbitant reparation demands threatened to destroy Germany's "willingness to work."[62] "If Germany is not at work," Davis warned Wilson, it would be "in a chaotic condition and unprosperous," making it "impossible for the rest of Europe to get to work and be prosperous."[63] Ironically, even as the United States in the postwar decade became more a consumer society, Americans framed European reconstruction in terms of work and production.

Although the Wilson administration sketched the outline of American reconstruction policy, it met little success in winning Allied adherence to it. Relations between the Allies and America turned sour in disputes over political debts, trade, mandates, and Germany. Concerned businessmen hatched schemes to tap the United States money markets, but little capital flowed to Europe. Since investors stayed away from unstable Europe, resentful Europeans saw little reason to shape policies to meet the wishes of the United States. Americans particularly disliked Allied intentions of collecting huge reparations from Germany.

The Senate's failure to pass the Anglo-American French security treaty[64] quickened French efforts to suppress Germany. France tried to manipulate reparations to gain both money and security. Under the Versailles treaty, she received payments on an interim basis until the victors determined the total German obligation. French strategy was to put the interim payments and final bill as high as the other Allies would accept. This would increase the likelihood of Germany's default, giving France the opportunity to wield further control over the enemy. Down to late 1923 the British were virtually prisoners of French policy. Britain wanted to weaken Germany with reparations, but not to destroy this valuable market and checkmate to France. By February 1920 Lloyd George had adopted Keynes's argument that Europe's economic recovery and British trade depended on a quick reparations settlement. He proposed that Germany make a lump-sum settlement, but France refused. Britain could not openly break with the French, for fear they would unilaterally destroy Germany. Therefore the British maintained the facade of Allied unity while trying to moderate French demands.[65] Disgusted, the Wilson administration sat out this squabbling.

In mid-1919 Wilson administration officials disappointed with the peace treaties still hoped to modify the treaty through participation in the league and the Reparations Commission. Picking an effective representative on the commission was "most important," Leffingwell affirmed, because the agency had the power "of world peace or war both industrial and commercial."[66] However, the Senate undercut American influence by rejecting Wilson's request for formal membership on the commission. Administration officials sidestepped this barrier with unofficial representation, a technique perfected by their Republican successors, but they could not change French policy.[67] "Nothing short of an earthquake" would make the French adopt "a sane policy," declared Norman Davis, newly appointed undersecretary of state. He defined American policy as "a waiting game," and rejected various Allied schemes that America pay Germany's reparations. "Allied obligations to us," Davis asserted, "have no relation whatever to the German obligations to them."[68] With this impasse, reparations and war debts remained deadlocked through the end of the Wilson administration.

For Wilson, furor over political debts was only further evidence of

Allied treachery. Bedridden and embittered, he talked more and more cantankerously about pulling back from an ungrateful Europe as his dreams dissolved. He charged that the British, who had reneged on promise of the open door in their oil-rich mandates, were "capable of as great commercial savagery as Germany."[69] When the Allies gave Fiume to Italy, contrary to what he had recommended at Versailles, the president threatened to withdraw the peace treaty from the Senate. The Allies complained that Wilson's "psychological condition was so uncertain," but backtracked by making Fiume a free city. Unmollified, Wilson remarked acidly that if war came, he hoped Italy would "get the stuffing licked out of her."[70]

Within the administration there were differences at first on the extent of American withdrawal from Europe. Wilson saw little reason to participate in councils where the "other great Powers are now mismanaging the world."[71] Houston agreed, but Davis and Leffingwell feared that such isolation would multiply "misunderstandings."[72] However, by early 1921 even Davis advised withdrawal. The Allies ignored America with regard to the spoils of war, Davis complained, "and only consult our views in cases where they look to us for assistance."[73] Frustrated with the Allies and defeated at the polls, the president in January and February 1921 withdrew from the Council of Ambassadors and the Reparations Commission.[74] Wilson's crusade was over.

Despite the deadlock on reconstruction and pullback from political cooperation, the United States did not isolate itself. Exports to Europe, though down from their 1919 peak, totaled $2.4 billion in 1921.[75] American businessmen began investigating investment opportunities. Artists and tourists discovered how cheap it was to live in countries with depreciating currencies.[76] In central and eastern Europe, Herbert Hoover's American Relief Administration (ARA), which Wilson termed the "second American Expeditionary Force to save Europe,"[77] struggled for order and stability.

The Political and Social Consequences of Relief

Hoover's relief program marked the transition from America's wartime, official, political involvement in European affairs to its post-1919, largely unofficial, economic and cultural penetration of Europe. Hoover helped pioneer the tactic of approaching thorny, largely political problems from an economic or technical perspective. The distinction was sometimes a matter of semantics, but important nevertheless, since the administrations in Washington shied away from overt political involvement, while many Europeans were awed by America's economic and technical prowess. This prestige was important in getting Europeans to accept American solutions to problems in areas where America had little political or military power. With a constant eye on public relations, Hoover cultivated American prestige in Europe. He also used publicity to raise private funds and facilitate quasi-public financing for his relief activities, again pointing to the path taken in the 1920s. Members of Hoover's staff aided the transition into the postwar decade by staying on in Europe as representatives of the Commerce Department or American businesses.[78] Hoover, whose rise as a hero in 1919–20[79] contrasted with Wilson's decline in popularity, became the single most important foreign policymaker from 1921 to 1933. He brought to that role proud memories of the ARA's success and resentment of Allied obstruction.

Hoover's ARA used food and technical skill to fight hunger and revolution and shape development in the new states of central Europe. The success of food, money, and technical know-how as tools of American diplomacy contrasted sharply with the relative failure of political and military power. Hoover held out the carrot of food to countries like Austria that remained capitalist, and laid down the stick on Bolshevik Hungary. But Americans soon realized that food alone was insufficient to stop revolution and build viable capitalist states. With approval of the Versailles conference delegates, teams of Americans reintegrated the transportation and communications systems of the old Austro-Hungarian empire and prodded the new nations to trade with their neighbors. As missionaries of American corporate capitalism, Hoover's men demonstrated the virtues of efficient management and planning, self-help, private enterprise, hard work, and good labor relations. Hoover's staff pushed Progressive reform in Central Europe,[80] much as Progressives had tried to do good in American cities.

Relief was Hoover's private empire. He held tight control by directing simultaneously the United States Food Administration, the United States Government Grain Corporation, and the ARA. He organized and dominated the Allied Supreme Economic Council, which appointed him director general of relief and trustee for the railroads and coal mines of the defunct Austro-Hungarian empire. From this power base, Hoover set up missions that reported directly to him.

As General John Pershing put it, Hoover was "food regulator for the world."[81] When the Wilson administration pulled back from close European cooperation and congressional authorization for the ARA ran out in mid-1919, Hoover transformed it into a private agency still firmly under his control. In 1921–23, he was a cabinet official in a government that refused to recognize the Soviet Union; nevertheless, he headed a massive relief program to that country and had close associates oversee technical assistance to Austria, Poland, Czechoslovakia, and Yugoslavia.

The relief czar amassed power by capitalizing on America's near monopoly of food and funds for relief. He rejected any plan "that even look[ed] like inter-Allied control" of these resources.[82] Although genuine humanitarian feeling inspired Hoover, his altruism was rooted in solid concern for America's interests and freedom of action.

Hoover asserted that "the whole of American policies" after the armistice was "to prevent Europe from going Bolshevik."[83] This was inseparable from feeding the hungry, for as Secretary of State Robert Lansing put it, "full stomachs mean no Bolsheviks."[84] Relief's task, Hoover explained, was "warding off Bolshevism on one side and reaction on the other, in order that the newborn democracies could have an opportunity for growth." If bolshevism triumphed in Europe, he warned, it would soon "attack our own institutions."[85] In the event of military aggression by the Bolsheviks, Hoover urged Wilson to be "prepared to fight."[86] More likely the enemy would choose subversion. Here food and technical assistance were more effective. As Joseph Grew analyzed the menace, "If you fight it with arms it will grow; if you fight it with food it will die a natural death."[87]

Relief was good business as well as good counterrevolutionary policy. As wartime food administrator, Hoover guaranteed farmers high crop prices. Production shot up to record levels, and when the war ended Hoover faced what he called the "nightmare" of disposing of surplus wheat, pork, and other commodities at prices high enough to fulfill the guarantee. Shipments of cheaper food from Argentina and Austria and the Allied blockade compounded the problem. Wilson and his advisers fought the Allies on the blockade and lobbied in Congress for a $100 million appropriation for relief to new nations. The treasury advanced the Allies money for food purchases (this competition Australia and Argentina could not meet) and bypassed a congressional ban on loans to ex-enemy states by funneling money to Austria through Britain and France.[88] Thus, the United States government advanced Europeans the money to buy food at high prices from Hoover's ARA, which purchased it from Hoover's United States Grain Corporation, which conducted such sales as part of Hoover's Food Administration. After several months of relief work, Hoover noted that the glut had eased: "Altogether, I think we will have cleaned up our pork situation, our cereal flour situation, our rye situation, and our wheat situation beautifully. We may be able even to clean up rice and beans."[89] ARA credit sales foreshadowed the 1920s when the United States used private and semipublic Federal Reserve Bank loans as a tool of foreign policy and way to finance exports. The aid missions also paved the way for the future by introducing to Europeans American equipment and methods and forging contacts between United States businessmen and the new countries.

Hoover piloted the ARA with a careful eye on America's prestige or moral power. American status in Europe had already risen when the AEF arrived to clinch victory for the Allies. Europeans were impressed with the Yanks' efficiency, energy, and money. George Creel, head of the Committee on Public Information, orchestrated propaganda campaigns in Europe that emphasized American power and ideals.[90]

Despite Wilson's trouble at Versailles, the United States still enjoyed considerable moral influence, especially because of its relatively disinterested neutral stance on most political quarrels. Both Czechs and Poles, for instance, could accept American administration of the disputed Teschen district confident that the United States had an alliance with neither side and did not covet the area for itself. Hoover, meanwhile, seized the opportunity to stabilize this strategic area and step up coal deliveries to places of unrest, thereby protecting broad United States interests at no political or military cost. However, this balancing act worked only so long as the European contenders were desperate for American aid and committed to the battle against bolshevism. To enhance U.S. moral power, Hoover insisted that all food carry prominent American labels and directed ARA missions to "firmly impress" on relief recipients the origin of their aid. Although Europeans paid for the great bulk of ARA food with credit or cash, Hoover shrewdly ran the highly publicized Children's Relief Fund as a charity. Aside from the humanitarian and prestige considerations, Hoover feared that "distorted minds" of "stunted children" were "a menace to all mankind."[91] More immediate was the danger that the Allies, disappointed with the peace, would "blame the United States." America could help "smooth out those ruffled feelings" with "baby feeding," he calculated, which had "touched the heart" of Europe.[92] "As a matter of protection," such goodwill was more powerful than "all of the battleships that could be floated upon the Atlantic Ocean." Child relief also had trade potential, as Edgar Rickard, a top Hoover assistant, explained: "The children of Europe will grow up with "affection for America as their benefactor[,] and these nations will trade with us preferably [*sic*] than with any other nation in the world. These youngsters are conscious of two factors today: 'Food'—'America.' "[93] Aid to the hungry boosted American prosperity, prestige, and security.

Economic assistance packed multiple consequences. For example, feeding the starving in Germany and Poland was a political act. The French hoped hunger would feed separatist movements in Germany, while Germans looked to Poland's early collapse. Food and supplies bolstered

Poland in its war with Russia, while denial of such aid weakened Hungarian Bolsheviks battling Rumanians. The ARA tried to use food relief to bring down the Russian Bolshevik regime. In the new states Americans assumed quasi-governmental power and on occasion mediated between labor and capital. All these activities were different aspects of the general fight against revolution. Such intervention was economic rather than political, Americans believed, because revolution, especially on the left, was by definition an economic disaster.

Fearing revolution in Germany, Americans at the Versailles conference tried to break the French stranglehold on German food imports. Controversy over how Germany should pay for this food was the opening round in America's fight in the postwar decade to regulate reparations in a way that would enable German economic recovery. Wilson and Hoover hoped that lifting the blockade on food would "tend powerfully toward the end of Bolshevism and the stabilizing of government." In return the Germans would hand over merchant ships for moving AEF troops home and food to Europe.[94] Relief in the new nations, declared Hoover's chief assistant, "is dependent to a large extent on the maintenance of good order in Germany," and access to the port of Hamburg.[95] Loath to see Germany's gold reserve go to Americans for food rather than to themselves for reparations, the French frustrated these plans. They prized the blockade as a weapon to force Germany to accept the peace treaty. France also hoped to manipulate food relief to strengthen German separatism.[96]

Frightened by Bolshevik success, Lloyd George exclaimed that French policy would lose all of Europe.[97] The French retreated, and at Brussels on March 14 the United States and the Allies agreed with Germany to ease the blockade. Germany would turn over merchant ships, open its port to the ARA, and pay for food with gold. In return the victors promised food supplies until the next harvest, lifted the ban on fishing in the Baltic, and allowed limited trade. If the Germans refused to sign the peace treaty, the victors would reimpose the full blockade.[98] Even before the German gold arrived, Hoover diverted a relief ship with flour to Hamburg. Mincing no words, the captain of the vessel warned that he would not unload if there were any Bolshevik disturbances in the city.[99]

Unable to save German gold for reparations, the French shifted to using food to divide Germany. They hoped to woo Bavaria with special food shipments. Lansing and Hoover defeated this move and a similar plan to nourish a Rhenish republic with a separate food supply.[100]

At Brussels, Germany traded ships and gold, which the Allies would take for reparations anyway, for desperately needed food and an economic link to the United States. As Berlin's Foreign Office perceived it, susceptibility to bolshevism was one of Germany's few diplomatic trumps.[101] ARA officials appreciated that the Germans were "shaking the red flag of Bolshevism . . . to frighten us," but they were trapped by their commitment to "good order."[102] Hoover feared that the Brussels accord to feed and stabilize Germany might backfire by encouraging a rejection of the peace treaty,[103] opening all Europe to renewed war and revolution.

The blockade controversy exposed the American and British commitment to Germany's economic recovery. In the 1920s this led to German friendship with the Anglo-Saxon powers. U.S. support for Germany was limited, however, because the diplomatic battles at Versailles drove home to Hoover and other Americans the peril of getting "dragged into detailed European entanglements." Rather than "police the world," Hoover argued, America should use its superior economic power and prestige to save the world from "misery and disaster worse than the dark ages."[104] For the next fourteen years he struggled to square the circle—to rebuild Europe while avoiding entanglements.

Hoover's relief agency wrestled with the difficulty of limiting intervention in the European quagmire. Effective action required ever deeper involvement. Indeed, the ARA could move maximum quantities of food and supplies only by assuming sovereign power. Hoover's men acted in the Progressive tradition as powerful administrators, above petty politics or personal gain. An American editor highlighted the Progressive concept of power when he observed that Hoover's agent in Austria was "more a real dictator than any man in their history, but because his reign was benevolent and his justice even-handed and his American purpose absolutely unselfish and disinterested, they submitted to him."[105]

The ARA used this power to reintegrate the communications and transportation networks of the old Austro-Hungarian empire. With regional headquarters in Vienna, the ARA and AEF took over the special telegraph lines used by the Austrian and German general staffs. By early 1919, the Americans commanded the only telegraph system that connected all of central Europe. At its peak, the Vienna office handled five hundred messages a day and often scooped the Allies in reporting news to Paris. With special ARA passports, Hoover's men passed easily across frontiers.[106]

Relief transport from Trieste and Hamburg to the interior required control of the railroads. Yet new boundaries had cut up the imperial network, and Italy manipulated food shipments from Trieste to advance political ambitions.[107] Hoover won from the Supreme War Council control of the railroads of the old empire, including the territory occupied by Italy.[108] Wilson backed Hoover by delaying loans until the Italians agreed to cooperate with the ARA. When the Yugoslav border question came before the conference in April, Wilson was already prejudiced against Italy.[109]

Hoover ran the railroads with engineers borrowed from the AEF. The new regime boosted rail traffic. Yet trade among the new states was stalled because each grabbed whatever rolling stock came across its borders. The ARA then stationed officers in the major railway yards and at the frontiers to ensure that cars and locomotives would return. Americans set up a clearinghouse to distribute rail receipts and barter equipment among neighbors.[110] In short, the ARA parlayed surplus food, resources of the AEF, and detachment from European politics into an effective agency to organize the central European economy and fight extreme nationalism and radicalism.

Hoover conceived of food relief as first aid against hunger and revolution. However, he did not stop there. Foreshadowing the economic diplomacy of the 1920s, the ARA took the second step in reconstruction by stimulating commerce among the new nations and with the United States. ARA officials negotiated barter deals with their counterparts in other countries: Austrian machines for Polish eggs and ham, Yugoslav wheat for Polish gasoline, German coal for Polish potatoes. They delivered Austrian munitions to Czechoslovakians battling the Hungarian Bolsheviks.[111]

While rebuilding European trade and institutions, Hoover did not neglect American commerce. Although the ARA sold food on credit to needy Europeans, the United States Grain Corporation, also under Hoover's direction, conducted "normal commercial transactions" with customers able to pay cash.[112] The relief czar was "anxious" to reestablish commerce "as fast as possible."[113] Businessmen had plenty of incentive. "If our American Packers and Sugar Refiners knew" the prices in Trieste, an ARA official reported, "they would go insane."[114] As soon as the Allies lifted the blockade on Turkey, Hoover revived trade with the United States.[115]

Hoover grounded all these activities on the assumption that America could carefully control the extent of its intervention in Europe. He believed the ARA culd stimulate commerce while avoiding accusations of crass jobbery. Americans could promote trade between Yugoslavia and Italy and yet stay aloof from border disputes. He tried to unit the impoverished, nationalistic new states in a consensus against revolution.

Yet the dynamics of involvement had a momentum beyond even Hoover's control. Americans did become implicated in political struggles. To stabilize central Europe, they found it necessary to assume increasing power. In early May 1919 the Americans expanded beyond communications and transportation into the area's most strategic resource: coal.

At Hoover's request, the Supreme Economic Council created an "Allied" Coal Commission of twenty-two members, which he packed with twenty-one Americans, including its president, AEF colonel Anson C. Goodyear.[116] The commission had a temporary mandate over coalfields allotted to the new nations by the peace treaties. Fighting between Poles and Czechs over Teschen and between Germans and Poles over Kattowitz halted production. The radical, predominantly Slav workers struck against the largely German mine owners. Each nation used what little coal it produced as a weapon against its neighbor. Goodyear's mission was to boost production and distribute coal according to need.[117]

The coal czar's power rested on his status as a "disinterested" American and, more to the point, his control of ARA food supplies.[118]

The coal shortage was most serious in Austria. Thousands were unemployed because of lack of coal in the factories. Without fuel, Hoover's Vienna agent warned, it would be impossible "to quiet the social and economic unrest which is now the principal factor to be considered in the old Empire."[119] Goodyear arranged short-term barter between Austria and its coal-producing neighbors, but long-term contracts, he reported, were "in no case carried out."[120] This pointed up a major flaw in the relief policy: Hoover expected the new states to perceive issues as he did, but contracts and cooperation appeared differently to precarious, embattled governments.[121] Americans were less frustrated when they applied Progressive labor policies to the restive and unproductive work force of the mines.

To Hoover, an engineer who had supervised mine construction around the world, coal production was faltering primarily because of a problem that plagued all of Europe: laboring men were not working hard enough. "Political, moral, and economic chaos" threatened. Compared to laziness and nutritional deprivation, wartime destruction was only a "minor" factor in Europe's economic malaise. He recognized, however, that European workers had legitimate complaints.[122] Redress of these grievances and increased productivity was the labor formula Goodyear brought to the coal mines.

Coal workers were "in an uproar," a mine owner wailed to Goodyear. In this revolutionary situation, "the only authority ... is the authority of the American Commission." The beleaguered capitalist begged Goodyear to "bring us back to good order again."[123]

Goodyear tackled the problem with what he described as "American methods of handling labor." He dispatched an officer, who reported that the mine owners provided good living conditions, but had failed to establish "direct personal relations" with workers. Labor was therefore alienated and radicalized. The Americans initiated a dialogue between employers and employees on how to increase productivity. Although willing to listen to labor's complaints, the Americans "stated very clearly" that they "would not countenance lack of discipline." This strategy apparently worked, for with the "interest and cooperation of the workers aroused," productivity jumped 20 percent. Not surprisingly, the mine owners asked the Americans to stay on even after the mandate of the Coal Commission expired. Neighboring owners "desire[d] to make similar arrangements,"[124] Goodyear reported. By steering a middle path between worker radicalism and employer authoritarianism, Hoover's men increased productivity and at the same time taught capitalists more effective means of "handling labor." Goodyear's success in introducing American labor relations techniques foreshadowed the deeper impact on European labor-capital relations in the 1920s when American-style assembly-line factories were built in Europe.[125]

As Goodyear demonstrated, American relief succeeded in impressive but limited ways. Armed with food, clothing, and sophisticated technical and managerial skills, Americans campaigned effectively against hunger and revolution. Europeans, particularly property owners, were impressed with their success. However, the Yankees were able to moderate nationalism and induce cooperation only when central Europeans were literally starving. Hoover's men became doubtful of their chief's dream to reform Europe with limited, nonviolent intervention. Efficient distribution, Goodyear decided, required "absolute authority." Hoover's railroad chief likewise concluded, "The only way to handle the whole situation in central Europe is to use a military dictatorship. These new nations can never be made to work by the use of moral persuasion alone . . . and nothing but a 'mailed fist' will appeal to them."[126] Thus, the dynamics of intervention led ultimately to total control. This was a Progressive dilemma equally perplexing in central Europe and in central cities back home. However, Hoover and Wilson backed away from the precipice of massive intervention, and, at the risk of ineffectiveness, continued the policy of limited action.

The logistics of limited intervention grew more complicated after mid-1919, when the Wilson administration cut back on public lending and relief. Hunger and revolution still plagued Europe, and U.S. farmers were about to harvest another bumper crop. Hoover jumped these hurdles with private organizations, thus maintaining relief and foreshadowing the 1920s.

On July 7, 1919, the relief czar announced the creation of the private

American Relief Administration European Children's Fund. He chose the name carefully. The first three words would "maintain the established prestige" of its official predecessor and reassure nervous Europeans that the United States was still committed to relief and to order. The last three words endowed the private organization with the sympathy and support due a humanitarian enterprise—while serving as a cover for more controversial projects, such as feeding White Russian armies. Hoover kept much the same personnel and, with Wilson's consent, endowed the private ARA with the equipment and assets of its governmental predecessor. Although "technically" the two organizations were distinct, he admitted that "the whole matter represents the continuity of American effort."[127] Government dollars best expressed the continuity. In addition to the old ARA's $8.3 million assets, the United States government in four years donated more than $81 million in cash, food, and other supplies.[128]

While the ARA stabilized Europe with food, an offshoot shaped development in the new nations along orthodox capitalist lines. Months before the Senate rejected the Versailles treaty, Hoover outlined a plan for technical assistance on a private and unofficial basis. With Wilson's approval, he urged the governments of Austria, Poland, Czechoslovakia, and Yugoslavia to hire ARA personnel as technical advisers, especially in transportation. These experts would create ties with American business and help "secur[e] finance and material." With his usual financial wizardry, he had tucked away $6 million, legally belonging to the four governments, to pay for the technical missions.[129] With the acceptance of the scheme, Hoover named the chief advisers: William B. Ryan in Czechoslovakia, Alvin B. Barber in Poland, William G. Atwood in Yugoslovia, and William B. Causey in Austria—all former ARA and AEF officers.

These advisers were in a delicate and strategic position: appointed officials of their host governments and agents of America's unofficial aid mission. Their effectiveness depended on the confidence of their respective governments. Thus, Barber insisted that his staff adhere "strictly [to] the Polish point of view."[130] This was relatively easy, for the United States' political aloofness enabled them to be loyal to a European state while promoting the broad American objective of a stable, prosperous Europe. The ambiguity of this dual role suited both sides. In negotiations with hostile neighbors, Austrians liked to bring along their "American official."[131] Hoover enhanced the prestige of the technical missions by appointing as liaison officer James A. Logan, United States government unofficial representative on the Reparations Commission and other inter-Allied bodies. After Logan left these positions, he used his contacts to secure loan business in Europe for Dillon, Read and Company, a Wall

Street firm. In the New York ARA office Hoover assigned two trusted aides to coordinate business contacts with central Europe and oversee the whole program.[132]

The technical advisers used their expertise, prestige, and disinterested position to build viable capitalist economies while easing nationalistic and class tensions. As Causey explained it, "The term 'Technical Adviser' is rather a broad one . . . [M]ost of my work has been in connection with transportation, coal and food matters, but I help settle difficulties with the labor leaders. I am . . . a liaison for the Austrians with the neighboring Succession States. Moreover, I am the connecting link between the Austrians and the American unofficial representation in Paris, and naturally with Hoover, to whom I feel a personal responsibility."[133] With the military communications network inherited from the ARA, [134] the advisers stayed in "constant touch" with each other to coordinate trade, transportation, and other matters.[135] Causey and Barber were among the delegates of Austria and Poland to the Genoa Conference of 1922, and each represented his government in other diplomatic negotiations.[136] At the instigation of the advisers, the central European states gathered at the Portorose Conference of October–November 1921. The meeting agreed to tear down some economic barriers, but foundered on the crucial question of tariffs.[137]

The technical advisers scouted mines, utilities, and railroads in response to inquiries from America or to promote investor interest.[138] Barber, perhaps the most successful in promoting trade, facilitated Poland's purchase of American railway equipment and coal-mining machinery.[139] But even in Poland, United States commerce and investment were "rather limited," Barber reported. Despite their efforts, the technical advisers were unable to solve the basic problems of depreciated money that could not buy foreign goods and international tension that discouraged foreign lenders.[140]

Such financial and political instability threatened chaos. Fear of "Social Revolution" plagued Causey throughout his three years in Vienna. If chaos swept central Europe, he warned James Cox, "the three thousand miles of Atlantic Ocean cannot prevent serious consequences for America."[141] He hoped to stem the tide by strengthening capitalist institutions while keeping labor under control. When workers threatened a strike that would shut down communications, Causey bluntly warned them that "all aid from America will stop."[142]

In Poland Barber pressured for an open door for domestic and foreign business.[143] The State Department echoed his appeal and threatened "radical action" if Poland carried out its plan to close foreign banks (most of which were speculating in Polish currency). The Polish government got the point and relented somewhat, allowing American banks to remain on condition that they "submit to supervision and inspection."[144] Poland did not dismantle economic controls until late 1920, at the end of the Russo-Polish war, but by 1922 it had become, Barber noted with pride, "one of the most liberal and progressive countries in Europe."[145]

The technical adviser missions and the ARA—in both its public and private capacities—expressed America's limited commitment to stability in central Europe. Economic and technical aid was a cheap, easy answer to surpluses at home and instability abroad. But such first aid could not heal central Europe's wounds of ethnic hatred, nationalist rivalries, class tension, and economic disorganization. Nor could the Hoover steamroller always crush radical governments. The ARA helped bring down a Socialist government in Poland by withholding food relief, but it encountered far more resistance in Russia and Hungary.

The ARA vs. Bolshevism

In December 1918 Hoover's assistant, Vernon Kellogg, reported from Warsaw that the Germans had carried off so much food that "people are actually dying of starvation."[146] Stamping out bolshevism required "food, clothing, and raw materials to put thousands of idle . . . men at work."[147] As price for such aid, Kellogg—backed by Hoover, Wilson, and ultimately the Supreme War Council—asked that popular wartime leader Jozef Pilsudski replace his leftist government with a government including both right and left. Anxious to maximize Western support and Polish unity, Pilsudski readily agreed.[148]

Americans continued food and medical relief to Poland throughout the Russo-Polish war of 1920, even at the risk of shooting incidents with the Bolsheviks. Most of the supplies to Poland went through Danzig, whose anti-Polish population threatened to cut off the flow. In cooperation with the British, the navy dispatched the flagship *Pittsburgh* to maintain order. Learning of the presence of Soviet submarines in the Baltic, the commander of the *Pittsburgh* asked Secretary of the Navy Josephus Daniels for permission "to treat as hostile Bolshevik submarines as it is the only possible way to defend American ships." "We are not at war with Russia," Daniels reminded the commander, but he did not withdraw American ships from the area, and gave the admiral orders to attack the Bolsheviks if he had "evidence of their hostile intent."[149] As Secretary of State Bainbridge Colby put it, Soviet Russia was an "enemy state."[150]

This was an enemy frighteningly resistant to Hoover's food relief weapon. The success of revolutionaries in Russia and—for a time—in Hungary challenged Americans' vision of a liberal capitalist order. It also demonstrated the limited utility of economic pressure as a diplomatic tool. Americans vehemently opposed revolution. Yet they feared that fighting it with U.S. troops would be expensive and unpopular, would strengthen the enemy's nationalist appeal, and would ensnare America in Europe's imperial rivalries. American leaders were caught in a bind between policy objectives and acceptable means.

Shortly after the Bolshevik revolution in Hungary engineered by Bela Kun, Hoover analyzed the dilemma. If revolutionaries refrained from armed aggression, he voted against "military intervention in . . . Hungary," which would only "make us a party to re-establishing the reactionary classes." Such injustice would "infect" American troops "with Bolshevik ideas" and provoke mass protest at home.[151] Yet the United States could not "even remotely recognize this murderous tyranny," for it would stimulat[e] actionist radicalism in every country in Europe."[152] Along with other Americans in Paris, Hoover sought a middle policy of destroying bolshevism with containment and food relief.

In early April 1919, Wilson's advisers developed a scheme for Russian food relief. Through the Norwegian humanitarian Fridtjof Nansen, the U.S. offered the Soviets food in return for their acceptance of a ceasefire in the Civil War and for turning over to Americans gold, raw materials, and control of railroads used in relief.[153] American expectations from the plan were variations on the theme of counterrevolution. House persuaded Clemenceau that relief would expose the misery of Soviet Russia and quench radical fervor elsewhere; William Bullitt wanted to co-opt and moderate the revolutionaries, and Hoover hoped to destroy the red menace, for "as soon as the fighting stops the Bolshevik army will disintegrate."[154] On May 7 the Soviets rejected the plan, but left the door open for further negotiations. The Americans and Allies were no longer interested, for the sudden success of anti-Bolshevik Admiral Kolchak had raised hopes of military victory.[155] Hoover delivered food to White Armies.[156] But with the White Russians' defeat in 1921 and the onset of famine, Americans turned once again to food relief to undermine the Soviet government. Meanwhile Colby and his successors reinforced economic and military pressures with political ostracism.[157]

As the Western powers struggled to contain bolshevism in Russia, the contagion leaped across to Hungary, on March 21. The shaken delegates at the Versailles Conference created the Council of Four to rush the peace treaty through. Charles Seymour, the American expert on Central Europe, endorsed Marshal Foch's plan to destroy bolshevism in Hungary with Allied troops, lest the menace spread to Austria, Czechoslovakia, and

Germany.[158] However, Wilson, Lloyd George, and Clemenceau rejected the idea as too expensive and dangerous. "To stop a revolutionary movement by a line of armies," Wilson argued, "is to employ a broom to stop a great flood."[159] Instead, the Western powers sent military supplies to Rumania, which was fighting Hungary, and clamped a blockade on the red republic. The blockade would demonstrate to other countries the perils of revolution. Without this threat, Hoover emphasized, we could not hope to "maintain the status quo of order."[160] He demonstrated the potency of this weapon when Austrian communists planned a May Day takeover. With Wilson's backing, Hoover announced he would cut off food shipments if radicals attempted any "disturbance."[161]

On May Day in Budapest, however, Kun rallied patriots to defend Hungary against Rumanian and Czech invaders. He had come to power in March only after the Allies had undermined the liberal Count Karolyi regime by slicing off piece after piece of Hungarian territory. Now one hundred thousand flocked to the colors, and Kun's generals swept into Slovakia and beat back the Rumanians. On June 13 Clemenceau ordered Hungary to withdraw from Slovakia and promised that Rumania would evacuate Hungarian territory. Kun complied, but Rumania did not honor the promise.[162]

Kun's resurgent strength frightened the Americans and Allies. Hoover feared that the Budapest regime undermined the stability of all central Europe. The region depended on use of the Danube, which "was impossible with Bela Kun in power."[163] The Hungarian radicals were sending money and propaganda to "industrial centers" in other countries. Unless the West overthrew Bela Kun, he warned, Czechoslovakia and Austria "will surely fall."[164] The blockade having failed to oust Bela Kun, Hoover and Lansing accepted the necessity to "throw him out by force of arms."[165] Hoover thus leaped one dilemma only to land in another. Whose troops were to crush Bela Kun? Two experts reported that a small number of American and British troops could land at Budapest and take the city unopposed. Anglo-Saxon flags, they asserted, "would be an open sesame to every difficult door in Hungary."[166] Other Americans, however, feared the consequences if the magic failed. Hoover strongly opposed sending Czech or Rumanian troops, which would only antagonize anti-Communist Hungarian nationalists. His solution was "two French divisions." Even as Hoover urged the Supreme Council to send troops, he desperately sought a "neutral" force to restore capitalism without inciting nationalist opposition or entrapping United States military power.

The French saw matters differently. "The world was sick of fighting," Clemenceau insisted. France was demobilizing and could not supply many troops. He urged the *cordon sanitaire*, but could not convince Lansing and Balfour, who wanted armed intervention. This opened the door for Foch to present the military realities: Bela Kun could field over 100,000 troops, which necessitated an Allied army of 160,000. France could contribute only 25,000, which meant some 85 percent had to come from Hungary's neighbors.[167]

As the West planned this assault, Kun's power weakened. The evacuation of Slovakia at Clemenceau's command alienated nationalist support. Peasants resented forced requisitions and Kun's failure to divide the nobles' estates. In 1919 grain productivity fell to less than a third of the prewar figure. Food shortages tightened the pressure of the blockade.[168] As Kun realized too late, Hungary lacked a "class-conscious revolutionary proletariat."[169] On July 20 Kun attacked the Rumanians in a desperate bid for food and nationalist support, but after three days the attack crumbled, and the Rumanians moved toward Budapest.[170] The defeat was a final straw.

Hoover seized upon the discontent as the way to break out of America's dilemma. T. T. C. Gregory, the ARA chief in Vienna, began talks with General Wilhelm Böhm, former head of Kun's army. In cooperation with British and Italian representatives, Gregory and Böhm agreed that Hungarian social democrats would throw out the Bolsheviks and establish a temporary "dictatorship" that would give way to a "government representative of all classes." Gregory promised to lift the blockade and send food immediately to support the new government.[171] Hoover proposed a general declaration to the Hungarian people promising food if they overthrew Kun, and the Supreme Council accepted.[172] If the scheme failed, Foch would begin the invasion. Under mounting pressure from Rumanians, hungry countrymen, and social democrats, Kun resigned on August 1 and fled into exile. As he concluded in a farewell address, the revolution had "been defeated economically, militarily and politically,"[173] by American and Allied pressures.

Hungary demonstrated the difficulty of segregating economic and military weapons in a war against revolution. Kun's fall from power rescued American policy from entrapment in a campaign of military repression. In the 1920s overoptimistic Americans concluded with Gregory that "bread is mightier than the sword,"[174] forgetting the problems of wielding economic might without a military backup.

Americans helped overthrow the radical left in Budapest, but they could not prevent Hungary from careening to the far right. The bloody White terror rooted out liberal as well as radical elements. Hoover was worried about the propaganda effect, for "the Bolsheviks were making much of it and claiming that the Allies were trying to re-establish a reactionary government."[175] The relief czar fumed that he would again clamp a

blockade on Hungary and Rumania, but never did. American leverage
had diminished with the ample Rumanian harvest of 1919.[176]

A deeper reason for inaction was that Americans could do business
with right-wing dictatorships. Like other United States leaders in the
1919–33 period, Hoover preferred liberal, democratic, capitalistic governments in Europe. Americans opposed leftist revolution as inherently
chaotic and hostile to their interests. Right-wing regimes—whether in
Hungary, Bulgaria, Italy, or, by 1933, Germany—were far more acceptable because, however unsavory politically, they secured order and
capitalism. Thus, in European domestic and international affairs, Americans favored political freedom and peaceful change, but when threatened
with upheaval, they quickly settled for order and stability.

The persisting dilemmas of order and change were part of the continuity in American policy from the Wilson to the Harding administrations.
Much of what became Republican policy was in place before March 4,
1921. Although still yearning for a League of Nations, even Wilson was
disillusioned with the real-life creature of the Allies. The Senate proved
it could effectively veto close, official involvement in European politics.
But the administration was soured on such "entanglements" anyway and
had experimented with unofficial means to represent United States interests. Hoover's ARA demonstrated that ostensibly private economic
intervention in Europe could work. Although disillusioned with Wilsonian diplomacy, many Europeans still looked to America for cultural models
and economic assistance. The Americanization of Europe proceeded without regard to change of administrations in Washington. Before Wilson
left office, then, the United States had already shifted toward involvement
that was economic and cultural rather than political and military, unofficial rather than official, private rather than governmental, and limited
rather than open-ended.

This continuity of means extended to the objectives of foreign policy.
America's burgeoning surpluses in agriculture, industry, and finance,
worsened by the 1921–22 recession, confronted each new administration
with the importance of securing outlets in Europe. Despite differences
over Article 10, administration Democrats and Root Republicans agreed
it was vital to strike a balance between revolution and rigidity. After
March 1921 Hoover and Hughes carried forward the policy of stabilizing
Europe with economic and technical assistance while seeking to undermine Russian bolshevism. Officials in the Wilson administration mapped
out future strategy on war debts, reparations, and loans. They experi-

enced the limits and frustrations of promoting peaceful change and liberal capitalism on a continent seething with social and nationalist tensions. America's European policy changed little when the Republicans came to power.

[2]

The Domestic Roots of
Republican Foreign Policy

Inheriting many of the Democrats' goals and methods, the Republicans sharpened the tools necessary to make those policies work. The first objective was cutting a path around the senatorial opposition that had rejected the Versailles treaty and hampered Woodrow Wilson's European policy. Secretary of State Charles E. Hughes and Secretary of Commerce Herbert C. Hoover, the two chief foreign policymakers in the Warren G. Harding administration, both believed that approval of the Versailles treaty with the Lodge reservations was important to stabilize Europe. They were disappointed when Wilson rejected such a compromise in 1920. Then, in his first weeks as president, Harding bowed before senatorial opposition to ratification of Versailles, even with reservations.

Hughes, Hoover, and many other top leaders in government, business, and the universities feared that congressional and public disillusionment with Wilson's crusade could cripple foreign policy, effectively isolating the nation from Europe. This would be disastrous. Most leaders believed that European prosperity was essential to America's health and that of America's other customers. Unless the European economies recovered, tensions would explode into another war or radical revolution. Conversely, Americans hoped that rising prosperity would lubricate peaceful change in Europe. Finally, they wanted to shape European recovery on an open-door, capitalist basis, conducive to U.S. economic penetration. In short, top leaders believed that American assistance and guidance were essential to Europe's proper reconstruction.

The techniques of unofficial, economic diplomacy tried out by Wilson and Hoover promised a way around congressional and public opposition to further European involvement. After 1921, Hoover and Hughes perfected those methods and, along with other elite leaders, advertised and packaged foreign policy in ways designed to minimize domestic opposition. This emphasis on economic diplomacy, informal business-government cooperation, and proper education of the public fit both the Progressive predilections of Hoover and Hughes and the popularity in the 1920s of "business" and "psychological" approaches to public problems.

New techniques in communication and advertising, coupled with semiprivate diplomacy, offered effective means to mollify public and congressional opinion. During the war, George Creel's Committee on Public Information had influenced opinion in America and Europe. Both in the United States and Europe, Hoover used public relations with great success. There was considerable irony here. At the very moment when mass education, wartime mobilization, and the Russian Revolution had awakened the masses to issues of high policy, radio and new advertising techniques gave elites a powerful tool to shape and pacify public opinion. In U.S. politics, for example, an advertising team (coiner of "Reach for a Lucky instead of a sweet") piloted Harding to a smashing victory in November 1920.[1]

Another businessman, Owen D. Young, head of the world-leading General Electric Company (GE) and Radio Corporation of America (RCA), expanded global communications. Young negotiated with foreign leaders to promote his business, defend the Monroe Doctrine, and settle reparations.[2] A Wilsonian Democrat, Young worked in harmony with the Harding administration. Private bankers and officials of the semipublic Federal Reserve Bank of New York (FRBNY) also tried to block public interference with their operations in Europe. Although some disagreement separated banking and administration leaders, the financiers' program paralled that of the government. These private, semipublic, and government officials agreed that, regardless of the league issue, limited involvement in Europe was essential to American interests and that public or congressional opposition should be minimized and sidestepped.

Harding's Policymakers

The league fight's final round took place after Warren G. Harding swept to victory with what was then the greatest popular majority in American history.[3] On foreign policy he had hedged the issues and won the votes of both irreconcilables and pro-leaguers. The president-elect continued this tactic by appointing Hughes and Hoover to head the State and Commerce departments while reassuring league opponents Henry Cabot Lodge and Philander Knox. Harding searched for what he termed

"common ground." After his inauguration, the president had Hughes
scout the chances of Senate acceptance of the league with reservations.
When anti-league senators threatened to ruin the new administration,
Harding conceded.[4] The United States would not join the League of
Nations.

This was a matter of tactics, not strategy. Rather than isolate America,
the Harding administration crafted a foreign policy to ease the problems
of economic surplus and political opposition at home while dealing with
the disorder in Europe. Hughes and Hoover were the master builders of
this policy, but they assigned important tasks to the Federal Reserve Bank
of New York and to private businessmen.

Charles E. Hughes overawed contemporaries with his extraordinary
intellect, imposing dignity, and stubborn righteousness. Even Hoover,
who doled out compliments like wartime sugar, praised the secretary of
state as his most able cabinet colleague.[5] Hughes's talent for lucid analysis
powered his rise as a prominent New York corporate lawyer. Aside from
two years as professor of domestic and international law at Cornell
University, Hughes devoted himself to his practice, where he gained first-
hand experience with domestic and foreign corporate expansion.[6] In
1910, after serving as governor of New York, Hughes resigned and
accepted a seat on the United States Supreme Court. Six years later he
won the Republican nomination for president.

Hughes enjoyed the respect of top leaders and had sampled the power
of the highest offices, but he ran a miserable presidential campaign.
Theodore Roosevelt dubbed him "a bearded iceberg."[7] His dull speeches
and political blunders lost the election to Woodrow Wilson. Hughes was
so chastened by this defeat, a State Department colleague observed, that
thereafter he was "terribly afraid of his own political judgment."[8]

The Senate's rejection of Wilson's peace treaty heightened Hughes's
sensitivity to the dangers of alienating public and congressional opinion.
As secretary of state, he shared Harding's determination not to divide
the party or nation over foreign policy. Domestic division would nullify
any foreign policy success, as Wilson's experience demonstrated. Hughes
worried about "maintaining an enlightened public opinion with respect
to international matters," particularly since the public was "still ill-ad-
justed to the magnitude of our financial power and to the international
interests accruing from the Great War."[9] This is not to say that Hughes
let concern for party unity, naysaying by irreconcilables, or the wishes
of vague "public opinion" dictate foreign policy. Rather, he acted on the
belief that sustained, successful action was impossible with strong opposition at home. Hughes put together a working consensus by carefully
staging events, cultivating legislators and political opponents, avoiding

sore points like the league, and relying on unofficial representatives beyond congressional and public reach. Hughes returned American influence to the Reparation Commission, for example, by sending unofficial observer Roland Boyden. Unofficial representatives also attended the 1922 Genoa Conference, the 1923 Lausanne Conference, and the 1924 Dawes Conference.[10] William Hard, a prominent journalist, observed that Hughes's concession on the league issue "outwit[ted] and outflank[ed] the isolationists for the benefit of internationalism and international law and order."[11] The secretary explained his policies in numerous public speeches, some over radio, held press conferences twice daily, and calculated the "psychological" impact of this or that policy.[12]

Hughes believed that involvement in Europe was vital to the United States and world peace. In 1916 he declared, "There is no isolation in the twentieth century."[13] As secretary of state he was more specific. "The prosperity of the United States," he asserted, "largely depends upon the economic settlements which may be made in Europe."[14] Here "the crux" was the perennial "reparations" problem.[15] Hughes "understands," an aide reported, "that this country is vitally interested in the whole [European reparations] settlement whether or not individual aspects of it appear to touch American interests." Hughes's formula compounded disinterested mediation by American businessmen and the money power of Wall Street.[16]

Despite the importance of an active foreign policy, Hughes prized American freedom of action and opposed entanglement in narrow European concerns. Unlike the isolationists, however, Hughes sought "a middle ground between aloofness and injurious commitments."[17] He marked out this arena carefully by refusing to bind the United States to the security of France or of any other nation. Unofficial representatives protected American interests while minimizing entanglements and opposition. Such delegates, Hughes believed, "represent[ed]" the United States government as "completely" as official ones.[18] The emphasis of Hughes and his successors on unofficial and economic diplomacy meshed with the semi-independent foreign policies of the Federal Reserve System and private businessmen. Although businessmen sometimes clashed with each other or with Washington, the general pattern was cooperation and interdependence. Like the businessmen, Hughes sought to expand American commerce through unconditional most-favored-nation trade treaties with industrial countries and the open door in the underdeveloped world. He was confident that once assured equal opportunity, the United States could "hold its own throughout the world."[19]

Hughes's "middle" policy of judicious action in Europe depended on economic and moral rather than political and military power. Moral power was not an illusion of naive men, but the prestige of America's predominant strength and political disinterestedness. "The world must accept [America's] moral leadership," stated the State Department's Western Europe desk chief, William R. Castle, "because back of that leadership is power."[20] Castle saw no conflict between American ideals and self-interest. Hughes recalled that in foreign policy decisions his "first" criterion was success.

Success was essential or else the "prestige of [the] State department and [the] United States would be damaged and [the] United States thereafter [would] be less effective in international affairs."[21] Hughes maximized prestige not by flaunting American power, but by using it efficiently. In the reparations imbroglio, for instance, he refused to intervene until the desperate Europeans agreed to an American-dictated solution.

Hughes shared power with Herbert Hoover, who accepted the Commerce post on Harding's promise of an important voice in economic and international affairs.[22] At times Hoover and Hughes conflicted, as on policy toward foreign loans. Hoover stood out as a practical idealist who had fed starving millions in a grand display of humanitarianism and engineering. Both Democrats and Republicans considered him for president in 1920, and shellshocked Progressives hoped he would pick up the liberal standard.[23] Despite protests from Old Guard Republicans ("Hoover gives most of us gooseflesh," one complained), Harding was determined to have him in the cabinet.[24] "He's the smartest 'gink' I know," the president once confided.[25] Hoover rebuilt the Commerce Department as an engine for business efficiency at home and abroad.[26] He poked into so many matters outside Commerce that another official dubbed him "Undersecretary of all other departments."[27] Under Harding, Hoover enjoyed substantial influence over administration policy.[28] Such power ebbed with the advent of Calvin Coolidge, who in 1928 sneered: "That man has offered me unsolicited advice for six years, all of it bad."[29]

In the 1920s, Hoover's advice on relations with Europe most often expressed the analysis he put forth in 1920. The United States had reached the position of Great Britain in 1860 when, despite growing raw material purchases, it could no longer absorb enough imports to cover burgeoning exports. This required long-term foreign investment to give foreigners the dollars to buy American goods.[30] However, with depreciating currencies, stagnated production, and rampant social unrest, Europe was neither a good market nor a fit field for American investment. Hoover wanted to rebuild Europe's economy and so save the continent "from social chaos."[31] This was a matter not of incidental concern, but "of daily importance to every worker or farmer in our country and the whole world."[32]

In the early 1920s and early 1930s, when depression withered foreign markets, Hoover sometimes talked about making the United States more self-sufficient. Yet he never tried to inaugurate the painful transition to an isolated economy. Neither as commerce secretary nor as president did Hoover enjoy the power to undertake such a restructuring. Moreover, his efforts during the 1918–33 period to expand markets and secure foreign sources of raw materials attested to his inability to promote simultaneously American prosperity and self-sufficiency. Hoover's great success as commerce secretary in promoting foreign markets and other ventures owed much to skillful public relations. "Publicity and advertising," he lectured, had "become an exact science."[33] Effective packaging of a policy was crucial, for "the world lives by phrases."[34] As wartime administrator, commerce secretary, and president, Hoover focused on efforts to "educate and direct public opinion." Such education linked centralized planning with cooperation by decentralized, voluntary groups. Publicity was essential to Hoover's dream of a stable, technological society knit together by concerned citizens and free of stifling bureaucracy.[35]

Private Policymakers

A cooperative, decentralized approach characterized the Republicans' economic, unofficial diplomacy. Semipublic officials like Benjamin Strong, governor of the Federal Reserve Bank of New York (FRBNY), and private businessmen like Owen D. Young and J. P. Morgan promoted American interests abroad, generally in accord with the administration's policy.

Hoover used public relations to guide citizen participation along lines laid out by elite experts. Benjamin Strong tried to shut out public participation altogether by making monetary policy the exclusive domain of Federal Reserve financiers. Agitation leading to the creation of the Federal Reserve System in 1914 had come mostly from two directions. Eastern businessmen believed that the United States needed one central bank, controlled by financiers, to stabilize domestic finances and aid foreign expansion. In the tradition of William Jennings Bryan, representatives of the South and West wanted to bust the New York "money trust" and decentralize finance.[36] The Federal Reserve Act created twelve regional banks with a supervisory board in Washington, but the power of New York's money market and Governor Strong's personality concentrated American monetary policy in the FRBNY.

In the 1920s Strong used this power to make the FRBNY the key unit among world central banks. Given the consensus of politicians and businessmen that financial stabilization was the first step in economic recov-

ery, the central bankers' role was crucial. Strong differed with Washington
on such matters as the tariff and loan supervision, but broad agreement
enabled central bank and central government to pursue semi-independent, parallel lines of foreign policy. Through the FRBNY, the administration oversaw financial aid to Europe and yet avoided responsibility
and congressional criticism. In cooperation with Governor Montagu Norman of the Bank of England, Strong made financial foreign aid conditional on the recipient country setting up a semi-independent central
bank. The creation of such institutions in each country gave orthodox
central bankers a channel for communication and influence. This development placed control of monetary policy, with its enormous consequences, in the hands of men largely free of public control. This was
necessary, Strong argued, to stave off "political" pressures—invariably
toward inflationary easy money.[37] Yet central bankers were susceptible
to the special pressure of the banking fraternity, which sought stable or
falling prices. British financier Sir Henry Strakosch spelled out the role
of central banks around the world in stifling popular control: "The trend
of political evolution the world over . . . is in a direction which makes
it less safe to entrust governments with the management of currencies. . . .
The tendency of political development in India is clearly in the direction
of increased popular representation. It takes an exceptionally enlightened
democracy to steer clear of the many pitfalls which beset the path of
currency management."[38]

In addition to the State and Commerce departments and the FRBNY,
private business shaped United States relations with Europe. Most businessmen operated small concerns and had little time or opportunity to
become involved in foreign affairs. They joined such associations as the
National Association of Manufacturers or the American Bankers Association that took stands on foreign issues and watchdogged their narrow
interests.[39] Such small businessmen, especially those of the South and
West, constituted much of the public opinion that Hoover and Hughes
hoped to direct along proper lines. Quite different were the leaders of
giant corporations and banking firms. Most of these men, with small
numbers but enormous power, believed that the reconstruction and stabilization of Europe was vital. Their economic decisions packed political
and sometimes military consequences. Such businessmen conducted many
of the negotiations and furnished much of the money that undergirded
relations with Europe.

In industry and finance the most influential figures in shaping and
implementing foreign policy were Owen D. Young, chairman of the board
of GE and RCA, and the partners of J. P. Morgan and Company. Young
masterminded the development of GE as a multinational corporation,

piloted RCA to a top position in world communications, organized American and European businessmen in the International Chamber of Commerce, engineered the reparation settlements of 1924 and 1929, and fathered the first world bank, in 1930.[40] He recognized the enormous political implications of such activities, but believed that economic relations among nations were the most important: "Whether the United States will join the League of Nations or the International Court, that is these man-made institutions, is a question which the people, acting through no wise Senate, may decide, but whether the United States will sit in the court of great economic movements throughout the world is not a question which the Senate, or even all of our people combined can decide. We are there . . . inescapably there."[41]

By 1920 GE and its international affiliates were already "there" as the dominant factor in the world's electrical goods industry. Young's ambition was "to obliterate the eastern, western, northern and southern boundaries of the United States," for, he explained, "the sphere of our activities is the world."[42] With assistance from the navy, GE in 1919 organized a group of corporations, including American Telegraph and Telephone, Western Electric, Westinghouse, and United Fruit, to funnel private and governmental radio technology into RCA. As chairman of the board of the new corporation, Young hoped to make America "the center of the world" for radio communication, thereby outflanking Britain's dominance of cables.[43] Radio communications promised political influence as well as profit. Woodrow Wilson's broadcast from New Jersey of the Fourteen Points was picked up in "remote districts in the Austrian and Balkan states," reported Admiral Bullard, navy representative on the RCA board, and the message "had been taught . . . to the school children like their catechism." Radio was crucial in Wilson's effort to reach "the people of those countries as distinguished from their governments."[44] This point was underscored by Walter Lippmann, who had helped draft the Fourteen Points, as "an attempt to exploit the modern machinery of communication to start the return to a 'common consciousness' throughout the world."[45] Such shared ideology, Young agreed, was essential to disarmament and peace: "When you can no longer appeal to the Armies of the world, you must appeal to the public opinion of the world, and there can be no public opinion in the world unless there be cheap and adequate communications in the world . . . underlying the success of any program of disarmament is inevitably the development of adequate communications."[46]

Businessmen had a more general function in stabilizing the peace. Politicians were handicapped in diplomatic negotiations by unstable parliamentary coalitions and public unwillingness to compromise. In postwar Europe and America people often had more confidence in business than discredited government. "We will not take any [unpleasant] facts from our political representatives," Young noted in 1926, "and yet there wasn't any particular difficulty about the people of Europe accepting the findings of the Dawes Committee [of businessmen]."[47]

American bankers also exercised tremendous power by negotiating with foreign governments and shaping opinion among investors. The House of Morgan enjoyed the position of top firm in the world's richest money market. Before the United States entered the Great War, Morgan and Company bankrolled the British and French governments. After the war, Morgan retained these gilt-edged clients and picked up business with Italy, Austria, and other governments. The firm set conditions for American participation in the Austrian and German stabilization loans of 1923 and 1924. Once Europeans agreed to his terms for security and interest, Morgan conducted a successful publicity campaign to get investors to purchase the bonds. With Europe's stabilization after 1924, however, Morgan lost control of the foreign bond market as hordes of smaller firms rushed to sell securities to emboldened investors.[48] But Morgan and Company remained the most august firm in an industry that valued prestige. Morgan's business with major European governments made it an important actor in foreign policy. Like Strong, Morgan partners Thomas W. Lamont and Dwight W. Morrow disliked the administration's tariff and war debt policies. Such differences, however, were relative, and often were matters more of form or politics than substance. On war debts, for instance, Hughes and Lamont were not far apart, but Hughes had to take a tougher stance in order to handle Congress and keep party and administration united.[49] Both bankers and government tried to co-opt each other's power. In 1923 with Austria and in 1924 with Germany, the State Department asked the Morgan company to stabilize the situation with dollars. Morgan insisted on adequate security and tried, unsuccessfully, to get an administration guarantee of the loans.[50] Partnership between the magistrates of government and finance was fitful, but grounded in common concern to revive Europe with minimum foreign entanglements and domestic opposition.

Congress

In 1921 Hughes, Hoover, Strong, Young, Morgan, and other top leaders faced the European opposition and congressional obstruction that had crippled Woodrow Wilson's foreign policy. Congressional rejection of the league and Versailles limited official political ties with Europe, but this restriction proved no serious barrier to administration policy. The two leading irreconcilable senators, Hiram Johnson of California and William Borah of Idaho, watchdogged American involvement with Europe. Yet their focus on the league, the World Court,[51] and other formal entanglements did not hamper unofficial, economic diplomacy. When Borah tried to stop Hughes from sending an unofficial observer to the Reparations Commission in 1921, Henry Cabot Lodge, chairman of the Senate Foreign Relations Committee, upheld the secretary's prerogative.[52] With the principle of unofficial diplomacy established, Borah's ascendancy to the chairmanship upon Lodge's death in 1924 did not throttle administration policy. Indeed, by the mid-1920s there was a growing consensus among legislators and the general public that the United States should actively promote world peace and prosperity while safeguarding its freedom of action. In Congress "isolationism" became more a slur than a badge.[53] Borah shared Hughes's and Hoover's concern to rehabilitate Europe and reform Versailles. The senator and administration officials agreed on the importance of American freedom of action, though they differed on what constituted an entanglement.

Despite this accord, Borah refused to follow the administration's lead on foreign policy. In late 1922, for instance, he called loudly for an economic conference to rebuild Europe, embarrassing—but not thwarting—Hughes's policy of waiting for Europeans to meet American conditions. Borah repeatedly urged recognition of Soviet Russia, a step anathema to the administration. He sought greater public participation in foreign policy formulation. Yet for all Borah's fireworks, he did not make American foreign policy,[54] nor did the Democratic minority in Congress—administration officials did. The Harding and Coolidge administrations packaged and advertised their European policy so as to bypass congressional obstruction. The administration's method "yielded results instead of ... fruitless ... controversy," Hughes explained.[55] In the 1920s, economic, unofficial diplomacy yielded the benefits of a rehabilitated Europe and a prosperous America. Yet the formula failed in the Depression. In the early 1930s, Congress crippled Herbert Hoover's European policy as it had Woodrow Wilson's. But in the sunny 1920s, the administration and its cohorts were able to manage Congress, because their management of America's foreign relations produced the expanded trade that leaders believed was essential to the nation's economic health.

The Economic Factor in American Foreign Policy

Especially after 1914, the American economy depended heavily on exports. United States sales abroad climbed to a dizzy $8.7 billion in

1920 and then crashed to $3.9 billion in 1922.[56] Surveying the wreckage, Americans realized that foreign trade revival depended on the revival of Europe, the number one customer. But Europe was sunk in an economic and political morass. Unless the United States government intervened with massive financial loans and political pressure—as realistic a proposition as Wilson's mutterings of a comeback in 1924—America had to wait for Europe to put its house in minimum economic and political order. In this frustrating situation, some Americans wondered aloud whether foreign trade was necessary after all. Alongside numerous assertions that foreign trade was vital to American prosperity appeared a few contrary statements.[57] "With fairly balanced relations between our own industries," Treasury Secretary Andrew Mellon concluded in 1923, "this country may enjoy a good deal of prosperity even when very unsatisfactory conditions prevail abroad."[58] "The basis of our prosperity," observed Vice-chairman William S. Culbertson of the Tariff Commission, "is in domestic finance and in domestic trade."[59] Herbert Hoover talked of national economic independence. Reading such statements, some historians have concluded that foreign trade was not of vital concern to policymakers of the 1920s.[60] But simultaneous with discussion of economic self-sufficiency, there remained a consensus which broadened in the 1920s. Those who moved beyond the simplest rhetoric recognized that "foreign trade" was not a simple entity, but the sum of literally thousands of transactions in the import and export of manufactured goods, raw materials, and food.

No one wanted to choke off American industry with massive imports of cheap manufactured goods. Despite political opposition from Democrats and warnings from some economists who thought the Republicans were overreacting, the majority party raised the tariff of 1922 as a dike against the feared flood.[61] Some historians have charged that the Republicans did not understand that the United States had become a creditor nation; but Hoover and Mellon realized full well that America's creditor position required that the rest of the world obtain sufficient dollars to pay its debts and buy United States goods.[62] At the same time they determined to shape United States foreign trade so as to maximize the power and profits of domestic industry. That meant protecting the huge home market for manufactures, pushing foreign sales of manufactured and agricultural goods, and importing noncompetitive raw materials and food. Protection enhanced domestic prosperity, the argument ran, which increased imports of noncompetitive goods. Europe would supplement its dollar earnings by marketing colonial products, hosting American tourists, and selling bonds and real property to United States investors. This system obviously stacked benefits heavily on the American side, but after 1924, as it seemed to work, domestic criticism abated. By 1928 even the Democrats endorsed the principle of a high tariff.[63]

A protected domestic market and mass production built the launching pad for manufactured exports. Foreign sales as a percentage of total industrial production fell from 13.9–14.6 percent in 1919 to 6.7–7.0 percent in 1923, and by 1927 climbed to 7.7–8 percent.[64] The United States was not Belgium or Great Britain: the primary industrial market was obviously at home. Confronted in the early 1920s with world turmoil, Hoover talked about "national industrial planning" and cooperative community to eliminate the need for exports.[65] But self-sufficiency remained a fantasy, as neither Hoover nor other leaders began the redistribution of wealth and planning of production necessary to insure domestic consumption of all production. In the real world, as Julius Klein, Hoover's long-time associate and Bureau of Foreign and Domestic Commerce (BFDC) chief, never tired of explaining, manufactured exports for many industries meant the difference between profit and loss. Without the 7 or 8 percent export market, a million workers would lose their jobs and the country would sink into a "severe depression."[66]

The gap between wishful thinking and economic reality was still wider in agriculture. Mellon observed in 1923 that with a "balance" among industries, the United States could do without exports. He admitted, however, that such a balance did not exist. Farmers, one-third of the nation's population, were mired in depression.[67] Farm exports, down from the record level of 1919, still absorbed 16 percent of the value of 1923's production. In major crops like wheat and cotton, exports were 25.6 and 48.7 percent respectively.[68] Even the domestic price of such commodities was, as Hoover put it, "dominated by the European situation."[69] Despite the growth of markets on other continents, Europe remained the number one customer, absorbing 80 percent of total farm exports in 1923.[70] Hoover and Mellon hoped that increased domestic population would eventually eat up the surplus, but Hoover acknowledged in 1926 that domestic consumption "obviously" had not kept up with production.[71] Hoover hoped diversification would reduce dependence on both exports and imports of agricultural products, but practical possibilities were limited.[72] Wheat and cotton farmers' reliance on foreign markets increased in the midtwenties. Exports as a percentage of the total value of agricultural production climbed to 18.2 percent in 1925, with wheat and cotton exports up to 26 and 61 percent.[73] For administration Republicans, defeat at the polls in 1922 sharpened the point of the statistics. Farm districts routed party regulars and slashed congressional majorities from 22 to 6 in the Senate and from 167 to 15 in the House.[74] William R. Castle blamed the defeat on the absence of "a prosperous

Europe which can buy American products."[75] To recoup their loss, Republicans in 1924 nominated for vice-president Charles G. Dawes, who, as journalist Mark Sullivan put it, was "the author of the [reparations] plan for the increase of the European market for farm products."[76]

The siren appeal of foreign trade as a way to ease domestic problems without structural change or extensive government intervention in the marketplace carried over to raw material imports. The voracious appetite of the new consumerism chewed up more raw materials than the United States could produce. Republicans designed the 1922 tariff as a package of economic rewards and penalties that induced the rest of the world to produce raw materials for American industry. With no tariff wall to climb, noncompetitive raw materials flooded in. By 1929, 65 percent of America's imports came in duty free, up from 47 percent in 1909. Europe benefited least, as only 38 percent of her exports enjoyed duty-free status, as compared with 81 percent for Asia and 84 percent for South America.[77] "Our standard of living," said Klein, "is absolutely dependent upon certain import commodities.... Without foreign trade, our industries would break down."[78] Hoover hoped to reduce this dependence. He especially opposed raw material cartels, such as the rubber scheme designed by the British to milk maximum dollars from American consumers, and encouraged United States corporations to develop alternative sources of supply.[79] Even here, however, American industry remained dependent upon materials brought in from overseas. Leaders such as Hoover who sometimes talked of self-sufficiency certainly would have liked to see America independent of foreign markets and supplies, but they were unwilling or unable to initiate the requisite adjustments, such as redistribution of wealth and planned production.

Hoover himself encouraged deeper economic involvement. "Further expansion of overseas trade," he stated in 1926, "is essential to continued economic stability in this country."[80] His Commerce Department bureaucracy powered such expansion. In the mid-1920s the BFDC answered over two million requests annually from exporters and sent out an additional four million trade circulars.[81] Such "booming" helped drive exports up to $5.4 billion in 1929, while the tariff wall restricted imports to $4.8 billion. The result was an annual trade surplus (averaging $732 million from 1921 to 1929) that, by means of the foreign trade multiplier, generated further prosperity and profit.[82] Affluent Americans invested in dollar-hungry Europe, and so fueled its recovery and payment for imports and past loans. By 1929 private investment around the globe totaled $17 billion. In that same year, the historian Charles Beard analyzed America's massive cultural "invasion of Europe."[83] Regardless of membership in the League of Nations, the United States was entangled in world affairs.

Calvin Coolidge heralded America's "foreign commerce unsurpassed in importance, and foreign investments unsurpassed in amount" and urged a larger navy. "Our interests," the president concluded, are "all over the earth."[84]

Shaping Public Opinion

Protection of these interests required careful but active diplomacy. To ensure public support or at least acquiescence to necessary involvement in the world, elite leaders in 1921 formed three organizations: the Council on Foreign Relations, the Foreign Policy Association, and the Williamstown Institute of Politics. The founders of these groups, Elihu Root, William Howard Taft, Bernard Baruch, Archibald Cary Coolidge, Walter Lippmann, Norman Davis, and other advocates of a careful but active foreign policy, hoped to tame unruly public and congressional opinion. They designed the organizations to reach opinion leaders, who would then convince the masses that America had a vital stake in Europe's reconstruction and stability. With their Progressive faith in education, the groups sponsored lectures and seminars, confident that the lesson would emerge in the exchange of ideas. Aside from their consensus favoring limited but effective involvement in Europe, these leaders divided on many foreign policy issues. Many favored joining the League of Nations, but differed on the question of reservations. Yet most were concerned that the league's defeats in 1920–21 could lead to real isolation.

The Council on Foreign Relations (CFR) defined itself as an organization to build consensus among the elite. In July 1918, a group of New York businessmen and lawyers formed a Council on Foreign Relations to study the prospects for postwar business. Several months later in Paris thirty-one of Wilson's advisers, including Edward M. House, General Tasker Bliss, Christian Herter, Hoover, and Lamont, joined with their British counterparts to form the Institute of International Affairs. Symbolizing postwar Anglo-American differences, this organization was stillborn. By 1921 it split into two national groups, the Royal Institute of International Affairs and the reborn Council on Foreign Relations.[85] The guiding hands of the reorganized council, Harvard historian Archibald Cary Coolidge, former under secretary of state Frank Polk, and *New York Evening Post* editor and former Harvard Business School dean Edwin F. Gay, determined to put together a membership "more influential . . . than that of any other organization of its size in America."[86] The first leaders included Elihu Root as honorary president and John W. Davis, former ambassador to London and future Democratic presidential candidate, as president. Hamilton Fish Armstrong, the *Post's* special correspondent in Eastern Europe, became general manager, and A. C. Coolidge served as editor of *Foreign Affairs*, the council's publication. By 1922 the council boasted some two hundred members of America's elite.[87]

Council meetings, open only to members, featured talks by domestic or foreign leaders followed by "frank and intimate discussion."[88] The council's prominent membership assured easy access to top-ranking leaders. Georges Clemenceau spoke the first year. Hughes recognized "the importance of . . . the Council on Foreign Relations" and accepted an invitation to speak before the group.[89] Hughes's successor Frank B. Kellogg carried on the precedent, and Henry L. Stimson used the council forum to deliver a major policy address.[90] When British prime minister Ramsay MacDonald visited the United States, he made his most important statement at the council dinner. The radio announcer noted, "Tonight MacDonald is meeting with the leaders, non-official I mean, in our country."[91] Meetings had two purposes, Armstrong explained: to discuss "the attitude which the United States should properly assume toward problems" and contribute "to the enlightenment of American public opinion."[92] The council commanded the attention of some of the most powerful men in the country. When opposition to the Washington Conference treaties developed in the Senate, the council quickly met "to focus public opinion, before final action by the Senate."[93] Press and radio coverage often broadcast council speeches to the rest of the country. This was important, for opposition to American involvement in Europe was concentrated west of the Hudson. Dominated by the northeastern elite, the council aimed for "a country-wide influence."[94] Armstrong reached out to the West for speakers, including Senator Brookhart, a "western radical who is 'agin' everything Washington might do in the foreign field." The purpose was to listen to Brookhart's argument while taking the "opportunity to educate him and refute some of his views."[95] The council had similar "educational" objectives in inviting German Nationalists and Russian Communists. The council paid full travel expenses, housed speakers in the best hotels, and offered a superb dinner besides the opportunity to address America's "non-official" leaders.[96]

Study groups supplemented meetings and offered the chance, a CFR official explained, to delve "more deeply into a few fundamental questions."[97] Most of these were serious affairs, with a dozen members who had extensive knowledge or interest in a subject spending a year in research, discussion, and preparation of a report to the general membership. The topics of these study groups pinpoint the central issues of the time: the relationship between domestic and foreign policy, international mineral resources, rehabilitation of Germany, relations with Japan, Anglo-American tensions.[98] The issue of league membership was conspicuous by its absence. The vast majority of members had favored Wilson's league or a league with reservations, but after 1921, despite the grumbling of diehards, it was a moot question. Coolidge saw no reason to waste "too much [in] support of the League of Nations."[99]

Coolidge and Armstrong planned *Foreign Affairs* as the "natural medium for the expression of the best thought" of America and Europe. Confident that in the marketplace of ideas it could "guide American public opinion,"[100] the journal offered diverse viewpoints; but almost all articles assumed the necessity of an active policy in Europe. For the first issue, appearing on September 15, 1922,Coolidge secured an impressive lineup of contributors, led by Elihu Root.[101] *Foreign Affairs* was an instant success, Lippmann congratulated the editor, instantly "an old established and indispensable institution."[102] Readership extended to Soviet Russia, where Vladimir Lenin and Karl Radek annotated several articles.[103] Coolidge stuck to a "highbrow policy," reasoning that with a "heavy" reputation, the journal commanded "consideration that we should not have if we were in the general scramble."[104]

The Foreign Policy Association (FPA) and the Williamstown Institute of Politics (WIP) both devoted themselves to "educating" a wider audience. The FPA originated in April 1918 at a conference of liberals including Charles and Mary Beard, Herbert Croly, Will Durant, John Dewey, Dorothy Straight, and Lillian Wald.[105] The organization drew up a list of "war aims" featuring a league to guarantee "security," peaceful change, and "equality of economic opportunity."[106] Under the banner of the League of Free Nations Association, the group rallied liberal support for the peace treaty, and after the first Senate defeat urged Wilson to accept the Root reservations.[107] Despite this stance in the league fight and wistful glances at Geneva afterward, the organization in the spring of 1921 "evolved" into the FPA. The league issue fell by the wayside as the FPA pursued what it termed an "adventure in adult education." By 1927 it branched out to fourteen cities, extending to Minnesota and Virginia in which more than twenty-seven thousand members attended lectures and discussions.[108] In contrast to the more conservative council, the FPA retained a liberal tinge. A measure of the difference was that women headed some of the FPA branches and made up almost one-third of its board of directors, while women at the council could be found only at the reception desk.[109] The FPA saw its duty as "disinterested" research and publicity. It ferreted out the "facts" with full-time researchers, a Washington bureau, foreign trips, and prominent speakers. In a steady stream of radio lectures and bulletins, the FPA got the news out to the "editors, college professors and others whose task it is to interpret our foreign affairs."[110] The message was America's "dependence on Europe," explained FPA chairman James McDonald. The "general problem" of the New York-based group was to convince "large sections of public opinion," especially in "the West and the South . . . that their stake in the restoration of normal economic conditions in Europe is in reality as direct and vital as that of the international banker."[111]

The WIP also assumed that publicized discussions would educate opinion leaders on the importance of America's role in the world. Like the council and the FPA, the WIP took final shape in 1921. Bernard Baruch funded a proposal by Williams College to hold an annual summer series of well-publicized discussions by American and foreign leaders. The college invited professors, lawyers, newspapermen, and businessmen to participate and "live together in Commons" with the speakers.[112] The caliber of participants suggests that top leaders regarded the WIP as more than an idle talkfest. Root and Chief Justice William Taft addressed the first gathering, and Taft served as honorary chairman.[113]

The mission of the WIP, declared the Williams College president, reflected the problem that "as a people . . . we do not understand world relations."[114] Taft picked up this theme and explained that foreign relations were affected not solely by "material, statistical and economic facts . . . but also by the interpretation of those facts . . . by the people of each country." Proper "interpretation" was vital, Taft believed, for "our own prosperity is to be dependent on our relations to other countries."[115]

Here Taft stated the policymakers' consensus. Regardless of the League of Nations, the United States was, especially for economic reasons, deeply involved in the rest of the world. The task for Republican leadership was to weave a foreign policy subtle enough to minimize domestic discord while promoting America's interests. The key question, Taft observed, was how people interpreted the "facts"—in other words, foreign policy was a matter not only of international negotiations, but also of packaging and selling the product to the public. This is not to say that American public opinion forced the administration to do its bidding in foreign affairs. Rather, Hughes and Hoover implemented policy in such a way as to minimize public interference. Organizations like the CFR, the FPA, and the WIP[116] sought to educate public opinion to the necessities of American involvement.

Leaders of the twenties, however, were not in agreement as to what constituted public opinion. The council defined its public as the narrow but powerful elite. The FPA and WIP reached out to what they considered the shapers of mass opinion: editors, teachers, influential businessmen.

Perceptive men like Elihu Root recognized that the United States was divided into class, sectional, and interest groups, each with its own set of ideas, yet they often referred to public opinion as a homogeneous mass with middle-class ideology or evolution toward it. One of the few who cut through the fog was Walter Lippman, who defined public opinion as "the voice of the interested spectators of action," who varied according to the issue.[117]

In the early 1920s, Lippman worried that the largely ignorant public ("the bewildered herd") had become *too* interested in public affairs.[118] Lippman's attitude was a commonplace in the aftermath of mass upheaval in Europe, social turmoil in the United States, rejection of Versailles by the Senate, and Harding's electoral victory, which irreconcilables claimed as a mandate for isolation.[119] The journalist despaired of "educat[ing] a people for self-government."[120]

Elihu Root, who commanded the lead article in the first issue of *Foreign Affairs*, shared Lippman's urgent concern. He began with the statement that "the control of foreign relations by modern democracies creates a new and pressing demand for popular education in international affairs." Mobilization of whole populations in the Great War had quickened interest in foreign affairs so that "public opinion" was increasingly an "active force in negotiations." Root genuflected before the shrine of democracy—"autocracies were utterly selfish ... democracies are generous"—but hurried on to warn of the dangers. "These plain people are our rulers," he told the WIP, but they were "untrained, uninformed and ... ignorant" folk who "must become internationally minded." This was important to the American economy, for "a large part of the influences which make for prosperity or disaster in our country consist of forces and movements which may arise anywhere in the world."[121] In this essay, Armstrong declared, "Root summed up the whole reason why *Foreign Affairs* was coming into existence."[122]

The development of sophisticated advertising and rapid communications complemented the efforts of the CFR, FPA, and WIP. From 1900 to 1930, national advertising revenue increased thirteenfold and reached $2.6 billion.[123] In 1928, advertising executive Edward Bernays recalled that only recently "the bourgeoisie stood in fear of the common people. For the masses promised to become king. To-day, however, a reaction has set in. The minority has discovered a powerful help in influencing majorities. It has been found possible to so mold the mind of the masses that they will throw their newly gained strength in the desired direction. In the present structure of society, this practice is inevitable."[124] Advertising was education of the plain people on a "scientific" basis. A nephew of Sigmund Freud, Bernays worked from the assumption that "the group mind does not *think*," but "has impulses, habits and emotions." This was a direct concern in foreign affairs, he observed, for "an international policy is sold to the public ... on the basis of the intangible element of personality."[125] Bernays "boomed" his industry just like any other product, but from an objective perspective Lippmann perceived that advertising offered "opportunities for manipulation." Lippman understood that advertising had now become "a regular organ of popular government." Lippman himself had helped shape Woodrow Wilson's Fourteen Points to publicize American war aims.[126]

This was part of the larger campaign to influence European public opinion. In 1918 and early 1919, the Committee on Public Information introduced the Italian public to relatively sophisticated advertising techniques. With a media bitz that included leaflets, photographs, speakers, newspaper subsidies, posters, postcards, movies, and lapel flags, the Americans helped stop Italy's slide toward defeatism and socialist revolution. For the twelve months after April 1918, Wilson replaced Lenin as Italy's savior. Italians prayed for peace and democracy before flower-framed altars made of a picture of Wilson. Politicians, including Benito Mussolini, tried to *"wilsoneggiarsi"* or "Wilsonize" themselves by adopting the American program of democratic reform. This passion for Wilsonism evaporated in April 1919 when the president, whom Mussolini had called "the *duce* of the peoples," opposed Italy's territorial claims.[127] The Wilsonian cult demonstrated the power of advertising and prepared the ground for longer-lasting American cultural influence in the 1920s.

Private Americans took up the publicity as tourists, artists, businessmen, aviators, film actors and actresses, and returned immigrants, whether intentionally or not, exposed Europeans to U.S. products, manners, values, and ideas. American advertising firms set up European branches[128] and contributed, in both form and substance, to the Americanization of Europe.

Advertising and other means of influencing public opinion were important tools for American foreign policymakers. Advertising executives Lord and Thomas bragged of their "massive advertising campaign" to "sell Harding and Coolidge to the country."[129] Coolidge linked advertising with "education ... It makes new thoughts, new desires and new actins."[130] Hughes stage-managed the 1921 Washington Conference; Hoover shaped public consciousness; Strong shielded central bank independence; Young organized business sentiment; Morgan sought to educate investors; and foreign policy organizations tried to mold a rough consensus. All sought to promote American interests in Europe while blunting domestic opposition or interference. In sum, American leaders aimed to sell goods in Europe and to sell their policy to the public. Their sales campaign had to succeed if they were to secure prosperity for America and peaceful change and economic reconstruction for Europe.

[3]

The Frustration of American
Policy, 1921–1923

In 1921–23, administration leaders enjoyed greater success in selling their policy to Congress and the public than in selling it to Europe. Secretary of State Hughes skillfully managed the Washington Naval Conference, imposing his disarmament and strategic program on both domestic and foreign opponents. Secretary of Commerce Hoover was equally adept at financing food and technical relief to Soviet Russia, whose regime the United States did not even recognize; but he failed to undermine the Soviet government as he had hoped. Similarly, Hughes restored American representation on the Council of Ambassadors and the Reparations Commission and signed with Germany a revised version of Versailles, but could not settle the German reparations controversy. He had to wait until the Dawes Conference of 1924 for that achievement. As long as Germany remained in turmoil, American efforts to revive Europe as a stable, prosperous customer made little headway.

Despite policy's slow progress, its direction was plain. Hughes and Hoover tried to move Europe toward slow, peaceful amelioration of the peace settlement, particularly by fixing reparations in a way that would facilitate Germany's recovery and reintegration into a prosperous Europe. Hughes pushed naval disarmament to ease naval rivalry, release funds for rebuilding Europe's economy, and set a precedent for land disarmament on that continent. Naval disarmament thus became an aid to European economic recovery, which in turn was essential to peaceful political change and America's own prosperity. America promoted European reconstruction on an open-door, capitalist basis, pushing the European nations to balance their budgets, settle war debts and reparations, reestablish stable currencies linked to gold, and reduce discriminatory trade barriers. The frustration of this program in 1921–23 had mixed consequences. Although currency depreciation destabilized Europe and hurt American exports, it subsidized many American artists, who found they could live cheap in Berlin, Vienna, and other cities. Many Americans engaged in food relief to Russia also discovered that a few dollars bought a lot of art objects in that inflation-struck country. Hoover undertook this food aid to the Russian people intending both to feed the starving and to establish an efficient American organization in Russia. If, as he hoped, the weakened Bolshevik regime collapsed, the relief agency would be there as an attractive capitalist model. But this hope was stillborn. American policymakers continued to yearn for democratic regimes while opposing leftist revolutions and accommodating right-wing dictatorships.

Americans steered a course midway between revolution and rigidity, between wholesale Versailles revision and unyielding enforcement, isolation and entanglement, Bolshevism and monarchism, inflation and depression. In war-torn Europe, however, this middle way was not always passable. In all the frustrating negotiations of 1921–23, Americans sought to help Europe while securing maximum benefits and minimum responsibilities for the United States. European nations, from anxious Britain to outcast Russia, just as consistently tried to use America's superior power for their own ends. In sum, Republican leaders in the 1921–23 period achieved a peace treaty and a naval arms limitation pact. Ideologically, they reaffirmed opposition to Bolshevism and welcomed stabilizing Fascist dictatorships. Aside from the British war debt settlement of 1923, the Republicans failed to stabilize and revive the European economy or even win Europeans to the American program for recovery. Despite the meagerness of these achievements, however, Hughes remained true to his principle of limited intervention.

In early May 1921, Hughes sketched this policy of restricted involvement in instructions to Georgy Harvey, ambassador in London. Woodrow Wilson had ended American participation in Allied organizations. Hughes renewed the effort to stabilize Europe by appointing Harvey to the Allied Supreme Council. Although America had "world-wide" interests, Hughes informed Harvey, it would not waste its power on "political questions of purely European concern." Yet the United States remained "interested in the economic questions which grow out of the war," since they affected "our prosperity." Echoing Hoover's advice of 1919, Hughes prescribed hard work and belt-tightening for Europe. Finally, he stressed determination to uphold American freedom of action and "the open door policy."[1]

The Separate Peace

This policy did not conflict, Hughes believed, with adoption with reservations of Versailles and the League of Nations. But irreconcilable senators vetoed league membership early in the Harding administration. By July 1921, Hughes concluded that the Senate would not ratify Versailles either. This put the secretary of state in a bind. League membership was not vital, but the Senate's Versailles rejection jeopardized America's victor rights. Moreover, a separately negotiated peace would draw the fire of Europeans quarreling over Versailles and destabilize the precarious postwar order. Hughes and Hoover hoped to reform the peace settlement, but not all at once and not with all the responsibility falling upon America.[2] Hoover feared that the Allies would "hate" America for negotiating a separate peace and "blockade . . . our already demoralized trade."[3]

Many congressmen did not sympathize with the administration's dilemma. Some legislators urged a unilateral peace declaration. Many farm state congressmen agitated for a quick peace and revived markets in central Europe.[4] Aside from the domestic pressure for a quick peace, Hughes wanted to stabilize relations with the Allies and Germany. Settlement of the peace treaty issue was essential to success for the upcoming conference on disarmament and the Far East.

Before 1914, Germany had been America's third largest customer, and the United States had been Germany's third greatest export market. Cotton, copper, and pork, three of America's depressed industries, enjoyed natural markets in the Reich. Germany's industrial exports offered fierce competition, but before 1914 American corporations like General Electric had found it profitable to divide world markets with their German counterparts.[5] After the Armistice, corporations renewed such ties, a development the German government welcomed.

Snaring American commitment to Germany's welfare was a major element in Berlin's strategy to throw over Versailles. The bait was trade and investment, the chance to profit from Europe's industrial powerhouse.[6] German leaders realized that politics and economics were inseparable, and in 1921 they hoped America's rejection of Versailles signaled a breach in the victors' encirclement. The United States commissioner in Berlin, Ellis Dresel, reported that many Germans "believe that it must fall into discredit, if we refuse to ratify it."[7]

Dresel's dispatches pointed up the fact that Americans had already renewed ties with Germany. Indeed, a number of American businessmen had stayed in Berlin throughout the war.[8] When representatives of the Interallied Control Commission first reached Berlin after the war, they found on a hotel bulletin board notice that the American Association of Commerce and Trade was already in operation.[9] Students trickled into Germany almost as soon as the firing stopped. During the winter semester of 1918–19, the University of Berlin enrolled twenty-one Americans.[10] Such examples were important symbolically, signifiying the tenacity of prewar ties and foreshadowing American economic and cultural penetration of Germany in the 1920s.

Other economic relations had immediate impact. Even before the separate peace of August 1921, New Jersey's Standard Oil, Averell Harriman's American Ship and Commerce Co., and Guggenheim's copper interests did business with Germany. Corporations like National Cash Register profited by building and buying factories. Speculating on the resurrection of the Reichsmark, Americans invested (and lost) some $700 million, most of it between 1919 and 1921.[11] Systematic trade and investment required an end to the technical state of war and settlement of reparations[12]—another reason for Hughes to make peace quickly. Ellis Dresel's difficult position in Berlin was a final factor. Since December 1918 Washington had maintained an unofficial mission. In March 1920, at the German government's request, Dresel publicly threatened to cut off relief supplies in the event of revolutionary outbreak,[13] but his unofficial status limited his effectiveness as a diplomat.

Economic and political imperatives, then, demanded prompt peace. Protection of United States rights and European stability required peace on the basis of Versailles, which the Senate rejected. The problem seemed insoluble.

But Hughes had not become a top corporate lawyer solely because of his dignified appearance. In early July 1921, the secretary proposed pasting together a treaty out of the peace resolution Congress passed on July 1 plus an enumeration of Versailles treaty clauses that established United States rights. This was a separate peace that did not separate America from Europe, offering the rewards of victory without responsibilities or controversy over interpretation of Versailles.[14] Hughes's treaty was "an extremely clever move ... because it will be almost impossible for the Senate to refuse to ratify it and yet we have saved what rights America had under the Versailles Treaty and this, I think, without undue cruelty to Germany."[15]

Despite this optimism, Hughes had trouble securing approval from the Germans and the Senate. Capitalizing on Hughes's need for a quick peace, the German Foreign Office tried to scavenge ammunition to attack Versailles. Hughes resisted, and Germany signed the Treaty of Berlin on August 25, 1921. The defeated nation had little choice, since hopes for recovery rested on friendship with what the *Deutsche Allgemeine Zeitung* termed "the most influential power in the world."[16] In the Senate, opposition arose from irreconcilables and bitter Wilsonians. Henry Cabot Lodge scotched William Borah's attempt to include a congressional veto over appointment of unofficial representatives.[17] Woodrow Wilson failed to mobilize Democrats against the separate peace. "The issue," declared influential Democratic senator Gilbert Hitchcock, was "between this treaty and a condition of uncertainty."[18] Frank B. Kellogg, Republican senator from Minnesota and future secretary of state, was more lurid: unless America approved the peace treaties, "the flame of revolution and anarchy which lights the skies of Russia today ... may sweep westward to the Atlantic and ... the Western Hemisphere." Moreover, he asserted, increased exports to central Europe were necessary for American prosperity.[19] Convinced, the Senate, including twenty Democrats, ratified the treaty. American diplomats negotiated similar treaties with Austria and Hungary that gave the United States the victors' rights specified in the St. Germain and Trianon treaties. Like the Berlin treaty, these pacts pleased the Senate by omitting mention of U.S. responsibilities and pleased the defeated nations by offering some revision, however minimal, of the hated 1919 settlement.

Senator Borah, who opposed the separate peace treaties, offered a perceptive analysis: the Treaty of Berlin amounted to Versailles with reservations. German revisionists gleaned some satisfaction, he explained, but the separate peace "propped it [Versailles] and strengthened it ... and thereby postponed the rehabilitation of Europe." Borah shared Hughes's and Hoover's desire to moderate the Versailles peace, but he was impatient for immediate, "far-reaching changes."[20] Partly because of sniping by such men as Borah, administration officials favored slower change, after first stabilizing Europe. The unanswered question was whether stability and change were compatible.

The Washington Conference

Hughes's greatest triumph as secretary of state took place at the Washington Naval Conference. His most spectacular success was mobilizing public opinion at home and abroad. The United States demonstrated that it would negotiate high policy with the Allies, if it could control the circumstances and outcome. The conference underscored America's regional approach to foreign policy: acceptable commitments in the Far East were unacceptable in Europe. At the same time, the Washington Conference launched a flanking attack on the problem of Europe's economic reconstruction. The meeting expressed American belief that an arms race would lead to war, a fear as deeply rooted as the desire for a navy second to none. Finally, the conference demonstrated the emphasis on results rather than rhetoric, or as Harding put it, on "something practicable."[21]

The Washington Conference came at a crucial stage in one of the most significant developments of the twentieth century, the rise of the United States and the decline of Great Britain as the predominant world power. This transfer of world leadership accelerated in the First World War and continued through the 1920s. In early 1921, the British ambassador in Washington analyzed the problem presented by the Harding administration: "The central ambition of this realist school of American politicians is to win for America the position of leading nation in the world and also of leader among the English-speaking nations. To do this they intend to have the strongest navy and the largest mercantile marine. They intend also to prevent us from paying our debt by sending goods to America and they look for the opportunity to treat us as a vassal State so long as the debt remains unpaid."[22]

Yet Britain could not afford open enmity with the United States. London's strategy was to co-opt American power for British ends while redressing the power imbalance by uniting the Empire. Dominion loyalties were already divided between Britain and the United States, and London desperately needed their resources and cooperation. Britain feared that if it pulled too strongly on imperial ties they would break, and the dominions would fall into the American orbit. In debating policy before the Washington Conference, as well as in discussions preceding the return to gold in 1925, British leaders agonized between desire to remain independent of America and recognition that they lacked the power to do so.

The American challenge complicated the issue of what to do about the twenty-year-old alliance with Japan, now up for renewal. Hughes, influenced by anti-Japanese officials in the State Department, opposed the alliance as delinquent in restraining Japanese ambitions and dangerous in the event of a United States–Japanese war.[23] Should Britain abandon the Japanese alliance and placate America? Or should it renew the pact that for twenty years had bolstered British power in the Far East?

Both choices posed economic, military, and political dangers. Wrestling with Britain's severe depression, prime minister David Lloyd George dreamed of a great China market that "might eventually total £4,000,000,000." America and Japan were both trade rivals, but America was the more serious economic competitor. Britain could make Japan a junior partner in the development of China, Lloyd George believed, but in any arrangement with the United States, America's superior economic punch might win "the whole of China's trade." U.S. economic dominance in the Far East would further encourage the dominions to look to Washington for strategic support.[24] Despite the cabinet's March 4, 1920 decision[25] to accept United States parity in capital ships, America's strength never rested easy on British minds. Lloyd George and Lord Curzon believed the Japanese alliance would force concentration of the American navy in the Pacific, thereby enhancing Britain's relative power in other seas. America's "bellicose attitude," the prime minister calculated, might require "a defensive alliance with Japan."[26] Other cabinet officials, including colonial secretary Winston Churchill, warned that the alliance would not intimidate America, but spur it to outbuild the combined English and Japanese fleets.[27] An exchange between Churchill and Lloyd George underscored the dilemma. " 'No more fatal policy could be contemplated than that of basing our naval policy on a possible combination with Japan against the United States,' " Churchill said. "The Prime Minister suggested there was one more fatal policy, namely, one whereby we would be at the mercy of the United States."[28]

Although concerned with independence, Lloyd George opposed breaking with America. Britain "could not fight the United States for economic as well as for military reasons," he concluded.[29] Some cabinet officials hoped that dropping the alliance might earn war debt concessions.[30] In late May 1921, the cabinet finally decided to deal with the dilemma of American power by trying to neutralize that strength. London would ask Harding to summon a conference of Pacific powers. If he agreed, Britain would invite the United States to join the alliance in a tripartite pact. Improved relations, it was hoped, would slow down the naval race in all three nations, and relieve the Exchequer. If America refused, Britain would reaffirm that the Japanese alliance was not directed against the United States, and renew it.[31] Unless America cooperated, then, the alliance would stand. The cabinet reached a decision. But London no longer governed the whole empire. Coordinated imperial policy now required agreement among the dominions, with divergent economic and strategic perspectives.

At the Imperial Conference of June–August, 1921, discussion of American relations exploded in a bitter debate that challenged the empire's unity. Canadian prime minister Arthur Meighen insisted that regardless of American concessions, the empire must drop the Japanese alliance. Meighen tore open the contradiction in British policy: If United States friendship was the "lodestar ... we must give foremost consideration to ... American relations."[32] Canada would not join a "combination against an American menace."[33] Canada could lean on the Monroe Doctrine in the event of a Japanese attack, however; Australia and New Zealand could not. Australian prime minister William Hughes denounced Canada's proposal "that the Foreign Policy of the Empire is to be determined by the United States of America," and declared, "I am for the renewal of this Treaty."[34] Opinion on opposite sides of the issue agreed that the empire's relations with America were all-important. Jan Smuts of South Africa warned that alienating America would eventually split up the empire.[35] The London Foreign Office feared that Canada "play[ed] into the hands of Senator Lodge and his party who hope to utilize the question of the Japanese Alliance for the purpose of detaching her and possibly Australia with a view to shift the centre of the English-speaking communities from London to Washington. Every effort should be made to prevent this."[36] Eventually Curzon and Lloyd George maneuvered Meighen to accept the idea of a tripartite pact including the United States. However, British leadership expected that the proposed Washington conference would fail, leaving the Japanese alliance intact.[37] These cabinet and imperial discussions pointed up Britain's problems in defending its empire in a world increasingly dominated by the United States.

In July 1921, British efforts to resolve the Japanese treaty issue intersected with the Harding administration's efforts to channel domestic demand for disarmament. Popular enthusiasm for disarmament blossomed after December, 1920, when Borah called for international agreement to slash naval construction.[38] Harding opposed such disarmament until the United States could float "the best that there is for the advance of our commerce."[39] However, the president soon encountererd strong disarmament pressure. Spurred by peace lobbies, Congress rebelled against the ship-building program.[40] Treasury secretary Andrew W. Mellon stated that arms expenditure threatened his economy drive.[41] Hoover warned that armament drained off too much capital and left "little hope of finding ... that surplus with which we can upbuild Europe." Echoing farmers and businessmen across the country, he told Harding bluntly that such spending "obstruct[ed] ... Commerce."[42] Hughes realized that the naval program stimulated more building by England and Japan, threatened to drive those two nations closer together, and heightened chances of conflict.[43] The Great War had taught that armaments were not deterrents, but weapons for war. In sum, conditions were ripe for a disarmament conference.

At the same time London asked Harding to call a Pacific conference, Hughes inquired informally whether the major naval powers would come to a disarmament conference in Washington. The secretary of state maneuvered to keep the meeting "our show" by publicly extending the disarmament conference's scope to include Pacific affairs.[44] The British accepted and congratulated themselves on manipulating Washington ("We have made history," Churchill chortled.)[45] Then came the painful discovery that, as Lloyd George lamented, "the Americans have manoeuvred us into a very bad position tactically."[46] He and Curzon had wanted a preliminary London conference where Britain could dominate the conclave and direct a favorable Far Eastern solution.[47] This Hughes refused.

He would not discuss the Far East except in the larger context of a Washington disarmament conference, in which he could set the agenda, bargain with American naval strength, weaken imperial unity, and sell the whole package to Congress as the means toward peace. The British cooled toward the conference. American dominance of the meeting, Lloyd George feared, meant "a newspaper campaign to force us into acceptance of the extreme United States position."[48] This proved to be an understatement.

Meanwhile Hughes faced a wide-based popular campaign for substantial disarmament. Concerned women, churchgoers, pacifists, farmers, students, radicals, and labor unions sent more than 13 million letters and petitions urging arms reduction. Well-informed groups petitioned for specific policies: representation of labor and of women on the delegation, open diplomacy, and emphasis on disarmament rather than the Far East.[49]

Hughes molded much of this popular sentiment into a tool of administration policy. The administration used Samuel Gompers to help regulate opinion at home and pressure leaders abroad. The problem, Harding and Hughes confided to the union leader, was that "too powerful and irresistible a demand from the American people" could cripple administration policy. Gompers could help by urging labor unions in other nations to "press upon their governments the same necessity of going to the limit." The labor chief eagerly complied.[50] With the advice of Hughes and Elihu Root, Harding appointed the American Advisory Committee to represent "the people" at the conference. Members included General John Pershing, Hoover, Gompers, governors, and representatives from the State, War, and Navy departments, including four women. Radicals, pacifists, and ordinary citizens were conspicuously absent. The committee, Hughes calculated, would satisfy "organizations and . . . supply dignified positions without permitting direct participation on the Conference." He detailed Hoover "to keep peace" within this "political repository."[51] This committee of "the people" effectively shielded Hughes from both public interference and charges of closed diplomacy. The facade wore thin when the Advisory Committee, on Hughes's advice, dismissed widespread agitation for total abolition of submarines as "alien"-inspired and "emotional" and advocated limitation instead.[52]

With the leashing of domestic public opinion, Hughes and Harding planned their strategy at the November conference. America would use naval disarmament, and the potential to outspend Japan and Britain, as levers to end the alliance and retain the Open Door. In September, Hughes told London the United States would accept a tripartite Pacific agreement with no binding commitments.[53] The Foreign Office was interested, but still feared, as one American expert put it, that the price of cooperation was "defer[ence] to the United States point of view on all occasions."[54] The tripartite pact would meet opposition in the Senate, Hughes realized. This influenced the choice of delegation members: Henry Cabot Lodge, chairman of the Senate Foreign Relations Committee, eager to demonstrate an alternative to Wilson's league; Elihu Root, widely respected and at seventy-six still a canny infighter; Oscar Underwood, Democratic Senate minority leader; and Hughes himself.[55] Neither Borah, who originally instigated the disarmament movement, nor navy officials received invitations. In preparation for the conference, Hughes dismissed the navy's policy recommendations and, despite doubts by his fellow delegates, secured Harding's approval for a "stop-now" plan. This would appeal strongly to public opinion at home and abroad, leaving the United States at a favorable stage in the naval race. A few days before the conference, Hughes incorporated the plan into what became the most notable speech of his career.[56]

The staging of the conference would have done the nascent film industry proud. On Armistice Day, with the foreign delegations assembled, Harding presided over the burial of the Unknown Soldier and, symbolically, the chaos of war. He asked for a "new . . . era of peace on earth." The next day he opened the disarmament conclave with emphasis on the need for "a better order which will tranquillize the world."[57] Instead of the platitudes that usually characterize such openings, Hughes made an electrifying statement. Displaying what a British delegate termed "a superb sense of the dramatic," the secretary offered disarmament now. He urged a ten-year naval holiday and the scrapping of thirty United States capital (battleship) vessels. As the delegates absorbed this shock, Hughes listed vessels Tokyo and London should scrap and suggested a 5:3:3 tonnage ratio for capital ships in the American, British, and Japanese fleets.[58] Hughes captured the imagination and approval of the world and with it, control of the conference. Awestruck, Balfour applauded this "great artist."[59] Robert Lansing mused that Wilson should have tried this at Paris, and even Borah acknowledged a "splendid beginning."[60] Now foreign delegates and Democratic senators could oppose the plan only at the risk of appearing to oppose peace.

The rest of the conference was almost anticlimactic. After some haggling, the British, Japanese, French, and Italians accepted a 5:5:3:1.67:1.67 capital ship ratio and the naval holiday, with modifications. The ratio expressed the Republicans' regional strategy and, along with the prohibition on fortifying Pacific bases, assured Japan naval dominance in the western Pacific. France had expected to mediate between America and

Britain, but finding those nations in accord on capital ships, Paris protested against its meager share and pleaded unsuccessfully for security
against Berlin.

In part, nations agreed to scrap capital tonnage because they suspected
that technology might soon render the giant ships obsolete.[61] Despite the
hoopla over sinking battleships, the delegates failed to agree on limitation
of cruisers or submarines. The naval lesson of the Great War taught the
importance of cruisers, which protected merchant ships, and submarines,
which sank them. Doubly resentful because the Anglo-Saxons dismissed
its third-class navy and criticized its first-class army, France insisted on
the right to build up to ninety thousand tons of submarines, over three
times its existing tonnage. Submarines were a cheap way to equalize other
powers' surface strength. Britain protested the threat to its commerce
and refused to restrict antisubmarine cruisers. Rather than jeopardize the
conference, Hughes agreed to leave open the number of submarines and
cruisers.[62]

On February 6, 1922, the five major naval powers signed the disarmament treaty. Hughes bargained away rights to build the largest battleship fleet and fortify Pacific islands (west of Hawaii), projects for which
Congress would not vote money, in return for the adherence of Britain
and Japan to the Four Power and Nine Power treaties. The former secured
the breakup of the Anglo-Japanese treaty and substituted a promise by
the powers (United States, Britain, Japan, and France) to respect each
other's territories in the Pacific and consult in case of controversy. This
was vague enough to satisfy the Senate, yet enabled Britain to placate
Australia and let Japan down gently. The Four Power pact was an important step in Britain's dependence on America, since it closed the option
of cooperation with Japan against America. Like the United States, Britain
now held only Japan's promise in the Nine Power treaty to keep the open
door in China. Like Japan, Britain obtained from America only the promise to consult.[63]

The Five Power disarmament treaty sweetened the package for the
Senate as well as Britain and Japan. Led by Lodge, administration forces
beat back Senate opposition to the Four Power pact by stressing that the
treaties were inseparable. Democrats sought revenge for Lodge's campaign against the league. Republican maverick Borah opposed the Four
Power treaty. Overwhelming support for the pact guaranteed his failure.
The administration had done its work so well that newspapers urged
ratification nine to one. Opposition came primarily from the Hearst chain,
but organized groups from the National Milk Producers' Federation to
the Parent-Teachers' Association endorsed the treaties. Underwood cor-
ralled Democratic votes, and on March 24, 1922 the Four Power treaty

passed with a thirteen-vote margin. The Five and Nine Power pacts then coasted through the Senate.[64]

Harding and Hughes were justifiably proud. Washington "demonstrated," the president confided to a friend, "that some of the things that we kept hinting at in the 1920 campaign can be accomplished by commonsense methods."[65] Harding still cherished romantic feelings about "an Association of Nations," but never found the "psychological moment" to commit himself publicly.[66] Perhaps like the president's mistress, Nan Britten, the "Association" was dispensable and not worth the political risk. The conference proved that outside the League of Nations, America could negotiate high policy and cooperate with other great powers while reserving freedom of action and blunting domestic opposition. The regional approach stabilized the Far East and prepared the way for United States action in Europe. The treaties undercut British independence and eased the threat of war and revolution. Harding concluded: "How simple it all has been."[67]

Yet the administration's success at Washington left problems untouched. Hughes had refused an invitation to the largest Far Eastern power, Soviet Russia, which challenged American policy to rebuild a viable capitalist Europe. Germany remained outside the circle of western industrial nations. The snubs France received at Washington strengthened its determination to suppress Germany. Italy's weak government gratefully accepted parity with France, but a few months later Benito Mussolini came to power. Trade and finance remained jumbled, and Americans and Britons differed over how to order a new structure. In 1921–23 United States leaders grappled with these problems by trying to undermine the radical left in Russia and eastern Europe, accommodate the Fascist right in Italy, settle political debts, and rebuild a world economy centered on America. This policy of seeking gradual amelioration of the peace settlement and orderly capitalist growth was frustrated by the problems of Franco-German tensions and Bolshevik Russia.

The United States and Bolshevism

Although Hughes himself negotiated the separate peace and conducted the Washington conference, he shared power in Russian affairs with Herbert Hoover. Despite bureaucratic rivalry between their two departments, the two men agreed on political and economic pressure to undermine the Bolshevik government. Some liberal groups, such as the Foreign Policy Association, urged political recognition of Soviet Russia, but members of the elite Council on Foreign Relations endorsed administration policy. Confiscated "American interests in Russia are much larger than has been generally imagined," a CFR study group explained, and "represent a major American concern." Like the administration, the CFR awaited Bolshevism's collapse and Russia's reestablishment "as a democratic republic and a ... friendly ally." This would secure "the established principle of the Open Door."[68]

For the present, however, Hughes and Hoover faced a dilemma in economic relations. If America withheld trade and investment, it might pressure the Soviets and weaken their economy. Yet American trade could moderate the Bolsheviks. Moreover, if the United States stayed out of Russia entirely, it would lose markets to European competitors. With no simple solution, Hughes and Hoover tried to limit Russian business to large corporations open to administration influence. Hughes continued Woodrow Wilson's policy of refusing political recognition until the Soviets acknowledged previous regimes' debts, compensated foreign property owners, and ceased propagandizing in America.[69] American rejection of Soviet moves to negotiate these demands pointed to the underlying prerequisite of recognition: the end of bolshevism.[70]

In the spring of 1921, the Soviet regime appeared on the verge of collapse. Hoover interpreted Lenin's New Economic Policy (NEP) as a confession of failure. Famine increased chances that the Soviets would "be overthrown." If that "much-to-be-desired change" occurred, officials of Hoover's American Relief Administration (ARA) were "anxious to show American good will at the earliest possible moment" with food relief.[71] When writer Maxim Gorky made an appeal for "bread and medicine," Hoover saw his opportunity to establish an American-run relief organization in Russia. How could he proceed, however, when the United States did not recognize the Russian government? Hoover sidestepped this problem by responding, as he put it, in his "entirely unofficial" capacity as ARA chief. He offered the Russians "food, clothing, and medical supplies" in return for release of all American prisoners, free transportation, and full freedom in administering relief. The ARA would "engage in no political activities,"[72] he promised, and he honored this pledge, realizing the ARA could not get far in either relief or politics if it overtly opposed the Soviet government. Hoover preferred the more sophisticated method of impressing Russians with America's generosity, efficiency, and productivity. His motivation for relief was both humanitarian and political. Unlike later historians, he saw little conflict between America's ideals and self-interest. The Soviet government agreed to Hoover's general conditions. After intense negotiations, Maxim Litvinov, deputy commissar for foreign affairs, agreed with the ARA representative on a "treaty."[73]

Hoover then faced the problem of how to finance Russian relief and explain it to the American public. Characteristically, he centralized power and steered a middle course between right- and left-wing critics. At Hoover's request, Harding publicly asked the ARA to coordinate all American relief to Russia. Hughes granted passports to Russia only to ARA-approved Americans. When pro-Soviet groups protested, Hoover enlisted the attorney general in a publicity attack. He resisted such right-wing critics as Henry Ford's *Dearborn Independent*, which labeled the ARA's staff pro-Bolshevik.[74] Hoover tried to stifle public discussion of aid to Bolshevik Russia, lest controversy destroy the administration's balanced policy. This complicated the problem of raising money. The ARA chief was a past master at dramatic appeals, such as the highly publicized ARA thousand-dollar-a-plate dinners at which donors ate relief rations.[75] But in the case of relief to Russia, an ARA official recalled, "an appeal ... might result not in funds, but in a violent reaction against 'foreign charity' in general and ... Russia in particular."[76] That would cripple an important arm of foreign policy. Moreover, Hoover believed that in the postwar depression, America's own poor should have first priority in fund drives.[77]

Despite these barriers, the ARA raised over $87 million, Congress supplying the largest single amount.[78] The Secretary of Commerce exploited his position as the public head of a "private" organization. At his request, Harding asked Congress to buy surplus corn for Russia relief. Friendly congressmen mobilized farm state support and blocked opposition by holding only abbreviated hearings. Congress appropriated $20 million, believing the purchase would revive the grain market. At a time of "depression," Hoover affirmed, "we are doing an act of economic soundness."[79] Equally astute politics netted the ARA $4 million of surplus medical supplies from the War, Navy, and Treasury departments. To secure funds and a commitment from the Soviet government, the ARA insisted that the Russians contribute some of their gold reserves.[80]

Despite "camouflage," as the ARA director for Europe observed, relief was "semi-official." At Hughes's request, the ARA assumed consular duties in Russia. Agency officials sent economic and political reports to Washington.[81] Hoover included ARA activities in his report as Commerce secretary. The army granted officers leave with pay to work with the ARA. The navy despatched ships to Russian Black Sea ports to assist with transportation and communication, and on one occasion a naval officer obtained from an informer details of defense fortifications. This breached ARA neutrality, but Hoover waited over a year, until naval facilities were no longer needed, to complain and ask the destroyers to leave.[82]

Soviet leaders understood the "semi-official" nature of the ARA. They did not realize, however, that Hoover and Hughes regarded relief as a substitute for rather than a prelude to recognition. Joseph Stalin and Leon Trotsky remained deeply suspicious, but Lenin enthused: "HOOVER is really a plus ... agreements and concessions with the Americans are super-important to us."[83] Lenin and foreign affairs commissar Georgi Chicherin regarded the ARA as a door on the West through which Russia could import United States capital and technology. Chicherin advised an ARA official that "Russia was anxious for cooperation and assistance from the United States."[84] America was Russia's proper model, Chicherin explained, because the United States "turned a gigantic virgin continent ... into a miracle of most perfect technique of production and culture."[85] Hoover and Hughes subscribed to the same analysis, except that for them Russia's emulation would come after bolshevism fell.

Although the ARA did not stimulate the capital flow the Bolsheviks hoped for, it helped end the famine. In August 1922, at the peak of the famine, 180 Americans supervised 18,073 ARA kitchens, which fed 10.5 million Russians daily. ARA operations extended from the Ukraine to Siberia and included aid to 1837 hospitals and several thousand other state institutions.[86]

Although the ARA had less independence than it enjoyed in Poland or Austria, its food relief still packed social, political, and cultural consequences. At Hoover's insistence, the ARA hired Russian employees regardless of social class. Thousands of bourgeois and others out of favor with the government flocked to the ARA for jobs. The relief organization sustained middle and upper classes with the food draft program, by which donors in America paid the ARA to deliver food to a friend or relative in the old country.

The ARA refused to accept the labor regulations of the Soviet trade unions, and thus remained a nonunion shop in a country governed (at least theoretically) by organized workers.[87] It had its way on the union question because the Soviets were desperate for food, but Americans adjusted easily to other aspects of the Bolshevik system. Rail transport improved dramatically after the ARA contacted the commissar, Feliks Dzerzhinsky. Dzerzhinsky knew little about trains, but he had, an ARA official recalled, a reputation of "legendary horror" as organizer of the secret police. ARA officials "found it satisfying to think" that he "might be able to terrorize the railways into greater usefulness." When ARA director William Haskell had trouble with some local Russian official, he invoked the name of "Mr. Dzerzhinsky." (Evidently the Bolshevik concept of civil rights made an impression on Haskell, who responded to a union leader's criticism by urging that the offender "be discredited and punished."[88])

Despite such contact with the central government, the ARA's real work was out in the villages, where young Americans undertook a program of Progressive reform to relieve famine and promote community development. The ARA, one American observed, "started waving the flag from one end of the Volga to the other."[89] So that even illiterate villagers would appreciate their benefactor, Hoover provided that all ARA food outlets display his picture and the words *American Relief Administration* in Russian and English. In the spring of 1922, with relief flowing relatively smoothly, ARA officials in many of the districts undertook public works financed with food. Americans organized "city and village improvement committees." To Russian bewilderment, the ARA ordered crews to clean up rubbish that had accumulated since the Revolution or even before. They allocated food for sanitary police and night watchmen, breeding farms, and venereal clinics. In one district ARA-fed teams built a flood canal, 279 new bridges, and 94 town water cisterns. In other areas they planted trees, drained swamps, and built roads.[90]

In return, Americans took home cultural treasures, which they were able to buy cheap because of the depreciating Russian currency. Archibald Cary Coolidge, Harvard professor and *Foreign Affairs* editor, served on the ARA staff. While in Russia he took advantage of rates of exchange "undreamt of before" to buy up books, manuscripts, and rare perioidicals for the Harvard library. Coolidge, who had made similar purchases in inflation-wracked Austria and Germany after the war, now traded dollars for the cultural heritage of impoverished Russian professors and nobles. Anna Louise Strong, a member of the American Friends relief team, reported that the Russians resented these ARA "speculators," but even she could not resist buying "a nice [4' × 8'] Caucasian rug for $2.00."[91]

An American reporter explained that the ARA was "in a sense competing with the Russian authorities," and although greedy at times, the Americans apparently impressed Russian peasants. "The people in the territory where we are feeding are deeply grateful to us, admire us, and depend on us." one ARA official wrote. "The contrast between us and their government is too striking. From the government they have never had anything but broken promises, from us they always get what they were promised. In such a situation it is obvious who will get their affection."[92]

Perhaps it was also obvious to Soviet officials, who in late 1922 attacked the ARA in a propaganda campaign. With good harvest prospects for 1923 and mounting difficulties with the Soviet government, Hoover ordered the ARA to pull out on July 20, 1923.[93]

For Hoover, the venture was a political failure in Russia and a political success at home. The relief effort demonstrated the administration's ingenuity in financing and implementing foreign policy. As head of the

"private" ARA and the public Commerce Department, Hoover tran-
scended each sphere and minipulated both. Yet the ARA saga did not
end as he had hoped. He had expected that with a food organization in
Russia when the Bolsheviks collapsed, the ARA could influence events.
After the Communists fell, a grateful Russia would turn to the United
States for "leadership." He dreamed of "the establishment of American
firms abroad, distributing American goods under American direction,
and ... the building of direct American financing and above all ... the
installation of American technology in Russian industries."[94] Soviet sur-
vival (aided by ARA food) trimmed these ambitions to a belief that
American generosity, efficiency, and productivity would invite unfavor-
able comparisons with bolshevism. Such may have been the case, but the
Soviet government endured. Their Progressive optimism led Americans
to clean up cities, build roads, and stimulate community action. They
hoped moderate reform could replace revolution. The ARA also illustrated a darker side of Progressive reform: the swift appreciation of secret
police efficiency. The ARA was a sophisticated element in the administration's anticommunism.

That stance persisted after the food relief program. Three days after
the ARA left Russia, Hughes reaffirmed nonrecognition. Throughout the
1920s and 1930s Robert F. Kelley, chief of the State Department's Division of Eastern European Affairs, watchdogged this Russian policy. He
designed training of the Department's Russian experts to ensure an anti-
Soviet perspective, encouraged diplomats at the Riga, Latvia listening
post to imbibe the "old Russian" culture of the White emigrés, and
detailed an agent to cultivate contacts with the intelligence services of
other anti-Soviet governments.[95]

United States officials also disliked radicalism in other parts of Europe.
The American minister obtained from the Austrian police extensive reports on European radicalism, which Hughes and other State Department
officials carefully examined.[96] The State and Justice departments cooperated with foreign police to watch domestic radicals who traveled abroad
and to prevent Communists from emigrating.[97] In 1926, during the British
general strike, U.S. diplomatic officials deplored the Labour Party's " 'Red'
principles and ideas." The strikers had to be put down, one ambassador
asserted, to preserve "the stabilizing and restraining influence of the
British Empire in world affairs."[98] Similarly frightened by agrarian po-
pulism in Bulgaria, American representatives welcomed a right-wing
takeover.

In 1919 a rough peasant leader, Alexander Stamboliiski, won election
as prime minister of Bulgaria. Stamboliiski, whom journalist Ernest Hemingway described as a "scowling Buffalo Bill," favored land reform and
progressive taxation while reducing the army's power and attempting

reconciliation with Yugoslavia. In a nation 80 percent peasant, Stamboliiski's Agrarian Union offered the most popular alternative to the Communists, the second largest party.[99] Charles S.Wilson, minister to Sofia under both Democrats and Republicans, concluded from these reforms that Stamboliiski had "gone over to the Communists.... Bulgaria is not a safe field for foreign capital and trade," he warned.[100] Wilson advised Stamboliiski that Bulgaria's "weakening" hostility toward Russia aroused "distrust." The State Department closely watched what Near Eastern desk chief Allen W. Dulles feared as "a tendency in Bulgaria towards communism."[101]

After Stamboliiski's victory in the April 1923 elections, a coalition of army officers, Macedonian nationalists, and conservative politicians staged a coup. The Communists remained neutral, and Stamboliiski was killed. Chargé Herschel Johnson explained the coup as a "fascist reaction" against the Agrarians' "demagogy and disrespect for law." He reported "that the majority of the nation is pleased and is experiencing the agreeable sensation of relief from an unpleasant strain."[102] Americans in Sofia certainly were relieved. Wilson still feared another "Communist-Agrarian uprising," however. Renewed radicalism could threaten the Standard Oil plant at Burgas. The American minister now urged an army increase to combat internal disorder.[103] Encouraged by this concern, Sofia's Washington representative appealed to the secretary of state, Frank Kellogg, for direct aid against Bulgaria's communists. Kellogg said no. Although the United States opposed communism, it was not willing to become directly tangled in European politics.[104] However, the State Department did offer concrete support to Poland, where it feared "a Bolshevist invasion." The department waived policy prohibiting loans for military purposes, because, as Western Europe desk chief William R. Castle explained, "the Polish army must be properly supplied with trucks if there is to be any chance of defending the country."[105]

In Europe's ideological conflict, American leaders preferred democratic capitalism, but consistently favored conservatism and fascism over communism and radicalism. America's antileft stance hardened in the twenties as business sought stable fields for trade and investment. In the postwar years, drastic change and revolution threatened from the left, not the right. Thus, Americans welcomed Benito Mussolini as a stabilizing force for Italy.

The United States and Fascism

The United States had important economic, political, and cultural ties with Italy that reached back to the Great War. Acting on the State

Department's fear that Italy might become "a second Russia," the Committee on Public Information (CPI) conducted a massive propaganda campaign directed to keep that country in the war and to build there "the edifice of Wilsonian democracy." This was Italy's first encounter with modern publicity techniques, and the people responded with almost religious fervor. Mussolini, at the time a prowar, moderate socialist editor, was the type of leader the Americans hoped to use in building a reformist middle alternative to the reactionaries on the right and the revolutionaries on the left. Mussolini sailed with the prevailing winds, declaring his "accept[ance] to the uttermost [of] the Wilsonian program for the reorganization of the world." Charles Merriam, the CPI director in Italy, offered appreciatively to subsidize the expansion of Mussolini's newspaper. "Find out how much money he needs," Merriam told an intermediary.[106] The CPI ceased operation early in 1919 after Wilson's triumphal tour; too soon, it developed. American aid had failed to create a vital center in Italian politics. Moreover, when Wilson opposed Italy's territorial demands at Versailles in April 1919, "Wilsonismo" evaporated and "son of Wilson" became a vicious insult. Politics polarized and by 1922, disillusioned with the millenial visions of both Wilson and Lenin, many Italians welcomed Mussolini. Il Duce had backed away from democratic reform, but even in 1922 he spoke of the "sad, sad decline of the prophet" Wilson.[107] The brief but intense interlude of Wilson's popularity had significant impact on the postwar decade. It helped secure Italy from radical revolution. It also illustrated the difficulty in finding a middle path in Europe's polarized politics. Despite this failure and Wilson's fall from grace, the propaganda campaign reinforced in Italian minds the importance of America's economic power, military might, and cultural example.

Mussolini lost no time reknitting his ties with the United States government. Shortly before his march on Rome, Mussolini talked with Richard Washburn Child, the U.S. ambassador, about the American attitude toward fascism. Upon taking power, he broke protocol by visiting Child rather than waiting to receive the ambassador. Mussolini termed "American cooperation . . . vital" and dangled investment "opportunities."[108] "Nothing but good can be said about the United States," he announced candidly. "One must always speak well of one's creditor, and we all owe the United States money."[109]

American political and economic leaders spoke equally well of the new dictator. The ambassador to London welcomed "the death blow to Bolshevism," and urged that Child show "notable friendliness and helpfulness."[110] Child labeled Mussolini's "enemies . . . a class of weak and halting men," and recommended a goodwill visit by the American navy.

Child's passion for Italian fascism later blossomed to the extent that he joined the party.[111] The ambassador did warn Washington that the Fascists would probably pursue a "chauvinistic hazardous foreign policy."[112]

Throughout the twenties and early thirties, Americans tried to use financial leverage to moderate that chauvinism. No one in the Harding administration questioned recognition of the new regime. Hughes and Mussolini exchanged greetings, and Harding sent the Italian leader a letter. "The great danger," warned the chargé in Rome, was Mussolini's "collapse." The State Department remained solicitous of Mussolini's welfare throughout fascism's first decade, fearing assassination attempts as "an upset."[113] Rooted in shared political and economic interests, Italian-American friendship grew. By 1931–32, secretary of state Henry L. Stimson recalled, Rome was "of all the greatest Continental powers the least difficult."[114]

American businessmen also found it easy to deal with Fascist Italy. The president of the Merchants' Association of New York praised the Fascists' defeat of "communism" by "substitut[ing] the ideals of individualism ... thrift and hard work."[115] Judge Elbert Gary of United States Steel suggested, "We, too, need a man like Mussolini."[116] Lured by Mussolini's talk of electrifying the railroads and selling them to private investors, United States Steel, General Electric, Bankers Trust Company, and the Mellon interests flocked to Italy.[117] Morgan partner Thomas Lamont enthused, "This is going to be a great country," and in 1926 backed that sentiment with a $100 million loan. By 1930, such borrowing totaled $462 million, and direct investment in utilities alone exceeded $66 million.[118] Perceiving "a special opportunity for American investment," Hoover urged the president to appoint as ambassador "a man of large industrial, financial and commercial vision."[119]

Mussolini's dictatorship did not trouble Americans who did business in Italy. Italians were politically naive and undisciplined, Americans argued, and threfore unready for American-style democracy. Fascism's program of efficiency, discipline, and progress would help them mature. Most business leaders, ignoring Mussolini's reign of terror, concluded that "the people are back of him."[120] Il Duce cultivated this benign image. "Mussolini no Napoleon, want fight, always mad; Mussolini laugh, gay, like good time, a Regular Guy," he assured Will Rogers.[121] A symbiotic relationship developed between the Italian leader and American journalists: he supplies them with news and interviews; they produced stories of adventure and success. In a decade engrossed by spectacles, the strutting dictator proved a sensation. Disdainful journalists like Walter Lippmann remained few.[122] Will Rogers observed: "Everybody in the world had either flew (*sic*) to the north pole this summer or was trying

to see Mussolini." He "took the Mussolini end, because there are two
poles but only one Mussolini." Rogers came away proclaiming, "This
Gent is a kind of cross between Roosevelt, Red Grange, Babe Ruth, when
the Babe is really good; the elder La Follette, a touch of Borah, Bryan
of '96, Samuel Gompers and Tunny."[123]

As Rogers humorously suggested, Mussolini reflected a variety of
American ideals and virtues. At a time when Americans were torn between agrarian past and industrial future, when war and revolution had
killed easy optimism, when Henry Ford and Frederic Taylor questioned
the need for reason and Sigmund Freud questioned its existence, Mussolini offered a satisfying dialectic. His image as a man of determined
action reaffirmed traditional American trust in common sense and human
drive. Simultaneously, he invoked the excitement of innovation and the
future. Mussolini appealed to Americans as a hero, whose gift to Italy
of progress and efficiency both reaffirmed America's own development
and promised that Italy would follow.[124] Mussolini answered Americans'
search for heroism and stability.

The United States and Economic Reconstruction

Mussolini's dictatorship provided Italian stability, but European peace
and prosperity, Americans believed, awaited the settlement of reparations
and war debts and reestablishment of the international gold standard.
The politics of economic reconstruction involved complex issues that
centered on governmental debts and the gold standard. The huge political
debts (some $27 billion in Allied war debts and $33 billion in German
reparations) depressed exchange markets and disrupted governments. A
workable settlement was essential to reestablish the international gold
standard.

These were economic issues with important political and sometimes
military implications. Americans favored moderate revision downward
of reparations so as to fix a burden that Germany could and would meet.
Similarly, Harding administration officials wanted to settle war debts on
a basis that would enable Europe to recover while paying America. They
hoped that their formula of moderate change and stability would rekindle
prosperity in Europe and safeguard it in the United States, while reducing
political tensions and chances for renewed war or revolution. American
and European leaders agreed on these goals of prosperity and security,
but fought over distribution of benefits and costs. Domestic conflicts
complicated the international ones. Britain, France, Germany, and the
United States each offered a program based on its own interests.

In both economic and naval power, Britain struggled to meet the American challenge. The war slashed London's overseas investments, forced heavy borrowing in America, and favored foreign competitors. British inflation outran American, and by 1920 the pound was off the gold standard and down to $3.38 from the prewar exchange rate of $4.86.[125] The pound's depreciation relative to the dollar and the flow of gold to New York undercut London's position as world banker. British financial officials determined to return to the gold standard at the rate of $4.86 and thereby recapture the happier times before 1914 when London dominated the gold standard and banking.[126] The British focus on the $4.86 exchange rate inadvertently admitted the dollar's hegemony: that currency had also depreciated, and was no fixed measure. London's financial renaissance required dampening the economy to depress British prices relative to American and so push the pound up to $4.86. Consequently, the Treasury and Bank of England followed a grim policy that aggravated unemployment and increased the national debt's burden.[127]

John Maynard Keynes protested this course. Britain should abandon the gold standard, "already a barbarous relic," and focus on domestic prosperity and price stability. Adopting the dollar-dominated gold standard meant that the "Federal Reserve Board of the United States" would determine "our price level and . . . credit cycle."[128] Treasury and central bank officials, however, dismissed Keynes's arguments.

Another alternative to deflation was to force inflation on America. In 1923, British Treasury officials urged sending gold to America as a war debt payment. The gold flood would engorge the United States money supply and push America into inflation. This would depreciate the dollar relative to the pound.[129] Montagu Norman, Bank of England governor, agreed "in principle," but doubted that with the Federal Reserve watchdogging "we can force their hand."[130] Nor did the central banker want to lose Britain's remaining gold. Norman's alternative was to co-opt United States financial power through close cooperation. Norman also sought to link European currencies with the pound and rebuild trade markets.[131] Suffering under the deflation policy of the Bank and Treasury, British industry urged a different formula. Unlike the financiers, the Federation of British Industry (FBI) wanted immediate stabilization of the pound regardless of the level. The FBI argued for lower taxes and wages, export credits, and systematic development of the empire. Battered by competition from German exports cheapened by the depreciating mark, industry urged that Britain and America "impose" world currency stabilization.[132]

Industry's and finance's difficulties aggravated the British government's dilemma with war debts and reparations. Britain could afford neither to pay America nor to ruin its creditor status by defaulting. Paying the debt, the cabinet feared, would "enable the American Government to reduce taxation and so place the American manufacturer in a favorable position as regards his British competitor."[133] On paper, England emerged from the war a creditor; in sad fact its $2.5 billion loans to Russia were uncollectable, and those made to France and Italy were dubious.[134] Reparations netted little money and much trouble. If Germany expanded exports to pay reparations, the treasury figured, it might "destroy" British foreign sales.[135] London hoped to escape this bind by inducing America to combine war debts and reparations, so that Britain's bad debts would cancel payments to the United States. While pressing this scheme on America, Britain tried to moderate French reparation demands. London defended Germany to restore the balance of power and an important trading partner. In contrast to the Treasury's concern for Germany, the Foreign Office tried to preserve the entente with France.[136]

The French army was Europe's most powerful, and Germany lay disarmed. As Walter Lippmann put it, the war and its aftermath corresponded to three men ganging up to knock out Jack Dempsey. "We then take [one man] and plant him firmly on Dempsey's chest, with his hand on Dempsey's throat, and leaving him in that triumphant position, we all go home."[137] France hoped reparations would bolster its precarious superiority. Huge economic claims would weaken Germany while financing reconstruction of war-devastated regions. French demands rested on the Versailles treaty, but that document gave Germany insufficient incentive to pay and Britain insufficient desire to back France. The gap between the aims of Versailles and the power to enforce it destabilized the postwar order. France could coerce Germany only by alienating Britain and America. This would leave Paris alone with Berlin and kill chances of war debt concessions from the Anglo-Saxons.[138]

Domestic politics aggravated the dilemmas of French foreign policy. Grouped around Aristide Briand, the center-left sought accommodation with Germany and Britain. Briand hoped that moderation toward Germany would buy a security commitment from Britain. This policy fell with Briand in January 1922. The right, under Raymond Poincaré, came to power promising that reparations would balance the budget and weaken the enemy. But whether under Poincaré or Briand, the French were boxed in by peace treaty contradictions, German intransigence, national debts, public expectations, political differences, and Anglo-Saxon disapproval. Poincaré saw an escape through America's cancellation of France's $3.8 billion war debt. He could then reduce reparations without suicide for his party or the franc.[139] For France, as well as Britain and Germany, America held the solution to domestic and foreign problems.

In both France and Germany, parliamentary governments struggled to apportion the domestic costs of the war and minimize payments to foreigners. The rise of German nationalist Wilhelm Cuno paralleled Poincaré's ascendency in 1922. Meanwhile French and German industrialists bypassed their crippled parliaments and dealt with each other.[140]

The paralysis of elected government and power of big industry went further in Germany, where the incomplete revolution of 1918 encased the old order in a republican shell. The large industrialists benefited after 1920 as the socialists declined, the middle-class parties splintered, and the government came hat in hand for hard currency. Businessmen used their clout to escape taxation and attack labor's gains from the revolution, especially the eight-hour day. The German government's strategy was to make an ostentatious but unsuccessful effort to pay reparations, thus demonstrating the impossibility of payment and winning American and British sympathy. Many businessmen endorsed this approach, especially representatives of light industry like Walther Rathenau and Felix Deutsch, who wanted an economic alliance with America. Some heavy industrialists who disagreed dared the French to invade or, on the contrary, sought security through marriage with French business. German business and political leaders endorsed the Anglo-Saxon idea of a business or economic solution to reparations.[141]

This approach testified to the growing semisovereign functions of business, but more specifically it changed reparations from a punishment to a common problem whose solution demanded German economic revival. In April 1919, Foreign Minister Brockdorff-Rantzau praised "the ideals of an honest businessman who considers the deal the best by which both parties gain."[142] While waiting for such idealism to grow, Germany supported the inflation policy which subsidized exports. Germans blamed the inflation on reparations, which was only half the story, since industry dodged taxes. They hoped inflation-subsidized competition would pressure America and Britain, and thus France, to reduce the Reich's burden.

The rapidly depreciating currency had broad consequences. It made living inexpensive for foreigners with dollars. By attacking established economic and social relationships, the inflation also contributed to the spirit of chaos and innovation that characterized postwar Berlin. Attracted by the cheap prices and exciting freedom, American artists found Berlin a city for creativity and enjoyment.[143]

By 1923, however, German leaders were in a less happy position. Trade declined after July; French invasion of the Ruhr in January 1923 severed the industrial heartland; and prolonged hyperinflation threatened social upheaval. Although unimportant at the time, Hitler's beer-hall putsch was symptomatic.[144]

Like France and Britain, Germany was headed toward an impasse. Germany would not end inflation without a foreign loan or reparations moratorium. France would not agree to a moratorium without guarantee of future payment and reduced war debts. Moreover, Paris continued to yearn for a security commitment from London. Britain would not help float a loan and write off receipts from Germany and the Allies without cooperation from the United States. Nor would London guarantee Paris's security without a joint commitment from Washington. "The European problem," English bankers concluded, had become "greater than the European countries alone can manage."[145] Only American dollars and disinterested intervention could break the deadlock.

The Gold Standard, Foreign Loans, and the Tariff

Americans believed that reconstruction hinged on the international gold standard. Europe's return to gold required an end to budget deficits and inflation. Americans expected that with this fiscal pressure, Europeans would cut armament and social spending and fund the political debts. Stabilizing European currencies would reduce dumping in American markets. The gold standard enhanced the importance of finance and required a gold loan. Americans made such credits conditional on establishment of semi-independent central banks and marketplace economic control.[146] Hoover explained the formula to President Warren Harding: "Currencies cannot be stabilized until inflation has stopped and inflation cannot be stopped until government budgets are balanced, and government budgets cannot be balanced until there is a proper settlement of reparations and until there is a reduction of expenditures including armament. Before these reforms can be carried into any other part of the continent they must first be obtained in France and Germany for chaos here is defeat everywhere."[147] Although they disagreed on details, most top political and business leaders concurred with Hoover's analysis. Businessmen might disagree with government tactics, but unlike the situation in Germany, the administration controlled policy with, of course, deep concern for business interests.

Common assumptions underlay United States reconstruction policy. United States leaders sought Europe's recovery without American sacrifice.[148] This matched Europe's hope to solve problems at American expense. Hoover tried to order the world economy in such a way as to allocate to America most of the benefits and to Europe many of the adjustment burdens. Future economic growth—what he foresaw as the doubling of trade "every fifteen or twenty years"[149]—would stabilize the lopsided framework. Thus, Americans founded their economic policy on the assumption that future growth was assured. This assumption proved disastrous after 1929, particularly since Americans assigned so much responsibility to the marketplace.

Economic diplomacy highlighted the marketplace's contradictions. Americans respected the wisdom and impartiality of that free enterprise court, and yet influenced the judge. Benjamin Strong of the Federal Reserve Bank of New York praised the automatic adjustments of the gold standard, but prevented the mechanism from inflating United States prices.[150] Hoover simultaneously argued that Europe's recovery required "forces entirely divorced from political origin or action: and yet urged that "the great public [central] banks ... formulate a plan."[151] Loans from the FRBNY to foreign central banks bridged the gap between the administration's reconstruction policy and opposition to government loans. Such ambivalence expressed contradiction between the dictates of liberal theory and economic interest. Americans were ideologically committed to marketplace control, yet when faced with practical problems, they often resorted to some sort of governmental intervention in the economy.

Economic diplomacy bore social and political consequences. America made financial aid conditional on Europe's adoption of deflationary policies such as debt repayment, which generally fell most heavily on lower classes. Such measures, an American diplomat admitted, "do not appeal so strongly to the proletariat of our different countries."[152] Emphasis on work and production ignored the problem of adequate income and demand. The flow of American surplus capital affected the shifting European balance of power. Wartime profits, embodied in America's tripled gold reserves, financed such loans.

The gold flow into America signified strength—but this power could be undercut. If Europeans, despairing at the concentration of gold in America, decided to forsake the gold standard, the United States would be left with a huge pile of yellow metal. It was important that Europe return to gold for a variety of reasons. With no gold backing, European paper currencies depreciated rapidly, thereby subsidizing cheap exports. As international lawyer John Foster Dulles explained it: "Europe, by inflating, is destroying its ability to buy from us, and is increasing its ability to compete with us." In a world of paper currencies, America risked isolation. Unless the United States could "get Europe back on a gold basis," Dulles warned, that continent would "gradually become wholly independent of us."[153] The American minister in Prague reported European sentiment for an "anti-American ... league of poverty" to "find new economic values other than gold."[154] At the helm of the Federal Reserve System, Strong feared that the "flood of gold" would "plunge us into inflation" by mushrooming bank reserves.[155] The British certainly hoped so. The international gold standard would reverse this flow and regulate, Strong expected, "both domestic and world price levels . . . automatic[ally]." That would shield Strong from domestic critics who urged that the FRS assume explicit responsibility to regulate prices.[156] Thomas Lamont warned that demonetization of gold in Europe would leave America "with a lapful of it and nowhere to go."[157] United States bankers promoted gold as the way to tie up foreign currencies with the dollar rather than the paper pound. Finally, the gold standard, with its easy, assured exchange of currencies, offered an open door for global expansion of trade and investment.

American leaders pressured other nations back to gold by means of FRBNY and private loans. The flood of private credits to Europe in the 1920s presented the administration with a problem and a temptation. The administration's ambitions for United States business and aversion to assuming responsibility for bad loans argued against government loan regulation. Yet such control seemed necessary to harness loans for foreign policy, minimize defaults, ensure sufficient capital for domestic industry, and prevent discrimination against American manufacturers. In 1921–22, top administration and FRBNY officials struggled among themselves and with private bankers to reach a compromise.

Opinion divided along a spectrum, with Hoover and other Commerce officials urging informal but broad regulation, Hughes and most of the State Department opting for narrower but formal review, and Mellon's Treasury Department and the bankers opposing government control.[158] The loan issue raised serious questions. Should the government control the private investment flow or leave that regulation to the marketplace? Could the government enjoy the fruits of financial expansion without paying the political price of incurring responsibilities at home and abroad? The Commerce Department affirmed governmental responsibility, but bankers resented any infringement on their profits or autonomy.

Hughes's compromise position prevailed. On March 3, 1922, the State Department publicly asked bankers to submit all foreign loan proposals. The State, Treasury, and Commerce departments would determine whether the loan violated government policy (by financing budget deficits, armaments, socialism, or other evils) and if so, pressure bankers not to make it. Despite Hoover's protests, government would not evaluate the economic soundness of loans.[159] The contradictions of this policy multiplied with the increase of German borrowing after 1924, but in the meantime loans aided American foreign trade.

Foreign trade needed such help. American exports to Europe fell from $5.2 billion in 1919 to $2.1 billion in 1921 (current dollars). The precipitous drop in the overall trade surplus (from $4.0 billion in 1919 to $0.7 billion in 1922) deflated the economy.[160] In 1921, the National Foreign Trade Convention, representing large manufacturers, bankers, and exporters, blamed "our business depression" on Europe's "unstable financial conditions." Prosperity required "an improvement of our foreign trade." This group feared that a higher tariff would cripple foreigners' ability to buy American goods.[161] Smaller manufacturers and other protectionists, eyeing the opportunity for protection and the danger of inflation-subsidized exports from Europe, clamored for a new tariff. Farmers, traditionally in favor of low tariffs, endorsed this demand, because of a frightening surge in agricultural imports.[162] The administration responded by imposing an emergency tariff to hold back agricultural and subsidized imports, financing farm exports through the War Finance Corporation, and planning for a permanent tariff that would both protect domestic industry and stimulate foreign trade.[163]

The key administration figure was tariff commissioner William S. Culbertson, who lined up the president, the State and Commerce departments, and influential senators behind the open-door tariff. Culbertson reasoned that America's diversified economy needed the widest possible export markets rather than the reciprocal tariff deals of the past. He urged a tariff that would impose an equal duty regardless of where the import came from. America would then offer and seek from others unconditional most-favored-nation status. This nondiscriminatory tariff complemented the traditional open-door policy in underdeveloped areas. Culbertson's measure included presidential authority to levy penalty duties on goods from countries that did not grant America unconditional most-favored-nation status. The president could also adjust rates by up to 50 percent to equalize costs of production. The administration rallied behind this measure, which promised protection at home, expanded markets abroad, and flexible rates. Although the executive branch framed the tariff structure, Congress covered it with logrolled rate increases. The final tariff bill was higher than Hoover, Culbertson, and others would have liked, but they applauded Harding's signature in September 1922 as inaugurating a new era of open-door or nondiscriminatory trade relations.[164]

Significantly, Hughes first approached Germany, which suffered the unequal trade treaties imposed by Versailles. The Germans snatched the precedent to strengthen ties with their hoped-for benefactor. The snag came from the Senate, which resisted administration pressure and ratified the treaty with a reservation favoring United States shipping.[165] This crimped Hughes's ambition "to apply the open-door everywhere throughout the world," especially in the French and British empires.[166] Nevertheless, throughout the decade, Hughes and his successors tried to dismantle the British imperial preference system and the French reciprocal tariff structure, efforts that met bitter resistance.[167]

War Debts and Reparations

The endless squabbling among Americans and Europeans over war debts and reparations eclipsed the bitterness generated by American trade expansion. These political debts hung over the exchanges and dominated political discussions. Aside from their political, military, and social impact, the debts symbolized for whole populations disappointment with the war and dissatisfaction with former allies and enemies. War debts and reparations assumed economic and political significance beyond their huge sums. Popular resistance to payments, and thus higher taxes, complicated compromise. Parliamentary instability in Germany and France and the precarious Republican hold in Congress underscored this problem. Political leaders made the situation worse with chauvinistic public claims that privately they disavowed.[168] Reparations and war debts presented public relations problems as well as economic ones.

The war debt issue boiled down to whether the United States should collect the money and whether it should link the obligations with German reparations. Behind the public debate on this emotional issue there lay substantial private consensus among most American leaders. Bankers like Strong and Thomas Lamont, fearing that payment would widen Europe's dollar gap, urged reduction or cancellation in return for reduced reparations and return to the gold standard. Borah would swap the debts for European disarmament and treaty reform. Virtually no important political or business leaders advocated collection with full interest or unilateral cancellation. Almost all valued the debts as an asset that America might barter for some combination of money and influence in Europe.[169] The Harding administration stood for partial collection and tacit linkage. It publicly denied any connection between war debts and reparations not because of economic blindness, but rather because it perceived that such linkage would anger Congress and unite Europe in an anti-American debtors' coalition. Succeeding administrations reasoned similarly,[170] and as late as 1975 the State Department repeated: "The United States has never recognized a link between payments of the debts owed us and German reparations."[171]

In June 1921, Treasury secretary Mellon sought from Congress broad authority to negotiate war debt agreements. Jealous of its power and taxpayers' money, Congress refused. Democrats contrasted the administration's concern for the Allies and opposition to a soldiers' bonus. Despite executive pressure, in 1922 Congress established the World War Foreign Debt Commission (WWFDC), with strict terms for settlements. Some senators left the door ajar with the suggestion that if the debtors deserved easier terms, the president should come to Congress with the facts.[172] Administration officials grumbled, but took steps to push open the door. Harding appointed Mellon as chairman of the WWFDC and Hughes, Hoover, Senator Reed Smoot, and Representative Theodore Burton as members. The cabinet officials easily dominated the group when it negotiated the agreement with Britain in January 1923, but throughout 1922 debt policy remained stymied.[173]

Struggling with economic and political problems, the United States and the Allies each turned the debt issue to best advantage. American leaders differed on how much the Allies should pay. Yet they agreed that in order to earn concessions, the Allies had to work harder and reduce reparations and armaments. Thomas Lamont expressed the American suspicion that unilateral cancellation would leave reparations festering and would "encourage slackness and extravagance."[174] Julius Barnes, Hoover's close associate and president of the United States Chamber of Commerce, objected to Europe's leftist experiments with public ownership of utilities, unemployment insurance, and paper money. "We have no right to impose our ideas of ... social ... structure upon other peoples," he admitted, but the Allies would get no concessions if they "wasted ... that generosity ... in inefficiency and extravagance, [and] in social experimentation which we know to be destructive of a people's productive impulse."[175]

The Allies ignored Barnes's warning. Furthermore, they insisted on war debt cancellation as the prerequisite to reparations reduction. In May 1922, Poincaré acknowledged France's debt, but refused to negotiate on the terms mandated by Congress.[176] In August, Britain issued the Balfour Note, which challenged American policy by urging outright cancellation of war debts and reparations. If that proved impossible, London promised to collect only what it "has to pay to America." Britain thus tried to trade bad debts from Russia, France, and Germany for relief from America. The Balfour Note explicitly linked war debts and reparations, made America responsible for both, and, Washington fretted, encouraged "a united allied front."[177]

Public outcry against the Balfour Note added to the tension. With his eyes on the November election and with Harding's blessing, Hoover rejected cancellation.[178]

Hughes tried to break the logjam by giving France a face-saving way to yield. He called Lamont to Washington "because I want to unburden my soul." The bankers' idea of reducing war debts and reparations in one operation was impossible, Hughes explained, "simply because ... Congress has not given us the power." His alternative was "settl[ing] Reparations first." This meant France had to reduce reparations before America reduced war debts. In order to get Paris to take this unpopular step, Hughes hoped to mobilize public opinion. He planned an international committee of private economic experts appointed by their respective governments "which shall sit down and determine the question of Germany's capacity to pay.... And whereas there might be no written agreement beforehand that the governments would abide by the decisions of that committee, the weight of public opinion behind it all over the world would force the government to accept its findings.... France must accept."[179] If France did not accept, Hughes told Castle, it could "go to h——l."[180] With a reparations reduction, the administration could go to Congress with the "facts" of France's lessened capacity to pay and probably get a liberal debt settlement.[181] "To start with the [war] debts," Hughes emphasized, "is to begin at the wrong end."[182] Hughes and Hoover recognized the link between reparations and war debts and, although publicly they denied it, based policy on that connection. Their conflict with Europe was which government should assume the unpopular debt policy. Here Hughes pointed to France and Germany.

America's interest in reparations extended deeper than the war debts connections. Reparations "lie at the foundation of economic recuperation," Hughes explained, and "the prosperity of the United States largely depends upon the economic settlements ... in Europe."[183] In late 1922, Hughes faced the dilemma of threatened German collapse and French resistance to his plan. After Poincaré in private negotiations rejected Hughes's scheme and Borah accused the administration of inaction, the secretary of state appealed publicly for a committee of experts. This December 29 effort also failed, and on January 13, 1923 the French marched into the Ruhr. France tried to go it alone and extract reparations with bayonets.[184] Hughes withdrew the United States Rhine occupation army and waited until the Europeans were desperate enough to accept an American solution.[185]

The administration's war debt policy won more immediate success with the British settlement of January 1923. In financial as in naval matters, Britain's American policy pivoted between need to cooperate and need to correct the power imbalance. Given Washington's refusal to cancel and London's ambitions as world banker, Britain had little choice but to settle. "The London [short-term] money market might have been superseded by New York," recalled a former president of the Board of Trade. The debt settlement reestablished London's credit.[186] Once Britain agreed to pay, it needed American support more than ever to rebuild European markets.[187]

Although American leaders disagreed on the amount Britain should pay, they concurred on the general shape of the settlement and the need to sell it to Congress and the public. In late 1922, Lamont acted as liaison between Washington and London. He urged a settlement easier than that mandated by Congress.[188] Through speeches and meetings with journalists, Lamont, Barnes, and other businessmen influenced American public opinion toward this view.[189] Hoover told Mellon, "There is no possibility of funding the debt within the terms enacted by Congress."[190]

Harding accepted this view, and sent a public message to Lodge that "if Congress really means" to help "with the European situation," it should "free the hands of the Debt Commission."[191]

Appraising the American climate, Stanley Baldwin, chancellor of the exchequer, shrewdly appealed for "discussion as businessmen seeking a business solution of what fundamentally is a business problem."[192] Hoover and Mellon, who dominated the WWFDC, agreed, but argued that their competitor could afford annual payments of $187 million. Baldwin and Norman bargained them down to $161 million for the first ten years and $184 million for the following fifty-two.[193] Baldwin remarked bitterly that the Americans deserved "a replica of the Golden Calf," but he accepted the terms. Prime Minister Bonar Law did not, and the cabinet agonized over the decision. "I never felt so miserable in all my life," Baldwin later recalled. Finally, British political and financial leaders decided they had no choice but acceptance.[194] Despite ratification, however, the debt controversy embittered Anglo-American relations for another decade.

British and congressional acceptance[195] of the debt settlement testified to the administration's skill in overcoming foreign and domestic opposition. Yet this success solved only a small part of the intertwined problem of war debts, reparations, loans, trade, and the gold standard. In 1920–24, fifteen interallied and ten German-Allied conferences struggled unsuccessfully to untangle reparations.[196]

The Genoa Conference

Analysis of the Genoa Conference of April–May 1922, probably the most important of these failed conferences, highlights the factors that kept Europe in turmoil from 1919 to 1923. In early 1922, Lloyd George planned a peace conference that would establish Britain at the center of a revived world economy. He envisioned a British-controlled consortium to develop Russia on a closed-door, privileged basis. As a junior partner, Germany would channel profits from Russian business into reparations to the Allies. Russian raw materials and food would reduce Europe's dependence on America. Fewer imports from the United States would boost the British pound.[197] British financial leaders devised a gold exchange standard centered in London.[198] Poincaré dampened these hopes by refusing to give power over reparations to a British-run conference in which Germany would participate.[199]

Germany's invitation signaled an end to its pariah status, but Poincaré's refusal to discuss reparations meant the meeting would not resolve Berlin's problems. However, the Reich's position between East and West offered other prospects. Germany had already begun secret military cooperation with Soviet Russia, and many Germans favored what Chancellor Josef Wirth called "a league with defeated peoples who bleed and starve as we do."[200] Despite doubts by Trotsky and left-wing Bolsheviks, Lenin and Chicherin believed such a league would divide the capitalist states and tap German technology. Lenin and Chicherin favored peaceful coexistence. They believed Russia could advance its security and development by exploiting the West's need for markets and raw materials.[201] Coexistence and the ARA experience also underscored America's importance. Trotsky argued that "Europe is ruined," and "the economic centre has moved to America."[202]

American leaders found Genoa offensive. Hughes spurned Russian overtures of coexistence and rejected Lloyd George's policy as "positively harmful" because it "diminished . . . pressures on Soviet Government."[203] The international consortium contradicted the open door and endangered American economic interests.[204] Strong's tepid reaction to the gold exchange standard soon cooled into solid opposition.[205] Hoover and Hughes condemned Poincaré's refusal to discuss reparations and Lloyd George's distortion of an economic conference with political representatives.[206] Hoover was anxious to rebuild European markets, but, he told Harding, Genoa did not meet American specifications. Hoover, along with Hughes and Lamont, saw no reason for cooperation with the conference.[207]

American opposition was not the only reason for Genoa's failure. Poincaré refused to lower reparations without simultaneous reduction of war debts.[208] Nor would the Soviets accept neocolonialism under the consortium. The French and Belgians, allied with Richard Washburn Child, Washington's unofficial observer, destroyed British plans for closed-door oil concessions in Russia. The gold exchange standard was stillborn, although London tried to revive the scheme in later years. On April 16, Germany and Russia signed the Rapallo treaty. The agreement did little more than formalize existing ties, but it emphasized that Versailles might lose Germany to the East. State Department officials condemned Germany's move as "extremely stupid," but cast most of the blame on Allied intransigence and Bolshevik intrigue.[209]

Genoa's failure and America's refusal to cooperate with it highlighted the diplomacy of 1921–23. The Harding administration dealt with Europe only on United States terms. Hughes and his colleagues used the Berlin treaty, the Washington Conference, and the ARA venture as vehicles for American power that safeguarded freedom of action. They minimized opposition by skillfully packaging and advertising these policies. Washington was in double jeopardy from official participation at Genoa: the conference's success would co-opt U.S. power; its failure would dissipate that power by weakening American prestige. Child explained to Harding: "We preserved by absence a *prestige* which will enable us to hold Europe together if a peril of cleavage matures. It is easy to say that we stay out of Europe to save ourselves. I think I could demonstrate that we stay out of Europe to save Europe."[210] Although Harding's selective intervention protected American prestige and freedom of action, it left Europe in a quagmire. Genoa underlined Europe's need for dollars and disinterested intervention. Britain lacked the power to impose its own political and economic solution. Russia refused to underwrite one by suffering economic exploitation. Germany had strength neither to fulfill the Versailles treaty nor to overthrow it. France could veto a settlement, but the Ruhr invasion subsequently demonstrated that Paris could not maintain an independent policy.

Genoa emphasized as well the basic challenge of change: what to do about revolution, Versailles, and depression. In place of revolution, Americans favored a stable world order open to gradual change. In the context of war-torn Europe, the United States opposed radicalism in Russia, Bulgaria, Austria, and elsewhere and accommodated stabilizing rightist regimes in Rome and Sofia. Norman Davis, a Democrat who assisted Wilson in 1919 and the Republicans in the postwar decade, expressed the central importance of peaceful change in the American conception of Versailles: "while we had to let ... defects go in order to get the Treaty, nearly at every place a machine was set up to eliminate that defect just as soon as public opinion and public conscience would permit and demanded."[211] However, such machinery as the Reparations Commission had rusted into instruments for rigid enforcement. United States efforts to reduce reparations and grant Germany most-favored-nation trade status were attempts to revise and liberalize the Versailles order. Americans hoped such peaceful change would head off war and revolution. The central dilemma, which plagued American policy in the entire 1919–33 period, was how to get European governments to accept gradual peace treaty reform without either entangling the United States or unleasing the forces of revolutionary change. Americans saw prosperity as a solvent that could lubricate change by easing tensions. This belief intensified United States desires to reestablish the gold standard and rebuild the world economy on an open-door basis. After 1924 these efforts finally succeeded with the Dawes Plan, Locarno, and financial stabilization.

[4]

Building the New Order, 1924–1926

After five frustrating years, America's European policy realized success in 1924. Before that date, Europeans and Americans were deadlocked over reparations, a key aspect of the central issue of whether and how to enforce the Versailles treaty. Europeans disagreed over how to apportion among themselves the financial costs of the war, but agreed on trying to get the United States to assume as much of the burden as possible. European wrangles culminated in the French occupation of the Ruhr in 1923, after which exhausted Paris and Berlin officials accepted the American and British idea of moderate reparations and a stabilized Germany.

The resulting Dawes Plan embodied the policy of peaceful change. It revised the Versailles treaty by sharply restricting France's ability to use reparations as a club over Germany. Americans achieved this breakthrough by advertising their scheme and backing it with their dollars. They believed this reform would help integrate a prosperous, peaceful Germany into the Atlantic community. As part of the scheme, a dollar loan revived Germany's economy and linked its currency to the dollar and the international gold standard. Furthermore, the plan set the basis for settlement of the Allied war debts and the return of most of Europe to the gold standard. Thus, the Dawes Plan was the keystone of American efforts to promote peaceful political change and healing economic growth in Europe. Building on its stability, Western Europeans, with American encouragement, moved further toward political peace in 1925 with the Locarno Pact. Within this framework of relative European peace and prosperity, American businessmen, tourists, and expatriates found new frontiers of profit, adventure, and creativity. Thus, the success of the United States' political and eocnomic policies in Europe facilitated Amer-

111

ica's cultural penetration of that continent. It was the economic and political environment created in 1924–26 that nurtured the cultural exchange.[1]

The American government used economic tools to help build this environment. This was a shrewd tactic since economic, unofficial diplomacy maximized America's strengths and minimized its foreign responsibilities and domestic divisions. Yet economics and politics were inseparable. Efforts to stabilize Germany through the Dawes Plan, stabilize the political debts through funding agreements, and stabilize the world monetary system through the gold standard all had political and military consequences. Americans believed that stability in each of these areas was essential to order in the other two. The Dawes Plan, the debt settlements, and the gold standard were three interlocking components in building a secure world open to trade, investment, and peaceful change. In keeping with this economic approach, the Dawes Plan dealt with reparations as a business problem.

A masterpiece of ambiguity and compromise, the Dawes Plan camouflaged Versailles revision as a business adjustment. It eased political conflicts by treating them as economic problems. The plan enabled the Coolidge administration to remain officially aloof while applying personnel, money, and political pressure. After resigning as under secretary of the treasury, S. Parker Gilbert, the plan's chief executive officer, stayed in close contact with administration officials and private bankers, but beyond congressional purview. Ostensibly a punishing device, the reparations scheme offered Germany an escape route. It culminated France's five-year quest for reparations, but signaled the defeat of its bid for hegemony in Europe. Written by pragmatic businessmen, the plan proposed what virtually all observers believed impossible. It tried to transform reparations from a burden on the world economy to a stimulus. The Dawes Plan marked American policy's greatest success. Ironically, it succeeded so well that it created new problems that eventually hamstrung U.S. policy.

Along with this scheme to revive Germany, Americans ordered the world monetary system and the political debts. The United States' economic superiority pressured Britain onto the gold standard, a step that only aggravated London's weakness. With the prod of a loan embargo, the Coolidge administration secured war debt settlements from most of the Allies. Americans believed the annual payments would limit Europe's military and social spending, stabilize the exchanges, and reduce the United States' national debt. Many Europeans resented such pressures, and, the achievements in peaceful change and economic reconstruction created problems that later undermined the new system. But in 1924–

26 most Americans were confident that prosperity and stability promised a bright future. They congratulated themselves, in the words of a top diplomat, on the "restor[ation of] our prestige and authority in the world."[2] The first chapter in this success story was the Anglo-American program to revive Austria.

Since 1919, William Causey and his staff of American advisers had worked at Austria's economic and technical problems. But Vienna still suffered from social unrest, runaway inflation, and covetous neighbors.[3]

British financial officials operated through the London-dominated League of Nations Financial Committee. They believed Austrian reconstruction would stabilize central Europe, expand British business, and secure a financial ally tied to the pound and the Bank of England.[4] These ambitions, however, depended on American investors supplying much of the money for a stabilization loan. Enticed by the high interest rate, J. P. Morgan and Company promised cooperation if Britain obtained from the European powers a guarantee for the bonds and Austrian territorial integrity.[5] As this deal demonstrated, in the early 1920s Morgan and Company worked closely with British finance. The association reassured still timid American investors. Morgan partners valued the Austrian loan as "very profitable" and "an object lesson for Germany." The problem was "sell[ing] it."[6]

The bankers jumped this hurdle with a vigorous sales campaign. In February 1922, with State Department backing and Causey's lobbying, Congress passed the Lodge Resolution, which postponed Austria's relief debt payments for twenty years.[7] This cleared the way for a fresh loan. Hughes urged Thomas Lamont, a Morgan partner, to float a portion of the Austrian loan in America. The banking firm now held back, asking for a State Department guarantee or endorsement of the loan. This would produce a "strong psychological effect upon American investors," the bankers believed, and enhance the loan's security.[8] In accordance with administration policy, Hughes refused.[9] Failing this tactic, Morgan and Company hired advertisers Bruce Barton and Ivy Lee. Although the bankers rejected some of Barton's more flamboyant promotions, they cultivated newspaper and public interest in Austria. Behind the scenes, the bankers underwrote public demand with subscriptions from the Rockefeller and Mellon interests and other large corporations.[10] On June 11, 1923 Morgan offered the Austrian loan to the public. Within fifteen minutes, investors oversubscribed the $25 million American portion.[11]

The loan was the initial victory of Woodrow Wilson's and Warren Harding's policy that Europe first ease political tensions and then come to private American investors for aid. Everyone recognized the precedent for German stabilization. The Lamont-Hughes exchange underscored the efforts by bankers and governmental officials to co-opt each other's power. London leaders enlisted support from New York for a largely British-run program, but United States bankers and investors gained confidence that encouraged later independence. The stabilization plan opened Austria to further American economic penetration.[12] In Austria, the loan stabilized the currency and put the budget under a "financial dictator," Alfred Zimmerman, appointed by Bank of England governor Montagu Norman.[13] As mayor of Rotterdam, Zimmerman had won a reputation as a foe of socialism. In Vienna he rolled back social welfare legislation.[14]

American businessmen approved Zimmerman's priorities. They believed Austrians had to "make many sacrifices" and "require[d] ... pressure from [bankers] to keep them on the right lines."[15]

For countries like Austria, stabilization meant an expensive loan and deflationary policies that depressed lower-class and national income. We are "rehabilitated to death," Austrians complained.[16] Such financial rehabilitation by bankers had social and political consequences. Yet in the 1920s country after country swallowed the bitter medicine because the disease of runaway inflation seemed even worse.

The Origins of the Dawes Plan

Germans pondered this dilemma in 1923 as the mark skidded to one-trillionth its prewar value, and Weimar democracy floundered. In January 1923, the French spurned Hughes's plea for a businessman's committee to settle reparations, and marched into the Ruhr.

For several reasons, Hughes fell back on a policy of watchful waiting. He realized that American intervention could succeed only if both France and Germany accepted it. Domestic opinion was divided. Hughes was loath to alienate France before ratification of the Washington Conference treaties. Moreover, some competing American industries benefited from Germany's crippling.[17]

In the second half of 1923, however, pressures mounted for American action. France finally ratified the Washington treaties.[18] A Commerce Department memorandum blamed Germany's reduced purchasing power for aggravating the decline in wheat prices. "Germany as a market," Commerce officials calculated, "is twice as important to this country as she is as a competitor." With a unified world economy the Ruhr disturbance "is equally reflected in all important markets." Hoover agreed. Even firms that had initially benefited now were pinched by reduced world buying power.[19] Hughes and other Americans feared that deals between German industrialists and French officials signaled the union of

Ruhr coke and Lorraine iron ore into a dangerously powerful steel combine.[20] A Council on Foreign Relations study group worried that French hegemony meant restricted "freedom to manufacture, to trade." Some members feared a "revolution that would be felt in other portions of the Continent, and eventually ... renewal of Germany's active war on France."[21]

Hughes responded to these problems by urging the Belgians and French to accept a businessmen's committee. He encouraged the shuttle diplomacy of Fred Kent, vice-president of Bankers Trust, and John Foster Dulles, an international lawyer, who tried to break the Franco-German impasse.[22] However, Hughes rejected the suggestion of Alanson B. Houghton, ambassador in Berlin, and William R. Castle, Western Europe desk chief, that America attack the falling franc.[23] Nor did he accept Poincaré's position that America explicitly recognize the linkage between war debts and reparations and reduce the former first.[24]

Germany's crisis deepened as the European deadlock continued. In September 1923, industrialist Hugo Stinnes outlined to Houghton plans for a right-wing coup, which prophesied the events of the early 1930s. Stinnes asserted that Germany could neither produce competitively nor pay reparations until business "forced" labor to abandon the eight-hour day. This required "a dictator and the abolition of parliamentary government."[25] Stinnes did not want to restore the monarchy; rather, he hoped for "a Fascist movement." He expected that the dictator would destroy the Weimar constitution and yet preserve appearances by pledging "to defend it." This dicator should be a man "who talks the language of the people."[26]

Ambassador Houghton worried that opposition to right-wing dictatorship could spawn a "Red Republic." However, if the new government were stable, the change from democracy to dictatorship "might easily be to Germany's advantage."[27] Along with Calvin Coolidge and William Castle, Houghton agreed that German economic recovery required eliminating the eight-hour day[28] In October 1923, the ambassador applauded the appointmnent of Reichswehr general Hans von Seeckt as temporary dictator. "Parliamentary government in Germany has not succeeded," Houghton reported, and without Seeckt, "I doubt if organized society would exist here today."[29] Although he did not want to see German democracy fail, Houghton accepted a dictatorship of the right, especially if it would prevent one from the left.

By means of political manipulation, financial juggling, and a measure of good luck, Foreign Minister Gustav Stresemann in late 1923 prevented overthrow of the Weimar Republic. In September, he ordered protesting Ruhr workers to return to their mines and factories.[30] But a permanent solution required a reparations settlement, Ruhr evacuation, and capital infusion. These depended on American intervention. On November 5, Hughes lost patience and shouted at the French ambassador that only a businessmen's committee could break the deadlock and determine Germany's capacity to pay.[31]

This time the French listened. The 40 percent fall of the franc in 1923 overshadowed France's meager economic and political benefits from the Ruhr occupation. Poincaré needed American or British money to bolster the franc, and reconciliation with his political opposition in Parliament and nominal ally across the channel. On November 13 the embattled French leader accepted Hughes's plan for a business or "experts" committee.[32]

Through the Reparations Commission Hughes appointed a powerful delegation headed by Charles G. Dawes, a Chicago banker and former director of the budget, and Owen D. Young, a Democrat and chairman of the board of General Electric and Radio Corporation of America, who conducted most of the actual negotiations. Henry M. Robinson, a Los Angeles banker and associate of Hoover, assisted. The group represented the major parties and sections. None of the three was vulnerable to attack as a Wall Street banker. Yet Dawes had won the lasting gratitude of J. P. Morgan and Company when, alone among Chicago bankers, he supported the Allied loan of 1915. Young enjoyed close business relations with the Morgan firm. Such ties aided flotation of a reparations loan. Dawes and Young appealed also to foreign interests. As a wartime general, Dawes had developed affection for and ties with the French. Young's European contacts and experience in international business negotiations helped push the American program through the conference.[33] In addition to these personal advantages, the delegates enjoyed unofficial but strong backing from the White House and Wall Street. This was crucial, since German revival depended on an American loan. Washington's efforts since 1919 to remain relatively aloof from the reparations controversy now paid returns, as Americans were able to mediate and lead the conference.

Americans used publicity to pressure the Allies and Germany to accept a workable reparations plan. As Young later explained, "a 'consumer demand' was built up for the Dawes Report before anybody knew what it was to be and before a line of it had been put on paper."[34] As "salesman," Dawes provided good copy for the press and advertisement for the plan. Dawes pitched the report to "the public conscience of the world," expecting that "public sentiment will overthrow any Government opposing it."[35] He cultivated French support, "the key" to a solution, with an opening speech that emotionally recalled wartime unity but emphasized German reconstruction as prerequisite to reparations.[36]

While Dawes did the advertising, Young "manufactur[ed]" the plan. Young reasoned that "confidence" was Germany's basic requirement. With that, Germans would "work" hard enough "to produce reparations." The reparations burden had to be light enough to ensure the Reich's acceptance and recovery, yet heavy enough to win Allied approval.[37] Since hyperinflation had wiped out Germany's national and corporate debt, Young argued, a reparations burden would protect the other industrial nations from excessive competition.[38] Young emphasized the importance of a balanced budget, a stabilized currency, and reparation funding. Like other Americans, he believed these three elements were inseparable and essential to economic and political order. "The heart" of Young's scheme, Houghton reported, was that once Germany collected the taxation revenue to pay reparations, these funds "will be left in Germany and the only method by which France and England can obtain these credits is by buying German goods." The plan would thus "take from Germany's back the burden of transferring these credits into foreign exchange."[39] The plan promised that Germany would pay reparations, but not that the Allies would receive them.

Young expected that German taxation revenue would yield the marks for reparations. If Germany held sufficient foreign exchange the American agent general in charge of reparations would transfer these funds directly to Britain, France, and other Allies. Anxious to spur world economic growth, Young hoped to use reparation moneys for "hot-housed trade." In French and Belgian colonies or in such underdeveloped areas as China, Germany would finance the building of electric power stations and other large development projects that would not otherwise be feasible.[40] The Allies might also take deliveries-in-kind, that is, German coal, dyestuffs, or other products. Young expected that in the early years of German recovery, as economy and export trade still underwent recovery, much of the reparations money would stay within the Reich, where capital-short industry could borrow it. Such "easy credit conditions," Young assured Hugo Stinnes, would generate a "great boom."[41] In short, Young recognized that Germany would have a hard time paying, and the Allies would have a hard time receiving, reparations. But he imaginatively sought to transform the problem by making reparations the engine for German recovery and world growth.

Young's plan included provisions for further reparations revision in the future. Young tried to build the Dawes Plan so that it could accommodate needed reform. Thus peaceful change would stabilize the structure rather than destroy it. The plan set a 5-billion-mark (roughly $1.25 billion) limit on the internal accumulation of reparations. If the Allies—by means of a German export surplus, reparation-in-kind, or "hot-housed" trade—drew on the balance, the Germans would replace the marks up to the 5 billion limit. But if, as most observers believed,[42] the Allies could not or did not want to accept large amounts of reparations, the balance would remain in Germany and the burden would automatically decrease. "Under the guise of control or supervision," Houghton reported, Young's scheme "has set up a machinery which is itself capable of bringing about a readjustment."[43] Looking over Young's handiwork, NYFRB governor Strong praised a plan that "proposes impossible things and sets up alternatives when the impossibility has been demonstrated."[44]

In order to win public acceptance and commence German growth, Dawes and Young promoted the plan as an economic document. Yet Germany's recovery could not get far as long as the French controlled the Ruhr, and the Dawes Committee had no jurisdiction over this political and military issue. Reparations required German economic unity and sovereignty, Young argued. France could keep armed forces in the Ruhr, "but they must not interfere with production, and France must pay for them."[45] France accepted this condition at the London Conference in August.

Stability and flexibility characterized this economic/political document. The scheme broke the reparations impasse and established some certainty as to German payments. The mechanism did *not*, as Young conceived it, require continued American intervention or loans. It did, however, assume a large international loan to get the machinery working. What Young and his associates failed to perceive was that their country's limited, initial loan to inaugurate the reparations plan would quickly and uncontrollably mushroom into a massive and ongoing obligation to keep the system going.

Americans hoped that the Dawes Plan would transform reparations from a political dispute to a business problem. Semantics aside, however, to separate politics and economics was impossible: reparations had both political and economic ramifications, touching deeply the basic questions of who had won the war and who would shape the peace. Officially, the committee and its report bore the name "Experts," but as Young later acknowledged, the expert technical economists "did not find the facts which were acceptable to the Committee, and would have ruined it but for . . . the horse trades."[46] Dawes quickly became "fed up" with "experts" who substituted "mathematics involving the fourth dimension" for practical experience.[47] The General Electric executive described the plan as "scientific,"[48] but his was the science of Thomas Edison, alive to the necessities of politics and possibilities of profit. Young and the other "experts" of the committee understood economics or business to mean the sphere of activities beyond the reach of popular or provincial control. With common stakes in a stable and prosperous capitalist order, practical businessmen could negotiate and "horse trade" settlements that compromised political conflicts. They could do this without penalty from disappointed legislatures or voters and with an aura of scientific, expert objectivity. Economic solutions assumed no irreconcilable conflicts and offered equal opportunity to profit from growth. Political solutions, such as the Ruhr occupation, implied market interference, continued tension, and atavistic imperialism.

As an economic scheme, the Dawes Plan accentuated Germany's industrial superiority over France. The London Conference of July–August 1924, called to implement the plan, then undercut France's dominant political position under the Versailles treaty. The economic settlement maximized the power of America's growing surplus capital and Britain's still formidable financial influence.

The London Conference

The London Conference of July-August 1924 highlighted these consequences. Its purpose was to implement the Plan. Young's adroit lobbying within the Dawes Committee secured a unanimous Report on April 9.[49] After five years of reparations deadlock, Europe was receptive to the report's answers, a mood that Dawes cultivated. The franc crisis in early 1924 drove home France's isolated weakness. Although the governments and bankers of the United States, Britain, and Germany did not purposely attack the franc, they were all, a Commerce Department official observed, "hoping and praying" for its fall.[50] Coached by Young and Houghton, German industrialists and their government endorsed the plan in principle.[51] The Dawes Committee had shied away from such explosive issues as default and renewed sanctions in order to project an image of calm unanimity. Nor could the committee deal with the details of the loan or the Ruhr evacuation. These issues occupied the London Conference, but in a deeper sense its delegates struggled over the fate of the Versailles order.

Determined to revise and eventually overthrow the Versailles system, the Germans appreciated their new prospects. The plan reduced payments, eliminated Germany's obligation to transfer them, and safeguarded the unity of the Reich. Germans welcomed America's commitment through sponsorship of the plan and loan. They calculated that with "the

support of the American financial and political world," the agent general
would prove that even the reduced Dawes annuities were unworkable
"and the Versailles Treaty must be changed."[52] The settlement was a
milestone along Germany's road to treaty revision, a path which, Stresemann recognized, might lead to war.

> I fervently hope that if it comes to that—and I believe that in the final analysis
> these great questions will always be decided by the sword—the moment may
> be put off as long as possible. I can only foresee the downfall of our people
> as long as we do not have the sword—that much is certain. If we look
> forward to a time when the German people will again be strong enough to
> play a more significant role, then we must first give the German people the
> necessary foundation.... To create this foundation is the most urgent chal-
> lenge facing us.[53]

Americans believed that moderate Versailles revision would lead to
peace, not war. With their Progressive optimism, they hoped that peaceful
change would eventually give Germany enough of a stake in the postwar
order so that that nation would want to preserve the system rather than
overthrow it. Unfortunately, the Depression cut the experiment short.
Whether, with enough time, continued prosperity and slow revision would
have pacified Germany is an unanswerable question. If the Germans had
developed a spirit of moderation, they might have used their preeminence
to achieve peaceful European economic integration.

In the actual situation of 1924, however, France saw Germany's economic and demographic superiority as a threat. The Gallic nation could
contain its larger neighbor only with the aid of the Anglo-Saxons, with
the club of reparations, or with the detachment of the Rhineland or Ruhr.
The occupation of the Ruhr was the last singlehanded attempt by France
to preserve its 1919 victory. Yet France lacked the power to stay the
course. Paris officials had to accept the Dawes Plan to stem further
decline.

The franc's depreciation emphasized the fallen confidence of domestic
lenders. The French government could no longer finance budget deficits
and war reconstruction with government bonds. French leaders' inadequate knowledge of economics and inability to collect sufficient taxes
made them dependent on American loans. Morgan and Company had
stepped in with an emergency $100 million credit in March, but further
aid required French compliance with what the bankers and Washington
believed necessary for European reconstruction. French financial trouble
symbolized the weariness after a decade of war and postwar strife. "The
French," Poincaré concluded after his defeat to reconciliationist Edouard
Herriot, "are too tired to follow me."[54]

Britain hoped that the franc's decline and Herriot's conciliation would produce French concessions at the London Conference. Declaring that "Germany is to us the most important country in Europe," British leaders determined to rebuild the Reich as a market and counterweight to France.[55] Division arose over how far to push France. Prime Minister Ramsay MacDonald and the Foreign Office wanted to keep Herriot in power and France as an ally; Chancellor of the Exchequer Philip Snowden and Montagu Norman sought more extensive Versailles revision.[56]

Norman's close relations with Thomas Lamont temporarily divided Americans at London. What Henry L. Stimson later criticized as Morgan and Company's "narrow banking axioms"[57] cooled its reception of the Dawes Report. Partner Russell Leffingwell inadvertently praised Young's negotiating skill when he criticized the report as "consistently two-faced." Leffingwell feared that the annuity "begins too early, mounts too fast and reaches too high a total," a defect Young accepted in order to get French approval. Sharing the general expectation that the plan would collapse within a few years, Morgan bankers focused on the issue of Allied response to German default.[58]

In contrast to Morgan and Company's reserve, the Coolidge administration and the media embraced the plan. Hughes "rejoic[ed]." Hoover predicted world "economic recuperation."[59] Calvin Coolidge endorsed the report and urged Americans to "participate in the requisite loan." Such investment, he explained, would "benefit our trade and commerce . . . and . . . expecially provide a larger market for our agricultural production."[60] As a capstone, Coolidge and the Republican party nominated Charles G. Dawes as vice-president.[61]

The government's selling of the plan was echoed by the campaign of businessmen like Fred Kent, who helped rally the International Chamber of Commerce and the National Foreign Trade Convention.[62] Newspapers and magazines gave lavish coverage. They praised the plan as an example of American business ingenuity and a vehicle for greater foreign trade and prosperity.[63] Such enthusiastic advertising had a tremendous, largely unexpected effect after bankers issued the Dawes loan in October.

In July and August, however, the London Conference controversy dimmed prospects for both loan and plan. Conflict centered on security. France sought security against Germany's industrial, demographic, and potential military superiority. America and Britain, especially their banker advance guard, wanted security against French punishment and disruption of Germany. Protection by the channel and the Atlantic accounted for some of the different perspective on Germany, but Anglo-Saxons also believed that stable prosperity and graduate change would tame Reich revisionism.[64] Sympathetic to France, Morgan partner Dwight Morrow explained the American thesis. He countered the French position that "reparations" and "security . . . are contradictory. . . . Such an antithesis really defines security as keeping your adversary weak. There is no real security that way. . . . The lessening of the likelihood of future war . . . can only . . . come by such treatment of Germany as will enable her to pay . . . as quickly and smoothly as possible."[65] Mindful of the French need for dollars to start up reparations and save the franc, Morgan partners asked France to choose between "a rehabilitated Germany" and American loans "and a broken Germany and what has been called 'security.' "[66]

At London, Morgan and Company and Norman made the Dawes loan conditional on French renunciation of renewed occupation.[67] Lamont informed Prime Minister MacDonald that the very name of the French-dominated Reparations Commission was "anathema to the American investment public. . . . If there was any possibility for that Commission to poke its fingers in and declare default, the American public would not take the bond."[68] After tortuous negotiations, Lamont and Norman, backed by the American and British governments, secured a complicated formula that transferred default decision making and overall control of reparations from the French to the Americans.[69] The Coolidge administration urged Lamont to accept the scheme. Lamont broke with Norman, who wanted still further French concessions, and advised New York partners that the Reparations Commission was effectively "scrapped."[70]

At London France effectively renounced the right, guaranteed by Versailles, to punish Germany with military and territorial sanctions. However, Paris could postpone evacuation of the Ruhr for one year. This victory salved French pride; nevertheless, after twelve months France would have to leave with little chance of return. The near ban on another Ruhr invasion underscored the temporary nature of Allied occupation in the Rhineland and hampered Allied policing of German rearmament. The franc's crisis impelled these concessions. As London Conference delegates realized, these economic difficulties had accelerated the "rewriting [of] Versailles."[71]

Although Lamont and other Morgan partners played the star roles at London, Coolidge administration officials also had a hand. Despite the administration's claim to a merely platonic relationship with the Dawes Plan, the government was, the agent general remarked, "committed . . . as much as it is humanly possible."[72] On supposedly private trips to London, Hughes and Mellon, along with Logan, Houghton, and Ambassador Frank B. Kellogg, mediated between bankers and delegates. Mellon staked his prestige as head of a private economic empire and chief financial officer of the United States government by recommending the loan to Lamont. The president repeatedly endorsed the plan and prepared to offer arbitration by the Supreme Court chief justice if the London Conference deadlocked.[73] Coolidge vetoed Morgan's and Norman's initial choice of Morrow for agent general because he feared that selection would fuel Robert La Follette's presidential campaign against Wall Street influence.[74] Administration officials, along with Young, Norman, and the Morgan bankers, finally decided on S. Parker Gilbert, recently under secretary of the treasury and, the Germans observed, "Mellon's protegé."[75] To insure final acceptance of the plan, Hughes reportedly informed Poincaré: "Here is the American policy. If you turn this down, America is through."[76] If they rejected the Dawes Plan, Houghton warned German nationalists, "it might be a hundred years" before America again "extended her hand to Germany."[77] The Coolidge administration backed the plan so vigorously because, Hughes stressed, the United States was "vitally interested" in "economic recovery abroad."[78]

The Dawes Loan

The administration's cooperation with Lamont heightened the frustration of smaller bankers eager to poach on Morgan and Company's preserve. The House of Morgan claimed to speak on behalf of the American bond-buying public. The important criterion, Leffingwell explained, was "what we ought in wisdom and conscience to require for his [the American investor's] protection." He dismissed claims by bankers such as Dillon, Read and company that they could float the Dawes loan without Morgan and Company's strict conditions: "American investors won't buy the German bonds unless we recommend them."[79] Despite such confidence, his firm's ability to speak for the investing public had already slipped. Morgan and Company's control depended on investors' caution and inexperience. In 1923, the firm had employed its prestige and an intense sales campaign to put over the Austrian loan, but investors rejected subsequent loans to Holland and Czechoslovakia by other bankers.[80] In June 1924, reparations expert Roland Boyden expressed the common business opinion that "the American investor is not eager for German loans."[81]

This sentiment changed as Coolidge and other political and business leaders stimulated public demand for the Dawes loan, and the Federal Reserve System lowered interest rates.[82] Cheaper money encouraged foreigners to borrow in the United States and enhanced the appeal of high-yielding foreign bonds. Meanwhile, the League of Nations Financial Committee had followed up Austria's stabilization with a similar, but less rigorous, plan for Hungary. In late May, Lamont refused to float a stabilization loan for Hungary because the European powers would not guarantee it and "all recent foreign issues here . . . have failed."[83]

Two months later, James Speyer, whom the Morgan partners belittled as "Jimmie,"[84] organized a banking syndicate to sell the Hungarian bonds. The bankers bought $7.5 million of the bonds at 80, marked them up to 87 1/2, marketed them to investors, and then sold an additional $1.5 million.[85] Speyer's success demonstrated the new opportunity in foreign loans and the end of Morgan's control.

The Dawes loan completed the transformation of investors' attitude toward foreign loans. Although low interest rates and the administration's public support had stimulated the bond market, Morgan partners still believed it necessary to give "the selling campaign every ounce of strength."[86] Before the firm finally accepted the Dawes loan, it angled for a government guarantee. Morrow wrote Hughes that the bankers realized the loan's importance, but feared that in the future Germans would "think not of the release of the Ruhr but . . . [that] what was once a first class power has been subject to foreign control."[87] Hughes answered that the plan's stillbirth would generate "chaotic conditions abroad." Those with "substantial interests in this country," he warned pointedly, "would not wholly escape the reactions of such widespread economic distress."[88] Morrow advised Morgan that the moral guarantee implied in Hughes's near request was "as good as we can expect,"[89] and on September 22 Morgan approved the loan. At 10:00 A.M. on October 14, a nation-wide syndicate of four hundred banks and eight hundred bond houses led by Morgan and Company opened the Dawes loan subscription books. By 10:12, the syndicate had received orders for over six times the total of the $110 million American portion of the loan. "How magnificent!" Lamont exclaimed.[90]

The new hunger for German bonds did not stop with the Dawes loan. While bankers scrambled to find investors, German local governments and corporations rushed to the trough of American capital.[91] In the years after 1924, American investors put up 80 percent of the money borrowed by German public credit institutions, 75 percent of that borrowed by local governments, and 56 percent of the loans to large corporations.[92] The market for foreign bonds, which American political and business leaders had so carefully nurtured, was already out of control. Houghton, who the spring before had encouraged American bankers scouting for future business in Germany, warned Stresemann in November 1924 that "Germany must be very careful not to abuse the credit she now enjoys in America." In December, Young publicly cautioned against excessive lending.[93]

Hoover's Commerce Department shared the apprehension and launched a campaign for administration restriction of the volume of German loans issued in the United States. The State and Treasury departments defeated this effort, refusing to "pass upon the merits of foreign loans as business propositions."[94] The loan flood and banker competition washed away the controls on which Morgan and Company had been able to insist. The administration's initial failure to stem the avalanche of German loans tied its hands for later action. As early as August 1925, the State Department feared that warning the public about the potential dangers in German bonds "would tend to injure the market value of the loans already floated."[95]

This reasoning assumed that the United States was economically committed to the continued flow of capital into Germany. The Dawes Plan generated quick profits for American business and long-term problems for the American government. The freedom of action that Americans had guarded so zealously before 1924 had already shrunk. Mellon argued that if the administration stopped the sale of German municipal bonds, the business would go to the British.[96] Grosvenor Jones of the Commerce Department emphasized that the loans bolstered the American and European economies and would "avoid communism in Germany."[97] By late 1925, even Hoover was wiling to accept an admittedly dangerous situation. "It seems," he confided to Henry M. Robinson, "clearly outside our functions."[98]

The torrential flow of capital to Germany was significant in that it irrevocably altered the character of the Dawes Plan. Although Young continued to talk into 1925 of using accumulated reparation balances to finance world economic development, large-scale plans were necessarily stillborn.[99] With the surge of foreign exchange into Germany, the Allies expected cash payments, and reparation balances did not accumulate in Germany.

It had now become vital to American interests that cash payments continue. Many United States exporters and bankers became dependent on the Dawes Plan's smooth functioning. The plan gave repayment of the Dawes loan priority over reparations, but the flood of loans made after the plan went into effect did not clearly enjoy such a priority. If Germany had insufficient foreign exchange to transfer reparations, a contingency Americans had once viewed with equanimity (a healthy demonstration of the "impossibility" of large reparations, as Strong put it in 1924),[100] the Allies would protest payment of interest and amortization on American loans and war debts. American investors would become frightened and cut off the vital flow of new capital. What Young and Houghton in early 1924 had prized as the plan's flexibility, Americans now feared as a "transfer crisis." The United States so valued the Dawes Plan as a vehicle for stabilizing change that it committed its economic and unofficial political support to the scheme. Ironically, that commitment gave Americans a stake in the reparations flow and made them opposed to further significant revision. This was a central dilemma of the peaceful change policy. The dilemma became worse in the late 1920s, but in the meantime Americans hoped to complement the Dawes Plan's economic stability with the political stability of the Locarno Pact.

Americans realized that the Dawes Plan rested on shaky ground. War might yet wreck Europe's fragile stability, ignite revolution, and jam the world economic growth essential to payment of reparations. Americans believed Europe's prosperity and political tranquility to be intertwined. For this reason, business and political leaders pressured Germany and France to adopt the Locarno security pacts. Locarno was the political expression of the Dawes Plan. Both expressed the peaceful change policy of slowly reintegrating Germany into a prosperous and stable Europe.

When the pact negotiations floundered, the Coolidge administration issued through Houghton, the newly appointed ambassador to Great Britain, "America's Peace Ultimatum to Europe."[101] European economic reconstruction depended on American loans, Houghton maintained. He warned "the peoples of Europe" to make a "permanen[t]" peace. Otherwise the flow of United States capital would stop, for Americans were not "interested in making speculative advances."[102] A temporary slowdown in American lending accentuated the warning.[103]

Houghton's "peace ultimatum" signified that the Coolidge administration would discourage foreign loans if Europe did not move toward peace and stability. This policy contrasted sharply with the administration's refusal to regulate loans according to their economic soundness. Coolidge urged "the people of the Old World ... [to] enter into mutual convenants for their mutual security."[104]

Lest there be any misunderstanding, Strong told the Reichsbank president "very plainly" that the Federal Reserve system would not discount German bills until Locarno was a reality.[105] Despite Houghton's disclaimer that the security pact "was a work which Europe must do for itself,"[106] the United States played an important role in the Lorcarno negotiations. American financial power was a potent weapon, since with London's loan market closed, France and Germany could get large amounts of money only in the United States.

Ironically, some Americans who had pushed for Locarno worried at the European accord. Houghton predicted that the pacts, which guaranteed only Germany's western borders, "fix[ed] the point where the next great war will begin, *i.e.*, the German-Polish frontier." Castle welcomed Locarno, but feared "another step toward uniting Europe as against the United States."[107] Castle's ambivalence expressed a recurrent American dilemma. A stable, united Europe enhanced trade and investment opportunities, but it also threatened concerted resistance to United States policy.

Anglo-American Rivalry and Britain's Return to Gold

Anglo-American agreement on Locarno and the Dawes Plan stemmed from mutual interest in a stable, prosperous, peaceful Europe. Even the Dawes Plan had elements of Anglo-American rivalry, however. Competition over whether to link the new German currency to the gold dollar or the paper pound demonstrated the connection of the debt and gold-standard issues.

Norman carefully cultivated American bankers to gain financial backing for ventures like the Austrian and Hungarian stabilization plans. These programs rehabilitated the local currencies, tied them to the pound, rebuilt markets, and gave London a voice in internal monetary affairs.[108] In 1923, Norman aided the Reichsbank in order to frustrate a French-supported separatist bank in the Rhineland and enlist a new financial satellite.[109] A year later he helped the Reichsbank president, Hjalmar Horace Greeley Schacht, in financing the new Gold Discount Bank. Despite its name, this institution granted to German businesses credit denominated in British pounds, not gold. This step promoted German independence and British influence. In return for British help in keeping the new bank "from the claws of the [Dawes] Committee," Schacht explained to Stresemann, German finance would respect London's control in Austria and elsewhere. Schacht hoped political entente would follow the financial one.[110] "It would be a *grand thing*," Norman wrote Strong, if the United States helped finance the Gold Discount Bank, but the New York banker refused to undercut the Dawes Committee.[111] Young eliminated this challenge by incorporating the Gold Discount Bank in the committee's reorganization of the Reichsbank,[112] but Norman countered with a more serious threat.

On March 12, 1924, Norman attacked American policy to establish a worldwide gold standard. He appealed successfully to French, Belgian, and Italian jealousy over Germany gaining a gold-backed currency while the victors remained with depreciated paper currencies. The British determined to put the Reichsmark "squarely upon the sterling basis."[113] This would encourage Anglo-German finance and commerce, while helping to exclude the United States. Germany would return to gold only when Britain did and, most serious from the American veiwpoint, the tie with Germany might convince London to stay off gold and build an independent sterling bloc. Along this line, Norman advised the president of the Netherlands central bank to remain off gold as long as the Americans dominated that standard.[114]

Some American bankers and the Federal Reserve Board worried "whether the Dollar shall permanently retain a predominant position, or ... surrender financial mastery to the Pound Sterling for good and all!"[115] Americans on the Dawes Committee fought for a clause in the report linking the Reichsmark to the gold dollar, but opposed by all the Allies, they won only a postponement.[116] The Morgan partners did not break with Norman on this issue; nor did Dawes and Young risk dead-locking the conference. Instead, Strong appealed to Norman's gold in-stincts with an offer to allow some inflation of American prices. This would enable the pound to return to gold at $4.86 without painful deflation.[117] Soon thereafter, Norman eased opposition to linking the Reichsmark with the gold dollar. Schacht cleverly maneuvered for finan-cial aid from both sides, and on August 30 put the Reichsmark on a gold basis de facto but not de jure.[118]

Anglo-American competition for the new German currency was one battle of the worldwide struggle over the postwar financial order. In 1922 at Genoa, British financial officials urged a global gold exchange standard. Under this plan, weaker countries like Austria or Germany would deposit gold in major financial centers (preferably London) and hold their mon-etary reserves in easily negotiable reserve country bills. These deposits would bid up the value of the pound, ease British balance-of-payments problems, and secure London's position as world banker. British financial officials hoped the gold exchange standard would prevent a disastrous drop in world prices,[119] and regulate the purchasing power and distri-bution of gold under the Bank of England.[120] Economically stronger, the United States favored not limiting currency blocs, but the open-door opportunities of a worldwide gold standard. America's huge gold reserves ensured predominance in such a system.

By early 1925, British efforts to build a gold exchange bloc linked with sterling had failed. Only such minor states as Austria, Hungary, and Danzig were tied to the British pound.[121] Moreover, several British Do-minions were about to break the tie with sterling and link up with the gold dollar. Unless Britain itself returned to the gold standard, London faced economic isolation from a growing segment of the world—includ-ing the British Empire. Britain's adoption of the gold standard in April 1925 was in large part forced by this American challenge.

Britain's return to gold involved three distinct but related decisions:

when and how to return, and at what rate. The discussion surrounding each reflected widespread concern with the power of the United States and hope that the gold standard would fortify Britain's ability to cope with the giant rival. The British feared that if they returned to gold at a rate lower than $4.86, foreigners would lose confidence in the pound and transfer even more of their business to New York. The pound's appreciation would also enhance the value of foreign investments de-nominated in sterling and facilitate British purchases from and war debt payments to America.[122] The question was how to get the pound up to $4.86.

For a brief period in the spring of 1924, Strong indicated to Norman that the United States would boost the pound's relative value by en-couraging some inflation of the dollar. At that time Strong faced the danger of a possible Anglo-German sterling bloc. Cheaper money would stimulate capital flows to London and encourage Norman to return to gold. In addition, lower interest rates would combat domestic recession and facilitate the forthcoming Dawes loan. By the fall of 1924, however, these dangers had passed. The Reichsmark was safely linked with gold. The American economy was on the road to recovery, and investors had snapped up the Dawes loan. Finally, domestic critics charged Strong with sacrifice of American interests to benefit Europe. Now Strong backed off from his earlier willingness to help the British. He urged Norman to return to gold before the British economy made the necessary price ad-justments, even though this would hurt Britain's already battered exports. Strong warned Norman that the Federal Reserve System would not main-tain for long the low interest rates that had stengthened the pound.[123] In March 1925, when Norman brought up the Genoa proposals, Strong indicated that he would cooperate. After Britain returned to gold, how-ever, Strong's opposition to Genoa hardened.[124] A conference to imple-ment Genoa "might be entirely wise" from [your] standpoint," he told Norman, "but I felt unwise from mine."[125] The United States, then, granted the British little latitude on how to return to gold. Americans refused to inflate. Nor did they adopt the Genoa proposals. To protect Britain's gold standard from speculative attack, the New York Reserve Bank and J. P. Morgan and Company, with the Coolidge administration's approval, arranged $300 million in credits.[126]

As the "average manufacturer" in England saw it, Norman's accept-ance of this arrangement made "Britain a vassal to America."[127] Niemeyer protested that the Americans were "requiring us to go to the pawnshop." Despite such complaints, Norman finally convinced the British govern-ment to return to gold as the Americans wanted. Threatened dissolution of the Empire pushed this decision.

Although postwar Britain depended more than ever on the resources and markets of the Empire, these imperial ties were endangered by growing American penetration.[128] Winston Churchill was especially sensitive to this problem. As colonial secretary in 1922, he had warned that United States naval supremacy "would indicate to the Dominions that a new centre had been created for the Anglo-Saxon world."[129] As chancellor of the exchequer three years later, Churchill suppressed his doubts about the wisdom of Norman's policy, largely because he hoped the return to gold would unify the Empire. By early 1925, South Africa seemed about to defect.

Several months earlier, the South African government invited an American-Dutch Commission, led by Princeton financial expert Edwin W. Kemmerer, to investigate conditions in the dominion and advise whether it should return to gold independent of Britain. British financiers were conspicuously absent. Kemmerer emphasized to South Africans the advantages of forming direct financial ties with New York and bypassing London.[130] This would be America's opening wedge. As South Africa's leading banker explained, "Trade really follows the bank, and if South Africa is financed by America, no doubt America will get a larger share of South African trade."[131] In January 1925, "against the advice of British financial circles,"[132] the South African government accepted the advice of the Kemmerer commission and decided to adopt the gold standard, regardless of whether Britain did so.[133] Australia was about to make the same decision, and Canada had substantially done so already.[134]

The threat to the empire posed by the expansion of a dollar-dominated gold standard helped convince Churchill to suppress his intuitive distrust of the orthodox, deflationary policies of the Treasury and Bank of England.[135] In late January 1925, Churchill presented Norman, Niemeyer, and other senior financial officials with a memorandum that fundamentally challenged Norman's policy of an immediate return to gold by means of American cooperation. Washington's "hard treatment of her Allies," Churchill charged, had led to a "glut" of gold. "Having got so much gold," America wished "to make it play as powerful and dominant a role as possible." He doubted "whether our interests were the same." The chancellor suggested instead a managed currency and shipment of gold to America to pay the war debt. This would force inflation and depreciation upon the dollar and raise the pound to parity. Churchill opposed an immediate return to gold if it meant tight money and industrial stagnation. In conclusion, he predicted that if Britain refused to adopt the gold standard, the Americans "will only become more anxious to persuade us to that course; and their persuasion may take the form of even greater facilities than are now offered."[136]

Both Niemeyer and Norman rejected as unworkable Churchill's idea of "overfeeding the United States" with gold.[137] "On a long view," Niemeyer affirmed, "the gold statndard . . . is likely to do more for British trade than all the efforts of the Unemployment Committee." Niemeyer and Norman warned that failure to return to gold meant worsening economic isolation. "The world-centre would shift permanently and completely from London to New York," Norman feared. He warned of "serious political results on the British Empire as a whole."[138]

This threat prompted Churchill to swallow his distaste for Norman's policies. In early May 1925, the chancellor publicly justified the return to gold as necessary for Britain's economic and social health and the only alternative to economic isolation from the Empire. "Australia would have trade with South Africa and all the Dominions would have trade with the United States on a gold basis . . . with the pound left out. . . . It would have been gold on the basis of the dollar and not of the pound. That would have been disastrous." Gold standard or no, Churchill acknowledged, Britain still confronted the United States, a nation "larger [and] richer than we are." The crucial question was whether "we ourselves would be stronger on the gold standard or off it." He put his hopes on "the British Empire united on this gold standard."[139]

As Churchill discovered to his chagrin, however, the gold standard linked the empire with America as well as Britain. The chronic weakness of the pound at $4.86 required that London cut back on loans to the dominions—thereby opening the door for New York.[140]

The return to gold at $4.86 signified the fulfillment of a long-held British policy goal. But the return must also be understood as part of Britain's effort to reinforce imperial ties, regain position as center of the world economy, and meet the American challenge. Unfortunately for their future prospects, Britons were so intent on meeting this threat that they failed to foresee the competitive danger posed by undervaluation of the French, Belgian, and German currencies.[141] After 1925, Britain failed to enter what Norman had promised as the "Golden Age," but remained instead in depression.[142]

The War Debt Settlements

Tension between the hard-pressed British and triumphant Americans was prominent in the next phase of economic reconstruction, the war debt settlements. This fulfilled Hughes's plan of 1922. Once the Allies accepted reduced reparations through the Dawes Plan and political peace through Locarno, Washington was ready to settle war debts on terms more generous than Congress had mandated in 1922. Countries usually borrowed from New York and adopted the gold standard after making a war debt settlement. Washington lifted the loan embargo from each of the Allies as it settled its debt. The consequent flow of dollars financed the return to gold. In sum, these arrangements stabilized—or rather, rigidified—financial relations with Europe and facilitated further American economic penetration. Under Secretary of the Treasury Garrard B. Winston, who conducted much of the war debt negotiations, explained this policy:

> Currency fluctuation was of course the greatest obstacle to putting the European house in order. Essential to a stabilized currency is a balanced budget and essential to a balanced budget is a determination of ... [a nation's] external debt. Until this could be settled, no assurance could be given that the budget was in equilibrium and that national currency would continue stable.... Washington let it be known that it would object to the flotation in the United States of loans of a country which had not negotiated a settlement of its war debt.... The economic restoration of Europe ... was not simply altruistic. American agriculture and industry was [*sic*] anxious to see Europe as a market for American products and with restored buying power.... Uncertainty was the curse of the economic world.[143]

Such dollar diplomacy yielded both success and bitterness. Most European debtors negotiated payment schedules and adopted the gold standard, but resented America's economic dominance. In 1926, France overtly challenged American policy while Britain denounced US. greediness. Germany and Italy grumbled quietly and sought further loans.

With the early success of the Dawes Plan and surge of foreign loans in late 1924, the Coolidge administration found loan control a sharp diplomatic tool. The administration blocked loans to the Allies until they allotted to America a small share of the Dawes annuities to repay occupation army costs.[144] Hoover was angered by European military spending and wanted to close the loan spigot to recalcitrant debtors.[145] His stance became administration policy in April 1925, a time when London's foreign loan embargo left New York as Europe's only major source of capital.[146] Although Morgan and Company at times criticized the administration's debt-loan policy, the firm in effect helped enforce it. Months before the governmental loan embargo, Lamont warned Paris that refusal to settle war debts "creates such a spirit of distrust" that further loans were "impossible."[147]

France and Italy

Of the various debtors who negotiated settlements in Washington during 1925–26,[148] France and Italy were the two most important. The loan embargo hurt France, which needed foreign credits to stabilize the depreciating franc. Yet most French citizens denied any moral obligation to pay war debts on top of their huge casualties in the common battle against Germany. French governments could not agree to any payment without risking political suicide. High officials in the French Foreign Office considered offering colonial territory or a naval base instead of cash.[149] Desperate for foreign credits, Finance Minister Joseph Caillaux decided to try to negotiate with England and America. Believing that a liberal settlement with London would pressure Washington, Caillaux negotiated first with Churchill.[150]

While awaiting the results of those negotiations, Coolidge and Garrard Winston warned French officials to prepare for Congress and the World War Foreign Debt Commission an airtight case for France's limited capacity to pay. Morrow and Strong also coached the French on how to deal with the WWFDC. Gilbert advised cooperation with Mellon, most sympathetic to a quick and generous settlement.[151] Hoover and Kellogg were far more suspicious and insisted on a tougher settlement. Kellogg complained of Paris's "deliberate justification of repudiation." Hoover focused on the excessive "Military budget."[152] Hoover distrusted Caillaux, whom he called "a roulette table croupier." The secretary of commerce urged a temporary five-year settlement. During this time French capacity would improve and America would keep the option of trading debts for disarmament. Europe's military spending "costs us $600,000,000 a year in defense expenditure." Hoover calculated.[153] Senator William Borah and President Calvin Coolidge endorsed Hoover's ideas. Mellon tried to mediate between Hoover and Caillaux, but could not strike an acceptable compromise. In the midst of these negotiations, the franc rose, easing the pressure on Caillaux to settle. Negotiations foundered on the amount of payments and French insistence on a safeguard clause. This provision would condition war debt payments on German reparations, thereby linking the two sets of debts and making the United States bill collector for both.[154]

American political and business leaders coaxed Italy with more success than France. Lamont reminded Italians that without fresh loans, they might have to ship $50 million in gold to pay an old credit. A war debt agreement would open the door to a $100 million loan.[155] Henry Fletcher, ambassador in Rome, encouraged Mussolini to settle, pointing out that without post-Armistice United States loans,"the Government might have been overthrown before [the] March on Rome."[156] Mussolini accepted advice to present Italy's case in a forthright, business manner. "I am just as much an American as anybody in that respect," he claimed.[157]

Italy's appeal for easy terms met a warm reception from the WWFDC. By the time of the Italian negotiations in November 1925, the pattern of debt settlements featured payment in full of principal over sixty-two years and payment of interest according to economic capacity. Americans agreed that "the Italians are very hard up,"[158] but this economic fact established only the agreement's parameters. The specific settlement reflected other political factors, what Young had termed the "horse trades" within the Dawes Committee. Mellon appreciated that "sound policies under the forceful direction of Premier Mussolini have radically reduced governmental expenditures." Unlike most of Europe, Hoover's staff calculated, Italy had cut military expenditures to below the prewar level.[159] Hoover was also aware that a generous settlement could win from Italian-Americans "hundreds of thousands of Republican votes."[160] Agreement with Italy was important to protect America's position in Europe. With failed negotiations, Castle feared, "we should never again see the French." If Italy joined France in rejecting Washington's terms, the Allies might unite into a bloc and refuse to pay. Europe's "political hatred" for America threatened "a very serious economic effect," Castle feared, and an accord with Italy would "break down in one little corner of Europe the growing hatred against us."[161] Mellon shared Castle's concerns. When Congress held up the Italian settlement, he warned Coolidge, "We can ill afford to hamper the customers which alone permit our large exports." Without such sales, "our own prosperity would be threatened."[162]

For all these reasons, the WWFDC gave Italy the easiest terms of any debtor. Low interest rates canceled 75.4 percent of the debt's current value (on a 4.25 percent basis). Annuities started at only $5 million, a sum Mussolini raised easily with an appeal to Italians at home and in America.[163] Soon after the debt settlement, the State Department approved Morgan and Company's $100 million loan, and further credits prepared Italy for return to the gold standard in 1927.[164]

As the administration hoped, an Italian agreement encouraged France back to the negotiating table. In 1926, the WWFDC negotiated the Mellon-Bérenger accord, which provided for annuities to begin at $30 million. An average interest rate of 1.64 percent canceled 52.8 percent of the debt's current value (on a 4.25 percent basis). Once more the Americans rejected a safeguard clause.[165] Unlike Italy, Bérenger complained, France lacked significant ethnic representation among American voters. He cabled Paris to accept the pact so that "France can regain her independence from America."[166] The carefully packaged French and Italian debt agreements enabled the administration to claim full payment and yet cancel substantial amounts through lower-than-market interest rates. The WWFDC settled with one eye on congressional opinion and treasury receipts and the other on European reconstruction. However, this compromise underestimated French resistance to any payment. The French government dared not ask the legislature for ratification.

In the summer and fall of 1926, the Mellon-Bérenger agreement was swamped in a whirlpool of British resentment, German treaty revisionism, and French crisis. Sunk in economic depression Britain resented its heavy debt payments to Washington. London still hoped for cancellation of war debts and reparations. Churchill had negotiated with Caillaux a war debt agreement that made future concessions to France conditional on parallel American generosity. Along with the Balfour Note, this made America responsible for the debtors' troubles. Churchill antagonized Americans by attacking their greediness in draining Europe of capital. "If the French debt settlement fails" of ratification, Strong complained, "it is largely to be charged to Winston Churchill."[167] In the summer of 1926, tensions over war debts exploded in bitter public debate between Churchill and Mellon.[168] Official documents dripped bitterness. Americans were "sunk in selfishness," Churchill complained to the foreign secretary.[169] Churchill "has always been ... violently anti-American," Castle commented.[170] "How your people hate us!" exclaimed Garrard Winston to a British Embassy official. Indeed, a British Embassy report described Winston as "a snake in the grass."[171] Cooler heads in the Foreign Office and the Treasury realized that public hostility was counterproductive. British policy soon reverted to the more subtle strategy of guiding the "natural evolution of American thought" toward realization that Europe could pay only by flooding the United States with imports.[172]

In the worsening financial and political crisis the French refused to ratify Mellon-Bérenger; on July 11, twenty-five thousand veterans marched in protest against the accord.[173] Later that month, maddened by the sight of rich Yankees sweeping up bargains with each fall in the franc, Parisians pulled American tourists out of sight-seeing buses and harassed others in the street. The government stationed gendarmes every fifty yards along major tourist boulevards. This offered no protection against determined Parisians who dumped water on tourist buses wending through Montmartre's narrow streets.[174] "A bunch of American tourists were hissed and stoned yesterday ... but not until they finished buying," jeered Will Rogers.[175]

Resentment of American power and pressure grew in Italy and Germany as well. "Americans are sowing ... hatred" by trying to "enslave a whole continent" with dollars, one Italian remarked.[176] Observing that the gold standard "subordinated" the world to America, Gustav Stresemann urged "close cooperation between European interests, in order to set a limit to the one-sided predominance of the gold power of the United States."[177] The State Department sent all diplomatic representatives a copy of Hoover's defense of the debt settlements, which stressed how Europe benefited from America's economic strength.[178]

The French populace and legislature did not direct foreign policy; yet they made ratification of Mellon-Bérenger impossible. The issue boiled down to whether France would subscribe to American rules in the postwar financial order. Backed by the Coolidge administration, the FRBNY and Morgan and Company made credits conditional on ratification. Despite their dollar shortage, a succession of French governments refused ratification before credits. France's carousel governments alarmed and disgusted American bankers. Strong, Lamont, and other New York bankers refused credits and told the French to unite in a strong government that could put through ratification, balance the budget, and return to gold.[179] American insistence on ratification and the legislature's opposition to that option meant that France could stabilize the franc only under a government sufficiently conservative to lure back expatriated capital.

On July 23, 1926, Americans got their wish for a vigorous French government. Yet the new ministry of Raymond Poincaré took a path independent of American and British financiers. Poincaré's government signaled victory by the moderate right over the moderate left of Herriot and Briand.[180] In late July, Frenchmen of diverse classes and interests rallied behind Poincaré's effort to save the franc with new taxes and a balanced budget. This action generated confidence. Within two weeks, expatriated capital was flowing back to France, and the franc had risen 50 percent.[181] Garrard Winston was confident that Poincaré would "soon realize that ... ratification ... is an integral part of successful monetary reorganization."[182]

To "furnish a bridge over which" Poincaré could "retreat" to ratification, Strong, Gilbert, Mellon, and Winston agreed among themselves to concessions. As part of a comprehensive plan involving credits from the FRBNY and Morgan and Company, Mellon offered the French a safeguard clause. Bank of France governor Émile Moreau was eager to accept the offer, but Poincaré still refused to submit the Mellon-Bérenger accord to the Chamber of Deputies.[183]

Frustrated by the deadlock, Strong and Gilbert recommended to Mellon a broad reappraisal of American policy. Both financiers believed that Allied agreement to pay was more important than payment itself.[184] They suggested that after French ratification and the November elections, the administration declare a three- to five-year moratorium on war debt payments, thus easing the exchanges and leaving Europeans sufficient dollars to buy America's agricultural surplus.[185] Mellon was sympathetic, but Hoover and Coolidge were not. Hoover honestly believed that payments were not an excessive burden, and Coolidge rejected even an ambiguously worded safeguard clause.[186] The Coolidge administration's policymaking style was collegial: powerful officials such as Mellon and Hoover could both initiate and veto policy moves, but the president was the highest court.[187]

Cut off from direct access to the United States money market, France turned to Germany. Berlin officials hoped to trade financial aid for Versailles revision. Loan-stuffed Germany planned to buy Eupen-Malmedy back from Belgium, revision of the corridor from Poland, and evacuation of the Rhineland and Saar from France. German leaders valued such changes as precedent for further revision and vindication of Stresemann's policy of Western cooperation.[188] Although opposed to extensive revision, French leaders favored financial aid without ratification. Backed by Strong, Gilbert and the Morgan partners at first tried to plug this escape route. The Franco-German deal would muddle financial stabilization with grave political matters and undercut Washington's debt-loan policy. Morgan and Company's habitual loyalty to the FRBNY and the administration usually paid returns. Now, however, it left France alone and receptive to sweet whispers by Dillon, Read and Company. In the spring and summer of 1926, Dillon representatives wooed both France and Germany with visions of $1 billion from floating German railway bonds created by the Dawes Plan, but not yet issued. According to this scenario, France would get the money and in return evaculate the Rhineland.[189] Lamont stonewalled the threat of France turning to a rival banker: "If the French Government want to commit Hari-Kari let them do it."[190] Strong rewarded such loyalty by urging the French to keep Morgan and Company rather than turn to Dillon, Read.[191]

Dillon's challenge to Morgan fizzled. But on September 17 at Thoiry, Switzerland, foreign ministers Briand and Stresemann bypassed the Anglo-Saxons altogether and arrived at a tentative independent Franco-German solution. Briand agreed to evacuate the Rhineland within a year. In return, Germany would float 1.5 billion Reichsmarks of railway bonds and give the proceeds to France.[192] This projected entente put the American and British governments in a dilemma. State Department officials wanted Franco-German peace, but feared the challenge to war debt policy and to "American financial supremacy."[193] The British Foreign Office shared the State Department's concern for European stability, but the

British Treasury and Bank of England opposed what it regarded as strengthening of the political debt structure. The sale of railway reparation bonds to private investors would decrease chances for future elimination of the political debts. British financial officials also disapproved of selling bonds in the London market to benefit France rather than British trade.[194] Disputing Stresemann's revision priorities, Schacht hoped for an end to reparations, and so opposed Thoiry.[195] Poincaré saw value in the scheme, but wanted more money and slower evacuation.[196]

Gilbert tried to limit Germany's revision while luring France back into the corral of United States financial influence. On October 8, he urged Strong, Mellon, and the Morgan partners to meet the French "half-way" by tacitly approving the railway bond issue before Paris ratified and stabilized the franc. Such approval would "sugar coat" these "pills." Gilbert suggested that the Coolidge administration simply refuse to comment on the railway bond issue. Having saved face, Poincaré could ratify and stabilize. Then the Germans would float the bonds. Thoiry would "carry Europe another stage . . . to reconstruction,"[197] Gilbert promised. Following Gibert's advice, the administration publicly remained silent on the railway bond issue, but privately still insisted on prior ratification.[198]

Gilbert's happy scenario underestimated Poincaré's determination to avoid American and British financial domination. The more concessions Strong, Mellon, or Gilbert offered, the more the French, especially Poincaré, suspected motivation from a "plethora of money" and world financial ambitions.[199] "Americans feared nothing so much as the possibility that France would not cooperate with them," observed Moreau.[200] By late October 1926, the hopes of Thoiry had perished through Franco-German disagreement and Anglo-American opposition.[201]

Throughout the Thoiry episode, funds flowed into France, strengthening the franc and gold reserves. In December 1926, Poincaré quietly arranged payment to Washington and London of the war debt annuities, but still refused to pay the political price of ratification. Moreau and Poincaré stabilized the franc de facto in December 1926, but did not officially embrace gold until June 1928.[202] In 1927, Americans tried to press stabilization loans on the French, but, Lamont reported to Strong, Poincaré "sees no need for ratification, he sees no need for stabilization."[203] French obstinance and war debt payments undercut the administration's loan policy. "The administration would be glad," Mellon finally told Lamont, to see bankers extend credits to France. Indeed, Mellon wanted to eliminate this "so called Government supervision of loans."[204]

Ironically, France's newfound independence and economic power established the basis for financial cooperation with American bankers. After 1926, Americans and French had common concern in preserving the gold standard and political debt status quo against extreme German and British revisionism. European resistance and resentment testified to the success—and the ironies—of American economic policy.

In the two years after 1924, United States political and business leaders broke the reparations deadlock, pressured Britain onto the gold standard, and settled most of the war debts. The reparations plan revised the Versailles treaty by sharply limiting French power over Germany. The scheme revitalized the German economy and elevated as overseer of reparations Parker Gilbert, a financier with close, unofficial ties to Washington and New York officials. By engineering the Dawes Plan and encouraging Europeans to adopt Locarno, American economic and political leaders believed they were relieving Germany's resentments and reintegrating that nation into a stable, prosperous Europe. With Germany linked to the gold dollar, United States leaders took the next step of pressing Britain and the rest of Europe to return to gold and settle war debts. This too would promote order and economic growth, Americans were confident These achievements of economic, largely unofficial diplomacy were won with minimal political commitments in Europe and opposition at home.

The successes were real, but flawed. The search for stability resulted in rigid debt settlements and a rigid monetary structure. Moreover, the new economic system assigned most of the adjustment burdens to Europe. This aggravated Europe's need for a continued flow of dollar loans. Yet the loan supply depended on a marketplace already out of control. Such economic weaknesses also threatened the political policy of peaceful change, which required prosperity to ease tensions and lubricate the adjustment of Versailles. In the early 1930s, these flaws undermined the American order, and most of it collapsed. Despite its later demise, the system was alive and vibrant from 1924 to 1929, a time of economic exuberance and cultural exchange.

The Dawes Plan, the debt settlements, and the gold standard opened the doors to Europe, and American business moved in with its methods and ideas, its goods and dollars. American bankers, lawyers, and accountants set up branch offices in Berlin, Paris, and other cities; businesses set up branch plants, converting Europeans to modern assembly techniques. Twentieth-century Yankee traders peddled goods the Europeans could now buy with their dollars. Businessmen and tourists stimulated demand for American products in Europe and provided employment for expatriate writers and other artists. This peaceful army, like its American Expeditionary Force predecessor, furthered the process that contemporaries perceived as the Americanization of Europe.

[5]

The Factory on a Hill: American Business Relations with Europe in the 1920s

In 1928 the National Geographic Society reported that this Americanization was far advanced:

> Travel where you will you can't escape American customs and fashions. Berlin flocks to its first elaborate soda fountain for nut sundaes, served by snappy soda "jerkers." American movies, automobiles, dental schools, typewriters, phonographs, and even its prize fights lead in spreading American fashions and customs throughout the world. American automobiles have spread the gospel of mass production.... Typewriters have pioneered the way for a whole battalion of office equipment devices which have converted many people to doing business according to American methods.... Won by Dempsey and Tunney ... young men, white, yellow, brown, black or red ... equip themselves with the necessary "gym" shoes from the "land of champions."[1]

As Owen D. Young, a leading manufacturer of such American products, perceived it, this United States-dominated cultural and "economic integration of the world" was the prerequisite to global peace and prosperity. Although his engineering of the Dawes Plan rescued the Republicans' European policy, Young was a Democrat and follower of Woodrow Wilson. He believed that Wilson's dream of "political integration [through the] League" had been premature, because it had come "in advance of any foundation of economics."[2] In the 1920s Young and other businessmen worked zealously to build such a foundation by expanding their operations around the world. Unfortunately, many lacked Young's sophistication and focused more on quick profits than on lasting economic or political integration.

140

Young's activities demonstrated the linkage of economics, politics, and culture. In 1924 he approached the essentially political problem of reparations from a business perspective. His success here laid the groundwork for the Locarno political accords. With Europe's political stability seemingly secured, Young and other businessmen expanded their sales, loans, and investments.

Responding to U.S. competition and example, many European enterprises adopted American-perfected techniques. The inroads of American business extended to the Soviet Union, which purchased Western technology and patterned its continental development in part on the U.S. model. Face to face with American economic power, Europeans regarded the giant to the west as a land suffering from excessive materialism, but enjoying technological preeminence and relative social harmony. Business and technology were the keys to understanding and emulating America's apparent societal success, and America's culture was the product of its technology. Hence, when important European artists looked westward for esthetic inspiration and societal models, they picked up on the American themes of mass consumption, production, and entertainment. This cultural and economic influence enhanced that prestige or moral power upon which much of America's unofficial diplomacy depended.

U.S. business expansion was aided by working consensus among most top economic and political leaders. Although some businessmen disputed Washington officials' tariff, debt, or loan policies, they agreed that European stability was essential to prosperity and peace on both sides of the Atlantic. The Dawes Plan, the gold standard, and the debt settlements—these were the cornerstones of the policy of peaceful change and stable growth. On this foundation, the businessmen built a structure of trade and investment that policymakers hoped would house a prosperous, pacified Europe open to further needed change.

The hope was realized only in part. America established an informal economic empire that suffused Europe with goods, capital, investments, technology, and expertise; but Europe was unwilling to become an economic colony. It resisted the business invasion by raising tariffs and adopting techniques like mass production, standardization, and rationalization. Americans then used direct investment and foreign loans to jump tariff walls and share in European industrial progress. Businessmen like Owen Young and Henry Ford, who sold factories to Soviet Russia, and Thomas Lamont, who loaned money to Fascist Italy, believed that these business deals could moderate the policies of those countries' governments. Reflecting their Progressive heritage, they anticipated that economic ties and rising prosperity would nudge the Communist and Fascist regimes along the road toward peaceful, democratic capitalism. These dreams did not come true. A more damning failure was that the American-dominated economic order collapsed in the early 1930s. A few farseeing businessmen, such as Owen Young, warned of the dangers, but most economic and political leaders lacked the foresight, and the courage, to change an economic system that by the mid-1920s was so profitable.

That economic system consisted of interrelated transactions in trade, loans, direct investment, and technology. Exports or imports were often the first phase of a corporation's foreign business. Later the corporation might build an overseas factory to produce for the host country, the United States, or other markets. Such investments, along with loans, imports, tourist spending, and immigrant remittances, gave Europeans the dollars to buy American goods. Aside from direct investments, United States corporations acquired influence through stock purchases, patent exchanges, and loans. Large corporations, joined by individual skilled workers and engineers, installed American technology and methods in Europe. This transfer of technology was especially important in helping the Soviet Union to industrialize.

Trade

Of all these interrelated economic activities, foreign trade was the largest in volume, and the most pervasive—in the first postwar decade, American goods penetrated every world market. Despite its high tariff, the United States became the number one market for many countries. While statistics cannot convey the color of this movement, they do sketch its magnitude. Total United States foreign trade jumped from $4.5 billion in 1913 to $10.2 billion in 1929. During this period, America's share of world exports increased from 12.4 percent to 16.0 percent. Its portion of world imports rose from 8.4 to 12.4 percent. In contrast, Britain's share of world exports dropped from 15.4 percent in 1911–13 to 11.8 percent in 1929, and its segment of world imports declined from 17.4 percent in 1911–13 to 16.3 percent in 1929. Germany's portion of world exports fell from 11.4 percent in 1911–13 to 9.8 percent in 1929, while its imports declined from 12.1 percent to 9.0 percent.[3]

In addition to winning a larger share of postwar world trade, the United States shaped much of the world economy to meet is own needs. As Herbert Hoover and other Republicans had expected, the 1922 Fordney-McCumber tariff (see page 103) encouraged the importation of non-competing raw materials and discouraged competing products. Although Hoover and others had anticipated that section 315 of the tariff would enable downward revision of rates, the protectionist Tariff Commission vetoed such aid to European exporters. By 1928 Hoover himself defended the tariff as essential to American, and hence world, prosperity. The combined effect of the tariff and low-cost mass production forced much of the world to become hewers of wood and drawers of water for the American industrial machine. Finished and semimanufactured goods increased from 46 percent of total United States exports in 1922 to 63 percent in 1929, while the proportion of duty-free imports rose from 60 to 65 percent. In the sluggish revival or world trade in the decade after the war, America's growing sales edged out trade rivals, especially Britain.[4]

Not all American gains came at British or German expense, of course. Markets expanded for all in developing countries and in newly developed products. But as the first and most efficient mass producer of new items such as automobiles, the United States benefited in the 1920s from its favorable position in the new products' life cycle. Thus, American competition contributed to the paralysis that hampered Britain's economic adjustment away from declining industries like coal and textiles. Former prime minister Arthur Balfour concluded after a parliamentary investigation that in many "markets American trade has increased to a considerable extent, it would seem, at the expense of British trade."[5]

Europeans reacted to the American challenge in various ways. Most increased tariffs or otherwise slowed the flood of United States exports. Balfour urged British businessmen to copy Herbert Hoover's campaign for efficiency through "large-scale production, elimination of waste, standardization, and simplification of practice ... 'rationalisation'."[6] In 1926–27, the German steel trust tried to dump steel in the United States market, but met a special tariff. More often, large German corporations agreed with their American counterparts to divide markets.[7] Some Britons, such as Dominion Secretary L. S. Amery and Lord Beaverbrook, urged a more comprehensive imperial preference system to reduce dependence on foreign supplies and markets. In 1932, this movement culminated in the Ottawa agreements. In the 1920s, however, it foundered on British unwillingness to pay high tariffs and risk, as Balfour warned, "widespread alarm and hostility" from other countries.[8] As in naval and financial matters, Britain was torn between need to redress a power imbalance tilted toward America and need for Yankee cooperation. From 1922 until 1928, Britain tried to ease the problem with the Stevenson Plan, designed by Winston Churchill to milk maximum dollars from colonial rubber resources.

The rubber scheme pricked the American at a sensitive spot, for its industrial machine depended increasingly on imported raw materials. Rubber was essential to the burgeoning tire and automobile industries.[9] The Stevenson Plan traced back to the postwar depression, when rubber

prices sank from 60.5 to 12.5 cents per pound. American rubber companies suggested an international cartel to stabilize prices and production,
but British rubber growers were unwilling to share control.[10] The Stevenson scheme restricted rubber exports under a formula regulated by
the British government. Churchill hoped higher prices would safeguard
British control of the plantations and furnish "one of our principal means
for paying our debt to America."[11] In response, Hoover encouraged the
Firestone Tire and Rubber Company to develop American rubber production in the Philippines or Liberia. The other three major rubber companies accepted the British plan as a means toward stability, and simply
passed the moderately higher prices on to the consumer.

In mid-1925, however, demand and speculation shot rubber prices up to
$1.10 a pound.[12] Ambassador in London Houghton warned: "Just as Eng-
land built up a new prosperity after the Napoleonic Wars by using iron
and coal, so, I think, she is planning to rebuild her fortunes and to obtain
world leadership again by making use of her raw materials to be found in
her tropical and sub-tropical possessions. Rubber is merely an item in this
general problem." He recommended that the administration recognize that
"England needs our capital" and encourage Anglo-American business cooperation.[13] For the immediate rubber problem, Houghton urged private
United States representation on the Stevenson control committee.[14]

Hoover shot down this recommendation, but agreed that rubber was
part of a larger issue. The Commerce secretary resented London's financing
of the Brazilian government's coffee monopoly and the French and German
governments' potash monopoly after the administration had vetoed such
loans by American bankers. "Thus," Hoover complained, "the British become parties to further impositions upon our consumers."[15] As Coolidge,
Hoover, and Secretary of State Frank B. Kellogg realized, potash was an
explosive political issue, because depressed farmers resented inflated fertilizer
prices. Hoover refused to "pay the cost of German reparations along the
lines which the British had attempted in connection with the price of rubber."[16] He especially objected to the British *government's* involvement in
the monopoly: "We are confronted with a most appalling vision of future
world relations. It will be a world in which governments are to be engaged
in negotiating and jockeying to secure favored positions in the distribution
of the very life blood of industry and the necessities of every day life.…
Thus the State Departments of Goverments are dragged into the bickerings
and higgling of the market with innumerable new frictions."[17] Hoover
attacked the British with publicity to reduce rubber consumption and waste,
develop new sources of supply, and legalize pooled buying.[18] Public posters
urged Americans to "Help Hoover Against English Rubber Trust" and drew
the parallel: "1776–1925."[19]

Hoover's public adamancy angered Britons and some Americans. "Hoover has simply infuriated these people," Houghton warned.[20] Hearing rumors of a congressional investigation, Foreign Office American expert Robert Vansittart snapped that Britain was "still an independent country, and we will not stand being 'investigated' by anybody."[21] Foreign Secretary Austen Chamberlain made changes in the rubber scheme conditional on United States tariff reductions. A Briton sent Hoover a Christmas present of an old rubber heel.[22] Despite the acrimony, the British increased rubber exports, and in 1926 prices receded. Chamberlain had to balance Britain's need for dollars with the necessity to "avoid the dangers which must arise to our international relations from the growing agitation in America."[23]

Houghton and Assistant Secretary of State William R. Castle opposed Hoover's rubber policy and protested his "influence" over Coolidge, Kellogg, and the cabinet.[24] Congress defeated Hoover's proposal to legalize pooled purchasing by the giant rubber companies. Legislators disputed the secretary's dramatic story of the victimized United States manufacturers and the greedy British growers. They cited evidence that in 1925 the industry paid an additional $88 million for rubber and charged consumers an additional $500 million.[25] Hoover sidestepped the congressional defeat, however, by securing Justice Department approval for informal pooled purchasing.[26]

Other domestic critics pointed out Hoover's inconsistency in fighting foreign raw material monopolies with America's surplus capital monopoly. Dulles pointed out that Hoover's strategy "in effect pitted one monopoly against another."[27] Despite this domestic and foreign opposition, however, Hoover controlled rubber policy until the British abandoned the Stevenson Plan in late 1928. Ironically, it was not Hoover's efforts but the rapidly expanded production of Dutch East Indies growers that undermined the British scheme.[28]

The rubber episode testified to the Coolidge administration's readiness to use loan policy as a diplomatic tool. But the British maintenance of the Stevenson scheme showed that this tool did not always work. Finally, Dulles's criticism underscored bankers' opposition even to Washington's limited loan regulation. Despite these problems, private American loans became vital to world prosperity and the vehicle of United States economic expansion.

Foreign Loans

Between 1924 and 1928, loans helped finance America's exports and prosperity, Europe's consumption and investment, and the world's return to the gold standard. Contrary to what Owen Young and others had expected in early 1924, United States loans financed reparations and war debts. American demand for foreign bonds added a weapon to Washington's diplomatic arsenal. As Dulles perceived in 1928, foreign lending was "how Europe has been saved from starving and we from choking." Morris Hillquit, international secretary of the Socialist party, underscored the consensus. Under existing conditions, he admitted, foreign loans were "absolutely indispensable."[29]

They were certainly indispensable to Germany. In 1919–22 the defeated nation enjoyed a capital infusion as foreigners dropped an estimated $1.7 billion (about half was the American share) in speculation on the mark's rise. From 1919 to 1932, the Germans received private bank credits and borrowed $1.28 billion in 135 public bond issues.[30] Germany's loan debt to America was triple that of France, the second largest European borrower.[31] The torrent of American capital transformed the Dawes Plan into a reparations machine fueled by loans. It financed all sorts of projects, from municipal housing to the steel trust.[32] Flush with dollars, Germany attracted American bankers, lawyers, and accountants, salesmen peddling the latest gadgets, and entertainers, who fed the mania for American boxers, dancers, and musicians.[33]

German loans had diverse benefits, but by the late 1920s Americans perceived a darker side to the business. America's growing stake in the Reich became hostage to Allied reparations policy. Controversy arose over whether payment on private loans or reparations should have priority if Germany lacked sufficient foreign exchange to cover both. In 1928–29, with this concern in mind, Americans pushed for Dawes Plan revision. The priority question grew serious because neither the administration nor the bankers were honest with the investing public. Both gambled on a sunny future, the administration unwilling to jeopardize the stability offered by the Dawes Plan and the bankers loath to limit profits.[34]

These returns were sizable. Of the $1.28 billion in German loans, United States bankers earned an estimated $50 million, or 4 percent, in net profit.[35] J. P. Morgan and Company organized the banking group that distributed the 1924 Dawes loan, but did not sell any of the $110 million in bonds itself. For its services it earned a $865,300 commission.[36] The House of Morgan also retained $900,000 for managing and pledging 20 percent of a $100 million standby credit to the British government (which London never used). The 143 participating banks earned an additional $1.6 million for pledging the remaining 80 percent of the credit. Of course, if the British had drawn on the credit, interest charges would have been additional.[37] Morgan and Company's preference for such gilt-edged customers as the British, French, Italian, and Belgian governments left less prestigious banks to scramble for weaker borrowers. Out for a quick commission, dozens of banks jostled for business that was profitable and safe. Banks did not commit their funds to the borrower. They paid for the bonds only after, and if, American investors bought them.[38] Germany "was full of American bankers who were offering loans right and left, often competing with each other as to terms."[39] Morgan partners publicly complained that such competition violated bankers' stewardship, but they too rejected national or international regulation of the vital capital flow.[40] As long as bankers were eager to loan money, Europeans found it "difficult," an American ambassador observed, "to resist the temptation offered."[41]

American loans had political and military ramifications. The American minister to Warsaw observed that "all money which comes to Europe turns at once into a political force." Without taking a direct part in European politics, a Polish diplomat concluded, America in fact decided if there was to be peace in Europe. Neither France, nor Poland, nor Germany could do without American money.[42] J. P. Morgan and Company acted as unofficial financial adviser to governments on both sides of the Atlantic. Morgan and Company used this influence to promote both its own interests and the stability upon which rested the whole American position in Europe. Thomas Lamont emphasized the importance of keeping an open and sympathetic ear: "In times of easy money like this almost anybody could do French Government or any other kind of decent French financing, therefore the contact that we have with the Government depends upon something more personal and intimate—that is to say, counselling with the Finance Minister from time to time, holding his hand and letting him feel that he has someone in America to whom he can turn for general counsel. That is the strength of our position today and if we fail to maintain that contact we shall loose [sic] our position."[43] When Kellogg became secretary of state, Morgan partners "outline[d] to him the contacts which we have had with the State Department."[44] In addition to work on reparations, war debts, and currency stabilization, Morgan and Company tried to pacify Benito Mussolini and improve the public image of fascism in America. The State Department and the FRBNY shared in this effort to stabilize Italy.

Morgan and Company's relations with Mussolini began with Lamont's meeting in early 1923. "Mussolini impressed me as a very upstanding chap," Lamont related. The firm had already established an Italian subsidiary, the Foreign Finance Corporation, and the banker envisioned closer relations.[45] Lamont counseled the Italians on their war debt negotiations and, as he promised, Morgan and Company granted a $100 million 7 percent loan after the settlement with Washington. In the next two years, the firm loaned money to the City of Rome, Fiat, and others.[46] The bankers stimulated investor confidence in Italy to safeguard this business. Morgan and Company bid up the sagging market price of already issued bonds.[47] During the acrimonious war debt ratification debate in Congress, partner Dwight Morrow asked Senator David Reed to say "something of warmth" about Italy and its leaders, who were "target[s] for everybody to keep kicking around."[48] As president of the Italy-America Society, Lamont publicly praised Italy's economic progress.[49] At his urging, Mussolini's government employed a New York publicity director to "interpret Italy to America."[50] Lamont himself challenged some unfavorable press stories.[51]

However, Il Duce's penchant for bellicose speeches made such public relations difficult. Americans wondered whether Mussolini "is bent on war," Lamont warned the Italians. He feared that warlike statements damaged the market for further loans.[52] Ambassador Henry Fletcher and FRBNY Governor Benjamin Strong echoed this warning.[53] Castle shared Lamont's concern for Mussolini's public image. When the assistant secretary learned that Ida Tarbell was writing magazine articles on Italy, he was "rather terrified of it . . . because I always think of her as a pretty red radical." Hoover assured him she was not. Relieved, Castle "hope[d] she will get the situation pretty straight because everything she writes is very widely read in America and if she should write articles which see the good in the Fascist regime, it will do away with a lot of subversive talk that goes on here."[54]

The partnership between Morgan and Mussolini peaked in April 1930. Lamont recorded after an interview with the dictator: "The role that we have from the start endeavored to establish—namely, that of being his loyal and disinterested counselors on all external finance problems— seems to be pretty well fixed. He looks upon us not as seeking business, but as honestly desiring to co-operate in the Government's important problems."[55]

Other nations also acquired American financial advisers. S. Parker Gilbert supervised the Dawes Plan and the German economy. In return for an international loan, Hungary accepted financial control by Jeremiah Smith, a Boston lawyer, who held veto power over its government's expenditures from 1924 to 1926. Charles S. Dewey, former assistant secretary of the treasury, advised Poland on the financial policies necessary to maintain stability and attract foreign loans. Walter W. Stewart, former Federal Reserve Board director of research and statistics, helped modernize the Bank of England and acted as liaison with the FRBNY.[56]

Edwin W. Kemmerer, the most widely traveled of these financial advisers, prescribed plans for a balanced budget and return to gold in a dozen countries around the world.[57] A Princeton economist, Kemmerer gained the reputation of "international money doctor." Nations sought advice from Americans rather than Britons or other Europeans, he explained, "because of our political disinterestedness, our financial progress, and because they think it will help them in obtaining American capital." Although he tried to avoid local politics, Kemmerer realized that "autocratic governments" had an easier time administering bitter financial medicine: the Chilean dictatorship made for "a beautiful situation to work with, no constitution to restrict the executive and no congress to debate its projects."[58] Although Kemmerer undertook his missions as a private citizen, he, like the other financial counselors, enjoyed unofficial support from Washington and the FRBNY.[59] The progress of Kemmerer's career, from his early activities in the Philippines and Mexico to later efforts in Europe, Africa, South America, and Asia,[60] symbolized the worldwide growth of American financial power. His monetary "sanitation" work[61] expressed the Progressive emphasis on stability as a prerequisite to economic growth and reform.

Direct Investment

In addition to loaning Europeans money and advising them how to use it, Americans bought and developed foreign industries in the 1920s. Purchases of direct investments gave Europeans dollars to buy American goods. Such investments involved Americans deeper in Europe and spread United States products and business methods throughout the Old World. Some American firms, such as Singer Manufacturing Company and International Harvester, had established European factories in Europe in the nineteenth century. This movement accelerated during the Great War and the first postwar decade. The book value of United States direct investment in Europe rose from $573 million in 1914, to $694 million in 1919, to $1.3 billion in 1929. Worldwide United States ownership jumped from $2.7 billion in 1914, to $3.9 billion in 1919, to $7.6 billion in 1929.[62] Americans penetrated former European preserves—in 1922, America's Canadian investments surpassed those of Britain, and United States Latin American holdings dwarfed Britain's by 1929.[63] This global expansion filled Europe with American goods and business techniques.

Although the electrical goods and automobile industries were the most important areas of United States direct investment by the late 1920s, thirteen hundred American-owned operations produced a variety of goods and services in Europe. With technological and capital advantages, International Telephone and Telegraph and its subsidiaries obtained control

of twenty-four equipment factories across Europe and the telephone systems of Spain, Rumania, and Istanbul. Ulen and Co., a global construction firm based in Indiana, constructed Athens's first adequate water
supply since antiquity. It then sold water to the Greeks for the rest of
the interwar period.[64] Kodak's three factories on the Continent and a
research laboratory in England helped it become the numer one camera
firm in the world. Many other corporations, such as International Business Machines, National Cash Register, Coca Cola, and Carnation Milk,
manufactured in Europe.[65] Innovative sales methods and services also
moved abroad. By 1929, F. W. Woolworth Co. had 350 stores in Britain
and was opening 25- and 50-pfennig outlets in Germany at the rate of
two or three a month.[66] J. Walter Thompson Company offered "market
analysis and foreign advertising" in fifty-eight countries.[67] In Germany
alone, American subsidiaries in 1930 operated five advertising agencies,
six accounting companies, and four insurance firms.[68] Some American
manufacturers allied with European competitors to share patents, divide
markets or produce jointly. Du Pont, for example, joined with Germany's
I. G. Farben and Britain's Imperial Chemical Industries. These accords
shielded Du Pont's domestic market from competition.[69]

In addition to these European operations, Americans invested in formerly European preserves in the underdeveloped world. Oil was the most
important example. In 1919 British companies nearly monopolized crude
oil output in Venezuela and the Middle East. Standard Oil of New Jersey
officials complained that British domination in oil posed a serious business threat.[70] Yet British oil interests were weakened by insufficient capital
and nationalist ferment. Under State Department pressure, and anxious
to win Yankee financial support, the British admitted American oil companies to a minority share of crude oil output in Venezuela, Persia, and
Iraq.[71]

The State Department and Jersey Standard appreciated that cooperation with the British would reduce political tension and stabilize crude
oil supplies for the refining and marketing business. To secure American
participation in Iraq, Secretary of State Hughes had to accept a closed-
door consortium. "Real assistance to American business interests," Hughes
explained to Coolidge, required a "practical rather than . . . theoretical"
perspective on the open door.[72] The trick was to adjust the open door
to meet such "practical" necessities and still insist on equal opportunity
in other parts of the world. Although American companies increased
their share of Venezuelan output from less than 5 percent in 1924 to
more than 50 percent in 1929, worldwide the British-Dutch companies
did better. Americans' share in crude oil production outside the United

States dropped from 38.8 percent in 1919 to 29.7 percent in 1929, while the British-Dutch portion rose from 35.7 percent to 41.0 percent.[73]

In a similar pattern, American mining firms gained a toehold in other British areas. After "a long siege" with British colonial officials, the Guggenheim interests commenced tin mining in Malaya with advanced equipment. In Africa as elsewhere, British firms tried to get American capital while avoiding Yankee control. London-based companies feared that U.S. investment in Northern Rhodesian copper would inevitably lead to American dominance. Nevertheless, American money and British financial need led to U.S. penetration in Northern Rhodesia, Australia, and elsewhere.[74] Union Carbide ingeniously used an all-British management to mask its ownership of the largest manganese mine in the Gold Coast and important chrome mines in Rhodesia.[75] The pattern of American challenge to British control reflected no special antagonism between the two countries, but rather the inevitable confrontation between declining and advancing economic empires. Oil and mining investments pointed the way to future United States domainance. And in the electrical and automobile industries, Americans by the 1920s were already number one.

These industries were the engine for American and European growth in the postwar decade. Electrification required huge amounts of goods and labor and stimulated demand for new products. Electricity powered the assembly lines of Henry Ford and those who copied them. General Electric (GE) was the innovative world leader of the electrical goods industry. Through its spin-offs, Electric Bond and Share and American & Foreign Power, GE promoted and helped finance electrification at home and abroad. The Radio Corporation of America (RCA), created by GE with assistance from the navy and participation by Westinghouse, American Telegraph and Telephone, and United Fruit, constructed a worldwide radio communications network. RCA dominated the domestic manufacture of receiver sets and stimulated demand for more electricity through the National Broadcasting Corporation and Victor Talking Machines.[76]

GE's wide-ranging expansion had greater significance because one of its two architects, Owen D. Young, crafted the reparation plans of 1924 and 1929 and pushed global integration of business through the International Chamber of Commerce. In 1929, at the height of his power, Young served simultaneously as board chairman of GE and RCA, vice-chairman of the FRBNY, director of Allgemeine Elektrizitaets Gesellschaft (AEG) and American & Foreign Power, and chairman of the New Experts Committee on reparations. While undertaking this last mission, he discussed with American and European business leaders merging Western Union with RCA to form a single domestic communications trust and uniting the world's electrical goods producers to form a cooperative group, led by GE.[77] Young was confident in the ability of enlightened corporations to reconcile class and national antagonisms through mass production, generous wages, market sharing, and global economic integration.[78]

GE's international expansion in the 1920s followed a tradition extending back to the 1880 formation of Deutsche Edison Gesellschaft, by GE's predecessor.[79] Even after the Great War broke such links with the Central Powers, GE, through its subsidiary International General Electric (IGE), had agreements with or control over thirty-four electrical goods manufacturers around the world. With technological and financial superiority, GE determined to become the global leader. "You have all the world at your feet, undeveloped," Young told a group of IGE executives.[80]

In October 1920, IGE held a conference for the leaders of its international associates. American executives discussed strategy for expansion and carefully educated foreign deputies in modern sales and management techniques. U.S. leaders stressed the utility of extensive advertising in "creating new demands." Maurice Oudin, IGE vice-president, detailed the advantages of "very close relations with government officials."[81]

A few months before this experiment in international corporate education, President Gerard Swope and other GE officials met with Walther Rathenau and Felix Deutsch of their prewar associate AEG. The Americans and Germans planned to share patents and divide markets. This would protect GE from cheap German exports and block AEG's negotiations with Westinghouse. To minimize alienation of customers in the still embittered Allied countries, GE delayed final approval of the pact until January 1922.[82]

Meanwhile, Young's negotiations for RCA had ramifications far beyond business profit. London's command of the world cable network meant, Elihu Root, Jr. explained to a Senate committee, that "no message which might be of value to the British Foreign Office or to the British Board of Trade is assured of secrecy if at any point in its journey it passes over a British line."[83] For this reason, the Navy and State departments wanted independent American lines. After protracted negotiations, however, American companies settled for two independent lines to the European continent and a larger share of business to South America.[84] Britain's continued preeminence in cables underlined the importance of international radio communication. Captain S. C. Hooper, director of naval communications, testified to Congress on the role of radio in shaping global public opinion.[85]

"The power of communications is a greater power than that of the combined armies and navies of the world," Young believed. RCA thus had an important role in world peace, since "no international under-standing ... can ever function adequately to preserve the peace of the world unless we can get communication so cheap, so free, that all the people of all the nations will understand all the questions and problems of the world. That is the business of the Radio Corporation of America."[86]

Young built up this business with international pooling agreements that ensured RCA's dominance. In late 1921, Young and British, French, and German businessmen hammered out a consortium plan for long-distance radio business in South America. "The British, French and Germans are ready to cooperate in ... South America under the leadership of the Americans—we always to have the final say," he reported at last.[87] The agreement covered only external South American traffic leaving the potentially rich internal business open to an RCA subsidiary.[88] The Japanese and British vetoed Young's bid for a consortium in China, but RCA installed long-distance equipment in Poland, Russia, and elsewhere.[89]

RCA's expansion fit with GE's sophisticated plan for global expansion. By 1928, Germany's low-wage, efficient electrical apparatus industry had recovered its prewar export lead. The resulting competition made for a "fearfully compressed" world, Young warned. Yet "there must be a leader," he believed, "because there is no such thing as equality."[90] De-spite the Germans' lower costs, GE could maintain its leadership by investing heavily in AEG. As Young outlined it: "Our future position and increasing success lies in making ourselves the crystalizing unit of strong concerns in all principal countries, and thereby ... share in all the business of the world, letting it take its normal flow and without trying to exercise financial or other power to secure unnatural allocation as between the different countries.[91]

Following this plan, in 1929–30 GE purchased roughly 25 percent of AEG's stock. Holding the largest single equity holding, GE put five di-rectors on the AEG governing board. In the same year, GE bought $11 million in debentures of Germany's other major producer, Siemens. These German investments followed the organization of GE-dominated com-panies in Britain to form the largest electrical goods firm in that country. GE likewise had strong influence with the leading producers in Japan, France, Holland, and Italy.[92] It even held significant ownership in the Soviet electrical trust.[93] From 1927 to 1930, GE's international invest-ments (excluding those in Canada) jumped from $24 million to $111.6 million.[94] Sensitive to nationalist opposition, Young and Swope preferred strong minority influence to majority control.[95] GE's patent agreements with major world producers and Westinghouse's similar though less extensive position made it almost impossible for United States competitors to lease foreign patents and challenge the two giants' domestic control.[96]

From his vantage point as a captain in international economic and political relations, Young worked for the international economic integration he believed essential to peace and prosperity. While the leaders of the American automobile industry did not share his involvement in international political negotiations, their industry's phenomenal success in sales and investments in Europe furthered the economic integration for which Young strove. The automobile makers also contributed to the Americanization of Europe by establishing branch plants on the Continent and forcing European manufacturers to become more efficient in order to survive the competition.

In the 1920s, motor vehicles were an American success story. Domestic annual production increased from 3.5 million in 1922 to 5.4 million in 1929; exports jumped from an annual average of $211 million in 1921–25 to $589 million in 1929.[97] By the end of the decade, United States automobile exports reached 71 percent of the world total, not counting the 13 percent share of Canada, where Americans controlled 83 percent of the industry. Journalists and Ford executives swapped storeies of "Tin Lizzies" chugging across the mountains of India and the sands of Fiji.[98] Ford, the leading exporter, established factories throughout Europe, South America, and the British Empire that assembled "knocked down" vehicles.[99] American producers outsold the British in every major empire market except Ireland.[100]

The Europeans struck back. They began to copy the Americans' assembly-line technique.[101] European industrialists agitated for higher tariffs and advertised "Don't-Buy-American-Products." Adam Opel, Germany's leading auto producer, forbade entrance into its factory to anyone who arrived in a foreign vehicle.[102] The anti-American campaign won some success, particularly when Ford and General Motors failed to produce the smaller, low-horsepower car Europeans wanted. In 1926, Model T sales to Europe fell below those to Latin America and the Far East.[103]

Determined to stay in Europe, the motor giants upgraded investment from simple assembly plants to full-scale manufacturing factories. Ford and General Motors followed different strategies. General Motors bought existing companies—Britain's Vauxhall in 1925 and Germany's Adam Opel in 1929—and tried unsuccessfully to purchase Italy's Fiat as well. GM's $39 million purchase of Opel, one of Germany's top ten industrial corporations, catapulted the United States firm to a leading position among European producers and outflanked the antiforeign campaign. Further investment installed the latest U.S. production methods.[104] Ford built its own manufacturing plants in Europe, and sought to minimize nationalist opposition by selling natives 40 percent of the stock of each subsidiary.[105] In May 1929, Ford Motor Company, Limited broke ground at Dagenham, England, for the largest automobile manufacturing plant outside the United States. Production at Dagenham gave Ford preference in exports to the British Empire. To meet rising competition in America and abroad, Ford in 1927 introduced the Model A, and in 1932 met foreign demand for a small car with the Model Y. Ford's later plans were frustrated by the Depression, however, and by growing nationalist demand for strictly domestic auto production. Thus, in 1931 Ford began manufacture in Cologne of an automobile with mostly German components.[106]

Manufacturers of tires, auto bodies, batteries, and other parts followed General Motors and Ford to Europe. Promoting GM products overseas, the Walter Thompson agency acquainted Europe with American advertising techniques.[107]

This migration of American business generated fears and resentment on both shores of the Atlantic. In response to protests by the American Federation of Labor and various congressmen, Louis Domeratzky, Julius Klein, and other Commerce officials warned business that branch plants might create unemployment at home and foster hostility in Europe. They admitted the lack of hard evidence concerning lost jobs, however, and acknowledged that branch plants were profitable. Commerce officials were reluctant to reduce such profits and intervene in the marketplace with a strong public statement against branch plants.[108] Their ambivalence reflected the dilemmas arising from the internationalization of American business, problems that did not end with the 1919–33 period.

Another long-lasting difficulty that intensified in the 1920s was European resentment of the Yankees' economic diplomacy and business success. This American intervention aided Europe, but in ways best suited to U.S. interests. Aristide Briand and Edouard Herriot feared that Europe "has already come to appear like a colony of young America," and called for an economic "United States of Europe" to redress the balance.[109] British conservatives urged self-sufficiency through a more extensive imperial preference system.[110] "The fear of *Ueberfremdung* [alienation of control] is preying upon the minds of the people like a nightmare," a top AEG official wrote after GE bought his company's stock.[111] Louis Domeratzky, a Commerce Department expert, listed "specific instances of economic hostility" in "the effort to overcome our lead."[112] The British tried to disfranchise American stockholders; the French wanted to double-tax foreign proprietors; Germans agitated against American products; the Swiss restricted stock ownership to nationals.[113] Such measures, however, had limited utility, as few major European countries could afford to provoke countermeasures against their investment. Despite fears of American takeover, Europeans still held direct investments in the United States equal to those of America in Europe.[114] More than the rest of Europe, Germany depended on American investments for its prosperity and political ambitions.[115]

Defense against the United States competition or takeover often led European manufacturers to rationalize production with American business methods. Europeans learned such techniques through contact with United States branch plants and proselytizing American businessmen, and by visiting America and attending scientific management congresses. German or French businessmen also developed practices that contemporaries credited to America.[116] *Rationalization*, a catchall term, usually referred to scientific, efficient production through simplification, standardization, time and motion studies, market analysis, market division, advertising, cost accounting, and mass assembly.[117]

In the 1920s, Henry Ford became the symbol for many of these practices. Journalists and public relations men broadcast his aphorisms and advice to millions in America and Europe eager to learn the secret of prosperity. Ford believed that the United States could teach the world "certain principles."[118] He urged partnership between workers and management, both committed to the greatest production at the least cost. Unions had no place in this scheme. Mass production required mass consumption, and Ford practiced and publicized a high wage policy.

Along with such industrial leaders as Owen Young and Alanson B. Houghton, Ford urged a consumption ethic.[119] In 1919, Ford advertisements urged: "Buy a Ford—SAVE the Difference." By 1923, the message had changed: "Buy a Ford—SPEND the Difference."[120] Former U.S. Chamber of Commerce president Julius Barnes lectured Europe against "over-emphasis on the savings of self-denial." America's prosperous mass consumption society pointed the way, Barnes asserted, that "must be followed by older peoples ... if they are to achieve the same progress."[121] Ford, Kodak, and other American corporations set an example with relatively high wages in their European factories.[122] Such advocacy of the consumer society conflicted with American pressures on Europe to return to the gold standard and endure the deflationary pains that cut consumption and encouraged saving. This contradictory advice reflected the broader conflict in America between bankers and other advocates of the work and thrift ethic and proponents of the newer consumption creed, which benefited industry.

Henry Ford's ideas and practices appealed to many Europeans. A Polish economist explained to the American minister that although his country needed "Ford dollars" or United States loans, "a hundred times more necessary for us are the Fords themselves ... the active cooperation of American industrialists" in Polish business.[123] In Germany, Ford's *My Life and Work* was a best-seller. Many interpreted *Fordismus* as a reincarnation of the old Prussian ideal of class unity and service to the whole.[124] German employers welcomed Henry Ford as an ideological ally against unions, welfare legislation, and Marxism. Business circles valued *Fordismus* as a means to greater worker productivity and reduced costs. Their enthusiasm did not extend to Ford's high wage–mass consumption doctrine, however. Partly because of constraints imposed by America's economic foreign policy, Europeans perceived more limits to the economic horizon than Americans. Germany could not risk high prices, the argument ran, because it depended on exports to pay reparations and import bills. Cartelized German industry's alternative formula was low wages, efficient production and limited output.[125]

French sociologist André Siegfried shared German business's evaluation of Fordism as a means of labor control. The assembly line transformed "millions of workmen into automatons.... France has the same instinctive fear of American methods as symbolized by Ford as she had of the German system on the eve of the War."[126] Despite Siegfried's fears, French industry was already adopting mass production, Henri Dubreuil observed. A French labor leader, Dubreuil visited America to work in a Ford factory and returned convinced that "scientific management is an indispensable tool of real socialism." Echoing Ford, he argued that the assembly line would free men of long toil and put "all the commodities created by civilization within reach of everybody."[127] Siegfried protested that these consumer goods lacked individuality. He lamented "a state of society that is doomed to disappear."[128] And so the argument ran. Whether Europeans welcomed or dreaded the advent of Americanization; whether they were entrepreneurs, laborers, or intellectuals; they acknowledged that the future lay mirrored in America.

American Business in the Soviet Union

Communists rejected Henry Ford's doctrine of class collaboration, but fervently embraced his principles of efficient mass production. The penetration of Russia by American technology and methods had enormous impact on economic development. *Izvestia* bragged of increased factory production through *Fordizatsia*. Articles entitled "Ford Conquers Russia" and assertions like "If Lenin is Russia's God today, Ford is its St. Peter" exaggerated, but the industrialist was a powerful symbol of achieving plenty through the use of machines.[129] During the interwar period, Russia industrialized feverishly. "We are fifty or a hundred years behind the most advanced countries," Joseph Stalin warned in 1931. "We must make good this distance in ten years ... or we shall go under."[130] The United States, because of its superior technology and continental dimensions, was the logical model. Like many other Europeans, Russians hoped to emulate Americans' progressive, materialist dynamism. Stalin reportedly defined Leninism as "the union of the Russian revolutionary spirit with the American practical spirit."[131] Despite basic differences, the industrial ideas of Ford and leading Communists converged in devotion to progress, hard work, pragmatism, confidence in the machine, and faith in its social impact.[132] Russians testified to Ford's importance—and their own wishful thinking—in a play presented by Moscow's Theatre of the Revolution in which Henry Ford, the lead character, became a Communist.[133]

But in real life Ford remained a capitalist, and deep ideological differences restricted United States economic relations with the Soviet Union. Robert F. Kelley, chief of the State Department's Division of Eastern European Affairs, believed that friendly governmental relations were impossible until the Communists "abandoned their world revolutionary aims and practices."[134] Although the Commerce and Treasury departments generally adhered to this hard line, they were more positive about controlled economic relations with the Soviets. Lower-level Commerce and Treasury officials favored loans to finance German exports to Russia, but Hoover overruled them and upheld the State Department ban. Hoover, Mellon, and Coolidge, however, ignored Kelley's opposition and approved long-term credits to finance American Locomotive Sales Corporation's large order from Russia.[135] By 1925, when such business began to accelerate, the administration had arrived at a policy of permitting— with some exceptions—short-term bank financing of sales and prohibiting long-term loans. The Commerce Department did not prohibit the large-scale sales of technology to Russia by large corporations. Not until the early 1930s did the American government actively discourage trade. This ambivalent policy reflected the administration's indecision whether to withhold large-scale economic aid until communism's inevitable downfall or to profit from Russian development while undermining bolshevism's basis in poverty. In effect, the government's ambiguous stance benefited large corporations, which could afford to finance Russian business and foreign, especially German, exporters, who reportedly sold to Russia with roundabout American financing.[136]

Businessmen like Henry Ford and Owen Young who helped Russia industrialize believed that with rising living standards, capitalism would gradually displace communism. Communism in their eyes was a disease that attacked the desperately poor. Increase the people's income, and they would naturally return to health—and capitalism. Economic aid, Young believed, handed the Communists the "very gun with which they will shoot themselves." Meanwhile the installation of American machinery and technolgoy insured future business in supplies and replacements.[137] Walter Rukeyser, an engineer who helped establish the Soviet asbestos industry, explained: "If we Americans didn't help them somebody else would. So we might as well teach them Yankee methods, make the Russian 'American-minded,' sell them American equipment when we design and build their plants, make, as we have done, 'Amerikanski Tempo' a by-word in Russia, and plant the seeds for a tremendous potential and future demand for American goods. Every American in Russia is an ambassador. And we maintain ambassadors, as I see it, primarily to establish good-will, *i.e.*, to sell our merchandise."[138]

Rukeyser's vision of Russia as a new frontier for American goods pointed to an important phenomenon. Americans of diverse ideology saw in Communist Russia a new West, a vast, virgin territory for profitable investment, cooperative communities, advanced technology, resource development, even missionary work. In 1922, two pioneers "follow[ed] the frontier still farther West," they explained, to build an industrial colony in the Kuznetsk Basin of Siberia. In the Depression, Russia appeared a new land of opportunity to those with "the optimism of the traditional pioneer." *The Magazine of Wall Street* reported, "Russia offers the United States something like a repetition of the exploitation of its own West in the swirling seventies and eighties." The new frontier appeared to extend even to American Christianity. Anna Louise Strong, a journalist with close ties to Leon Trotsky, advised her father, a minister in Seattle, of the chance to modernize the beliefs and practices of forty thousand Orthodox priests who theretofore preached "religion little better than paganism."[139] Some Americans regarded the Russians, and other native peoples, as not fully adult. The Russian was "hardly awake, confused and undeveloped . . . a man-child," *Commercial and Financial Chronicle* explained. American engineers referred to Russian construction workers as the "babies," and Rukeyser doubted "whether the Russian temperament is *psychologically able* to master the intricacies" of an assembly line factory.[140] Shepard Morgan, an assistant in Parker Gilbert's reparations office, suggested that "Russia could be a fine country without the Russians."[141]

Americans like Parker Gilbert and Owen Young believed that developing this frontier was essential to world prosperity and stability. Gilbert emphasized "the vital relationship of Russia to the immediate economic future of Europe and the United States." He believed Europe could pay reparations and war debts only by expanding trade with Russia. In 1926, he pictured the alternatives as "either the early economic reconstitution of Russia or some form of cancellation." Gilbert sought "some way out," a Berlin embassy official reported, "almost desperately." The reparations agent urged that Owen Young head an economic commission to direct the Soviets along the road to capitalism.[142] When this idea died aborning, Gilbert tried unsuccessfuly to arrange for American financing of German exports to Russia. In July 1930, Young blamed the Depression on "crippled consumption" in Russia and China.[143]

From the Russian perspective, imports from America were highly important. The Soviet Union bought tractors, industrial machines, cotton, and other products from the United States. Yet U.S. exports to Russia never exceeded 1.4 percent of total sales abroad. For the Soviet Union, however, America was the largest source of imports in 1924–25 and 1930–31 and the second largest in the years in between. Most of these imports were capital goods.[144] Industry-by-industry analysis demonstrates that the Soviets borrowed rather than developed nearly all their industrial technology. American firms supplied most of the help, signing sixty-four technical assistance contracts compared to thirty for Germany, the second most important source.[145]

American technical assistance started soon after the revolution. Russian-Americans trickled back to see the new Russia; deportees and fugitives, such as "Big Bill" Haywood of the International Workers of the World (Wobblies), sought refuge in the workers' state; other Americans with a radical or pioneer bent wanted to participate in the experiment. Many of these American expatriates had technical expertise and managerial skill. One hundred American Communists used a half-finished Moscow automobile plant to repair and then produce motor vehicles.[146] With financial help from Lincoln Steffens and the Soviet government, a group of American agricultural experts brought tractors and other equipment to instruct peasants in mechanized farming.[147] Finnish-Americans demonstrated farming, fishing, canning, and lumbering techniques. Deportees arrived with textile machinery to found the Third International Clothing Works.[148] One of the most important Russian-Americans was "Bill" Shatov, who graduated from Wobbly agitator to construction boss of the thousand-mile Turksib railway. Shatov owed much to America: "When I work in the railways here, they call me a railway expert, when I work in the army, they call me a military expert. But hell, I'm no kind of expert; I'm just an American. . . . You learn a certain trick of organizing work in America, a way of doing things without waste motion, that is good for any job."[149]

In the Kuznetski Basin (Kuzbas), a group of four hundred immigrant and native-born Americans, many of them Wobblies, poignantly demonstrated the possibilities and the pitfalls of colonizing Soviet Russia with Yankee expertise. The Soviets needed increased coal production at Kuzbas to build the Ural steel industry. The Russian government signed an agreement with Wobbly leader Bill Haywood that promised American control of the Kuzbas coal-chemical complex. Once the Americans arrived at Kuzbas in 1922, however, the Soviets rejected as anarchic and inefficient the Wobblies' insistence on worker control and equal pay. Protesting what they termed Communist authoritarianism and wage slavery, many of the Wobblies struck. When the other American colonists refused to support the strike, some of the Wobblies left and the others accepted differential wages and supervision of a government-appointed Dutch engineer. Kuzbas was a failed labor experiment, but an industrial success. The United States colonists, one of them reported, got "rid of the horde of Russian employees infesting the industry and installed American methods of administration throughout." Without any new equipment, they boosted coal production 80 percent.[150] Yet American methods produced hostility as well as coal. Anna Louise Strong, who sympathized strongly with the Communists and worked on a number of Soviet-American projects, asserted "that most Russians resent Americans working here."[151]

In spite of such friction, Sidney Hillman, head of Amalgamated Clothing Workers of America, formed the Russian-American Industrial Corporation (RAIC) to provide technical assistance to the Soviets and managerial training for his union. By late 1923, the RAIC, in cooperation with the Soviet clothing trust, operated twenty-five plants in Moscow employing fifteen thousand workers, plus factories in seven other Russian cities. Lenin's formula, Hillman explained, was "American machinery and American executive ability combined with Russian labor and Russia's almost limitless resources." Hoping for social change in America, Hillman "expect[ed] to learn an enormous amount about the management of industry."[152]

Despite these and other earnest efforts, the most important technical transfers came after 1928, when Russia embarked on the Five Year Plan and enlisted the masters of American capitalism. GE, Ford, and other United States corporations sold industrial equipment, licensed patents, and built factories. Other individual Americans and engineering firms designed and supervised construction of the industrial infrastructure.

Petroleum was the single most important export with which the Soviets paid for their imports,[153] and in the early 1920s International Barnsdall and other U.S. corporations increased Russian production and refining capacity.[154] American capital participated in the British-controlled Lena Goldfields concession, another big foreign exchange earner, which produced gold.[155]

The Soviets allocated precious foreign exchange for purchases from GE and other electrical goods producers. This was essential, for as Lenin defined it, "Communism is the Soviet power plus the electrification of the whole country."[156] During the Great War, GE displaced the Germans and established a manufacturing subsidiary in Russia. After the Soviets nationalized this property, GE operated in Russia through its European affiliates, especially AEG. In October 1928, the American company signed with the Soviets a direct contract calling for $25 million in sales over six years on a 75 percent credit basis—by far the largest credit any American corporation had extended to the Soviet Union. By agreeing to pay high interest, the Russians tacitly indemnified GE for its nationalization losses. The following year GE and Moscow negotiated a ten-year technical assistance contract. The Russians established an office at company headquarters in Schenectady, and the corporation did the same in Moscow.[157] After obtaining clearance from the Coolidge administration, RCA sold apparatus for international radio communication.[158] Such technological and economic aid would eventually weaken rather than strengthen communism, Owen Young believed. Besides, the business was highly profitable.[159]

Henry Ford was equally confident that Russian economic development would undermine communism. When told that the Russians "want to go back to work," Ford concluded that they wanted to move toward capitalism. "The sooner we can get started in Russia industrially, the better ... because they will draw on us for supplies of all kinds."[160]

In 1919, during the hysteria of the Red Scare, Ford officials secretly sold 238 automobiles to a private Russian firm. Private agencies made other small purchases until 1924 when Amtorg, the trading corporation operated by the Soviet government in the United States, bought 3,323 units and 11,140 the following year. Most of these were tractors. By 1926, more than 80 percent of the 25,000 tractors in Russia were Ford made.[161]

In May 1929, Ford agreed to assist in construction of a Russian-owned, 100,000-unit-per-year automobile plant. Russian engineers traveled to America to learn assembly-line techniques, and Ford technicians went to Nizhi Novgorod to set up the factory. The Soviets paid salaries and expenses for the Ford employees on loan and, more important, promised to purchase seventy-two thousand knocked-down Ford vehicles at cost plus 15 percent within four years.[162] Henry Ford asked his chief technician in Russia to cable "when the first car comes off the assembly line.... It means very much to this company."[163]

This American involvement meant very much to the Soviets also. "With Ford and the General Electric investing in our Country," the commander of the Soviet army in Central Asia told an American, "I don't think we need fear war for two or three years."[164] The analysis was a bit simplistic regarding big business's influence on U.S. foreign policy, but it illustrated one aspect of the political and military implications of the American sales.

In addition to contracts with Ford, GE, and other industrial corporations, the Soviet government negotiated with individual engineers to build the giant dams and factories of the Five Year Plan. In 1930 an estimated two thousand American engineers, workmen, and technicians were in Russia, and the following year Amtorg anounced plans to hire an additional six thousand. Hugh Cooper bested German competition to become chief engineer on the Dnieprostroy dam, the most powerful hydroelectric project in Europe. Others played key roles in the development of the Russian steel, coal, asbestos, and other industries.[165] Most American engineers in Russia saw the advantages of society by blueprint, but believed that communism would eventually fall.[166] American specialists appreciated the Soviets' work ethic and ambition. "I don't give a damn about Communism," one exclaimed, "but building the biggest blast furnace on earth—that's a job."[167] Devoted to efficient production, United States advisers and Communist party officials often cooperated against Russian workers who resented American intrusion and Soviet control. For this reason, foreigners were an important Red weapon against White sabotage and obstruction.[168] The Soviets demonstrated their appreciation—and heightened Russian workers' resentment—by housing their foreign experts in an "American City," often set off from the workers' quarters and with a special store selling goods at extra low prices.[169]

Although both sides in the Cold War later blotted out these episodes of the 1920s and early 1930s, Americans, in seeking a new frontier, played a pioneering role in building Soviet industry. This was especially so, a Russian worker recalled in 1967, "in teaching us mass production."[170] Whether Americans in Russia sought an equalitarian society, efficient production, enhanced profits, or evolution toward capitalism, what they accomplished was the installation of United States technology and equipment.

Despite their different interpretations of the American dream, corporate executive Young and Wobbly leader Haywood shared the Progressive faith that economic growth would enable Russia to share the dream.

Both succeeded in introducing American advances, but both failed to influence the Soviets' ideology. The Americans overestimated the universality of their formulas and the impact of their technology.

The Weaknesses of the International Economy

Despite his naiveté with regard to Russia, Young was astute in pointing to underconsumption as a fatal flaw in the international economy of the 1920s. Unfortunately, he was no more successful in solving this problem than in influencing Soviet communism. More than most contemporaries, Owen Young understood that mass production required expanded markets. Yet the relatively high wages paid by GE, Ford, and other efficient producers were not earned by most American workers. In the 1920s U.S. workers' productivity increased far more rapidly than their wages.[171] European businessmen insisted that they could not afford to pay even the American scale. Reparations and war debts aggravated the trend toward overproduction, for the United States and the Allies resisted payment with competitive products. Where was the outlet for surplus goods? Unless the increasing output was consumed, eventually the factories would have to close. Gilbert looked longingly at Russia as a largely untapped market, but Washington forbade the necessary financing. At the Dawes Conference, Young sketched one imaginative answer: Use reparation money to finance early construction of railways, power plants, and other infrastructure in Asia and Africa. Such "hothoused" economic development would create purchasing power and absorb the surplus. Young's idea was creative, but the Dawes Plan developed differently than he had expected. The surge of American lending to Germany transformed the plan into a scheme dependent on continuous loans. The reparation money that Young had hoped to use to finance hothoused growth did not accumulate in Germany.[172] Compounding the overproduction problem was Europe's chronic dollar shortage, a product of America's competitive advantage and its tariff, war debt, and monetary policies.

And so the overproduction and balance-of-payments problem hung over the international economy, a sword of Damocles suspended by the thread of American lending. Once that broke (as it did in 1928), Europe was cut off from much of its dollar supply and American exporters were cut off from much of their market. In the 1920s economic and political leaders entrusted private business with enormous responsibility in regulating the international economy. As a leading U.S. businessman put it, the overproduction and balance-of-payments problem "was the acid test as to whether modern business is competent in itself to solve its own problems." Failure threatened "the maintenance of international peace."[173]

On June 25, 1925, a trio of American economic leaders launched a campaign to revive the idea of hothoused growth. Owen Young spoke at a dinner given by Stone and Webster, the international electrical engineering firm; on the same day Henry M. Robinson, a former Dawes Committee member and Los Angeles financier, addressed a group of bankers; again on the same day S. Parker Gilbert, the agent general for reparation, talked to a group of European and American businessmen. All three urged the necessity, as Young put it, of developing "enterprises which will make a market for those goods which we do not want to take ourselves."[174] Two days earlier, an association of European and American businessmen emphasized the importance of stimulating growth and pointed to the inevitable connection between war debts and reparations.

Unfortunately, the hothoused growth idea died aborning. Coolidge focused on, and publicly protested, the linkage of the two sets of debts.[175] The Allies were afraid to stimulate German industry. American loans made for easy payment of reparations with foreign exchange. Most important, too few leaders grasped, as Young did, the importance of generating sufficient effective demand to consume the burgeoning production. With political opposition and dim vision, business failed the "acid test." After 1925, production increased further. Prices dipped slightly, but the European economy kept afloat with American loans.[176]

This stillborn initiative to bolster the international economy epitomized the flawed success of American businessmen in the 1920s. Corporate leaders spun a global web of trade, loans, and direct investment, which generated profits at home and political and cultural infuence abroad. The United States became a factory on the hill, with the eyes of capitalist and Communist industrialists upon it. Europeans met the trans-Atlantic challenge by copying American business methods and perfecting their own mass production techniques.

Yet United States success was limited in scope and time. Americans failed to moderate fascism or undermine Soviet communism. As Stalin remarked, Leninism—not capitalism—was the offspring of Russian revolution and American technology. Democratic-minded Wobblies revitalized the Kuzbas coal mines, but did not prevail against Communist authoritarianism. Similarly, Owen Young and Henry Ford did not convince most European—or American—businessmen to adopt the high wages essential to full consumption. Underconsumption and the international payments imbalance eventually helped destory the stable prosperity for which American businessmen worked so hard.

The rebuilt international economy rested on the foundation of the

Dawes Plan and Locarno. Americans built a structure of prosperity, hoping it could accommodate further peaceful change. This interdependence of politics and business continued in the 1930s when the economic crash brought down the policy of peaceful Versailles revision. American cultural influence in Europe also flowed and ebbed with the economic tide. Unlike the political policy of peaceful change, however, the cultural impact of American technology persisted, in transmuted form, into the future.

[6]

The Americanization of
Europe in the 1920s

In the 1920s, American economic, political, and cultural influence washed over Europe. The first cultural wave came in 1917–19 with the two-million-man American Expeditionary Force, which brought Europeans face to face with the United States' power and creativity, the development of which they had watched for over two centuries. A second swell of cultural influence followed the Dawes Plan, Locarno, and the financial stabilizations. These achievements, the fruit of the peaceful change and economic reconstruction policy, opened Europe to American business and cultural penetration. Tourists, expatriates, and Hollywood films flooded Europe, serving as missionaries for American life-styles and products. The United States' rank as the world's most powerful nation induced Europeans to pay attention to American culture. That culture's vitality, and its appropriateness to the machine age, made it all the more attractive to Europeans struggling with modernization. American models influenced Europe's popular entertainment, its artistic development, and its thoughts about the future. In cultural matters as well as in economic and political ones, the United States was the engine, the leading nation whose independent and pioneering course Europe was compelled to follow.

Perhaps because Europeans were so fascinated by the United States' economic power, they interpreted aspects of American culture, whether literature or life-style, as the products of a machine-dominated society. Increased mechanization, they believed, was the central element of Americanization. For many Europeans, American culture was above all technological. *Americanism* suggested materialism, efficiency, largeness, mechanization, standardization, automation, mass production, mass consumption, mass democracy, technocracy, uniformity, pragmatism, reformism, optimism, spontaneity, generosity, and openness. *Americanization*

167

had two overlapping meanings: the spread eastward of Yankee influence and the modernization indigenous to both continents but more advanced in America.[1] Some Europeans favored the Americanization of their continent, others opposed it; but nearly all believed that the United States was setting the path along which they would have to follow.

After 1917 American culture penetrated Europe in various ways. The American Expeditionary Force prepared the way for post-war cultural exchange by introducing Europeans to jazz and doughboys to the charm of the Old World. The doughboys' machines, their efficiency, energy, and innovativeness, impressed Europeans. Exhausted by the war, disillusioned with their own societies, many Europeans wondered whether they should not adopt the methods of these highly successful Americans. After the war, many former soldiers returned to the Old World as artists, tourists, or businessmen, each in his own way spreading U.S. culture. Along with Herbert Hoover's American Relief Administration, smaller private aid teams initiated Progressive reforms. Hollywood films stimulated demand for America's products while exposing Europeans to its speech, its manners (and mannerisms), and its values. Fads swept Europe as boxers and dance troupes pioneered this cultural and economic frontier.

Yankee popular culture excited many European artists, particularly avant-garde Germans of the *neue Sachlichkeit*, or new objectivity school, who sought modern cultural models to replace discredited imperial ones. Although many of these artists, like other Europeans, feared domination by the machine, they welcomed Americanism as a way to increase the Old World's economic productivity while resolving its social and ideological conflicts.

America's mass culture seemed democratic and progressive, the wave of the future. Many German leftist artists saw little contradiction in paying simultaneous allegiance to Bolshevism and Americanism. Both creeds preached popular sovereignty, mass culture, and technological development. In the heyday of U.S. influence, such German artists as Bertolt Brecht decided that Americanism, not bolshevism, offered the surer and more comfortable road to progress.

The United States was not only Europe's competitor, creditor, and occasional political mediator, but also the leader of Western civilization; and what happened in America was of intense, often personal interest to many Europeans. They watched closely, and reacted with near-hysterical joy, to Charles Lindbergh's solo flight across the Atlantic and, only a few months later passionately repudiated the Massachusetts trial and execution of Nicola Sacco and Bartolomeo Vanzetti.

America's influence in Europe had great impact also on its own artistic development. American painters, writers, composers, and other artists made pilgrimages to Europe, looking for freedom and esthetic inspiration. There they found many artists fascinated with the technologically dominated culture they had scorned. Moreover, significant numbers of expatriate artists ended up financing their adventures by working for compatriot businessmen and tourists. In the Old World, then, many Yankee artists found both esthetic validation and financial support for developing an indigenous American art.

Just as America's power led Europeans to heed American culture, so too did such prestige or moral power enhance the effectiveness of the United States' unofficial economic diplomacy. Washington officials realized that America's reputation for success and efficiency, coupled with its lack of interest in most European political rivalries, gave the nation a subtle but important moral authority in the Old World.

The State Department valued this asset because it yielded influence abroad with minimal cost or responsibility. Department officials tried to maximize America's moral power by making sure their foreign policy initiatives would succeed.[2] In 1927, the department countered European resentment of U.S. power by using Charles Lindbergh as a goodwill ambassador. Like the AEF a decade earlier, Lindbergh riveted Europeans' attention on Yankee boldness and technology, and thus quickened the pace of Americanization.

The American Expeditionary Force

AEF soldiers did more than fight. They impressed allies and enemies with American motor vehicles and American know-how. In Germany the doughboys helped suppress bolshevism; in Poland they fought typhus. As good Progressives they believed that with enough "soap, clean towels, and above all clean underwear, we can wash Poland."[3]

The first American troops paraded through Paris on July 4, 1917, a time when the French army faced mutiny and exhaustion. Prefects throughout France reported that arrival of these American "saviors" raised civilian morale. George Creel, director of the Committee on Public Information, tried to undermine German morale by dropping behind enemy lines pamphlets that promised American-sized rations for prisoners-of-war and pictured the huge AEF buildup in France.[4]

The buildup made good propaganda, but it snarled traffic in the French ports allotted to American traffic, St. Nazaire and Nantes. AEF engineers tackled the difficulty by building new port facilities, stringing telephone lines, and constructing a reservoir. French newspapers admired the Americans' superior "boldness" and "initiative," and found French accomplishments wanting by comparison.[5] Struggling to comprehend the invasion, journalists defined "Americanism" as a "method of procedure ... more concerned to do things well and quickly than to follow old-fashioned regulations." Many argued that adoption of this attitude "will do us good."[6] The AEF introduced the French to jazz as well as American methods, whetting appetites for the jazz bands that flocked to Paris in the twenties.[7] Although not all Frenchmen and women liked jazz, most appreciated the doughboys' sense of humor, kindness to children, and generosity. Marriage statistics perhaps best convey the closeness of the personal ties between many Yankees and the French. In St. Nazaire, Franco-American nuptials in 1919 reached 21.7 percent of the total, climbing to 37 percent in June.[8] Although most soldiers brought their wives back to America, some fifteen hundred remained with their spouses in France, forming a link between the two societies and a vanguard for the 1920s expatriates.[9]

Less happy relations also foreshadowed the 1920s. Although trigger-happy soldiers and hostile French peasants caused incidents throughout the AEF's two-and-a-half-year stay trouble worsened after the Armistice. Americans awaiting transport home were bored, and irked by gouging merchants; many French chafed at the foreigners' continued occupation. Local newspapers condemned Woodrow Wilson's stance at Versailles.[10] On the second anniversary of Congress's declaration of war on Germany, street fighting broke out between AEF soldiers and natives of St. Nazaire. Anti-American demonstrations followed in other cities. In Nice a gang ambushed and killed American military police.[11] Such hostility exposed the reverse side of French admiration for America and foreshadowed the difficulties between the two nations from 1919 to 1933. In 1919 as in later years, the United States' riches and efficiency excited envy and fear as well as adulation.

Specific complaints against the AEF paralleled later ones against American businessmen and tourists. Although Americans tried to improve transportation facilities, the heavy AEF vehicles angered natives by clogging traffic and damaging highways. Many French people later condemned the mass production methods, imported from America, that forced changes in their lives. The French complained of AEF requisitions and later war debt demands, even though the United States tardily paid for the requisitions and reduced the burden of the war debt. Proper Frenchmen and women deplored the doughboys' sometimes crude and violent behavior. Working-class Frenchmen charged that the free-spending Americans bid up the cost of living and corrupted the local women. In the 1920s, tourists and expatriates drew the same charges.[12] Thus, the AEF's impact in the postwar era increased both cultural exchange and the tensions between Americans and French.

The American army's experience in occupied Germany was a happier one, and it too foreshadowed the 1920s. After initial hostility, soldiers of the American Forces in Germany (AFG) and civilians of the Rhineland soon developed cordial relations. In mid-1919, the *New York Times* repeatedly criticized American soldiers who loudly compared German hospitality with French hostility.[13] Doughboys found Fräulein even more attractive than Mademoiselle. Commanding General Henry Allen stated that one-third of his men had married German girls. The venereal disease rate hit 423 per 1000.[14] Germans both welcomed and resented the free-spending Americans. In marks, an AFG private's pay exceeded that of some German bank president. Despite the Reich's technological achievements, AFG personnel demonstrated to the Germans superior methods for drilling wells, maintaining sanitation, building bridges, and repairing roads. American forces also maintained order, suppressing a strike and Communist agitation.[15]

The Rhineland occupation from 1919 to 1923 underscored America's decisive role in the war and doubtless heightened Germany's receptivity to U.S. methods, ideas, and products. In 1931, a German observed: "Victors in war always become the unconscious ideal and model of the conquered: America, which has conquered the whole world, has stamped its childish version of mechanistic style on our era."[16] Although Germans and other Europeans found it easy to criticize American culture, it was harder to deny that culture's pervasive influence in the Old World.

In 1917–19 other Americans influenced Europe. Convinced that "American theories" were essential to European reconstruction, American women formed the Committee for Devastated France, which undertook social work and reconstruction in the Aisne, one of the worst battlefield areas.[17] André Tardieu (later prime minister) recalled that the committee molded much of the social reorganization of Aisne; it introduced community "public spirit."[18] With the committee's guidance the French organized agricultural cooperatives, public libraries, Boy Scout troops, and nursing schools. These institutions offered services and, the Americans calculated, opened new career opportunities for French women. Local peasants and townspeople came to appreciate the new institutions, and maintained them after the Americans left in 1923. Although the French had at first resisted American social service techniques, the committee concluded, they had "bent to the contact of our methods."[19] With similar Progressive idealism, the Young Women's Christian Association (YWCA) trained women of Czechoslovakia and Poland in recreation and social service work.[20]

Other Americans set up schools and hospitals. Probably the most influential was the American Red Cross Albanian Vocational School (AVS) in Tirana, established upon completion of wartime medical relief. Under

American direction, the AVS operated in English, which Albania had adopted as its second tongue. The school provided Tirana with electricity, operated a printing press for the government, improved agriculture, installed the nation's first indoor water tap, and trained hundreds of young Albanians. Oriented toward American ideas, methods, and products, AVS graduates challenged Italian domination of Albania. Despite the Americans' sincere protests about the "disinterested character" of their involvement in the school, such cultural influence had unavoidable political implications, which did not escape the Italians. In 1933 they insisted that the Americans leave.[21]

As the AVS demonstrated, there was direct linkage between America's participation in the Great War and the subsequent economic and cultural penetration of Europe. The soldiers and social workers awakened Europeans to the advantages of American products. Observing the AEF's mobile antityphus campaign in Poland, the minister of health remarked, "One Doctor plus one Ford makes six Doctors."[22] Some 10,000 AEF and AFG soliders plus ARA veterans remained in Europe, and others returned in the 1920s as tourists and representatives of U.S. firms. The AFG newspaper called the troops "but a vanguard of millions of Americans who will ... invade the several states of Europe. We are paving the way for the men who will enter the European markets of the future.[23]

That invasion accelerated after the Dawes Plan and Locarno stabilized Europe. American tourists, expatriates, and movies broadened Europe's exposure to Yankee products, life-styles, and ideas. Along with the loans that flooded Europe after 1924–25, tourists provided Europeans with the dollars they needed to pay their debts and buy American exports. The annual pilgrimage of as many as a quarter of a million tourists, plus the presence of eighty thousand U.S. expatriates, stimulated consumption in Europe of American products. Tourists and expatriates demanded the same goods—cokes and chewing gum, typewriters and Ford—that they knew at home. Their example, highlighted by the consumption patterns portrayed in Hollywood films, aroused European desires for the same amenities. Tourists and expatriates who fled Main Street found much of the Old World entranced with Wall Street and Hollywood. The economic and cultural exchange was a dynamic process. As Europe became more Americanized, more tourists felt comfortable vacationing there. Similarly, Europe's Americanization stimulated demand for U.S. exports, which in turn enhanced the prosperity that financed tourists' trips to Europe.

Tourists and Expatriates

Tourists constituted the largest and economically most important American group in Europe. The number of United States visitors jumped from roughly 15,000 in 1912 to 251,000 in 1929. In the latter year, American citizens in Europe spent close to $323 million and immigrants visiting home expended an additional $87 million. By the end of the 1920s, foreign travel became possible for middle-class Americans.[24]

Visits to Paris nightclubs and the Louvre seemed a painless answer to America's balance-of-payments dilemma. Tourists' dollars helped Europe pay its debts and the United States maintain its tariff. Herbert Hoover's Commerce Department noted happily that worldwide American tourist expenditures of $770 million in 1927 more than matched $714 million in war and private debt receipts.[25] In addition to the financial dividend, tourism had a beneficial "political effect," American officials told the Germans, "leading to a normal resumption of relations" between the two nations.[26]

The flood of travelers generated resentment as well as dollars. Always the tourists' favorite, France in 1926 attracted foreigners who picked up bargains as the franc fell. Americans commonly asked waiters and shop-keepers "How much is that in real money?"[27] A few even papered their train compartments or luggage with franc notes. Such insensitivity aggravated tensions over the war debt, and in July Paris erupted in several antiforeign, and especially anti-American, demonstrations. Both French and American officials tried to calm emotions. Calvin Coolidge balanced a rebuke of "bumptious" tourists with a warning that badly treated Americans would stay home.[28] But probably the majority of visitors had pleasant tours that never made newspaper headlines—in any case, France remained the number one American tourist attraction in Europe.

In 1929, the combined expenditure of American tourists and residents in France totaled over $137 million, creating an American economy in Paris.[29] In the French capital one could be born in the American hospital, attend one of several American schools and churches, belong to the American Legion, the YMCA, the Cornell, Harvard, or American Women's Club; read one of three Parisian-American newspapers, in a favorite café or at the American Library; sip whiskey in the many American bars, drink milk delivered by American milkmen, eat sweet corn and ice cream produced by local Americans; go to hockey games, boxing matches, and other imported sport events; receive care from American dentists and doctors and be buried by an American undertaker.[30] With fewer United States tourists or permanent residents, Berlin still supported an American church, student association, newspaper and, intermittently, chapters of the American Medical Association, Daughters of the American Revolution, and the Harvard Club.[31]

The forty thousand American residents in Paris created teaching, writing, and translating jobs that helped support expatriate artists. For American writers who matured in the decade after 1919, residence in Europe, especially on the Left Bank in Paris, was almost an initiation rite. The city was "our 'university,'" Matthew Josephson recalled.[32] The "lost" generation was on a quest for personal freedom and revitalized American art. Although many American writers, painters, and composers mocked Main Street's materialism, these largely middle-class sons and daughters did not entirely abandon its values. Most artists who sailed to Europe were confident in their own capabilities and in America's esthetic potential. In Paris they found themselves, and they found European artists entranced by America's technocratic civilization. The fruit of this cultural cross-fertiization yielded, in such diverse artists as Ernest Hemingway, Gertrude Stein, and Virgil Thomson, a reaffirmation of their Yankee heritage and a recommitment to developing an indigenous American art of which they could be proud.

American artists in Europe seemed light-years away from the less colorful U.S. diplomats and bankers. Yet ties bound the two groups. Each was confident in the power of the individual and the potential of American development. Neither put much faith in political reform or politics generally, and this abnegation strengthened the status quo. The artists who left for Paris and the administration leaders who struggled for a policy of limited involvement in Europe each felt constrained by provincial America. Personal ties, not always harmonious, also linked artists with the business-governing elite. Writer and publisher Harry Crosby secured a position at Morgan et Cie. from Uncle J. P. Morgan and researched the poetic effects of hashish while guest of Cousin Joseph Grew, ambassador to Turkey.[33] Another Crosby cousin, Walter Berry, won renown as an international lawyer and bibliophile and, as Edith Wharton's confidant and lover, inspired the novelist to new heights. Between his failed diplomacy of 1918–19 and ambassadorships to Moscow and Paris in the 1930s, William Bullitt married John Reed's widow and cultivated the friendship of artists. Banker Otto Kahn helped finance Hart Crane's *The Bridge*. Americans like reparations expert Fred Bate and International Chamber of Commerce official Lewis Galantière combined such Right Bank work with active encouragement of the artists on the Left.[34]

In October 1918, Walter Damrosch, an officer in the AEF and former conductor of the New York Symphony, established a music school in France to train military band leaders. After the war, the Conservatoire américain continued to educate American composers. Damrosch hired Nadia Boulanger, a prominent French musician, who encouraged composers like Virgil Thomson to take pride in and develop their native musical traditions.[35] Thomson was part of that generation of American composers, born between 1890 and 1910, which went to Paris in the 1920s. Like other artists, many were attracted by Europe's cheap prices.[36]

Harold Loeb, the editor of a lavish literary magazine called *Broom* published inexpensively in Berlin, explained that "literature, as well as finance, is sensible to the trade balance."[37] Encouraged by the United States government, Austria stabilized its currency in 1923, Germany in 1924, and France in 1926. While it reduced the dollar's extraordinary buying power, stabilization attracted American businessmen and tourists to Europe. This meant jobs for artists, especially in journalism. Warren Susman calculates that almost 70 percent of American expatriates in Paris gained at least a partial living from writing articles printed in the United States or Europe.[38]

Loeb, Matthew Josephson, and other expatriates looked for inspiration from European artists. "Instead," Josephson recalled, I found "a young France that . . . was passionately concerned with the civilization of the U.S.A., and stood in fair way to be *Americanized*."[39] Other expatriates sharpened Europe's image of America as the land of technology and business. Assisted by Ezra Pound, George Antheil composed and conducted in Paris the *Ballet Méchanique*, an orchestration of nine machine-played pianos, electric bells, and a whirring airplane propeller.[40] Gerald Murphy, a wealthy painter and a leader of the expatriate colony, chose such themes as machines and smokestacks.[41] Ernest Hemingway, whose writing in the 1920s was translated into French, German, and Italian, embodied a work ethic as strong as Herbert Hoover's. Jake's parsimonious outlook in *The Sun Also Rises*, Hemingway's novel on expatriate life, paralleled American leaders' moral view of debts and currencies.[42] Anna Louise Strong, an American journalist in Moscow who helped establish the John Reed technical school for Russian youths, brought along her "Ford . . . electric toaster, percolator, etc. etc."—for her own convenience and to "show the folks here American stuff."[43]

Although the expatriates' idiosyncrasies defied rigid categorization, most self-exiles were the figurative sons and daughters of General John Pershing, Henry Ford, and Herbert Hoover. America's business/machine civilization had provoked their rebellion, but America remained their cultural homeland just as surely as the culture of business suffused their art and thought.

Malcolm Cowley chronicled how these inadvertent "trade missionaries" stimulated, by their life-style, demand for American goods.[44] A few expatriates urged more explicit ties between economic and cultural expansion. Walter Lowenfels argued that "American intellectuals must take their place beside the businessmen to guide the intellectual future of the world."[45] F. Scott Fitzgerald also anticipated an imperial future. "Culture follows money," the novelist declared; "we will be the Romans in the next generation as the English are now."[46]

The esthetic and business spheres intersected in other ways. Well-paying European audiences helped support black jazz bands.[47] Europeans read American authors like Sinclair Lewis and Ernest Hemingway in part because they believed it essential to understand the giant across the Atlantic. In 1930, Lewis won the Nobel Prize in recognition both of his own abilities and America's coming of age.[48]

Europeans often addressed American writing in terms of Yankee economic predominance. American poetry had "skyscraper creativity," a German reviewer wrote. A French analyst compared Hemingway's style to "modern buildings: girders and concrete"; another labeled it "the very essence of American genius ... reaching the first rank by jostling one's way to the fore."[49] Whatever the metaphor, young Europeans hastened to copy the American novelist. A German critic remarked in 1932, "Young European authors write like Hemingway."[50]

Hollywood Films

During the Great War, Hollywood invaded European and other world markets. YMCA representatives entertained Allied trops with American films, and the "movie habit" caught on among civilians and soldiers.[51] In the 1920s, American films were an international box-office hit. Assured of the domestic market, which netted 60 percent of total world film revenue, Hollywood produced extravaganzas with which Europeans could not compete. By 1925, United States films made up 95 percent of the total shown in Britain, 60 percent of the total in Germany, 70 percent in France, 65 percent in Italy, and 95 percent in Australia and New Zealand.[52] In Germany, the number of cinemas increased by 35 percent from 1920 to 1929, while the production dropped from 646 films to 175 films.[53] Americans owned three-fourths of the most fashionable movie theatres in France.[54] Hollywood's profits depended on foreign screenings, since domestic revenues covered only production costs, and frequently not even that.[55]

"Trade follows the film," Americans and Europeans agreed. Greek appliance wholesalers and Brazilian furniture dealers found that their customers demanded goods like those pictured in the American movies.[56] Although direct correlation between films and trade was hard to prove, Congress, parsimonious in most matters, established a Motion Picture Section in the Bureau of Foreign and Domestic Commerce in 1926. Bureau chief Julius Klein and his officials attested that United States films "stimulat[ed] the desire to own and use such garments, furnishing, utensils, and scientific innovations as are depicted on the screen." Will H.

Hays, Hollywood czar, boasted of the power of these "silent salesmen of American goods."[57]

American films not only sold United States goods, but, many Europeans feared, threatened independent national identity. "America has colonized us through the cinema," one Frenchman complained.[58] Another French critic testified to the secularization of John Winthrop's city upon the hill: "Formerly US preachers ... deluged the world with pious brochures; their more cheerful offspring, who pursue the same ends, inundate it with blonde movie stars; whether as missionaries loaded with bibles or producers well supplied with films, the Americans are equally devoted to spreading the American way of life."[59] Charles Pomaret, a member of the Chamber of Deputies, remarked that Europeans had become "galley-slaves" to American finance and culture—appropriately, an image taken from the Hollywood hit *Ben-Hur*.[60] British groups worried that the many Hollywood films shown throughout the empire led to "American domination in the development of national character or characteristics."[61] After a concerned speech by the Prince of Wales, the London *Morning Post* warned: "The film is to America what the flag was once to Britain. By its means Uncle Sam may hope some day, if he be not checked in time, to Americanize the world."[62]

After 1925, Britain, Germany, and France tried to check the trend. Governments enacted measures to limit the number of imported Hollywood films and encourage domestic production. This policy diminished but did not eliminate Hollywood's dominance in Europe.[63] Required by law to produce domestic films if they wanted to import the popular American ones, German and other European producers responded with "quota quickies," often subgrade efforts produced only to meet the letter of the law. American filmmakers circumvented the restrictions by investing in Europe, especially Germany. They imported European directors and performers and remained preeminent in world film exports.[64] The State and Commerce departments vigorously supported Hollywood's diplomacy.[65] In the late twenties film exporters faced a new danger, with talkies. How could they screen English-language movies in polyglot Europe? Hollywood responded with multilanguage production. In collaboration with a Berlin company, Paramount filmed *The Blue Angel* in English and German versions. In France, Paramount worked on an assembly-line basis: sixty-six features in twelve languages for the first year. Dubbed sound tracks helped, and by 1931 United States films had regained all but 10 percent of their 1927 market in England and Germany.[66]

Hollywood films were a hit in Europe because they projected modern culture in a vivid and attractive light. Film embodied the era's emphasis on mechanical, simultaneous, and concentrated production. The message was mass entertainment. As Adolf Behne, a German avant-gardist, recognized, "Film is ... democratic.... This ha[s] been recognized by the German masses, which flock to see Charlie Chaplin films.[67] As the industry's global leaders, Hollywood producers had budgets large enough to pay for the casts of thousands and other spectacular effects calculated to please those masses. Finally, the films portrayed an image of life in fabulous America, the giant of the contemporary world and the pioneer of Europe's own future.

The American Impact on Europe

From Switzerland to the Soviet Union, Europeans acknowledged America's cultural leadership. "Mrs. Lenin," Anna Louise Strong reported from Moscow, "wants ... American ideas on education through doing; manuals about ... various things."[68] Jean Paul Sartre reflected, "Skyscrapers ... were the architecture of the future, just as the cinema was the art and jazz the music of the future."[69] André Siegfried, a French sociologist, concluded that America had replaced Europe as "the driving force of the world."[70]

American cultural influence probably went deeper in Germany than anywhere else in Europe. "Berlin Goes American," a journalist reported from the German capital, where cafeterias offered "griddle cakes mit syrup" and theatres featured Broadway hits.[71] Germans, especially Berliners, eagerly borrowed almost anything American: shorter hemlines and hairdos, flapper styles, soda fountains, prizefights, Hollywood films, the Charleston, jazz.[72] In the business and technological fields, many German industrialists, particularly the larger and more successful ones, adopted the efficient techniques of Henry Ford and Frederick Taylor. Other small businessmen, unable to install or compete with mass assembly lines, protested Germany's transformation. Some intellectuals and members of the middle class sided with the smaller entrepreneurs and defended the virtues of *Volk*, *Kultur*, and *Heimat* against the invasion of foreignness, functionalism, and modernity. The mania for things American became an issue in the sharp debate over Germany's future.[73]

In this controversy many left-wing intellectuals and artists, particularly those of the *neue Sachlichkeit* or new objectivity school, embraced the technocratic vision of Americanism, but not for the same reasons as the industrialists.[74] The businessmen sought greater productivity and profits, most of which they were unwilling to pass on to workers. The intellectuals and artists viewed increased efficiency and productivity as a vehicle toward greater social justice. Struggling to throw off the constraints of the past in art and architecture, many Germans—like the Frenchmen observing the AEF—admired the Americans' success, inventiveness, and practicality. Avant-garde Germans welcomed American mass culture as democratic and appropriate for the machine age. In designing new structures, some of which were built with American loans, German architects incorporated efficient design elements also borrowed from the United States, such as wall closets, folding beds, and self-service restaurants.[75] *Der Querschnitt*, an avant-garde journal, interpreted jazz in terms of machinery: "Man became mechanical, rigorously ruled by a strict, rhythmically syncopating present, which call itself the jazzband."[76] Germans made similar analogies in describing the fad for American synchronized dance troupes, such as the Tiller Girls. Siegfried Krakauer, Berlin cultural editor for the *Frankfurter Zeitung*, explained: "The Girls were artifically manufactured in the USA and exported to Europe.... Not only were they American products; at the same time they demonstrated the greatness of American production.... When they formed an undulating snake, they radiantly illustrated the virtues of the conveyor belt; when they tapped their feet in fast tempo, it sounded like *business, business*; when they kicked their legs high with mathematical precision, they joyously affirmed the progress of rationalization."[77] Whether intentionally or not, Krakauer parodied German fascination with that factory upon the hill.

The strength of this appeal was demonstrated by left-wing artists' simultaneous allegiance to Americanism and bolshevism. Both paths offered an alternative to the discredited past; both promised a democratic, technocratic, peaceful, and abundant future. Especially during the years of the quasi-capitalistic New Economic Policy in Russia, the two paths appeared to some Europeans to merge into a single road. Indeed, the contrast in the early twenties between Russia's distress and America's success led some left-wing Germans like Bertolt Brecht to pick the Western route: "I am now very much against Bolshevism . . . universal service . . . rationing of food, control.... I would like an automobile."[78] Others adhered to bolshevism while also reaching for the Americanist dream. Maria Piscator recalled that her husband's Communist theatre group

invented "America." Everything that was useful, effective, expedient, operative, performing properly and instrumental for productivity was called American. Even time had an American tempo.... None of them had seen America.... They admired what seemed real to them: the objective existence of the land of plenty, its material genius, with its prosperity, its slogans, and the great god—the machine. It is impossible to understand the complexity of Epic Theatre without taking into account this capture of the imagination by America, while, at the same time, the period was idealistically entangled with the new Russia.[79]

The Lindbergh Flight

Although the creator of the Epic Theatre admired American civilization for its efficient practicality, many other Europeans condemned it as cold, soulless, and repressive. Lindbergh excited and reassured Europeans because he had conquered the Atlantic with his machine and yet remained endearingly human, showing the world that mankind could enjoy technological progress and yet retain its soul. "Lucky Lindy's" feat met a tumultuous welcome in Europe, a reception that the hard-pressed State Department swiftly turned to diplomatic advantage.

In May 1927, Secretary of State Frank Kellogg characterized Franco-American relations as "bitter."[80] The year before, French resentment of the United States' war debt and foreign loan policy had exploded in anti-American demonstrations. Ill-feeling flared up again when Charles Nungesser and François Coli, popular French war heroes, disappeared in an attempted flight from Paris to New York. French newspapers charged, falsely, that the United States Weather Bureau had impeded Nungesser's takeoff by withholding meteorological reports. The French papers then printed as fact rumors of Nungesser's and Coli's New York arrival. Parisians rejoiced in the streets. Thousands massed at the Paris *Herald* office grew angry at the newspaper's refusal to acknowledge the French feat. When it became apparent that the arrival stories were false, Parisians demonstrated against newspapers in general and pulled down American flags. Ambassador Myron T. Herrick warned Washington of the "lamentable effect" of any American attempt for the transatlantic prize while Nungesser and Coli were still missing.[81]

Despite Herrick's fears, more than one hundred thousand people massed at Le Bourget airport to witness Lindbergh's landing. Appraised of growing French excitement as the lone pilot's plane neared Paris, the ambassador saw the public relations potential of a transAtlantic flight in a plane named after Louis IX. Although Lindbergh had made hotel reservations from New York, Herrick urged him to stay at the American Embassy, in order to lend the flight "official character."[82] Lindbergh's first visit outside the embassy was to Nungesser's mother,[83] and on behalf of "everybody in our country" he publicly mourned the disappearance of

Nungesser and Coli. Coolidge's public cables to Lindbergh and to the French president also honored the lost pilots.

The French responded to Lindbergh's achievement, and his courtesy, with greater warmth than they offered "crowned heads or visiting potentates," Herrick enthused. The Foreign Office flew the American flag, the first time it had ever so saluted anyone not a head of state.[84] "Lindbergh's personal popularity," an embassy official informed Kellogg, "has been translated into popular enthusiasm for this country."[85] Now was the time to settle the tariff dispute that had soured Franco-American relations, he suggested.[86] The State Department encouraged the young pilot to accept invitations to Belgium and England. The Belgians honored him as they did only few heads of governments, and the British House of Commons gave him a standing ovation—the first, an embassy official reported, in British history.[87] American representatives accepted such adulation as America's due. "Thanks to Captain Lindbergh," one observed, "America has come into its own here." Europeans were "compelled," another reported, "to admit the genius of the American race."[88]

The rhetoric with which Europeans praised the flight emphasized mankind's triumph over the natural world through use of the machine. Testimonials from such diverse groups as the Rumanian Ministry of War and the Marseilles Chamber of Commerce spoke of the pilot's "vanquishing the atmosphere" and "dominating space," his "conquest of the air" and "master[y of] the wild forces of nature." A radio cantata by Bertolt Brecht and Kurt Weill, "Der Lindberghflug," sang of man's triumph over nature. Lindbergh had used a machine to overcome these "wild forces" and still emerged an independent individual—in fact, still a boy. Europeans applauded "the American people as a whole" for their youthful "audacity" and technical skills. Although the glory reflected on all mankind, it originated "in the American national ambition, whose propelling force carried Captain Lindbergh across the ocean. . . . This aeroplane was inspired with the ambition of the American nation, with the enthusiasm of Young America, with the spirit of enterprise of the young American, setting thereby an example to the whole of mankind.[89] This was an example Europeans took to heart.

The Sacco-Vanzetti Trial

Three months later, the execution of Sacco and Vanzetti stimulated equally impassioned European protest.[90]

Although ethnicity figured in domestic reaction to the anarchists' trial, Europeans saw the issue in terms of the worldwide struggle between revolution and capitalism. Conservative, liberal, and radical Europeans all agreed that America was the bulwark of capitalism and democracy. Could the United States contain radicalism and still retain its democratic tolerance? The question was of direct importance to the Europeans. If the powerful United States could not strike a moderate pose between reaction and revolution, how could Europe's democracies hope to do so?

At first only European radicals protested the Massachusetts court decision. In late 1921, after the first guilty verdict, militants bombed four American diplomatic offices in Europe and demonstrated in front of several more. Police killed several Portuguese in a demonstration at the United States Consulate in Oporto. Rioters tore down American flags in Amsterdam, and Parisian workers roughed up American expatriates and tourists.[91] United States diplomatic representatives received threats. If Sacco and Vanzetti were executed, one message warned, you "will also be a corpse."[92]

Dismissing the furor as Bolshevik agitation, the State Department reaffirmed the verdict's justice and routed a threatening letter from Spain to the department's Division of Russian Affairs.[93] Washington prepared a defense of the verdict and asked diplomatic representatives to publicize it.[94] The department asked the German government to ban films glorifying Sacco and Vanzetti.[95]

In 1926 moderate and conservative Europeans joined the protest. Regardless of the anarchists' guilt, influential individuals and newspapers argued, six years on Death Row was punishment enough. Some of the outcry simply vented resentment of what a Viennese financial newspaper termed America's "arrogant preponderance."[96]

Many Europeans believed that the ideological issue had global relevance. Nonsocialist labor groups feared that the United States had abandoned its liberal tradition.[97] Conservatives "deplored" the sentence of execution, the consul in Brussels reported, because it "would furnish much ammunition to radical agitators everywhere."[98] Benito Mussolini, speaking personally as a "friend" of Ambassador Henry Fletcher and the American people, urged speedy clemency. The left's agitation "throughout the world is increasing in intensity," he warned. If Massachusetts prolonged the case and then did not execute, radicals would conclude that they had broken America's resistance, and this could hurt United States "prestige." Significantly, the Italian dictator viewed the issue as ideological rather than ethnic. Leniency, he argued, would point up the difference between Russia and America and "strike from the hands of the subversive elements an instrument of agitation."[99] Although the United States shared Mussolini's anticommunism, its ideology stood closer to Europe's small democracies. A prominent Danish newspaper concluded that "liberal" Europe saw its own social institutions at stake. Liberals feared that execution would undermine the "bourgeois ideals of humanity and justice.... By its whole bourgeois character [the American people] should be the opposite of and the bulwark against subversive tendencies which can send the world back to barbarism, a people for which we feel racial and cultural kinship.... *If our faith in America's ability to participate in the upholding of a common culture which has its roots in Western Europe is weakened our own hopes for the future of our own social culture are also weakened.*[100] If America moved rightward to suppress revolution, how could such countries as Denmark keep to the middle road of tolerance?

What happened in America affected the whole world. The United States had become John Winthrop's city upon the hill, though not for the religious reasons that he had expected, and Europeans could not avert their gaze. Whether they welcomed the prospect or dreaded it, most Europeans believed than American civilization portrayed the future course of their own societies. The United States was the metropolis, the hub of the modern cultural system, and Europe now figured as a satellite.

Stabilized by the Dawes Plan, Locarno, and the gold standard, Europe was a beckoning frontier for American business and cultural pioneers. Cultural and economic influence enhanced America's prestige and thus the effectiveness of its economic, unofficial diplomacy. Yet ironically, the very success of the peaceful change and economic reconstruction policy created conditions which, by the late twenties, were undermining the new order.

[7]

The Limits of the
American Order, 1927–1929

This central irony, that the very success of America's peaceful change and economic reconstruction policy produced contradictions that after 1926 undermined that policy, are illuminated in the analyses of two contemporaries, Bertolt Brecht and Ogden Mills. They were an unlikely pair—Brecht was a brash, radical German playwright who eventually became a Communist, Mills a conservative American politician who eventually became secretary of the treasury. From different perspectives, both men in 1930 surveyed American relations with Europe in the 1920s. Taken together, their accounts chalk out the boundaries of America's awkward dominion. Both men focused on what Mills termed America's "preponderating power and influence . . . on the interests, thoughts and imagination of mankind." Unlike Mills, however, in 1930 Brecht used the past tense:

> What men they were! Their boxers the strongest!
> Their inventors the most adept! Their trains the swiftest!
> *So we imitated this renowned race of men*
> Who seemed destined
> To rule the world by helping it to progress.[1]

This reputation fell with the stock market crash and the decline in foreign lending. Under Secretary of the Treasury Mills—like the Calvin Coolidge and Herbert Hoover administrations, of which he was an important member—failed to perceive that the economic, unofficial diplomacy that had worked so well from 1924 to 1926 was less suited to the changed conditions of 1927 to 1930. He worked together with Hoover, Andrew Mellon, and Federal Reserve officials to guide economic foreign policy in those years, and in 1930 reemphasized the vital importance of Amer-

184

ica's international economic ties. Despite the problems of the preceding
three years, Mills insisted that the United States could still succeed with
limited, economic, and unofficial diplomacy.

> The day of isolation in world affairs is over. The prosperity of each member
> of the world community is, in a large measure, dependent upon the prosperity
> of all. We are vitally concerned in the maintenance of peace, order and
> stability throughout the world ... and in the welfare and economic health
> of the other nations, with which our commerce and economic life are so
> closely interwoven. As a nation, we must not shirk our responsibility as a
> world power, but we are entitled to ... define what those responsibilities
> are, and to decide under what circumstances we shall use our power and
> resources.[2]

The fact that after the financial crisis of 1927–30 Mills was still so
confident in the formulas of 1924–26 betrays the rigidity and myopia
that beset American foreign policy in the late twenties.

Such shortsightedness stemmed in a large part from American leaders'
smug satisfaction with what had become a profitable status quo. This
narrowed the range of what they considered acceptable change.[3] After
1926 the war debt settlements, the adoption of the gold standard, and
the growth of foreign loans all bound the United States to the international financial order, while at the same time reducing the flexibility
within that system. Ironically, seeking stability through the beneficient
change of economic growth, the Americans had helped build an international order whose stability was undermined by the narrowed scope
for such change.

That system was also weakened by the unequal distribution of costs
and benefits, which favored the United States over Europe. Resentful of
this imbalance, British financiers sought redistribution of the world's gold
supply and international regulation of the vital flow of capital from New
York. Americans rejected such attacks on their wealth and freedom of
action, reaffirming their faith in the marketplace (the collective judgment
of individual investors) as the regulator of loans. In 1928–29, this trust
proved misplaced when the stock market boom and crash played havoc
with foreign loans. The puncturing of the loan market deflated Germany's
economy, intensifying its demands for Versailles treaty revision more
rapid and drastic than Americans thought proper. Thus, by 1927–29,
these flaws—the limits of acceptable political or economic change, the
unequal distribution of economic benefits and burdens, and the dependence of the international economy on foreign loans regulated only by
the marketplace—undermined the postwar order.

These flaws also marked the cleavages that divided Americans and

Europeans. Great Britain and Germany schemed, respectively, for financial and treaty revision beyond what Americans wanted. Backed by the resurgent franc, France shared U.S. concern for the financial status quo. Yet Paris officials failed to get a binding American commitment to the Versailles treaty. Soviet Russia simultaneously insulted American capitalists and sought their money, a contradiction that the U.S. government refused to overlook.

The Americans and Europeans played out their rivalries in a series of conferences: economic and naval meetings in 1927 at Geneva, a central bank conclave the same year on Long Island, a treaty signing in Paris in 1928, and a reparations meeting there the following year. At these conferences Americans tried to consolidate the gains won in 1924–26 through the peaceful change and economic reconstruction policy. Enjoying the fruit of past success, Americans now favored only very limited change in the postwar order. Whether represented officially or unofficially, the United States sought stability for Europe and preeminence without entanglements for itself.

The 1928 Kellogg-Briand Pact renouncing war, probably the best-known product of late twenties diplomacy, symbolized this American approach. The pact was, journalist William Allen White observed, "a world corporation with a limited liability to underwrite the peace."[4] Although the United States limited its liability, it determined to be the single largest stockholder. The Kellogg-Briand treaty fit nicely with America's economic approach to foreign relations. If the world's nations did forsake war, that would enhance both the importance of America's economic superiority and the security of its worldwide business. The pact was a cheap investment in world peace.

The 1927 Geneva Naval Conference

Americans also invested in a navy second to none. Calvin Coolidge enunciated the American military formula: "preparation, limitation, and renunciation."[5] Preparation came first, and at the 1927 Geneva Naval Conference the president insisted on cruiser parity with Britain. American officials were eager for peaceful change like that which ended London's naval superiority. Simultaneously, they frustrated Paris officials' efforts to snare a strong American commitment to the territorial status quo. The 1927 naval negotiations and the 1928 pact talks demonstrated American concern for preeminence, stability, and nonentanglement. This diplomacy also illustrated the difficulties in American policy, since the naval conference failed, and the peace pact offered no substitute for war. Finally, these negotiations pointed to the connection between military and economic matters. The pact's banishment of war boosted confidence in the future and, perhaps, Wall Street speculation. Unable to compete with America economically, Britain could not outspend the giant in a naval arms race either.

Although the 1922 Washington Conference naval treaties had granted the United States parity with Britain in capital ships, they made no provision for cruisers. Economic rivalry and sour relations intensified a race in cruisers between the two navies.[6] British officials were torn between unwillingness to abandon naval supremacy and uncertainty whether they could afford to keep it. In cabinet discussions, Winston Churchill, chancellor of the exchequer and former Admiralty chief, opposed conceding to American cruiser parity. "We have come through a series of perils," he remained the cabinet, "and seen the end of many giants in the past."[7] Yet Foreign Office officials warned that Britain was ill equipped to race America. At the request of Foreign Secretary Lord Cushendun, American expert R. L. Craigie analyzed the American challenge. Britain faced in America, Craigie reported, "a State twenty-five times as large, five times as wealthy, three times as populous, twice as ambitious, almost invulnerable, and at least our equal in prospertiy, vital energy, technical equipment and industrial science."

Other high officials, though divided on the parity issue, shared this sense of diminution by and dependence upon America. Churchill saw America's "mighty economic structure towering up on our western flank." Leopold Amery, Dominion Secretary, feared the "terrible ... danger" of "the American menace." Foreign Office officials compared the tension "to that existing as between this country and Germany" before 1914. Craigie warned, "War is *not* unthinkable."[8] London officials worried about their dependence upon America. They calculated that victory in a future world war would require access to American money and material. Cruiser parity was a vital issue even if the two countries never became enemies. Both U.S. and British strategies foresaw a situation in which London would be at war with a third power like Japan, and Washington would be neutral. Cruiser parity would enable the United States to insist on full neutral rights, and thus thwart an English blockade. British peacetime power was also hemmed by America. The pound's stability depended on American loans. A Foreign Office memorandum concluded that containing German ambitions "must depend more than ever on the state of our own relations with America."[9]

To make matters worse, London had few ways to redress the power imbalance. Amery and Craigie believed that an economically integrated British Empire could surpass the United States. Other Foreign Office officials warned that this would require a closed-door, imperial preference system that would antagonize "the United States, whose policy since the war has been to entice the Dominions away from Britain." Indeed, the Pacific Dominions, apprehensive of Japan, applauded America's growing naval might.[10]

London faced the paradox that self-contained imperial development would alienate the dominions, which sought increased economic and naval ties with America. Negotiations were doubly difficult, Craigie explained, since Britain needed the United States more than vice versa. Largely because of this imbalance, Churchill complained, Britain had deferred to the United States in regard to the Anglo-Japanese alliance, the war debts, Irish independence, and the Genoa proposals. A policy of further concessions irked Churchill and others who refused to be, as Cabinet Secretary Maurice Hankey put it, "blackmailed or browbeaten." Some Foreign Office analysts saw a way out in co-opting American power for British ends. By means of adroit diplomacy, Craigie argued, London "could utilise the better elements in the United States for the purpose of advancing our own world-wide interests."[11] In 1927–29, Anglo-American naval rivalry crested as British officials struggled to meet Washington's demand for parity while preserving London's world position.

Both American and British officials worked from the assumption that essential foreign trade required a strong navy. "We have . . . a foreign commerce unsurpassed in importance and foreign investments unsurpassed in amount," Coolidge emphasized. "We too have far-flung lines of communication which are equally necessary to our economic life," asserted Hilary Jones, United States admiral.[12] Naval vessels scouted trade opportunities, transmitted commercial messages, and protected trade and investment. The navy declared itself a "good investment."[13]

Although committed to naval parity, the Coolidge administration and Congress believed naval limitation offered a chance to get naval parity and still save money. In 1925–26, Coolidge hoped to repeat Warren Harding's success with a second Washington naval conference that would extend the 1922 tonnage ratios to cruisers and other auxiliary vessels. Before the president could act, however, the League of Nations called a preparatory land and sea disarmament conference in Geneva. Skeptical, Secretary of State Kellogg suspected the Allies would try to "blame the United States" when the conference failed.[14] Germany asked the United States to participate, hoping to direct American influence against heavily armed France. Although the administration expected little from the negotiations, it could not refuse to attend. Congress and the press were "practically unanimous" in favor, Kellogg reported, and the legislature would vote money for participation.[15]

As the administration expected, the Geneva Preparatory Conference produced little but platitudes and paper (one subcommittee alone used almost four million sheets of typescript, enough to paper the path home for the Swedish or Polish delegations). Since it depended on colonial troop supplements, France insisted that land, sea, and air armaments were inseparable. France also wanted to limit Germany's industry and war-making potential. The Americans and British rejected these French demands, fearing German restiveness and unwanted commitments.[16] Impatient with the deadlock, on February 10, 1927 Coolidge invited the major maritime powers to a naval limitations conference in Geneva. Ever cautious, the president did not invite the powers to Washington or appoint a prestigious delegation. France refused to attend, arguing that one could not separate naval from land disarmament. Paris also opposed Washington's plan to extend the 1922 ratio to all classes of naval vessels. This would give Italy parity with France while fixing the latter in an inferior position relative to the Anglo-Saxons. Italy also declined the invitation.[17]

With this poor outlook, the conference opened on June 20, 1927. Naval officials dominated both the American and British delegations, and negotiations immediately bogged down in technical disputes. Underlying the squabbles, however, was the central question of United States naval parity. Although some British leaders, such as Prime Minister Stanley Baldwin, originally wanted to concede parity in cruisers, Churchill and the Admiralty successfully resisted this policy. If the United States had parity, warned David Beatty, first sea lord, "the Admiralty would no longer be capable" of protecting British interests.[18] London naval officers proposed limitation of the 10,000-ton, 8-inch-gun cruisers the United States wanted to patrol the Pacific, with no limitation on the smaller 6-inch-gun cruisers suited to British needs. The British dreamed they "still ruled the waves," a U.S. admiral complained.[19] With Coolidge's support, the Americans insisted on parity. The conference could not resolve this issue and ended with bitterness on both sides. Hugh Gibson, the chief American delegate, described the meeting as not "negotiations at all, but merely a form of hostilities." Austen Chamberlain, British foreign secretary, complained that the Americans were "a terrible lot of people to deal with."[20]

Anglo-American relations worsened from the time of the conference's breakup in August 1927 to Hoover's inauguration in March 1929. The Coolidge administration submitted to Congress a long-term seventy-one-ship building program designed to achieve cruiser parity by 1936.[21] In July 1928, the British further incensed Washington by negotiating a disarmament compromise with France. London agreed to French conscription, which decreased Germany's willingness to remain disarmed. The British dropped opposition to submarines and accepted French parity in two classes of fighting vessels. In return, Paris supported London's aim to restrict only the larger cruisers desired by the United States Navy. The compromise aligned France and Britain against the United States and Germany. Furious, Coolidge refused to hear the British explanation. At the president's orders, Kellogg dropped plans to visit London after signing the Paris peace pact.[22]

The Kellogg-Briand Pact

Neither Coolidge, Kellogg, nor a majority of congressman saw any serious contradiction in signing a multilateral pact to renounce war and building a war fleet second to none. Preparation, limitation, and renunciation, American leaders believed, was the formula for United States preeminence in a peaceful and prosperous world open to limited change.[23] Coolidge viewed the Kellogg-Briand Pact from a practical Yankee perspective. It did not eliminate the need for adequate defenses and arms limitation, nor did it guarantee peace; yet it was an important step in evolution toward a warless world.[24]

Although antiwar pacts were discussed on both sides of the Atlantic in the decade after the war,[25] serious negotiations began on April 6, 1927, the tenth anniversary of American entry into the war. Aristide Briand, French foreign minister, proposed that France and the United States sign a treaty outlawing war between the two nations. Such an assurance of American neutrality or cooperation in a future war would strengthen France's hand against Germany. Briand hoped it would also neutralize American resentment over French refusal to participate in the naval conference or ratify the war debt agreement. Hoping to enlist the powerful American peace movement, he made his proposal public.[26] This manipulation of U.S. public opinion put Coolidge and Kellogg in a dilemma. The administration was trapped between Briand's diplomatic motives and the American peace movement.[27] In December 1927, Senator William Borah suggested a way out: make the pact multilateral by inviting the whole world to renounce war. "That was the best way to get rid of the damn thing," growled one senator.[28] Outmaneuvered, Briand tried to retreat, but Kellogg pressed on, partially for revenge and partially because he began to take the pact seriously.[29]

Stresemann favored the pact as a means to earn American support for Versailles treaty revision. An essential principle of German foreign policy, he told Washington's ambassador, "*is to eliminate all warlike conflict and instead to create a regulated peaceful procedure for all kinds of conflicts between states.*" Hungary was also eager to for treaty revision. The Danubian state praised peace while pointed to the "unjust and unnatural" peace treaties and the need for change.[30] Of course the pact lacked any reform machinery, but the revisionists evidently hoped that the Americans eventually would remedy this defect, especially to protect their investments from war and revolution.

In mid-1928, the major nations adhered to the pact after tortous negotiations. Kellogg overcame French and British objections by pointing to the Germans' immediate acceptance. Stresemann personally demonstrated this loyalty by rising from his sickbed to attend the signature ceremony in Paris.[31]

Stresemann's courtship of America underscored the central issue of Versailles treaty revision. Germans hoped to parlay American investments into support for further change in the peace treaty. Making a virtue of necessity, Berlin officials echoed American condemnation of land armaments and applauded the peace pact. Germany was motivated by "a sense of past favors and the hope of more,"[32] a diplomat observed. However, future favors in the form of American support for Versailles treaty revision depended on the Allies' acceptance of peaceful change. Yet the Kellogg-Briand Pact condemned war without offering an alternative means of change. The treaty lacked what Article 10 of the League of Nations Covenant originally contained before Woodrow Wilson deleted it: a vehicle for peaceful revision.

Failure to provide for peaceful change was the pact's major flaw, not, as most critics subsequently charged, failure to provide enforcement. In the late 1920s, American leaders opposed a military commitment to peace as a contradiction in terms, a sacrifice of freedom of action, and rigidification of the status quo. Yet, because they were unwilling to become directly entangled in European politics, they failed to produce what Walter Lippmann termed "the political equivalent of war." For all its horror, war resolved differences. "Peace implies change as well as stability," Lippmann stressed; peace required a "hospitable guidance of changes that sooner or later are inevitable." Treaty revision through the Dawes Plan and Locarno had preserved order thus far, he noted. Yet the "curse of rigidity" would overhang the world "until there is an international government strong enough to preserve order and wise enough to welcome changes in that order." Neither Congress nor the administration favored such a superleague. Lippmann acknowledged it would limit America's freedom of action, and confessed sadly: "I am not wholly sure that I am prepared to pay the price which the establishment of peace" would cost.[33]

More optimistic than Lippmann, State Department officials believed that with continued prosperity, European tensions would gradually disappear, making way for peaceful change. Castle valued the pact for its "moral and psychological" value in the evolution toward peace. Kellogg believed it "important to get people and governments thinking in terms of peace.... There will be a rapid spread of the treaty's sphere of peace."[34]

The Kellogg-Brian Pact expressed American policy to pacify Europe without risk or responsibility. Significantly, at the signing of this limited investment in peace, William Allen White counted only a few diplomatic costumes in a sea of "gray business suits."[35] The United States was equally undaring at the 1927 Geneva Economic Conference, a missed opportunity to shore up the world economy.

The Geneva Economic Conference

The need for an international economic conference arose out of a central contradiction in the American policy of financial stabilization through the gold standard. The French and British asked the League of Nations to call the meeting to deal with what Louis Loucheur, Paris's delegate, termed the "curious paradox that, as money became stabilized ... economic crises seemed to arise." And such economic trouble threatened the peace.[36] European and American leaders hoped the Geneva conclave would ease such crises by stimulating world trade. With financial stabilization nearly complete in the major countries, expanded trade was essential to ease the pain of returning to gold. Americans confidently assumed that they could enhance European stability and their own profits while blocking unwanted changes or burdens. The trade conference, it was hoped, would point the way to commercial revitalization, just as the 1920 Brussels financial conference had sketched the outlines of monetary stabilization.[37]

This first step in commercial revitalization did not get far, however. The conference endorsed the most-favored-nation tariff principle and urged low tariffs within Europe. Although most contemporaries did not realize it, the meeting was a lost opportunity at a critical time. Complacency and conservatism on both sides of the Atlantic killed chances of increased consumption through lower tariffs, higher wages, or Russian development. In Europe, economic interests and military strategists vetoed tariff reduction, seeing a threat to jobs and security. Anti-Soviet policy in America, England, and France prevented large loans, and Germany had little to lend. Soon after the conference, European economies slumped. Russia's failure to obtain significant Western capital bolstered Joseph Stalin's argument that the Communists had to wring it from the *kulaks.* One cannot put sole blame for the Depression or for Stalin's brutality on the failed Geneva Conference. Yet the world economic conclave was the 1920s' last chance to broaden Europe's boxed-in economies and ease Russia's capital shortage.

The May 1927 meeting was significant also in that it highlighted the pattern of United States–European diplomacy in the 1920s. The State Department believed that participation was vitally important so as to block anti-American "conspir[acies]" and win worldwide acceptance of the open-door, most favored-nation tariff principle.[38] Such selective involvement with Europe and the league, however, was American policy. Also characteristic of the 1920s was the delegates' unofficial status. Although they championed its policies, these delegates did not formally represent the administration. As with the reparation and central bank negotiations, this arrangement enabled the administration to promote American interests with minimal congressional interference. Herbert Hoover nominated his friend Henry M. Robinson to head the United States delegation, with the understanding that Robinson would pay his own expenses. "Otherwise," Hoover explained, "we shall have to go to Congress for an appropriation and throw the whole of many complex problems into acrimonious discussion."[39] Anxious for American attendance, Britain and France agreed to exclude from discussion war debts, immigration, and non-European tariffs.[40] Predictably, the Europeans then tried to bring up these issues anyway.

This met united American opposition, with Democrats and financiers backing up administration Republicans. Norman Davis, a delegate and former under secretary of state in the Wilson administration, blocked European efforts to discuss debts, immigration, and the American tariff.[41] The delegation's solidarity testified to the Republicans' creation in the 1920s of a *working* foreign policy consensus. Alonzo Taylor, a close Hoover associate, reported: "How faithfully and efficiently Norman Davis and Roland Boyden [International Chamber of Commerce representative from America] labored. Davis is a Democrat and Boyden practically a Mugwump; Davis is a pro-Leaguer and Boyden at least sympathetic; Davis is a free-trader and Boyden close to it. But no two men could have worked for the viewpoint of the Administration harder than these two men did. ... We called Norman Davis 'the noblest Republican of them all.' "[42]

The American stance at Geneva exemplified U.S. policy in substantive as well as procedural ways. Confronted with Europe's stagnated economy, Robinson and Davis emphasized stability and growth within the open-door context. Brushing aside debtors' complaints, Davis told the Austrian delegate: "You really seem to be very much concerned about the creditor nations. After all, there aren't so many of us."[43] The Americans prescribed rationalization of industry, a remedy in which many Europeans also had faith. Robinson and Davis had no such cure for agriculture, which languished overseas as well as at home. Finally, Americans firmly rejected, as they had since 1917, any suggestions of large credits to or political coexistence with the Soviet Union.

The United States entered the conference aiming for an endorsement for the open-door principles of unconditional most-favored-nation tariffs and no commercial restrictions. These precepts had support from most countries, except France, which favored reciprocal tariff agreements. Paris levied special low tariffs on goods from a country if that nation gave France the same privilege. The U.S.-backed most-favored-nation method offered all countries the same tariff level—a level that was too high, the French and others charged.[44] At Geneva, Davis and Boyden (who earned the nickname "Steam Roller") led a "bitterly fought" campaign for the most-favored-nation principle, a State Department official reported. Americans also pushed for condemnation of raw-material export limitation schemes, such as the Stevenson rubber plan.[45] With these goals won, the American delegates argued that tariff stability was more important than the particular level of duties. They declared that the conference's main business was elimination of "disorder" and "chaos." Changing tariffs "are more burdensome to commerce than the actual duties themselves," Robinson told the meeting; "even though the level may be high."[46]

This statement expressed American faith in stability. Whether it was foreign exchange rates or tariff levels, Americans believed that with certainty and order, economic growth could surmount almost any obstacle. The United States delegates supported the conference's final declaration supporting lower tariffs. Given their own protectionist policy and emphasis on the open door and stability, however, Americans could not and did not lobby for significant reduction in European tariffs. Nor did the European countries do more than talk about lowering tariffs after the conference disbanded.

If the conference's espousal of the most-favored-nation principle meant a victory for United States tariff policy, the meeting's endorsement of industrial rationalization testified to America's existing preeminence. A State Department official reported that other delegations were "anxious for any guidance from American experience and opinion."[47] At the league's request, Robinson enlightened the opening plenary session with a definition of rationalization: "stabilization, standardization, and simplification . . . also the correction of economic wastes and irrational operations in industry and commerce resulting from governmental activities."[48]

Dominated by industrialized Western Europe and the United States, the conference largely ignored the problems of underdeveloped, agricultural nations. We "expected nothing from [the] Agricultural" committee, a State Department official reported, "and were not disappointed."[49] Polish and Chilean appeals for an international agricultural credit bank met United States, British, and German opposition.[50] Nor did the conference satisfy Soviet Russia's plea for credits and political coexistence.

For the Soviet Union, the economic conclave came at a critical moment. Rival Bolsheviks fought over control of the Russian economy. Maneuvering first to the right, then to the left, Joseph Stalin insisted that obtaining industrialization capital required squeezing the peasantry, especially the prosperous *kulaks*. After 1925, Leon Trotsky moved to the right and supported Gregory Sokolnikov, Nikolai Bukharin, and others whose strategy emphasized less rapid industrialization and less repression. Trotsky urged purchase from the West of light machinery for such industries as textiles. The regime could manufacture clothing and other consumer goods, exchange them for grain, and export the agricultural produce for additional machinery. This development required large Western credits to prime the pump.[51] Sokolnikov and N. Osinsky, delegates to the Geneva Conference, were in Trotsky's camp. As commissar of finance, Sokolnikov had reestablished the gold standard and encouraged a measure of private enterprise. Osinsky came from a noble family (he was related by marriage to the Astors) and had tried unsuccessfully to get a visa to the United States in order to hunt up a loan.[52]

At the conference, the Russians tried to cultivate Robinson and other Westerners who might help them get loans. A Soviet delegate confided that Moscow regarded the conference as a "serious step" in the search for "investment of foreign capital in Russia."[53] The Russians also sought Western acceptance of bolshevism's parity as a legitimate social system. Americans and other Westerners rejected both bids. The conference yielded no loan negotiations. Julius Klein dismissed Soviet viewpoints as "doctrinaire bunk." Robinson read a newspaper during Osinsky's speech. Davis slept.[54] The Soviets felt that they were treated like "a wild animal which everybody is interested to see but none dares to touch."[55]

Osinsky pressed the legitimacy issue, urging that the conference endorse the "peaceful co-existence of the capitalist and socialist economic system." Boyden, the Western spokesman on this matter, agreed only to "pacific commercial cooperation." Despite Osinsky's persistence, Boyden rejected "peaceful co-existence."[56] The difference was not semantic. Official U.S. policy welcomed Soviet trade, but denied the regime's permanence or legitimacy. Sokolnikov and Osinsky failed to establish new economic and political ties with the West. Instead, Norman Davis reported on May 23, 1927, the capitalist world's "sentiment for political cooperation has diminished."[57]

A few days earlier, Great Britain broke off relations with the Soviets after raiding their London trade mission. Trotsky's political enemies declared that the incident proved that Western capital was a chimera. In July 1927, important party leaders defected from Trotsky's camp and recommended the financing of investment through wholesale price increases rather than capital imports. In October, French loan negotiations collapsed, and in November the party expelled Trotsky. By 1928, Stalin began forcibly to collectivize the peasants. This action further alienated the West, Bolshevik leaders recognized, but in any case the "chances of foreign credits" were "already insignificant."[58] The Trotskyite failure at Geneva was only one of many factors that led to Stalin's war on the *kulaks* in the Five Year Plan. Had Osinsky and Sokolnikov returned from Geneva with some measure of Western economic and political support, however, the anti-Stalinists might not have met such swift and total defeat.

At Geneva, the United States gained an endorsement of the open-door most-favored-nation principle, but the world economy lost an opportunity to reintegrate Russia or reduce tariff walls. Satisfied with the postwar status quo, Americans opposed radical change, whether it involved accommodating Bolshevism or initiating tariff reduction. Thus, United States leaders greeted Geneva's meager results with sighs of relief rather than disappointment.

The Financial Crisis

The Dawes Plan yielded many benefits. In 1924, it transferred reparations control from the Allies-dominated Reparations Commission to the American-dominated agent general's office. The plan substituted relative certainty for destabilizing crises. It facilitated Germany's recovery, pacification, and integration with the West, and at the same time kept Germany under control. S. Parker Gilbert, the agent general, cultivated close but informal relations with Washington and FRBNY officials. This protected U.S. interests without congressional criticism. Despite American denial of any legal connection between reparations and war debts, Germany's payments financed Washington's receipts. The plan's stability encouraged American investors to purchase German and other foreign bonds. With borrowed dollars, countries financed balance-of-payments deficits and returned to gold. Capital outflows also helped finance U.S. export surpluses, which further increased profits and prosperity at home.

U.S. exports to Germany, for instance, jumped from \$317 million in 1923 to \$482 million in 1927.[59] The centerpiece of American policy in Europe, the Dawes Plan demonstrated the benefits of moderate Versailles treaty revision.

The international gold standard was a kind of Dawes Plan for the whole world. The system replaced fluctuating, unstable foreign exchange rates with fixed, ostensibly secure ones. In countries like Poland, American advisers supervised the return to gold. Usually, however, such direct control was not necessary to ensure financial sobriety. Strong and Montagu Norman, governor of the Bank of England, would not make currency stabilization loans without the establishment of at least semiautonomous central banks staffed with orthodox bankers. These institutions offered a channel for communication and influence. The gold standard enabled investors to repatriate profits, thereby opening new frontiers for international business. When Poland returned to gold, American and European bankers rushed in, the United States minister reported, "all with their noses to the wind to take advantage of [the] strengthened credit position."[60]

By 1927, both the Dawes Plan and the international gold standard were in trouble. With conflicting interests, leaders from the United States, Britain, Germany, and France argued over the nature and extent of needed change. Americans believed the structure was basically sound and needed only minor reform.

John Foster Dulles, partner in a top Wall Street law firm and negotiator of loans to Germany, Poland, and elsewhere, analyzed the problem from the American perspective. In the postwar decade foreign loans had enabled America to enjoy "great prosperity, entirely disproportionate to the rest of the world." In 1928–29, however, the stock market boom lured investors away from foreign bonds. This threatened "a collapse which will mean the realization of the dangers which were forecasted ten years ago, but which since then have been so successfully avoided."[61]

Even before the stock market boom, however, leading New York bankers mapped out the dangers facing the Dawes Plan. In July 1927, Strong, J. P. Morgan, and Russell Leffingwell, a Morgan partner, agreed that, despite the original conception of the plan, it had become "wholly dependent" on foreign loans to Germany. Soon such borrowing would be insufficient to pay Germany's import, reparation, and private loan bills. In the 1927–28 Dawes Plan year, Germany would receive from the United States government \$250 million for wartime confiscated property. Thereafter a breakdown was "inevitabl[e]." This meant a general financial crisis, for with the stoppage of reparation transfers, the Allies would protest dollar payment on private American loans. Thus, American self-interest demanded speedy revision. Yet negotiation of the emotional issue before the French, German, and American elections in 1928 would fire enormous controversy and consequent instability. The Dawes Plan would have to continue until after the November 1928 U.S. election, the financiers agreed, and this required control of public information. If investors realized the true situation, Leffingwell and Dwight Morrow acknowledged, "there would be no more foreign loans to Germany, and therefore no more Dawes remittances."[62] For all its benefits, Leffingwell lamented, the Dawes Plan amounted to a "house of cards."[63] In sum, financiers understood the precariousness of the Dawes Plan. They realized, too, that private loans propped up the Dawes Plan and the gold standard. Yet in the very letter in which he described the financial crisis, Leffingwell reaffirmed the bankers' opposition to loan regulation by the United States government or the League of Nations. Business and political leaders insisted that the marketplace—that is, the sum decision of individual investors—exercised the most effective control.

London officials had a different perspective. Suffering a weak economy, the British wanted fundamental change in war debts, reparations, loan control, and the gold standard. Monetarily strong after 1926, France shared America's interest in preserving the financial status quo. Germany was torn between desire to overthrow Versailles and the hated reparation payments and determination to keep American friendship and support.

Political and military rivalry complicated the financial crisis. Many Americans feared that if Washington cancelled the war debts, the Allies would spend the extra cash on armaments.[64] London Foreign Office experts warned that financial dependence on New York required settling the naval arms race with Washington.[65] Anglo-French competition for political influence spilled over into financial rivalry in Eastern Europe.[66] In 1928–29, the Allies made German acceptance of a permanent reparation settlement the condition for military evacuation from the Rhineland.[67] Essentially, reparations were a club to keep Germany weak and enforce the Versailles treaty—the Dawes plan wrapped the weapon in velvet and entrusted it to American administrators. Yet the French and Germans still viewed reparations as an instrument of control rather than a contractual debt. Elimination of reparations remained a key element in German plans to overthrow the Versailles order; conversely, the debts were equally important to French ambitions to preserve that system. These conflicting national interests formed the backdrop to the growing financial crisis.

Problems with dubious loans and declining prices beset the Dawes Plan–gold standard financial structure from the start. After lengthy discussion, the Coolidge administration decided in 1925 not to warn investors about the risks of German bonds. "It might shake confidence in foreign loans," a treasury official explained.[68] Washington officials feared, moreover, that if they vouched for the soundness of foreign loans, investors would hold them accountable for bonds that were defaulted. As overseer of the Dawes Plan and the German economy, Gilbert feared that excessive borrowing might undermine both. Loans to German states and municipalities were especially dangerous because Article 248 of the Versailles treaty made reparations—not private loans—a first charge on revenues of the Reich's constituent states. In a transfer crisis, reparations to the Allies had clear priority over repayment of state loans and perhaps municipal ones as well. Gilbert and Jacob G. Schurman, the United States ambassador, also objected to loans that funded the local governments' "state socialistic enterprises." Although the Germans were eager borrowers, the "principal pressure" for loans, Gilbert concluded, "has thus far come from New York."[69]

Some Wall Street bankers misled investors in order to sustain demand for German securities. In September 1926, Harris, Forbes and Company offered United States investors a $20 million bond issue of the Prussian state government. The loan prospectus denied Article 248's relevance and falsely declared the bonds a first charge on Prussia's public revenue. Giblert complained to the bankers and German government about the distortion, but did not raise the issue publicly.[70] Dulles, the bankers' attorney, argued the importance of loans in financing reparations but skirted the legal fact of Article 248.[71] Commerce Department officials also kept the issue quiet. "Publicity" might "incur the ill will of powerful financial houses," one of Hoover's assistants explained, and "make holders of German State bonds panicky." He was confident the Dawes Plan would not break down. Some State and Treasury department officials wanted to eliminate any government review of foreign loans, but Hoover blocked this total abdication of responsibility.[72]

At Gilbert's request, the State Department urged the German government to regulate municipal and state loans. Gilbert feared that overborrowing would dim chances for orderly Dawes Plan revision and the issue of a large block of reparation bonds to inaugurate the new plan. Germany's governmental and central bank officials divided on the private loans. Municipal and state governments wanted the golden flow to continue. Hjalmar Schacht, president of the Reichsbank, feared that the loans made payment of reparations too easy, thereby undermining his hopes for a drastic revision of the Dawes Plan. The result was an impasse. The central government wrung its hands, but did not stop the loans. Schacht led what one of Gilbert's assistants called "a double life," trying to undercut the Dawes Plan while protesting his loyalty to it.[73]

In late 1927, the bankers proposed a second Prussian government loan, for $30 million. This time Gilbert protested publicly about Article 248. The resulting furor exposed the weakness of the Dawes Plan and the contradiction of United States loan policy. Wall Street had "pour[ed] money more or less indiscriminately into Germany," Gilbert complained to Strong. Strong admitted the "moral question" of hiding "facts" that probably would make "the loan unsalable," yet he put the primary blame on "failure of German self-control." He defended the bankers as men of "varied ability and experience" who were "bewildered" by the lack of "laws, treaties, lawyers, or officials to guide them."[74] This was a powerful, if inadvertent, indictment of marketplace wisdom. The marketplace could not regulate foreign loans in the interests of long-term growth and stability.[75] Investors panicked at the controversy and many Americans sold their German bonds, even those of sound industrial firms. A reparations priority crisis had been "inevitable," Strong acknowledged, but it had come too soon. In order to rebuild the market for "sound and necessary German loans" and "protect our investors," Strong and Gilbert sought to revise the Dawes Plan by fixing Germany's total obligation and abolishing transfer protection.[76] In other words, their solution to the problem of inadequate regulatory machinery was elimination of all regulation except that of the marketplace.

Although investors' confidence improved in early 1928, Gilbert spent all of that year shuttling from capital to capital to prepare a new reparations settlement. While Gilbert tried to stabilize the financial order through controlled reparations revision, the British sought more radical change of the gold standard.

The problems of the Dawes Plan and the gold standard were interconnected. Both depended on United States capital exports to fill Europe's dollar gap. Both increasingly involved central bankers who realized the stakes for international stability and national advantage. A severe crisis in one would destroy investor confidence and likely bring down the other. London appreciated the stability both offered, yet chafed at the burdens they placed on the undercompetitive British economy. In 1927–29, the British hoped to ease this pressure through international regulation of prices and loans, establishment of the gold exchange standard, and continuance of the Dawes Plan until its collapse brought down the whole war debts–reparations structure. Americans successfully opposed these aims and capped their victory with establishment of the Young Plan for reparations and the Bank for International Settlements (BIS). Emerging from the Young reparations conference, the BIS illustrated the close correspondence between reparations and the gold standard. This connection was apparent throughout the international negotiations from 1927 to 1929.

Some of the most important of these discussions took place at the central bankers' conference of July 1927. Like the Geneva Economic Conference, this gathering demonstrated how reluctant Americans were to change the international economic order. Despite rhetoric of cooperation, the central bankers—Strong of the FRBNY, Norman of the Bank of England, Charles Rist of the Banque de France, and Hjalmar Schacht of the Reichsbank[77]—each jockeyed for national advantage. All four had a stake in world financial stability, yet each perceived the international situation from his own perspective, and none was willing to sacrifice major domestic interests.

In early 1927 the franc surged in value as speculators repatriated funds and bet on a further rise. The capital inflow flooded the Banque de France with foreign exchange, especially British pounds, and threatened a renewed bout of inflation. The French central bank sold pounds for gold, hoping to force the Bank of England to raise interest rates and stem the tide of money into France.[78] Burdened with an overvalued pound and heavy unemployment, Britain could not afford to lose the gold or to raise interest rates. Bank of England officials accused the French of "homicidal mania," and indeed Governor Moreau was glad to repay the humiliation that Norman had long inflicted. Yet neither Moreau nor Premier Raymond Poincaré wanted to press Britain so hard as to endanger the Conservative government or the pound's stability. In June, Moreau, Norman, and Strong worked out a formula that eased the strain on London and shifted French balances to New York, a development that would threaten the dollar in 1931–33.[79] Although the central bankers had averted one crisis, the pound remained weak. Strong convened the central bankers to deal with the problem.

The resulting conference underscored the weakness of central bank cooperation in the late 1920s. The group met at the Long Island home of Under Secretary of the Treasury Ogden Mills but, it seems, never actually gathered to talk business. Schacht recalled that Strong met separately with him, Norman, and Charles Rist, Moreau's deputy. This fit New York's and Washington's preference for dealing with the Europeans one at a time and so avoiding a united debtors' coalition. The bankers divided on an Anglo-German and Franco-American axis. Norman and Schacht crossed the Atlantic together and were united by common dependence on New York and discontent with their financial burdens. The Englishman resented the financial entente between the two creditors, New York and Paris. Strong "would do anything to help the B[ank] of F[rance]," he noted in a diary of the conference. In contrast, Strong had little "sympathy" for Schacht and left the German situation to Gilbert. Rist and Strong were "drawn together by Poland," where New York and Paris had defeated London's bid for financial control. Norman complained of other factors that put England at a "disadvantage": the abortive Geneva Naval Conference, Anglo-American financial competition, and "resent[ment]" of Winston Churchill. Strong did respond to Norman's and Schacht's plea for lower U.S. interest rates to encourage money flows to London and Berlin; but the New York banker had "little interest" in the long-term problem of declining prices. Weighing the divergent national interest and continued financial turmoil, Norman concluded that "C[entral] B[ank] cooperation" remained "a pretense."[80]

Even before the Europeans arrived in New York, Strong had decided that, for a variety of reasons, the Federal Reserve System needed to reduce interest rates. He feared that Europe's dollar gap threatened the Dawes Plan, the gold standard, and United States farm exports. Cheaper money would combat the developing recession. Lower interest would also facilitate Treasury debt refinancing and boost the American acceptance market. Finally, Strong wanted what he termed a "good alibi" against the accusation by some Britons that United States gold policy and the international gold standard depressed world prices.[81] Cheap money promised these benefits, but it risked excessive stock market speculation. At Strong's urging, the FRS reduced interest rates. "To hell with the stock market," one board member exclaimed.[82]

The increased interest differential between the United States and Europe stimulated foreign loans. Net U.S. short- and long-term capital exports jumped from $506 million in 1926 to $985 million a year later, with most of the increase coming in the latter half of 1927. The loan boom continued into the first half of 1928. Foreign nations built up gold reserves as American stocks shrank by $509 million between mid-1927 and mid-1928. Strong's cheap money policy temporarily relieved the world's dollar and gold shortage, but it also fueled the stock boom and weakened the dollar. Total brokers' loans for stock speculation climbed from $3.3 billion in 1926 to $6.4 billion in 1928. Some of the funds that fed the bull market came from foreigners who reinvested the proceeds of long-term loans floated in New York. Net foreign short-term capital inflow into the United States rose from $455 million in 1926 to $934 million in 1927.[83]

Strong feared that sudden withdrawal of these huge foreign balances, coming on top of the half-billion in gold losses, might endanger the dollar. This apprehension hardened the Federal Reserve System's opposition to the British-proposed gold exchange standard, which envisioned even larger foreign balances on deposit in London and New York. Such foreign balances restricted America's freedom of action. In sum, the cheap money policy stimulated the capital movements that Strong desired, but the magnitude, he confessed, was much greater "than I had expected."[84]

Although the costs of the cheap money policy were higher than FRS authorities had anticipated, the benefits were less than the British desired. London's relatively high interest rates attracted foreign balances, which strengthened the pound. But short-term deposits, whether in London or New York, were volatile and could be withdrawn suddenly. Basically the pound was still weak.[85] World commodity prices continued to slide, stifling producers and forcing Britain to deflate still further in order to compete. British wholesale prices dropped 12 percent from 1925 to 1927 and an additional 5 percent by 1929.[86] Chancellor of the Exchequer Churchill charged that Norman's deflationary policy smothered the economy with a "vast wet blanket." R. G. Hawtrey, a Treasury official, feared that because London was still a world commodity center, the effort to reduce British prices only depressed world prices, leaving the United Kingdom's relative position unchanged. Philip Snowden, who would become chancellor of the exchequer in 1929, complained that America's gold "sterilization" forced Europe to deflate. Many Britons worried about world gold shortage, aggravated by the concentration of reserves in America and France. This shortage would tend to depress world prices, a development feared in the Bank of England, the Royal Mint, and the League of Nations Financial Committee (LNFC).[87]

Since the existing system offered bleak prospects, British leaders pressed for sweeping change. Specifically they sought a regulated gold exchange standard, canceled political debts, foreign loan supervision, and international price control. Britons hoped to coordinate these changes through the LNFC and the Bank of England. These proposals touched two thorny issues: marketplace control and United States cooperation.[88]

Norman supported these measures to regulate the world order and redress Britain's weakness. Yet dependence on America did not permit an all-out fight for the proposals, all of which the FRBNY opposed. Nor did Norman abandon the dream of returning to the automatic marketplace regulation of the prewar era.[89] Despite these contradictory impulses, Norman recognized that the existing gold standard machinery needed repair. In 1927–28, he tried to get American agreement to international regulation of loans, prices, and the gold standard.

For ideological and political reasons, Strong objected to such regulation. Like Norman, Strong dreamed of automatic marketplace control and distrusted governmental interference. Financially secure, America did not share Britain's perspective on the world economy. As a creditor nation with a trade surplus, the United States had less to fear from future price decline. From this perspective, Strong rejected national or international price regulation. He also opposed control over foreign loans, particularly by the British-dominated League of Nations Financial Committee. "In central bank circles," our "influence . . . is almost predominant," Strong explained, but the FRBNY's power in the LNFC "would be almost negligible."[90] Similar reasoning set the New York banker against a formal central bank conference. The United States would be "the only lending market" in a meeting of debtors. I "would have to be sure," he told the British, "of having one more vote than all the borrowers combined."[91] Like the administration in Washington, the FRBNY found safety in bilateral rather than multilateral discussions.

The FRBNY also shared the administration's interest in minimizing Congress's influence in monetary and foreign policy issues. Strong and other FRBNY officials campaigned against congressional bills favored by debt-ridden farmers that charged the FRS to maintain stable prices. This price control issue replayed the 1896 presidential election, with the New York financial interests pitted against deflation-stricken farmers. This time, however, a Boston financier observed, the British "talked more like William Jennings Bryan."[92] FRBNY officials feared that once they accepted responsibility for prices, they would be attacked by dissatisfied groups and suffer tight political control. Of course, the system's countercyclical monetary policy did affect prices, but FRS officials denied any formal respsonsibility. As a group, American financiers were more concerned about inflation than deflation—the condition of the late 1920s—and so were inclined toward a hands-off attitude. These domestic considerations hardened Strong's opposition to British proposals for international regulation of prices. Domestic factors also strengthened his antagonism to the gold exchange standard. Large foreign deposits, he warned, would expose the FRS to "the hazards of political developments abroad and to the even greater hazard of political . . . control at home."[93]

These conflicting domestic interests shaped Anglo-American differences in the late 1920s. Americans either rejected British proposals outright or attempted to derail them. For example, FRS officials agreed to unofficial participation in the LNFC, and then appointed Jeremiah Smith, Boston financier, with instructions to block its intended inquiry into the gold shortage.[94]

British frustration increased in mid-1928 when, after a year's respite, Europe's dollar gap again widened. In early 1928, FRS authorities raised interest rates so as to slow down the feverish pace of foreign loans, gold outflow, and stock speculation.[95] By mid-1928, foreign loans fell off, and pressure built on London and Berlin. Now, however, Wall Street's boom ruled out another dose of cheap money. Moreover, FRS authorities emphasized, the United States could not afford to lose much more gold. Much of European's meager capital was sucked into Wall Street's boom as deflationary pressures throttled the British and German economies.[96]

As the 1928 crisis worsened, Strong's health faded and deputy governor George L. Harrison assumed more responsibility. Although Strong and Harrison worried about the pound's stability, they joined with the French to defeat Norman's effort to make Poland and Rumania fiefs of London. Cooperation with Paris opened the door for American influence and business in these countries.[97] Despite years of friendship with Norman, Strong in the last months of his life grew increasingly hostile to the Englishman's scheme to redress London's weakness.[98] This souring of Anglo-American monetary relations, accompanying the naval rivalry, increased the difficulties of revising the Dawes Plan in an orderly way. Critically ill, Strong left the FRBNY in August 1928, and died a few months later.[99] At the moment of deepening crisis, American finance lost its helmsman.

Revising the Dawes Plan

To fill the gap, Owen Young, acting for the FRBNY directors, turned to Agent General Gilbert. "Universal opinion here that you are the best qualified of any man in the world," Young cabled. The choice of Gilbert underscored the man's high prestige and America's deep involvement in the Dawes Plan. Gilbert refused the offer,[100] but remained in close touch with Washington and New York as he negotiated the Dawes Plan revision. Gilbert's "hold ... on Prime Ministers and Finance Ministers is quite amazing," Leffingwell said admiringly. "The Dawes Plan works because he makes it work."[101] A holdover from the Wilson administration, Gilbert at the age of twenty-nine had become under secretary of the treasury under Andrew Mellon. He maintained ties with Mellon and other Washington officials after he went to Berlin in 1924. "There is the closest relationship between the work here [Berlin] and the work of the Federal Reserve Bank," he explained. Borrowed personnel and frequent correspondence strengthened this intimacy with the FRBNY. Gilbert cultivated connections with prestigious banking firms like J. P. Morgan and Company, which he joined in 1931.[102]

In sum, Gilbert stood at the nexus of American financial power in Europe. He coordinated the negotiations leading to the Young Conference of 1929. In these discussions the agent general regarded himself as an international expert above petty national rivalries. Yet the broad outlines of Gilbert's program conformed closely to American economic and political requirements. "My first duty," Gilbert declared at a difficult point in the Young Conference negotiations, "is to the American experts."[103] By such informal channels, the Republican administrations protected U.S. interests with minimal responsibility in Europe and opposition at home.

Gilbert's loyalty and power helped safeguard the American position in the acrimonious reparations–war debts issue. For the United States, Germany, France, and Britain, reparations and war debts touched the basic questions of who had won the war and who would dominate the peace. As symbol and as substance, the political debts incited powerful domestic reaction in each of the countries.

Reparations presented Washington with the dilemma of how to reconstruct Europe and collect war debts and yet not get stuck with paying Germany's reparations bill. The Allies refused to pay war debts unless they received reparations from Germany. Washington denied responsibility for Germany's reparation burden and worried about an anti-American debtors' coalition. If the Allies succeeded in linking war debts and reparations, feared Henry L. Stimson, Hoover's secretary of state, Europe would form "a solid front . . . including Germany" agitating for cancellation. This would anger Congress and the American public, thereby eliminating any future chance for war debt reduction.[104] For these political reasons, successive administrations insisted that reparations and war debts were separate and distinct. This was a difficult position to maintain, especially since America's economic stake in Europe dragged it into the reparatitons controversy.

By 1928, Americans had loaned Germany well over $1 billion.[105] In the event of a transfer crisis, this money would be hostage to the Allies' claim of priority for reparations. Although the war debt agreements did not mention reparations, the Allies still insisted that payment to Washington depended on receipts from Berlin. Thus, the administration's debt funding policy reduced uncertainty, but it rigidified the Allies' reparation requirements. Payments to Washington and French demands for reconstruction costs set a floor beneath reparations.

The Coolidge and Hoover administrations handled the explosive issue gingerly. Both delegated to private, unofficial representatives the responsibility for revision of the Dawes Plan and protection of American interests. This was ironic, for Gilbert, Strong, Young, and the other financiers who shaped the new reparations plan had privately criticized both administrations' war debt collection policies.[106] Similarly, Gilbert railed against American bankers' shortsighted greediness. Yet in reparation negotiations with the Europeans, these financiers upheld and protected as best they could America's creditor interest in war debts and private loans.[107]

American determination to collect the war debts and Allied determination to tie them to reparations placed the burden on Germany. Germans realized that elimination of war debts would probably eliminate reparations. "That the United States 'holds the key to the situation,' " an American diplomat reported, "is firmly fixed in the German mind."[108]

Theoretically, Berlin could join Paris and London in an attack on United States policy. In August 1928, Poincaré proposed such an assault. "All of us in Europe," the French premier complained to Stresemann, "are suffering from the situation in which we find ourselves as regards the United States." He argued that Europe should insist on a "general settlement" linking the two sets of debts. Concerted action was necessary against "the dangers of American mammonism and Russian Bolshevism." Stresemann rejected this suggestion. Germany depended on U.S. loans, he emphasized; without such credits, "we could no longer feed the 64 millions of our population."[109]

Stresemann also anticipated American support for further Versailles revision. The Rhineland occupation and reparations remained the Allies' principal weapons to enforce Versailles.[110] Although Washington kept officially aloof from such political matters, Stimson, Gilbert, and Ambassador to London Alanson Houghton favored Rhineland evacuation. In the Dawes and Young plans, Americans reduced the amount and the punitive nature of reparations. Many Americans sympathized with Germany's territorial claims against Poland. In 1931, when the postwar order was collapsing, leaders including Hoover and Secretary of State Stimson urged the Europeans to undertake this border revision.[111] German dependence on American goodwill deepened in mid-1928 when Britain, Germany's chief European friend since the war, edged closer to France in reparation and disarmament issues.[112] Karl von Schubert, the Foreign Office state secretary, pleaded to Ambassador Schurman that Germany wanted "to avoid anything which the United States would find unacceptable or disturbing." Berlin would meet "the requirements of the American situation," he promised.[113] In practical terms this meant financing the Allies' war debts and not attacking the ultimate creditor. Dependent on America, Germany rejected Poincaré's idea of a debtors' coalition.

France's happy financial condition enabled it to choose an attractive alternative, cooperation with the United States. As fellow creditors interested in preserving the financial status quo, French and American financiers worked together to revise the Dawes Plan, established the Bank for International Settlements (BIS), and defeated the British-backed Genoa proposals. Such amity did not extend to the disarmament issue, and President Herbert Hoover's resentment of France in this matter later soured the financial entente.

But in 1928, Moreau and Poincaré cooperated with Gilbert's efforts to chalk the outline of a revised reparations plan. Moreau judged the agent general France's "friend."[114] No wonder, since Gilbert tallied Germany's revised reparations bill so as to cover war debt payments to America plus an amount for French war damage. This fulfilled Poincaré's ambition to endow France with a stabilized currency and secure debt arrangement. After the new reparations plan assured payments from Germany, Poincaré would ask the Chamber of Deputies to ratify the 1926 Mellon-Bérenger war debt agreement. Unless France ratified by August 1929, it would have to pay the United States $400 million in cash for war stocks it purchased in 1919. Along with the national elections, this deadline set a time constraint on the reparation negotiations. In return for Germany's payments, Poincaré promised early evacuation of the Rhineland. Like the Americans, he hoped that moderate treaty revision would satiate German ambition.[115] Pleased with Poincaré's cooperation, Gilbert explained French requirements in a cable to Kellogg, Mellon, and Coolidge. France needed enough reparation money to cover its war debts and reconstruct the war-devastated areas. These demands, Gilbert asserted, were "really a recognition of the war debt and not at all ... a drive against America to reduce the debt."[116]

Not everyone in the Coolidge and Hoover administrations endorsed Gilbert's acceptance of a tacit linkage between war debts and reparations. Arthur N. Young, State Department economic expert, went along with Gilbert, advising Kellogg that "we cannot prevent their [the Allies'] figuring on such a basis, and I see no gain in trying to do so." Kellogg, Mellon, and Coolidge concurred with this analysis, or at least did not protest it.[117] Although Gilbert favored the tacit connection of the two sets of debts, he wanted to prevent the linkage from becoming "too direct."[118]

Yet a direct connection was the central assumption of British policy. London's stance rested on the 1922 Balfour Note, by which Britain promised to reduce its demands on Germany and the Allies in pace with Washington's reduction of London's debt. In the absence of such American concessions, British Treasury and central bank officials preferred the Dawes Plan to continue until it broke down. They expected that in the ensuing crisis the United States would slash war debts, if only to protect its private loans. The end of reparations would also help British coal and other industries that suffered from Germany's deliveries-in-kind and industrial effort to pay the debts. These British financial officials, Gilbert complained, presented the "greatest obstacle" to moderate reparations reform.[119] Gilbert sidestepped this barrier by appealing to the Foreign Office and the prime minister, who had their own reasons for orderly revision. Faced with an election in May 1929, Conservatives calculated that a reparations settlement and Rhineland evacuation would win votes.

The British also realized that without a final reparations settlement, Poincaré could not get ratification of the Mellon-Bérenger agreement. In that case, France would pay the $400 million war stocks debt by selling its sterling holdings. This would cripple the pound. By mid-October 1928, even Churchill had dropped his plan of "a united European position" on the debts and accepted Gilbert's plan for a settlement large enough to cover war debt payments to Washington.[120]

One by one, Gilbert herded the European nations into support for a reparations settlement that would protect American interests and international stability.[121] Gilbert expected that the elimination of transfer protection would secure existing American loans and enable the marketplace to appraise Germany's credit worthiness. Moderate treaty revision, it was hoped, would satisfy German ambitions. Tacit linkage of the political debts would meet Allied demands yet protect the administration from European or congressional attack.

The bill for these benefits was presented to Germany, which hoped to pass it on to American investors in German securities. Gilbert warned Stresemann that the settlement would be "expensive." Germany could not expect much reduction from the Dawes Plan annuities of 2.5 billion marks. Stresemann protested that Germany needed relief fom such burdens; it "was sitting on a volcano."[122] Nonetheless, he could not reject Gilbert's plan. "We are not only militarily disarmed," the German leader lamented, "we are financially disarmed; we have no kind of resources left." American and Allied cooperation were essential for the immediate goal of Rhineland evacuation and the Reich's long-range ambition of resurgence.[123] Gilbert assured Stresemann that the final reparations settlement would generate a burst of world confidence and economic growth, thereby reducing the relative weight of the debt.[124]

Future prosperity was the magic ingredient of the new reparations plan. Owen Young calculated that the scheme required "the greatest economic development which the world has yet seen."[125] In the short run, however, American investors would have to finance Europe's dollar gap. Yet the stock market boom, priority controversy, and disarmament issue had cooled investors' ardor for foreign, and especially German, bonds.

To rekindle that ardor, Gilbert turned to the device that had worked so well in 1924, a committee of impartial economic experts. Such a committee promised something to everyone. The Allies would be able to disguise their reparation demands as the businesslike conclusions of neutral arbitrators. With little maneuvering room, the Germans hoped for leniency from an experts committee that included their private loan creditors. And as in 1924, the expert committee offered a vehicle for United States participation without official responsibility.[126] Although every country found protection under the mantle of expert objectivity, none would give the experts sufficient independence to arrive at a truly objective settlement (if such could exist). "In effect," Charles Dawes observed, the committee would "conduct a diplomatic negotiation, not . . . an expert research." The new plan needed, Dawes predicted, not just "skillful surgeons, but . . . consummate beauty doctors."[127] Americans trusted that skillful advertising could camouflage the contradiction of an independent committee of economic experts dependent on the political policies of governments.

Since he was vice-president, Dawes could not attend the 1929 experts conference, but Washington followed the 1924 precedent by informally nominating United States delegates whom the Europeans then appointed. Owen Young's commanding role in the 1924 negotiations and prestige on both sides of the Atlantic made him "indispensable" to the conference.[128] Essential to any future commercialization of reparation bonds, J. P. Morgan was the second American representative, with Thomas Lamont as his assistant. Central bankers filled the European delegations, underscoring the connection between monetary and reparation politics. The Europeans could not agree on one of their own as chairman, and Young assumed leadership of the conference, which thereafter bore his name.[129]

The Young Plan and BIS

Young's task was formidable. He had to reconcile Allied demand for money with German reluctance to pay, while protecting America's position on war debts. The challenge was to guide Versailles revision so as to strengthen rather than undermine the postwar order. A master dealer who helped negotiate General Electric's global expansion, Young realized he needed some "magnet" to hold the conference together during the bitter fights over money.[130] Early in the meeting Young and his American assistants drafted plans for such a device, the Bank for International Settlements (BIS). Established in 1929–30, this world bank proved to be the capstone of American reconstruction efforts, pointing up the flaws and ultimate failure of U.S. policy. Discussion leading to the creation of the BIS proceeded in lockstep with reparation negotiations, which resulted in inauguration of the Young Plan. Thus, the BIS became a focus for the major issues of the 1929–33 period: war debts, reparations, gold standard, capital distribution, economic growth, and treaty revision.

The idea for an international bank arose on February 25, when the French and Belgians proposed an organization to administer the reparations agreement and give it what Young termed a "commercial color." Berlin could not repudiate these "commercial" obligations without destroying its national credit, the Allies hoped. The next day Hjalmar Schacht suggested to Young an "international clearing house" to finance world development and trade. Such growth would help Germany particularly, Schacht calculated. Young also wanted accelerated world development, but he balked at Schacht's radical proposal of a wholesale, possibly inflationary, credit expansion. Nor did Young accept the Franco-Belgian idea to commercialize and rigidify the entire reparations debt, thereby eliminating the possibility of later reductions.[131] Instead, he and his advisers drafted the blueprint for a bank for central banks to stabilize the international financial structure. The bank plan expressed Young's idea that tariffs were not the worst barriers to foreign commerce. "The great paralyzer in the development of world trade," he asserted "is the fluctuation of the currencies."[132] The gold standard was supposed to calm such disturbances, but the standard itself was shaken by the decline in American foreign lending. By means of central bank cooperation under American auspices, the BIS would strengthen the gold standard and thus stimulate world economic growth. As an added bonus, the BIS offered an American alternative to the Genoa proposals.[133]

The bank also promised political and social benefits. If the BIS "centralized ... the whole credit structure of the world ... in one place," Young predicted, "the Kellogg Pact ... would become practically effective, because nothing except peace could exist."[134] Lamont reported that Europeans hoped the BIS would help their "vexing ... social questions."[135] More bluntly, Young pronounced the new bank "a powerful barrier against the spread of Bolshevism."[136] In its narrower, reparation function the BIS signified a further step in the transformation of the indemnity from a weapon against Germany (the Versailles concept) to a business debt owed by Germany. The new bank replaced the Reparations Commission mandated by the Versailles treaty and the agent general's office established by the Dawes Plan—what Young's assistants termed "war and postwar machinery"—with "machinery essentially commercial in character." The new bank would administer reparation payments and issue reparation bonds.[137] For the Germans' benefit, the bank plan in-

cluded a vague provision that if the institution had sufficient resources—
a big if—it would finance world trade. This was an "optional" function,
in contrast to the "inherent" ones of reparation administration and central bank coordination.[138] Its American architects designed the BIS as an
institution to promote stability through economic growth, global integration, and peaceful change.

Accordingly, the bank scheme illustrated both the basic principles of
postwar foreign policy—that is, the emphasis on unofficial, economic
relations—and the basic flaws of this American approach: the narrow
definition of proper change, the skewed distribution of benefits and burdens, and the dependence on marketplace-regulated loans. Eager to integrate a pacified, prosperous Germany into the community of Western
nations, Americans often sympathized with that nation's ambition to
ease reparations and other strictures of Versailles. The Yankees tried to
shape such reform so as to strengthen international stability rather than
overthrow it. Yet because of their conservative view of acceptable change,
Americans rejected Schacht's credit expansion proposal, which might
have stimulated world economic growth. Similarly, Young's success in
securing American domination of the BIS meant that the bank was un-
responsive to German and British proposals in the early 1930s to revive
the global economy through wholesale creation of credit. Apprehensive
of such European initiatives through the BIS, and particularly fearful of
further entanglement in reparations, the Hoover administration in April
1929 vetoed formal Federal Reserve participation in the planned bank.
Yet Young, Federal Reserve officials, and the Hoover administration soon
patched together a working arrangement, again repeating the pattern of
the 1920s. As Young suggested, the BIS was the financial arm of the
Kellogg-Briand Pact. Both were limited investments in global peace and
economic integration that assumed continued prosperity. More specifically, the BIS's effectiveness in Europe depended on an adequate flow of
capital from New York. (Indeed, Young and his associates intended the
BIS and the reparations revision to revive the foreign loan market. Unfortunately, the bank, like so much else, became a victim of that market's
collapse.) Finally, the BIS illustrated the pattern of diplomacy in the 1920s
in that the Europeans had to accept American involvement on U.S. terms,
since they believed they could not solve major problems without the
world's preeminent power.

Despite its later failures, in the sunny days of early 1929 the BIS seemed
a valuable instrument to stabilize the world economy. The Allies were
pleased that a "commercial color" would shade the "political color" of
reparations, Young reported to Kellogg. The BIS would benefit Germany
by easing "temporary strains on her exchange." Advertising the BIS as

an instrument for peaceful financial cooperation and the reparation plan as a final solution to the controversy, Young and his associates hoped to rebuild American confidence in foreign investments. With sufficient dollars flowing into a stabilized financial system, the world economy could grow, thereby reducing the debts' burden. This vision, Young cabled Washington, helped save the conference from breaking down over the question of reparation annuities.[139]

In comon with Gilbert, Young envisioned a German annuity of about 2 billion marks.[140] This would cover Allied payments to Washington plus an indemnity for wartime damage suffered by France, Belgium, and Italy. The Allies and Germans, however, had different figures in mind. The Allies insisted on a 2.67-billion-mark annuity and quarreled among themselves as to its distribution. Schacht offered only 1.65 billion marks annually. He refused to give up transfer protection unless the Allies returned Germany's colonies and the Polish corridor, and opened markets for German goods. These demands for radical treaty revision he presented as the "economic" prerequisites for reparation payments. Furious, Moreau pounded the table and hurled his ink blotter; Schacht refused to back down, and the conference neared collapse.[141] Lamont, press manager for the American delegation, could not keep this acrimony secret. Leffingwell warned from New York: "The newspaper despatches from Paris have failed to reproduce the atmosphere of economic study which was so admirably created five years ago, and instead have created an atmosphere of political bargaining."[142] Such squabbling would not rekindle investors' interest in European bonds.

Young moved decisively. He agreed to clauses in the experts' report that alluded vaguely to Germany's need of expanded economic opportunities. The American industrialist then outlined a schedule of annuities that eventually became the Young Plan. Germany's obligation would average 2.05 billion marks annually over fifty-six years, but begin at only 1.675 billion. This offered an immediate saving from the Dawes Plan's 2.5 billion marks. Berlin would pay 660 million marks unconditionally, that is, without transfer protection.[143] This met French desires for at least partial commercialization of reparations. Yet the end of transfer protection for most of the annuity upgraded the relative status and security of private loans.[144] By reducing reparations and eliminating foreign control, Young offered Germany substantial reform of Versailles. Simultaneously, he and Morgan undercut Schacht's bid for drastic change and French refusal to compromise by threatening to cut off future American credits.[145] By early June, the experts accepted Young's plan, Schacht adroitly shifting to Stresemann responsibility for agreeing to the heavy burden.[146]

An analysis of the plan prepared by Morgan and Company noted the "great care ... to avoid marked coincidence" between war debts and reparations. Despite such attention to cosmetics, the plan divided reparations into two categories: a larger, postponable portion corresponding roughly to the war debt obligations and a smaller, unconditional annuity. In a special agreement outside the report, the Allied and German delegates—but not the American—agreed that Germany would receive a substantial portion of any reduction or cancellation of war debts granted by the United States.[147] This linkage violated United States policy, but, Young explained to Hoover, Stimson, and Mellon, the Allies had tallied their demands "on that basis and there was no other way ... to develop discussable figures."[148]

Allied insistence on this point was not news. Throughout 1928, Gilbert kept Kellogg, Mellon, and Coolidge informed of negotiations. They had not objected to a tacit linkage of the two sets of debts, and Gilbert had promised to camouflage the connection as best he could. On March 28, Young submitted to the Allies his schedule of annuities. On the same day, Stimson, who admitted he knew little about reparations, became secretary of state. Policymaking shifted to treasury officials, with whom Kellogg had not fully shared Young's telegrams for fear of "leaks."[149] Under Secretary of the Treasury Ogden Mills denounced Young's linkage of reparations and war debts in a stinging message that Stimson, with Hoover's approval, cabled to Paris:

> If the settlement goes through as planned, the whole burden of the collection and transfer of reparations payments will fall on our shoulders and the allied debtor nations will have succeeded, by including Germany in their ranks, in creating a solid European front which will exert continued pressure for the reduction and eventual repudiation of these debts. In the meantime they will have created a most unfavorable popular atmosphere in this country for the capitalization of future payments and for the ultimate settlement of these debts on a fair and reasonable basis.

Administration officials underscored their anger by refusing to permit any FRS official to serve on the BIS, which would receive and disburse reparation payments.[150] Young found the administration's outburst personally "offensive" and threatened to resign.[151]

Despite this acrimony, the Hoover administration and the American experts soon reached a working agreement. Young, Gilbert, and Lamont appealed to Elihu Root, Republican elder stateman and Stimson's mentor. Root agreed that the connection between the two sets of debts was a "coincidence of fact" and warned the administration that the conference's collapse meant "breaking down the credit situation in Europe."[152] Hoover, Stimson, and Mills soon reverted to the Coolidge administration's more moderate position. "We understand fully their [the American experts'] difficulties in this matter," Stimson cabled Paris; the primary concern was preventing *"any bald statement"* linking war debts and reparation.[153] Although the Hoover administration did not sign the Young Plan, it concluded a separate agreement with Germany that lowered United States Army and mixed claim receipts in accord with the general plan. The government withdrew its opposition to the BIS, asking only that American representation be through private bankers rather than FRS officials. The administration has "gone a long way to reversing their first position," Morgan noted with satisfaction. Official aloofness was essential, Stimson explained, if the administration were to "prevent" its "friends on the Hill from running amuck."[154]

This working consensus proved important in the latter half of 1929, when Americans struggled to get the Young Plan and BIS approved by the disgruntled British and Germans. In the by-now-familiar lineup, a relatively satisfied America and France confronted a revisionist-minded Germany and Britain. The Conservative party's defeat in the May 1929 elections brought into power Philip Snowden as Labour chancellor of the exchequer. In 1927, Snowden publicly protested America's gold sterilization. Now he urged that the BIS undertake "control of credit and economy of gold."[155] Snowden and Norman wanted to transform the BIS into a vehicle to reorder the international monetary system. Paris allied with New York, endorsing the American conception of the BIS as a nonpolitical bank for central banks to administer reparations and stabilize the gold standard. In a series of conferences, American and French financiers put through their version of the BIS and placed their nationals in command.[156] "In the Bank itself French and American interests will more or less coincide," a Morgan economist predicted.[157]

Governmental wrangling over the Young Plan was still more hostile. The scheme met "violent opposition" in Britain, Lamont reported.[158] Snowden demanded a larger share of Germany's payment and nearly disrupted the August 1929 Hague governmental conference to implement the plan. Once again, British Treasury officials calculated that if the Dawes Plan were allowed to continue, it would soon collapse.[159] Snowden held out until the other Allies met nearly all his financial demands. His intransigence symbolized the decline of Anglo-French cooperation and the demise of the Locarno spirit. German frustration also focused on the Young Plan. In a bid for right-wing political support, Schacht denounced the scheme he had helped negotiate. I would never invest a penny of my own money in German government bonds, he told startled American bankers.[160]

The United States became involved in the fight when France protested the separate agreement with Germany. Once again the administration defended its position through unofficial but effective observers, Edwin Wilson and Dawes, the new ambassador to London.[161] Although Hoover and Stimson did not like the Young Plan's tacit linkage of war debts and reparations, they were "very glad" about the Hague agreement, the secretary of state told the British ambassador. Settlement "was of overwhelming importance."[162] After another Hague Conference in January 1930, the Young Plan and the BIS came into effect. Both became cockpits for the battles of the early 1930s.

The bitterness of the Young Plan negotiations doomed the bankers' efforts to invigorate the foreign bond market with renewed investor confidence. Lamont warned shortly after the Young conference: "It is important for the public not to get the impression that the annuities had been reached through bargaining rather than scientific examination.... It would have a very bad effect on them [investors] to have all these memoranda made public." A couple of months later, he and J. P. Morgan commented that everything depended "on an atmosphere yet to be created." Dwight Morrow suggested that "some Prime Minister will have to kiss the other on both cheeks in order to create just the right background."[163] This "atmosphere" never materialized, despite lavish press coverage of the Young Plan as a "treaty of peace" and "the first chapter of a new era."[164] Favorable publicity was unable to camouflage growing national differences. The Hoover administration did not give the Young Plan the enthusiastic public support Coolidge had extended in 1924 because of the tacit linkage with war debts and reluctance to sink more money into reparations bonds. As the American reconstruction effort neared completion, its contradictions and weaknesses became more serious. After years of quiet, Congress, beginning in 1929, challenged the policy of limited economic involvement in Europe.[165] These domestic and international differences were aggravated by sagging national economies and rising armament tensions.

From 1927 to 1929, Americans sought to complete the work of stabilizing Europe through peaceful change and economic growth. Confident that the world economy was essentially healthy and concerned to protect the benefits they had built into the postwar order, Americans approached this task in a conservative way. The U.S. government limited and shaped its involvement so as to obtain the maximum return of European stability and peace at minimal American cost. This seemed like a sound strategy, but it failed to correct or even perceive the flaws which undermined the international system. Americans' vision of acceptable change was limited by their determination to preserve the economic benefits of the international gold standard, the war debt settlements, the foreign investments, and the trade surplus. Thus, they opposed British efforts to reapportion the benefits and burdens of the international economy. Despite Americans' faith in investors' wisdom, the financial markets fluctuated wildly in 1927–28. First the loan market flooded Europe with dollars and gold, then the stock market drained funds back into Wall Street. Thus, in 1929–30, when Americans created the BIS, the structure was already fatally undermined by its flaws.

Yet these defects did not negate the real American accomplishments of 1927–29. In the late 1920s the Coolidge administration urged the world to think about peace while telling Britain to stop thinking of itself as sole mistress of the seas. Unofficial delegates represented the administration at the Geneva Economic Conference, winning a victory for open-door, most-favored-nation tariffs while helping defeat Russia's bid for peaceful coexistence and large loans from the West. Protective of the FRBNY's near independence, Strong joined with fellow creditors in Paris to promote financial influence in eastern Europe and safeguard the status quo against British assault. Meanwhile Mellon's protegé, Gilbert, operating from his outpost of American power in Europe, worked to revise the Dawes Plan and protect U.S. investments. The resulting Young Plan promised to accomplish these objectives. The plan also spawned the BIS.

All this added up to an impressive display of economic, political, and moral power. The leadership that wielded this strength was decentralized, but in the 1920s it came together in a working coalition that pursued peaceful change and economic growth as the means toward peace, stability, and prosperity. As Brecht observed, these were grand accomplishments; the Americans "seemed destined to rule the world." Yet their creation could not withstand the storm of Depression and, indeed its defects contributed to the severity of that upheaval. Brecht's epitaph was apt: "It all looked like lasting a thousand . . . but endured a bare eight years."[166]

[8]

Depression and Disintegration, 1930–1933

The Depression, following those eight years of American ascendancy, destroyed the postwar political and economic order while dimming United States cultural influence in Europe. Hard times deepened and exposed the flaws of the international system: its fatal dependence on prosperity fueled by marketplace loans, its unequal distribution of benefits and burdens, its reliance on slow, peaceful change in a revolutionary era, and the inability of its American fathers to launch a rescue through wholesale intervention in Europe. The Depression intensified such problems of the previous decade into a nightmare from which American leaders could not awake. The spectacle of Herbert Hoover, the humanitarian and engineer of the new era, applying the nostrums of the 1920s to the crises of the 1930s pointed up the confines and the constancy of American foreign policy.

As throughout the 1919–33 era, the primary international issues in the early 1930s were whether and how to revise the Versailles treaty, how to revive and sustain world prosperity, and, on a more subtle plane, how Europe would adopt and modify the American cultural pattern. The Depression melded the political and economic problems into a single, deepening crisis. Meanwhile the American economic collapse deflated Europe's mania for Yankee culture while leaving American production techniques in place and in some countries under authoritarian control.

The Hoover administration became more deeply involved in the international crisis than Republicans in the 1920s had thought proper or necessary. Yet the administration adhered to the old strategy of seeking solutions through gradual Versailles revision and stable capitalist economic growth and seeking influence without responsibilities or entanglements.

218

Unfortunately for Hoover, American power to win such goals had dwindled. As the crisis worsened, the loans dried up and Europeans abandoned the gold standard. Washington officials' remaining financial leverage was a promise to reduce war debts. This asset diminished too as the Allies edged toward default and Congress gagged at any mention of war debt relief. The severity with which the Depression struck America undercut the nation's prestige as a model and leader. During Hoover's administration American moral authority received no such boost as followed Charles Lindbergh's transatlantic flight or Owen Young's engineering of the Dawes Plan. Instead, Europeans booed the Smoot-Hawley tariff or witnessed the failure of American solutions to debt and disarmament issues. This decline in image was doubly ironic since Hoover, an accomplished public relations manager, was sensitive to the problem and packaged his initiatives so as to win public acceptance in American and Europe. Yet such advertising backfired, and the president became a captive of his own publicity efforts.

Hoover foresaw such failure. Shortly after his five-to-one electoral victory over Alfred E. Smith, the president-elect mused that he had "overadvertised" himself. "The American people think of me as . . . a superman," he said. "They expect the impossible of me and should there arise . . . conditions with which the political machinery is unable to cope, I will be the one to suffer."[1] Hoover did suffer, personally and politically, for his inability to stop the Depression that struck months after his inauguration.

As the Depression deepened, nationalists in England, Germany, and Japan challenged the American conception of a world open to trade and investment through nondiscriminatory tariffs and the gold standard and open to treaty revision through gradual, peaceful change. Hoover and other American leaders struggled desperately to contain these forces of upheaval and conjure anew the 1920s promise of peace through treaty reform and prosperity through economic growth. When the well-worn tools of financial diplomacy, unofficial representation, and managed publicity failed to cut through toughened congressional obstruction, European intransigence, and domestic economic failure, Hoover did not surrender. Instead his administration became more deeply involved in European politics through direct governmental negotiations, pressure to revise Versailles, and a willingness to link economic, political, and military issues. Deepening depression and public opposition defeated these efforts as well, however. In 1930–33, the ailing political economy yielded neither the lendable capital nor the popular confidence that had enabled leaders from 1924 to 1929 to carry out foreign policy largely unimpeded by Congress and the public.

Despite America's weakened economy and Hoover's faulty political leadership, the United States and its president were at the center of world efforts to check the economic and political storm. Americans generated many of the proposals to deal with world problems, and American power was essential to any global solution. Yet as these proposals failed and that power faltered, Britain, Germany, and Japan built closed-door blocs. This trend continued into 1933, when President Franklin D. Roosevelt aimed for domestic recovery by severing America's tie with the international gold standard. Roosevelt's brief experiment with an insulated domestic economy wound up a two-year national debate over self-sufficiency and testified to the Depression's terrible severity.

Historians disagree on the Depression's causes, but most concur that a major factor was the sharp cutback in United States foreign loans after 1928 and imports after 1929. This forced the rest of the world to deflate at home and restrict purchases and investments abroad. Retrenchment snowballed, aggravating the decline in raw material prices and world income. Destruction of confidence and wealth in the New York stock market crash reinforced these deflationary pressures. United States unemployment jumped from 3.2 percent of the labor force in 1929 to 15.9 percent in 1931. The gross national product fell from $104.4 billion in 1929 to $76.3 billion in 1931. World trade slumped from $2.8 billion in September 1929 to $1.6 billion in September 1931. After 1931, things got worse. At the trough in 1933, unemployment stood at 24.9 percent, the gross national product at $56 billion, and monthly world trade at $1.1 billion. Both in the United States and abroad, farmers and raw material producers suffered most. From 1929 to 1933, world prices of foodstuffs plummeted 54 percent.[2]

This economic crisis depreciated Yankee cultural and political influence in Europe. Europeans saw less need to heed Yankee wishes or examples, and expatriates sensed a new seriousness in hard-times America. Checks from home shrank, fewer tourists came, many expatriate newspapers and magazines folded, some businesses closed their European branches—and the army of self-exiles sailed back to the United States.[3]

With this retreat, Europe's love-hate relationship with America took a new twist. Although the crash hurt Europeans by slashing U.S. loans, imports, and tourist expenditures, many were gratified by the giant's fall. French writers such as Robert de Saint-Jean and Bernard Faÿ, who in the 1920s had denounced the Americanist vision as materialistic and machine-dominated, now claimed victory over the god that failed. They believed that with economic adversity, Americans would turn toward the spiritual, esthetic values embodied in France.[4] In Germany, divided by cultural, economic, and political debate between advocates of Americanist modernity and proponents of a return to *völkisch* traditionalism, the United States' decline favored the latter group. America's fall from grace removed a major cultural prop of the *neue Sachlichkeit* just as the collapse of the foreign loan market cut off funds for housing and other projects that had incorporated new objectivity architecture.[5] Bertolt Brecht, who had begun shifting from Americanism to bolshevism even before the stock market crash, declared in 1929: "The Ford factory is, considered technically, a Bolshevik organization; it does not fit in with bourgeois individualism; it fits better in a Bolshevik society."[6]

This pointed up a central irony of the Americanization movement: Communists, Fascists, and others could easily separate the technological advances from the reformist components of the vision. In the 1930s, factories with the latest mass production techniques, installed with American money and example in Germany and Russia, were at the disposal of totalitarians who rejected democracy and mass consumption as decadent and unnecessary. Before taking power in January 1933, the Nazis denounced modernity and capitalized on Germans' yearning for a pastoral society of craftsmanship and community. Once in control, however, the totalitarians utilized the advanced factories and accelerated the modernization process to build German power.[7] Similarly, in his five year plans Stalin used the factories and dams built with American technology and expertise to construct a rigid, repressive society with low mass consumption.

When the Depression drove raw material prices through the floor, Stalin, desperate to pay for the imported technological equipment, dumped wheat, lumber, and other raw materials on the world market. This depressed prices still further, angering competing producers in America and elsewhere. Stalin also raised cash by selling a treasure trove of European art masterpieces, accumulated over the centuries by the czars and Russian nobility.

This dumping of wheat and art produced in the Hoover administration a contradictory response that demonstrated the convoluted connection of economics, culture, and politics. During the 1920s, the Soviets tried to outflank the United States government's ostracism and win American friends by exhibiting Russian art treasures. In 1928, when the Soviets began to sell their art collection, Americans bought some $10–15 million worth of masterpieces. The largest single buyer was Andrew W. Mellon, secretary of the treasury and a multimillionaire, who in 1930 purchased twenty-one paintings worth $6.7 million. This amounted to one-third of total Russian exports to America in that year. The collection came from the Hermitage, private museum of the czars, and included paintings by Rembrandt, Van Eyck, Titian, and other European masters.

While Mellon the private collector took advantage of Soviet dumping of art works, Mellon the treasury official was responsible for blocking the importation of stolen goods or dumped raw materials. Secrecy and some convenient chronology prevented any public embarassment—until 1935, when the art purchases were exposed during Mellon's prosecution for income tax evasion. In May 1930 M. Knoedler and Company, the secretary's art agents, completed most of the negotiations to purchase the paintings.[8] No doubt the Soviets concluded from their Marxist ideology that Mellon personified the capitalist equation of wealth with political power. He could be a powerful friend.

On June 17, Hoover signed into law the Smoot-Hawley tariff. The tariff included Article 307, which required the Treasury Department to embargo competing Russian products made with slave labor. Since the importer had the burden of proving that a Russian export was *not* the fruit of forced labor, Article 307 made it easy for American raw material producers to block Russian competition. Mellon responded to popular pressure and embargoed Russian wheat, asbestos, and lumber. This pleased congressmen like Hamilton Fish, Republican of New York, who spoke for many leaders when he condemned "short-sighted dollar-chasing American capitalists [who] do not count the cost of promoting world revolution."[9] However, Mellon refused to embargo Soviet exports of manganese, a material vital to the steel and aluminum industries, of which he owned a sizable share. Although Mellon welcomed Soviet sales of paintings and manganese, most Soviet exports to the United States were suppressed. In response to the American embargo, the Soviets reduced total imports and shifted purchases to Germany, which offered sizable credits. This shrank America's share of Russia's imports from 25 percent in 1930 to 4.5 percent in 1932.[10]

Mellon's private and public postures on Russian trade offer several lessons on the Depression's impact. Hard times caused desperation in Russian exporters and their American competitors; yet those with money could benefit from the crisis. Both the deflation of the early 1930s and the European inflation of the early 1920s offered opportunities to American art collectors. Despite the Depression, Americans—at least an elite few—had the wealth to enhance the United States' cultural endowment at the expense of Europe's. Mellon's actions also demonstrated that the U.S. government responded to distress in important sectors of the economy while protecting the special interests of those in power. Finally, the Russian trade episode demonstrated the United States' steadfast oppo-

sition to left-wing governments. In 1930, Washington officials tightened
the limits on trade with the Soviets and continued to deny Russia political
recognition. Meanwhile Americans worked closely with the right-of-cen-
ter Heinrich Brüning government in Germany and maintained cordial
relations with the Fascist regime in Italy. However, the decline in the
nation's economic clout and cultural prestige made it more difficult for
Americans to channel the rightist, revisionist tendencies in Germany and
Italy toward peaceful change. Opposed to leftist revolution, U.S. officials
did not even consider enlisting the Soviet government in that endeavor.

Aside from its economic and cultural impact, the Depression bred
political and ideological tension. In much of the world hard times hamstrung political leadership and threatened upheaval. Hard-pressed taxpayers were less willing to sacrifice for war debts, reparations, or tariffs.
Frightened investors shifted their assets from one country to another,
aggravating balance-of-payments difficulties, deflationary pressure, and
political turmoil. Political paralysis at home and in international conferences undermined the liberal doctrine of solution through compromise
and bolstered the extremists' appeal. Economic experts lost credibility
even as expertise became more crucial. Hoover echoed voices on both
sides of the Atlantic when he declared that arms reduction would help
restore prosperity. Yet the Depression undercut moderate elements in
Germany and Japan, strengthening demand for radical treaty revision in
those countries and weakening support for disarmament in the United
States and Britain. These economic, political, and military problems linked
together into what British Foreign Office analysts termed a "chain."

> The *monetary crisis* leads inevitably back to the *economic chaos* in Europe.
> The economic chaos, and all attempts to deal with it, involve in their turn
> the political questions of *reparations* and *war debts*. These are linked by the
> United States with the question of *disarmament*, and the latter, in the eyes
> of the French Government, depends upon the problem of *security*. The
> problem of security, in its turn, raises the question of the *territorial status
> quo* in Europe (e.g., the Eastern Frontier question), which brings us to the
> conflict between the *maintenance or revision of the Peace Settlements*.[11]

In the end, everything boiled down to Versailles treaty revision, the
issue of whether to preserve, reform, or overthrow the existing order.
The dilemma had not changed since 1919 when Woodrow Wilson backed
down from his original plan to build flexibility into the postwar system
because he feared upheaval and revolution.

Herbert Hoover

In 1919–20, Herbert Hoover criticized the rigidity of Versailles and the League of Nations, but urged American ratification, preferably with mild reservations, because the threatened alternative was uncontrolled change and uncertainty. As president, Hoover opposed unilateral, violent overthrow of Versailles or American entanglement in European politics. Yet he railed against the treaty's provisions. "Evidently you don't approve of the Versailles Treaty," concluded Secretary of State Stimson. "Of course I don't, I never did," Hoover snapped.[12] Hoover and Stimson pursued the middle path of moderate revision, believing that such slow, limited reform of Versailles would safeguard American interests and secure stability abroad. Despite frequently conflicting ideas and temperaments, the two men shared this consensus on the central political issue. The president and secretary of state had a stormy, but enduring, relationship. Each moderated the other's extremes, and for the most part they worked together effectively.[13]

Neither Hoover nor Stimson had much taste for or experience in back-slapping, baby-kissing politics. Even at the height of his popularity, Hoover was painfully shy. "I dread these shows," he murmured as he went out to make a public appearance.[14] As food administrator, relief czar, and Commerce secretary, Hoover operated from behind the scenes, coordinating decentralized activity through a centralized public relations machine. As administrator and as president, Hoover promoted what he called the "American system" of "American individualism." The latter name was misleading, for Hoover wanted Americans to join together voluntarily in local and national organizations. Orchestrated by government appeals, Hoover hoped, such organizations would bridge the gap between the technical expertise necessary to run America's complex industrial society and the individual initiative essential to democracy. At the inauguration, Hoover expected that his administration would fine-tune the economy and nudge Americans toward constructive voluntarism.

Confronted instead with the Depression, Hoover telephoned businessmen and local government officials, begging them to increase construction and not cut wages or employment. Simultaneously, he resisted congressional and popular pressures for massive direct relief spending. Hoover believed his policies were essential to promote "American individualism" and forestall a bureaucratic welfare state. This approach undercut the administration's effectiveness at home and abroad.[15] As Walter Lippman observed, the president "spends his energies lavishly in fields where under our political system the President has no powers and no responsibility; he is unable to use his energy successfully on the major political tasks where he alone has the power of leadership and the consequent responsibility."[16] The president was a superb administrator in organizing work and giving orders, but incompetent and thin-skinned in the world of logrolling politics. Nor did his attitude help—he viewed politicians as "reptiles," Stimson recorded.[17]

Hoover's political weakness, aggravated by the Democrats' victory in the 1930 congressional elections, hamstrung foreign policy. As long as America's European policy reinforced domestic prosperity, Congress gave the Republican administrations wide scope in which to pursue their economic and unofficial diplomacy. In the 1930s, however, Congress derailed plans for careful tariff and war debt revision. Congressional opposition also checked the president's efforts to fight the world depression, which Hoover feared thwarted domestic recovery.

Hoover's attitude toward American dependence on foreign trade has puzzled historians.[18] In 1928, he bragged of his "organized campaign to build up the exports of our products." Foreign markets for surplus production were essential to "ensure continuous employment and maintain our wages," he declared. If the United States could not export "the 9% or 10% of our total production which is now sold abroad ... we might survive as a nation, [but with] lower living standard and wages." Exports also purchased essential raw material imports, without which "our whole standard of life would be paralyzed and much of the joy of living destroyed."[19] In time of prosperity, then, Hoover concluded that economic self-sufficiency was possible in theory but costly in practice. As Commerce secretary he tried to reduce economic vulnerability by broadening the sources of imported raw materials. Yet he also focused efforts on foreign trade promotion.[20] Europeans who reviewed Hoover's record in the Commerce Department were "apprehensive" at his election to the presidency, British diplomats reported. They expected "an aggressive policy of commercial development." Hoover realized "that continued American prosperity depends upon the growth of American foreign trade." Similarly, a French journal explained that Hoover believed in "America for the Americans ... and the world for America."[21]

Confronted with reduced exports in the Depression, Hoover tried to revive the international economy and foreign markets. His activity here was limited by the failure of the global economy to respond and the squabbling among nations over how to distribute painful adjustments. Simultaneous with these actions, Hoover assured the American people that their "remarkably self-contained" domestic economy could "make a large measure of independent recovery." The president's reminder that

America's primary markets were at home skirted the fact—which he fully realized—that even a small surplus of wheat, cotton, or pork could drive down the prices received by all producers.[22]

Hoover's homilies on self-sufficiency must be read in the context of three factors: his continual concern with the international situation, his despair of being able to improve it, and, most important, his belief that *confidence* was essential to recovery. No matter if the United States economy really *was* self-sufficient; if Americans believed it to be, their faith could lessen the impact of international trouble. "Repeated shocks from political disturbances and revolution in foreign countries stimulate fear and hesitation among our businessmen," the president feared. "Confidence" was the "transcendent need," because fear had a direct economic impact: "We are suffering today more from frozen confidence than from frozen securities." That "cooperative action" on which so much of Hoover's "American system" depended required "faith and courage." Hoover's entire public career focused on shaping such psychological factors. He tried unceasingly, and unsuccessfully, throughout the Depression to stimulate the confidence necessary for prosperity. Hoover's assurance that America could recover regardless of world conditions fit alongside his assertions that prosperity was just around the corner and that Americans needed a joke to get them smiling. In mid-1931, with unemployment at 15.9 percent, the president declared, 'Over 95% of our families have either an income or a bread-winner employed."[23]

Hoover's actions spoke louder than his words, however. Despite congressional and European opposition and pressing domestic problems, Hoover tried persistently to rehabilitate the world economy. Naturally, in times of severe domestic crisis, the president put foreign problems aside, delegated them to Stimson, and sought optimal benefit for American interests. After Hoover left the presidency and world problems worsened, he swung closer to a stance of self-sufficiency. Yet he concluded his administration convinced that "a full and secure recovery" required the "cooperation of other nations." America could not isolate its prosperity from that of the rest of the world. Hoover's focus on preparations for the 1933 London Economic Conference attested to this belief.[24]

The Secretary of State

Although Hoover and Stimson agreed on the necessity of an active policy in Europe, they often conflicted. Stimson was a protegé of Theodore Roosevelt and Elihu Root and owed his appointment partly to the latter's influence. Descended from patrician New Yorkers with a long military tradition, "Colonel" Stimson was proud of his battlefront action in the Great War. Stimson disparaged the president's "Quaker nature" and disarmament ideas derived "from Alice in Wonderland." This aristocrat was no vote-getter, having met defeat in his sole bid for elected office. Nor did he win over the press, represented, he complained, by "an inferior bunch of young men." Stimson relished the role of colonial governor in the Philippines from 1927 to 1929, and in Washington he maintained a twenty-acre estate. His views on presidential leadership harked back to Teddy Roosevelt, and he had little respect for congressional capacities. Thus, Stimson neither appreciated Hoover's political frailties nor alleviated them. Helping Hoover agonize through an issue "was like sitting in a bath of ink," Stimson complained, and arguments often "got quite tense." But the two men soon came to a working arrangement on most issues. In general, Stimson acceded to Hoover's wishes on large issues, such as the response to Japanese aggression and disarmament. And he often moderated the president's angry responses to European opposition.[25]

Underlying agreement facilitated this working relationship. "It was my business to develop foreign trade," Stimson explained. He believed that confidence was the key to economic recovery and emphasized the "psychological" aspect of the political debt moratorium, world economic conference, and other measures.[26] Like Charles Evans Hughes, Stimson believed that the United States should limit intervention in European politics to dramatic, deus ex machina performances. "We would lose our influence and moral power," he explained, "if we ... had to discuss on equal terms with other nations the routine problems and squabbles of Europe." America reserved its might and prestige for "major emergencies."[27] Hughes had succeeded with this strategy at the Washington and Dawes conferences. Hoover and Stimson failed with similar dramatic proposals to suspend governmental debts and slash armaments.

The London Naval Conference

Even before the Depression reduced governmental receipts and raised international tensions, Hoover decided to slow the armaments race. His faith in disarmament reflected the American formula for security and peace in Europe. Disarmament would reduce tensions and promote prosperity, Americans argued, thus facilitating peaceful change and security for all. The French disagreed, insisting on security in the form of a strategic commitment from Britain and America as the prerequisite for disarmament. Partly because of this impasse with Paris officials, Hoover focused first on the cruiser race with Britain. The Anglo-Saxon powers "were really at each other's throats," Stimson recalled.[28] Conflict centered on whether London would concede Washington parity, and whether the United States would build or Britain would scrap to achieve equality. In February 1929, Congress passed the massive naval construction bill. This demonstrated to British leaders that America could and would build a superior fleet.

Admiralty and Conservative government officials, who at the 1927 conference opposed conceding cruiser parity to the United States, now reconsidered. V. C. Bridgeman, first lord of the admiralty, admitted that despite the "risk" of United States parity, "absolute security against U.S.A." was impossible. Since Britain could not fight this giant, it had best reconcile it. However, other cabinet officials still refused to abandon naval superiority, and the Conservative government left office without settling the naval dispute. Ramsay MacDonald, the incoming Labour prime minister, grounded much of his foreign policy on cooperation with America. Like Hoover, he had long advocated arms limitation and disarmament. The prime minister wangled an invitation to visit the United States and there disarmed audiences: "What is all this bother about parity? Parity? Take it without reserve, heaped up and flowing over."[29]

MacDonald could afford such generosity because Hoover had already broadened the definition of parity. Since the collapse of the 1927 conference, desultory naval discussions had continued at Geneva. Soon after taking office Hoover injected what he termed a "bold and unexpected proposal." Delegate Hugh Gibson suggested a way around the parity deadlock: a "yardstick" to reduce 8- and 6-inch gun cruisers to a common denominator. This enabled both the United States and Britain to build the size ships they needed and still attain parity. Coming from the engineer president, the "yardstick" seemed the simple, yet scientific, way to disarmament. Foreign and domestic opinion applauded the plan.[30] The "yardstick" approach expressed Progressive confidence in measurable, scientific reform. Yet it also reflected the limits of this approach, for as Europe soon learned, Hoover and Stimson in truth had no such magic ruler; the yardstick was a public relations device to reconcile the conflicting naval demands. Gibson explained how the measure would be cut to fit the cloth: "The first thing is to find out how little the British can get along with, and how much we are obliged to build in order to attain a reasonable parity that will satisfy the Senate and the man-in-the-street; then all we have to do is to make a yardstick to fit that situation"[31] The Anglo-Saxon powers invited Japan, Italy, and France to meet in London for a naval conference to limit tonnage in auxiliry vessels and thus complete the work of the 1922 conclave.

The London Conference "was the last of the great conferences done in the tradition of the Congress of Vienna," reflected United States diplomat Hugh Wilson. Hoover underscored the conference's importance and his own interest by sending a high-ranking delegation and then monitoring negotiations personally. Stimson, the chief delegate, was accompanied by Dwight Morrow, Charles Lindbergh's father-in-law and a former J. P. Morgan partner. Morrow had just reconciled United States–Mexican differences, and at London he applied the same skills to reconciling the French. Democratic senator Joseph Robinson and Republican senator David Reed protected the congressional flank. In contrast to the 1927 conference, the admirals served only as technical advisers, thus facilitating broad political agreement. As in the 1924 reparations conference, Charles Dawes, now ambassador to London, helped keep the meeting in the public eye.[32]

Shaping American public opinion became a key factor, especially when negotiations stalled on the French demand for security. Since London accepted United States naval parity, the Anglo-Saxons cooperated at the conference.[33] Negotiations with the Japanese proved more difficult, but eventually Reed and Matsudaira, Tokyo's representative, agreed to a moderate increase in Japanese naval power.[34] Most difficult was the French insistence on security before disarmament. Stimson generously recommended that Britain offer such security in the form of a Locarno Pact for the Mediterranean. More cautiously, he suggested the possibility of a consultative pact that the United States might join. The significance of such a pact was that if France were attacked and Britain went to its aid, the United States would consult—and probably cooperate—with Britain to the extent of forgoing American neutrality rights to trade with the aggressor nation. Although in conversations with MacDonald the previous September Hoover had suggested adding such a consultative clause to the Kellogg Pact, he now vetoed Stimson's suggestion of consultation with disarmament. Hoover feared—and Stimson subsequently agreed—that if Washington agreed to consult in return for Paris's disarmament, the United States would have a moral obligation to aid an attacked France. Nor were the British willing to grant France a security pact. Buffeted by antipact opinion, led by Senator William Borah, and propact peace groups, Hoover struggled to retain public and congressional support.[35] "Due to French propaganda," the State Department cabled Stimson, "the support of the peace groups we are losing rapidly." Hoover urged an "offensive ... before the American public shall have become completely prejudiced against us through the French."[36]

Since the Anglo-Saxons rejected the consultative and security pacts, the French refused to accept Italian naval parity. This doomed a five-power accord, and the conference ended on April 22, 1930 with only a three-power naval agreement. It provided for limitation until 1936 of auxiliary vessel tonnages in the ratio of ten for Washington and London and seven for Tokyo. Since Britain refused to scrap, America had to build up to the British level. Peace-minded congressmen were dismayed that naval parity required $1 billion in construction expenditures, more than twice the total of the previous eight years.[37]

Attacked by both hawks and doves, Hoover tried to shape public reaction to the treaty. He ordered that news releases ring with "a clear note of exultation." Each delegate received instructions to declare himself "satisfied . . . and proud."[38] The State Department solicited endorsements of the treaty from prominent Americans: Owen Young, General John Pershing, and Charles Lindbergh ("a few whispered words from Papa Morrow would probably do the trick," a State Department official suggested.)[39]

Despite this publicity campaign, critics condemned the treaty for doing either too much or too little. Hoover called a special session of the Senate to pass the treaty. Numerous naval officers, echoed by the Hearst press, warned that the treaty overly restricted the American fleet. Rear Admiral Mark Bristol pointed to the task of protecting "foreign markets. When foreign markets close to us American prosperity ends." Other officers acknowledged the importance of trade, but denied that the treaty hampered its defense. Finally, on July 21, the Senate ratified the treaty, 58 to 9.[40]

Despite this victory, the Hoover administration for several reasons found later foreign policy initiatives more difficult to achieve. Opposition to arms reduction increased after the Japanese invasion of Manchuria in September 1931. The Republicans lost control of Congress in the November 1930 elections. Other foreign policy measures such as war debt reduction dug into taxpayers' pockets and aggravated antiforeign feelings. As the Depression deepened, Hoover's political clumsiness became crippling. Failure to control tariff revision in 1929–30 demonstrated the disastrous interaction of presidential weakness, congressional opposition, and foreign problems.

In his inaugural address, Hoover had called for legislation to encourage cooperative marketing and raise the agricultural tariff. This fulfilled a campaign pledge and was essential, Hoover believed, to help farmers who generally had not benefited from the prosperity decade. Higher tariffs would protect the domestic market and reduce gluts by encouraging crop diversification. As an engineer, a Progressive, and an administrator, Hoover wanted to replace congressional logrolling with a revitalized Tariff Commission, responsible to the president, that would adjust rates through expert analysis of the costs of production. As politicians, congressmen resisted. When Congress took up the tariff question in May 1929, it ignored the president's plan. Instead, special interest groups, as in 1921–22, horse-traded rate increases so as to hike the entire tariff. Democrats voted for specific rate increases, then attacked the bill as a whole. Focusing on the Tariff Commission and the flexible rate principle, Hoover exercised no leadership as to particular rates.

The end product was a disaster. Passed at a time when foreign trade was already sinking, the Hawley-Smoot tariff raised rates to an average of 40 percent, up from the average 33 percent rate of the 1922 tariff. Congress did include the flexible provision the president had demanded, however. Many businessmen and economists denounced the new tariff and urged Hoover to veto it. Europeans raged and threatened boycotts. Despite this, fearing that a veto would prolong business uncertainty and the Depression, Hoover signed the measure on July 17, 1930. In an election year the president could not repudiate what had become a Republican tariff. Moreover, he believed that a high tariff was essential to high wages and prosperity. Hoover convinced himself, as his speeches and memoirs attest, that the increases were neither great nor dangerous. The president "had got himself boxed in."[41] What Hoover intended as moderate tariff revision mushroomed into wholesale change, which he shrank from controlling. In the context of worsening depression, the flexible clause did not significantly reduce the tariff, despite Hoover's intermittent efforts to adjust some duties. Expert analysis proved more difficult than the president had assumed. Domestically, the tariff episode pointed up Hoover's political ineptitude. Internationally, it intensified European resentment and balance-of-payment difficulties. Economically, its impact was hard to measure, but it did not help, especially since other nations retaliated.

The brief U.S. economic upturn in the first half of 1930 probably encouraged Hoover to endorse the higher tariff. Overseas economies continued to sink, however, and sharply falling raw material prices slashed incomes in much of the world, including the U.S. farm belt.[42] After June 1930, all economic indices nosed down. With only a few weak rallies, the world economy from mid-1930 to 1933 dropped ever lower, undermining the economic, political, and military stability of the 1920s. The Depression reduced American economic leverage and multiplied international political tensions.

Nevertheless, Americans tried to carry out the formula of the 1920s. They encouraged peaceful change and prosperity in Europe while defending U.S. interests and minimizing political entanglements and domestic opposition. As in the 1920s, American efforts to strike a balance between revolution and rigidity centered on the issues of reparations, the gold standard, Versailles, and disarmament.

The Reparations Crisis

Despite the Young Plan's "final" settlement of reparations, controversy continued. At first the Hoover administration distrusted the plan and the Bank for International Settlements (BIS) because the two devices tacitly linked war debts and reparations. Administration officials also worried that proposed sales of reparation bonds would leave "American holding the bag" and benefit France, chief reparations recipient. France misspent such money, they believed, on excessive armament. Furthermore, Hoover was vulnerable to attack from Representative Louis McFadden (Republican, Pennsylvania) and other congressmen who challenged financial diplomacy and its loose management by the bankers and the State Department. McFadden's public assault on the Young and BIS bonds shook investor confidence and threatened the administration's informal loan policy.[43]

Despite this initial apprehension, the Hoover administration soon embraced the Young Plan and the BIS as pillars of stability in an increasingly unstable world. In effect, the international bank became an American outpost. Hoover adjusted America's small claims for army costs and war damages to fit the Young Plan's requirements. Hoover and Stimson approved attendance at a BIS meeting by George L. Harrison, governor of the Federal Reserve Bank of New York. Stimson's lieutenants, Under Secretary of State Joseph Cotton and his successor, William R. Castle, had close ties with Gates McGarrah and Leon Fraser, president and vice-president of the BIS. Fraser informed the State Department, through the American consul, of the BIS's inner workings.[44] During the German financial crisis, Fraser served as Hoover's banking adviser.[45] McGarrah and Fraser consistently "defend[ed] American financial policy and the position of our currency," the consul reported.[46] In practice this meant defense of the gold standard and America's investments.

Such a conservative stance conflicted with German and British financial revisionism. The Depression soured Germans on the Young Plan, and Berlin sought drastic change. Governing by decree with the backing of President Paul von Hindenburg and the Reichswehr, Chancellor Heinrich Brüning was a determined revisionist. Like Stresemann, he succeeded in enlisting American and British support.

The chancellor sought backing from the German people in the September 1930 elections. Candidate Brüning declared: "We realize that no

German accepts the Young Plan; the idea of revision is before our eyes."[47] Yet such statements did not match the virulence of the Nazis and Communists, who shouted for ouster of the Versailles treaty and the moderate parties. Voters were suffering from Brüning policy of deflation. With the votes tallied, the Nazis became the second largest party in the Reichstag, multiplying their seats from 12 to 107. The Communists placed third with 77, a jump of 23. The Social Democrats lost 10 seats, but remained the largest part, with 143. Brüning's coalition included only 171 out of the total 577 deputies, fewer than before the election.[48] Extremist success accentuated Brüning's political weakness and dictated a policy of more rapid revision. The subsequent flight of capital aggravated Germany's financial problems and highlighted reparations as an obvious revisionist target.

In the 1920s, Walther Rathenau and Gustav Stresemann had chalked out the basic German strategy: enmesh powerful American-British economic interests in Germany's welfare and thus secure allies for revision. American and British bankers were willing accomplices, and by mid-1931, total United States investment in Germany totaled several billion dollars. Nine hundred million dollars in short-term credits were especially precarious. After long-term loans slacked off in mid-1928, Germans borrowed huge amounts through short-term bills, using the credits in place of long-term loans. Most credits became frozen; Americans could not withdraw the money without a German financial panic.[49] In a conversation with bankers in January 1931, Frederick Sackett, ambassador in Berlin, reported that the huge volume of illiquid short-term credits resulted from "competitive effort by American bankers working independently of each other to secure attractive earning power for surplus funds showing only meager returns in the home loan market." So much for what administration and banking officials touted as marketplace wisdom.

The crisis threatened America's own financial structure, since key United States banks had much of their capital involved. The Chase Bank, for instance, had $190 million of short-term German investments, about half its total capital. Sackett urged Stimson and Hoover, both of whom read this dispatch, to say nothing that might make investors "nervous" and cause them to withdraw their money.[50] Sackett's suggestion of official silence and further loans paralleled the administration's response in 1925–27 to reports of over lending. Committed to marketplace control of capital flows, administration officials courted panic if they leveled with investors. In sum, America's investments and own financial stability stood hostage to investor confidence and German policy.

Germans, especially Hjalmar Schacht, exploited American vulnerability. Although he helped negotiate the Young Plan, Schacht, a twentieth-century Talleyrand, soon repudiated it. Later dubbed a wizard when he conjured up the finances for Hitler's public works and rearmament program, Schacht's expertise and imagination were exceeded only by his ambitions and wiliness. In October 1930, he conducted an American lecture tour. He made some forty addresses, blaming Germany's economic problems and the Nazis' rise on reparations, lack of colonies, and Versailles. He suggested that Americans protect their investments and moderate government in Germany by seeking an end to reparations.

He advanced another proposal, which foreshadowed John Maynard Keynes's theories. Schacht pointed to the problem of the liquidity trap[51] and emphasized that central banks could create new money without serious inflation as long as unemployment persisted. He suggested that central banks form an international authority to finance "new markets" in the underdeveloped world. The plan harked back to the "hothoused" trade that Young had hoped would develop out of the Dawes Plan and Schacht had pushed for the BIS. Only with access to such a new economic frontier, Schacht insisted, could Germany pay reparations. This was an ingenious proposal by which capital-rich nations like America and France would finance German penetration of new markets and counter growth of closed-door colonial systems. A few months later, the British advanced the Kindersley Plan, which similarly demanded that America and France transform their idle gold into international loans to restart the world economy. Both these plans fell flat because they went far beyond what American financial and political leaders considered acceptable change. These schemes pointed up the growing differences between the conservative Americans and the increasingly desperate Germans and British, who were ready to move beyond marketplace orthodoxy to stimulate growth.[52]

Despite Schacht's private status, the German government approved his visit and revisionist message. In a major policy address on October 16, 1930, Brüning questioned whether Germany could fulfill the Young Plan.[53]

To Americans, German instability seemed part of the global threat of revolution. Discouraged, Stimson counted "the seventh Latin-American revolution, six of them successful, since this administration took office." The New York *World* described the Nazis' electoral victory as "an outburst ... similar to recent overturns in Latin America." Listing "reasons for pessimism," a Morgan partner included "chronic revolution" and "epidemic revolution." An American diplomat in Berlin warned that the Nazis regarded themselves as "revolutionar[ies]." In early 1933, Hoover characterized Hitler's regime as "monarchical and reactionary," and "very radical."[54]

For most of the 1930–33 period, American leaders viewed the Nazis as a force for chaos, similar to the Bolsheviks. Consul George Messersmith drew a parallel between Hitler and Lenin rather than between Hitler and Mussolini. The Nazi and Communist threats in Germany were linked, Ambassador Sackett explained. After the Nazis' inevitable "failure," the ambassador feared, the radical faction under Goebbels and Strasser "would immediately group itself with the Communists and . . . plunge the country into a national Communism of a disastrous type." Chancellor Brüning was "a strong bulwark" against such dangers, Stimson hoped.[55] Brüning played on such fears to justify revision of the status quo.

Washington officials approved Germany's Austrian customs union proposal of March 1931 because it seemed a peaceful way to help central Europe economically and rectify one of Versailles's errors. Brüning, however, saw the venture as primarily political. Close economic ties would keep Austria from joining any French-sponsored group and lead to political union. This would boost the chancellor's popularity at home and further undermine the Versailles order. Some German Foreign Office analysts expected that Czechoslovakia would gravitate toward the German-Austrian union, thus isolating Poland and improving chances for corridor revision. Although Austro-German negotiations began in 1927, Berlin sprang the proposal suddenly, antagonizing London as well as Paris and Rome.

Despite Allied disapproval, Hoover, Stimson, and Julius Klein, the president's long-time economic adviser, favored the plan. A customs union for central Europe had figured in American thinking since 1918. The project would "benefit people who were good custsomers of ours," Stimson declared. This blessing was limited, however, by a central dilemma of American policy. The unilateral announcement without prior Allied approval set a destabilizing precedent. Stimson and Hoover worried that "the repercussions of Germany's actions on our Naval Treaties and on our efforts for peace might be quite bad."[56] Nor would they risk intervention to overturn the Allied veto.

Hoover could not afford such aloofness when the German financial crisis broke in June 1931. On May 11, the Kreditanstalt, a pillar of Austrian finance, announced severe losses. This signaled the failure of Allied and American efforts since 1919 to prop up the truncated state. When France refused further loans until Vienna repudiated the customs union proposal, the Bank of England and BIS supplied the money. "Austria stood up like a man," Stimson cheered, "and told France to go to Hell."[57] Disgusted with French rigidity, the secretary sympathized with what seemed peaceful, sensible Versailles revision. Financial panic soon resumed and spread to Germany. On May 26, the Berlin stock market plummeted, and German murmurs about ending reparations grew louder. Although Hoover hoped the United States economy would pick up in May, it too nosed down. "This slump was a crushing one to the President," Stimson observed. Prospects for domestic recovery faded as the international situation worsened. "We were tied up with Germany's situation," the secretary told the president. Hoover was more cautious, but he agreed "that we, of course, are vitally interested."[58]

Entangled in the German problem, Hoover and Stimson concluded after agonizing debate that they had to act. They aimed to preserve America's creditor position, stimulate economic recovery, and control change. Stimson, Hoover, and others stressed that the crisis was fundamentally a "psycholog[ical]" one, a matter of "influenc[ing] public opinion here and abroad." War debts and reparations were dwarfed by trade and capital movements and were not "the source of our troubles," concluded Owen Young, Parker Gilbert, and Ogden Mills. However, "the fact that people believe them to be important makes them so."Economic theory also suggests that the political debts had impact beyond their dollar amounts. According to the trade-capital-asset view of international transmission of economic forces, war debts and reparations may have aggravated Germany's difficulty in obtaining foreign capital, America's reduction in foreign lending, and the rising demand for gold, which depressed prices.[59]

The political debts were also emotionally charged symbols of the conflict and sacrifice since 1914. Attention centered on this issue because it was an aspect of the world's ills which governments—in particular the most powerful one—could directly affect. Pressure by New York bankers was an important factor pushing Hoover toward a political debt moratorium. Thomas Lamont emphasized the "fantastic total" of American credits and the need for the "courage-giver" of a moratorium. Hoover did not carry out bankers' orders. Rather, he shared their analysis that a German crisis would cripple America. The administration had to intervene, State Department economic adviser Herbert Feis explained, "to save the financial and perhaps political order in Germany" and prevent "a crash of important banking houses here." The situation demanded that America act prior to and independent of Germany and the Allies. If Germany declared a reparations moratorium, investors would panic. If the Allies seized the initiative, they would shape revision so as to burden the United States.[60]

For all these reasons, Hoover, worried about the prospects of the domestic economy and his own reelection, gambled on a government debt moratorium. The desire for maximum psychological impact ruled out extensive prior consultation with Europe. A newspaper leak of such negotiations would spoil the surprise effect. In mid-June Hoover conferred with congressional leaders. When senator William King (Democrat, Utah) released a hostile version of the plan on the nineteenth, Hoover cursorily notified the Allies and then dramatically announced a one-year suspension of war debts and reparations. Although the president made war debt relief conditional on a parallel reparation concession by the Allies, he denied any connection between the two sets of debts. Similarly, Hoover's moratorium ignored the Young Plan's relief procedure, yet he intended the measure to strengthen the existing financial order.

These contradictions haunted the president for the rest of his administration, but initially the moratorium seemed to work. "The psychology is completely changed," Stimson enthused. Stock markets around the world jumped, and the press excitedly reported a surge of exports.

The curve of Hoover's political fortunes also swung upward. Pro-administration newspapers welcomed the "return of the wartime Hoover whom the country so much admired."[61] Indeed, the moratorium announcement fit the pattern of Hoover's prepresidential successes as an above-politics administrator. After agonizing analysis with his staff, the president launched a carefully tailored, well-advertised offensive.

Amidst this enthusiasm, France reacted with what the German ambassador reported as "extraordinarily great agitation, ill-humor, and nervousness"[62] Paris, the other great creditor power, was peeved at Washington's unilateral, deus ex machina action. As chief defender of the status quo, France feared that America's bypassing of the Young Plan poked another hole in the Versailles order. The financial effect of the moratorium benefited America far more than France. Per capita, France's sacrifice on the political debts equaled America's. Yet private French investments in Germany totaled only one-ninth of America's. As one French deputy noted, America's moratorium sacrificed 6 billion francs to safeguard 250 billion francs in private investments.[63]

Although Hoover asked the French to accept immediately "to help the psychology of the situation," Paris held out until July 6. France wanted to limit revision by obtaining political concessions from Germany and safeguarding the Young Plan. Washington and London condemned this injection of politics into the financial crisis. Then the Anglo-Saxons asked for "voluntary" German concessions in return for reparations relief. The British wanted abandonment of the customs union proposal, and the Americans begged Berlin not to build a planned pocket battleship. The latter request was not political intervention, the State Department rationalized, but a legitimate American concern, since it affected disarmament. Realizing that Anglo-American economic interests required a debt moratorium, Brüning rejected the pleas.[64]

German resistance demonstrated that the Anglo-Saxons could not fine-tune the pace of revision. The antirevisionist forces fared better with regard to the Young Plan. France won American approval of a scheme whereby Germany paid the unconditional annuities into the BIS, which then reloaned the money to Germany.

These negotiations both intensified Hoover's Francophobia and illustrated the underlying cooperation between the White House and Wall Street. "We are all fed up with the French," Hoover exploded to Lamont. He ordered the banker to "get the French in line." Lamont tried to explain the French view, but recorded that he "always backed up the President's argument to the limit" when talking with Paris.[65]

Despite these efforts, the moratorium did not stop the slide. The bloom of public confidence withered. On July 3 Germany suffered a domestic banking crisis, which hastened foreign credit withdrawals. Hoover learned that the German short-term foreign debt amounted to over $5 billion, including much of the capital of America's leading banks. He feared "wholesale bank failures." Yet he could say "not a word to the American people," he recalled, "lest I precipitate runs." Hoover had wrestled with this dilemma since 1925, but now the problem had become "a question of saving ourselves." Although Hoover stayed at the helm during this crisis, he delegated much of the actual negotiations to Stimson, who at the end of June went to Europe to prepare for the 1932 disarmament conference. Stimson's talks demonstrated, first, how economic, political, and military factors melded together, and second, as one newspaper put it, that "we are back in Europe up to our ears."[66]

Disarmament and Financial Crisis

The galloping financial crisis overturned American hopes for an orderly passage to prosperity and stability. European differences widened. Germany's demands for treaty revision rose as its economy sank. Desperate to lessen economic burdens, some Britons looked to wholesale financial and political revision. France distrusted Germany's laments and Britain's fidelity, and stood firm against treaty revision or disarmament.

Disarmament was the key in the jam, Hoover and Stimson believed. The European economy would recover if freed from the armaments burden. The Allies would not grant further reparations relief without a war debt reduction. This, too, required European disarmament, since neither the administration nor Congress wanted the Allies to spend on arms money saved on debts. The League of Nations' called for an international conference in early 1932 offered a chance.

Despite fear of European entanglements, Hoover and Stimson realized that they could not remain entirely aloof and still promote disarmament. Hoover did not dispute Stimson's conclusion that "the only way we can get at the question of European peace with disarmament, is to get at the underlying problems which lie between France and Germany. Those are the real problems of a general disarmament conference, *the question of the revision of the Versailles treaty. On that point the question of disarmament and European peace lie hitched together and they also closely touch the economic depression.*" Thus, Stimson went to Europe intending "to force the nations of Europe to settle their . . . political disputes before the [disarmament] conference."[67] The secretary expected to play the role of disinterested mediator, but U.S. intervention was not neutral. Hoover and Stimson sympathized with the demands of Germany—the center of Europe's economy and America's investments—for revision of the Polish corridor. The Hoover administration also conflicted with France by favoring Rome's bid for nominal naval parity.

Consonant with Italo-American friendship, Stimson sailed to Europe on an Italian ship and granted Mussolini the first spot in his itinerary. Il Duce responded by coming to dinner at the American Embassy. "Everybody was all agog," Stimson recorded, since this was Mussolini's first official appearance in any embassy. After the dictator piloted the Stimsons "for a spin" in his speed boat, his guests decided they "both liked him very much." More substantively, Mussolini and Dino Grandi, his pro-American foreign minister, praised the debt moratorium and promised to cooperate in the disarmament conference. Stimson agreed to urge France to reach a naval arms accord with Italy. Since the Italians were asking the French to concede parity, pressure for a settlement would probably help Rome.[68]

As Stimson traveled from Rome to Paris, London suffered huge gold and foreign exchange withdrawals. British officials called an emergency conferencne to meet in London. In this storm Hoover and Stimson tried to protect U.S. investments while instilling in Europeans a sense of confidence and compromise. Hoover's approach repeated that of the debt moratorium: sudden presentation at the conference of a detailed American plan. Specifically, the president recommended a standstill agreement by which Germany's short-term creditors would agree not to withdraw their money. He wanted private and central bankers to implement this plan, following the 1920s policy of insulating the United States government from direct responsibility. This scheme offered financial relief to Germany without further loans and closed out discussion of more extensive financial revision.

Getting the Europeans to accept this plan was difficult. Hans Luther, the Reichsbank president, made a spectacle of Germany's financial frailty by flying from capital to capital in an unsuccessful bid for further loans. The French Government offered the Germans money, but only in return for a ten-year acceptance of the political status quo. In contrast, Montagu Norman and the British Treasury hoped to parlay the crisis into wholesale financial and treaty revision.

On Hoover's orders, Stimson, who at first considered further loans, told Berlin to "buck-up" and "turn to courage and self-help."[69] Americans did not regard these as empty words. Stimson emphasized the supreme importance of "psychology" since the Europeans were "all scared to death." Dissatisfied with Berlin's public relations, Hoover asked Sackett to help Brüning "advertise." Sackett edited some speeches of Brüning and other officials and the result, Stimson noted, was "a good deal of favorable publicity." Yet Stimson and Hoover did not want Berlin, as the secretary put it, to "hide behind our skirts." Instead of depending on American aid, the Germans should aim for lasting stability through reconciliation with France.[70] A Franco-German rapprochment based on moderate treaty revision was central to American hopes for disarmament and financial stability. Thus, on the one hand Stimson warned Brüning about German "militarism" and squelched Norman's plans for wholesale treaty and financial revision at the upcoming London conference—and on the other hand rejected as "immoral" and impractical the French thesis of a ten-year moratorium on treaty revision.[71] The trick was how to promote gradual change and protect American interests.

Hoping to safeguard United States investments in Germany, Washington launched a publicity blitz to sell what the newspapers proclaimed the latest "Hoover Plan." Administration leaders brimmed over with optimism that this standstill agreement "would permit the world to return to the normal conduct of business." The time was long past, however, when Hoover's publicity guaranteed success. Wall Street bankers were pessimistic. The stock and foreign exchange markets remained flat. In Paris, Hoover's public crowing about an American plan worsened Stimson's difficulties. The French still smarted from the President's unilateral moratorium announcement. After harrowing negotiations, the London Conference concluded on July 23 with agreement to renew the $100 million central bank credit to the Reichsbank and establish an international bankers' committee to implement the standstill.[72]

Albert Wiggin, president of the Chase Bank with $190 million in Germany, chaired this group. Just as the governments threw the German financial problem to the bankers, the bankers in their August 18 report threw it back. The Wiggin Report provided for the standstill, but emphasized that the lasting solution required reduction of reparations and war debts.[73]

The agreement to leave the credits in Germany helped Berlin, but hurt London, the next weakest financial link. The standstill froze $300 million of British money. Worse, it tied up the assets of other Europeans, who now pulled funds out of London to regain liquidity. Confidence in the pound plummeted with the publication on July 13 of the *Macmillan Report*'s statistics on London's huge short-term liabilities. On July 31, Parliament's May Committee aggravated the fright with the announcement of a large government deficit. In August, American and French banks loaned London $650 million, but the run on the pound continued. Meanwhile Norman, frustrated in his attempts to overturn Versailles and the political debts and overcome by Britain's crisis, had "broken down under pressure,"[74] MacDonald informed Stimson.

While Norman sailed to Maine to recuperate, the world economy suffered the deflationary impact of the pound's collapse. London officials tried to restore foreign confidence by cutting public spending and raising interest rates. This was the orthodox prescription to deflate the economy and bolster the currency. Berlin went the same route to save the mark and demonstrate the impossibility of reparations. Countries believed they had to endure this pain to minimize currency sales by citizens and foreigners. Thus, financial scares in Berlin and London generated deflationary shock waves that aggravated the decline in other countries. As Britain demonstrated, the deflationary burden often weighed most heavily on public workers and the unemployed.

Although Britain's outlay for unemployment relief (the dole) amounted to 10 percent of the budget and interest for the national debt consumed 50 percent, conservative officials in America and England focused on the former as the unnecessary expense. Disturbed by the veterans' bonus agitation in the United States, Castle and other State Department officials found the dole a similar inducement to "idleness." Cutting the dole was better than cutting bond interest rates. "God knows this 'bond holding class' has been hit hard enough," Castle commented.[75] State Department officials did not translate such views into official policy. Yet J. P. Morgan and George L. Harrison made loans to the Labour government conditional on a budget reduction program acceptable to British bankers and the Conservative and Liberal parties. When MacDonald tried to pin responsibility for specific budget cuts on Morgan and Harrison, the bankers shrewdly backed off and reiterated that they would accept any program acceptable to British bankers. No conspiracy existed, but the Americans understood and shared their British colleagues' prejudice against the dole.[76] With backing from the bankers and the other political parties, MacDonald cut unemployment benefits by 10 percent, a step that the Labour left wing and its union allies rejected. Thereupon the Labour party split. MacDonald formed a National government with Conservative and Liberal backing, and the new government slashed the budget.[77]

Despite these sacrifices, the run on the pound continued. On September 18, desperate London officials asked Washington and New York for a large additional loan. Hoover, Stimson, Mellon, Lamont, and Harrison agreed that further banking credits were impossible and governmental aid required congressional action. Asking for relief to London, Stimson told the British, would "release a flood of legislation for domestic relief." As Stimson's remark illustrated, antirelief, antiexpansionary policies ricocheted between the domestic and foreign spheres.

Then the secretary of state gave directions for Britain to follow to get war debt relief. This formula remained the Hoover administration's policy until it left office. First Germany, following Young Plan procedures, should ask for relief. After reducing reparations, the Allies should singly ask Washington to consider their reduced capacities to pay. Stimson warned that the Balfour Note, the basis of British policy since 1922, was still unacceptable. Under this policy, Britain passed on to its debtors any relief it obtained from America. This united the debtors against America and benefited France, which the Hoover administration believed was already too strong financially.[78]

Meanwhile, British officials on September 21 gave up the gold standard. With typical British understatement, the acting head of the Bank of England explained "that in 1914 they had many powers which they do not now possess."[79] Many of those powers had passed to New York, which in the 1920s had refused to restructure the international financial system so as to buttress London's weakened position.

The New Sterling Bloc

As Harvey's long perspective suggested, Britain's leaving the gold standard was a turning point in twentieth-century history. It signaled the end of the 1920s' stable exchange rates and easy international capital movements. It ushered in the 1930s' disorder of competitive devaluation, chaotic exchanges, and economic blocs. Only after years of depression and world war did the global economy again come together under American hegemony—this time under the firmer, though no more permanent, system of Bretton Woods, established in 1944. Britain's departure from gold undermined the American-dominated postwar order, as did Japan's invasion of Manchuria three days earlier and Germany's demand for armament a year later. Going off gold meant giving up the dream of a return to the market-ordered Eden of pre-1914. Yet American and British central bankers had already tried to manipulate the gold standard to avoid inflation or deflation. This prevented the market system from working its harsh efficiency. Coupled with the establishment in 1932 of an imperial preference tariff system, leaving gold enabled Britain to renew the option of pre-1925. Once again it could build an independent sterling bloc to challenge the dollar-dominated gold standard. Although it was financial weakness that drove Britain off gold, leaders turned their position to advantage by seeking, as a worried State Department analyst described it, "a new international deal and a new balance of power."[80]

This new deal featured what a joint committee of the Federation of British Industries (FBI) and the Empire Economic Union (EEU)[81] termed an economic Pax Britannica. This group argued for an "empire monetary and financial policy." The National Government's overwhelming victory on a platform pledging a protective duty cleared the path for imperial preference tariffs. Citing the Macmillan Committee's judgment that the Depression was "primarily a monetary crisis," the FBI-EEU focused on the "maldistribution" of gold owing to American and French balance-of-payment surpluses. Ironically, Britain's huge trade deficit with America equaled 85 percent of the latter's export surplus. "Our free trade policy has, in fact, proved a misfortune for the world as a whole, as well as to ourselves, by handing over the gold, which we should have steadily diffused by consistent overseas investment, to others less capable of using it for world purposes." Since America proved incapable of responsible world leadership and effective international cooperation seemed unlikely, the empire should create an independent system. A sterling bloc might well become the nucleus for a world economic order, the FBI-EEU hoped. The essence of the plan was to "divert" imperial trade "from the United States to this country or to other parts of the Empire."[82]

British financial leaders tried to implement this imperial policy even before they left gold. The day before the suspension, the Bank of England asked the Reichsbank and other central banks to join it. The Germans refused, afraid to isolate themselves from the United States. After leaving gold, Britain continued to recruit. British firms threatened to bar Finnish wood exports unless Finland abandoned the gold standard. Although Greece tried to shift its banking to New York, the influence of London bankers forced it to join the sterling bloc. An American diplomat reported the Swedish view that, financially, "England now has the ball at her feet again." At the Ottawa Conference of July 1932, Britain and its dominions established a system of tariff preferences that discriminated against non-empire producers. By November 1932, the British bloc included some thirteen countries, primarily dominions and trading satellites.[83] Countries joined the sterling bloc to share the export advantage of devaluation. As the pound sank in value, the goods of sterling bloc countries became cheaper in foreign markets. In Palestine, for example, the American consul contrasted the expected "revival of British trade" with the abrupt "cancel[lation] of "American orders."[84]

Rather than scurry back to the gold standard, as Americans expected them to do, the British found life comfortable with a managed currency and a sterling bloc. L. P. Amery, former dominion secretary, described sterling as "a world by itself." By January 1933, British financiers asserted that while the pound was stable, the gold standard currencies were fluctuating.[85] This recalled the apocryphal London headline: "Fog Closes Channel; Continent Cut Off," but it also attested to the success of Britain's independent policy. In April 1933, Franklin D. Roosevelt finally matched London's bet by devaluing the dollar and severing its link with gold.

An ideological attack accompanied the commercial and financial drives. London newspapers ran stories and sent dispatches to the dominions contrasting Britain's economic revival with America's imminent financial collapse. These "malicious rumors," a London embassy official reported, originated chiefly with Montagu Norman. The widespread currency of such stories stemmed from real uncertainty about the dollar, British efforts to bolster the pound, and what one American consul reported as satisfaction "that the people of the United States are now experiencing hard times."[86]

Threatened by Britain's departure from gold, from 1931 to 1933 Americans pushed for a return. Thomas Lamont felt "the worst shock ... since ... 1914." Immediately after the event, Herbert Feis warned of a "socialist regime" and an end to the British Empire's "stabilizing place in the world." Other State Department officials worried about the "growth of really revolutionary sentiment among the masses." The Conservative National victory eased such apprehensions, but some Americans remained concerned about the financial and commercial offensive. State Department officials perceived the United States as "the big outsider ... principally affected" by the imperial preference system. *American Exporter* labeled the rise in imperial tariffs "the Ottawa tragedy."[87]

The abandonment of gold on September 21, 1931 was one of three great shocks that hit Washington almost simultaneously. On September 18, the Japanese invaded Manchuria. This violent, sudden overthrow of the Asian status quo threatened a precedent for Europe. Japanese aggression underscored the necessity for easing tensions through peaceful change, yet ironically it strengthened resistance to such revision. Stimson recited the formula to the Italian ambassador. Although America would not recognize change through "force or war," it also opposed any "strait-jacket against ... peaceful revision."[88] Since Stimson hoped for coop-eration with London on treaty revision, the Far East, and disarmament, he skirted the economic differences that flowed from September 21.

One consequence of that event, however, the Hoover administration had to confront directly. On September 22, the United States suffered the largest gold outflow in its history. In the next five weeks, currency and gold losses mounted to $1.1 billion. More than eight hundred banks failed in September and October. The dollar suffered a similar run the following spring, when American and European investors panicked at the inflationary threats posed by Congress's consideration of the veterans' bonus and refusal to pass a national sales tax.[89] This crisis pointed up the interdependence of the American and world economies and the failure of Hoover's moratorium and standstill to restore prosperity.

Disarmament and Treaty Revision

By late September 1931, the president feared domestic "social trouble." Hypersensitive to congressional criticism and justifiably nervous about reelection, Hoover was reluctant to aid Europe, especially with the budget deficit so large and Europe so uncooperative. The president wanted to "tackl[e] the question of reparations ... and ... war debts," Stimson recorded, but first he had to shore up the domestic banking structure. Hoover turned his attention to what became the Reconstruction Finance Corporation, a government agency that lent money to ailing banks. On September 29, Hoover told Stimson "it would be impossible to get the American people to approve any more sacrifices in Europe unless it was tied up with a plan to alleviate distress in this country."[90]

These domestic and foreign concerns revolved around the issue of Versailles treaty revision. Resentful of foreign debt evaders, Congress would accept war debt reduction only as part of a comprehensive plan to pacify and disarm Europe.[91] Confidence, that elusive psychological genie that the Hoover administration pursued as the key to prosperity, also required European tranquillity. These problems of "finance and armament and politics combined," Stimson concluded, but "the whole situation underneath is political and ... the political obstacles must be solved before ... either the financial or the disarmament." Stimson was more specific when he told Hoover: "The political questions of the East-ern Boundary of Germany underlay the whole question, not only of disarmament but of the economic rehabilitation of Europe and of the whole peace of Europe."[92] The Hoover administration used the visit of French premier Pierre Laval to intervene in the explosive issue of the Polish-German border.[93]

In preparation for the Laval visit, American financial and political leaders reviewed and refined the peaceful change policy. Stimson and Dwight Morrow, a friend of France whom the administration designated to head the disarmament delegation, reiterated the tenets of peaceful change. "The American Government could entirely agree with the French that security was a prerequisite to disarmament; the rub came in the definition of ... 'security.' If the French meant the perpetual freezing of the post-war status quo, including the maintenance of unjust and bitterly resented treaty solutions and a preponderant military force to guarantee it, then we could not agree with them. Our idea of security was a tranquilized Europe, which meant the solution, one by one, and by peaceful means, of the problems that were preventing it from settling down."[94]

Given the intense agitation within Germany, American leaders believed that the Polish corridor was the first such problem. Woodrow Wilson had made a restored Poland with access to the sea one of his Fourteen Points. After 1919, the United States steered an ambivalent course. American technical advisers and businessmen helped build Poland, and officials at first stayed out of its border dispute with Germany. By 1931, however, many Americans had concluded that Germany's stability and Europe's peace were more important than Poland's corridor. As Thomas Lamont put it, "It might settle a lot of things if Germany could have back the darned old Polish corridor." Robert F. Kelley, chief of the State Department's Eastern European desk, believed that the corridor would inevitably be returned to Germany.[95] The Germans cultivated such sentiment. Touring East Prussia as a guest of the German foreign minister, Ambassador Sackett met some "charmingly hospitable" Junkers and afterward described the corridor as "very unfairly designed."[96] Walter Lippmann promoted the idea that Poland should peacefully absorb Lithuania as compensation for surrendering the corridor. Stimson and Hoover considered seriously banker Paul Warburg's suggestion of a German-run elevated railroad across the corridor.[97] The secretary told Polish diplomats that although America was uninvolved in any German-Polish "political questions"—the wording implied that the international border *was* an issue—America was "vitally interested ... that the solution should be by peaceful methods"—phrasing that again leaned toward unarmed Germany.[98]

The Polish corridor was precisely the kind of political issue that the

United States had tried to avoid since 1919. Yet Hoover and Stimson believed that political tranquillity in Europe was essential to economic recovery. At least one figure close to the Hoover administration suggested a solution that harked back to the successful approach of the 1920s, that is, an expert, economic inquiry. Although a Democrat, Norman Davis staunchly defended Republican policies at the 1927 Geneva Economic Conference and the 1932 General Disarmament meeting. In the fall of 1931, Davis was the unofficial American member of the League Financial Committee. In a conversation with the German foreign minister, Davis doubted that the United States would participate in a conference to revise the Versailles treaty; yet it might attend a meeting that considered the Polish border as an issue whose resolution was necessary to "get the world definitely back on its feet at peace and at work." A variant on this business approach to political revision, Davis continued, would be for the league to appoint a "committee" with American representation to examine the issue. Then "it would be politically possible for the governments concerned to make concessions which would be more difficult in any direct negotiations." Davis envisioned some compromise of shared sovereignty over the corridor or guaranteed German access to East Prussia.[99] Davis's idea reflected American success with this approach in the 1920s; yet in the 1930s political tensions were too tight to accommodate a business solution.

Although the British and French governments had considered revision of the corridor in the 1920s, they had been unable to move the Poles.[100] Alarmed by growing revisionist sentiment in America, Marshall Józef Piłsudski in October 1931 sent what Stimson termed "an ultimatum" to "keep hands off the Polish Corridor." If Warsaw's rights "were tampered with," the Polish representative warned, "she would defend them by force, treaties or no treaties." This was "a typical Polish production," Stimson sniffed, "characteristic of the wretched little troublemaker."[101] The exchange demonstrated the depth of American feeling about peaceful change and the difficulty of achieving it.

In conversation with Laval on October 23, Hoover defied the Polish "ultimatum" and "plung[ed] into the ... political questions of Central Europe." Instability in that quarter, Hoover asserted, "affected ... disarmament and ... the depression." The corridor was only "a local condition" that blocked Franco-German harmony, Stimson told Laval. The "oscillations of history" demanded revision of the "extreme" peace settlement. France should pressure Poland to compromise with Germany. Laval admitted that the corridor was an "absurdity," but insisted that changing it was "a political impossibility." Appeasement would "only whet Germany's appetite."[102] Given America's unwillingness to become politically entangled in Europe and its reduced economic leverage over the Continent, French opposition doomed the peaceful change policy.

Differences with Laval over treaty revision led to conflict over disarmament. French policy demanded security (a guarantee of the status quo) as the prerequisite to disarmament; the American stance was that French security demanded a pacified, contented Germany. Americans opposed any guarantee of the status quo because they believed moderate change was inevitable and desirable and they did not equate French security with American security. This was not because the United States lacked vital interests in Europe. Rather, those vital concerns pertained to the peace and prosperity of Europe as a whole—Americans did not assume that if they became involved in another European war, it would be on the French side. Thus although Stimson, with Hoover's lukewrm support, considered restricting U.S. neutrality rights so as not to benefit a future aggressor, neither official contemplated a security guarantee to France or to any other European nation. Moreover, in the Franco-Italian naval arms dispute, Stimson took the side of Rome. "France was more in the wrong than Italy," Stimson told Laval, "and the concessions ought to come from France." The secretary did not record Laval's response, but when the Frenchman suggested that an American "promise of consultation" in the event of war would promote disarmament, Hoover replied that this was "a political impossibility." Discouraged by French intransigence on the Polish border and disarmament issues, Stimson did not even mention to Laval the possibility of a change in American neutrality policy.

Despite the impasse on political and disarmament issues, America and France—the two major creditor and gold standard powers—agreed on a formula to reduce the political debts. Germany would ask the BIS to convene the expert relief committee provided for in the Young Plan. This was financial revision, but within the confines of the postwar treaty structure. Hoover would then ask Congress to recreate the World War Foreign Debt Commission (WWFDC) to negotiate bilateral agreements to reduce war debts. Although most of the president's advisers wanted a permanent debt reduction, his formula was for relief only during the Depression. The Hoover-Laval accord was "subject of course to Congress'" approval. This reservation proved portentous.[103] Given congressional sniping and European intransigence, treaty revisionism was dangerous business, and the already beleaguered Hoover administration publicly denied that it had proposed corridor revision.

Senator William Borah illustrated the explosive possibilities with a public interview in which he predicted treaty revision "either by peace or by force" and denounced the German and Hungarian borders as particularly unjust. Revision was prerequisite to disarmament and war debt relief. The United States could not ignore these problems, the senator insisted, since "we are economically affected by the situation in Europe and will continue to be." Borah, who had discussed these issues with Stimson, publicly echoed the private Laval conversations. The domestic reaction was loud and divided. Europeans vehemently praised and pilloried the senator, demonstrating that American intervention in such issues meant entanglement in age-old hatreds. German newspapers crowed: "United States attacks Versailles Treaty" while Poles labeled the senator "a German agent." Borah's name was cheered by Prussians celebrating the seven hundredth anniversary of the Teutonic Knights' conquest of Poland. Adolf Hitler welcomed the end of Washington's "political isolationism" and praised Borah's "genuine Americanism."[104] Americans' public and private prodding yielded noise and protest, but no revision. Stimson complained that despite United States urging that Europeans make the compromises necessary for disarmament, "they hadn't done it."[105]

Stimson was pleased, however, that the flurry of diplomacy and visits "cement[ed] Italy to us." Hoover welcomed the November visit of Foreign Minister Dino Grandi as "a foil to the French." Italy shared the American thesis of moderate revision, Grandi told his hosts. He assured Americans that fascism "had nothing in common with" the radical Nazis and explained that Italy desired close relations with "the most powerful nation in the world." Stimson reiterated hopes for corridor revision and a reparations reduction, promising that war debt relief would follow.[106] Despite the Italo-American accord, the dilemma of peaceful change remained.

Nineteen thirty-one's disappointments exposed the basic elements that comprised American foreign relations for the remainder of the Hoover administration. In 1932–33, Hoover and Stimson continued their uneasy partnership, annoyed by each other's ideas and temperaments but usually able to reach a working agreement. The domestic and international economies spiraled ever downward. As the crisis worsened, the intertwined economic, political, and military stands tightened further, knotting domestic and international affairs. The middle road of peaceful revision became increasingly narrow with nazism's rise. This new threat of upheaval amplified Japan's challenge of the existing order, and in late 1932 American policy swung closer to the French thesis of upholding the status quo. Growing domestic problems also choked international cooperation.

Hoover and Stimson, like every nation's leaders, were unwilling to make domestic sacrifices without a promise of greater return from the foreign sphere. Specifically, Hoover had to balance the domestic budget deficit against war debt relief, United States naval strength against disarmament prospects, and American freedom of action against European security. Other factors aggravated these dilemmas. Committed to the existing distribution of wealth in the United States, American leaders feared that international debt relief or default would endanger domestic debtor-creditor relationships. Nervousness about a run on the dollar led Hoover to seek a tax increase and increased his resistance to the veterans' bonus. Opposed to direct domestic relief, administration leaders could not go to Congress for European relief. Thus, deflationary, antirelief policies bounced between the domestic and international arenas.

Domestic and foreign problems aggravated one another in other ways. Congress challenged the president's policy on war debts, taxes, farm policy, and domestic relief, especially after the Republican defeat in the 1930 elections. Gone were the happy days of the 1920s when the administration enjoyed wide latitude in its economic, unofficial diplomacy so long as it steered clear of explosive, yet irrelevant issues such as League of Nations membership.[107]

Hard pressed, Hoover sometimes talked about America's potential economic self-sufficiency. Yet such statements were chiefly public relations ploys to bolster confidence. The president was of course concerned primarily with the nation's domestic welfare, but he never implemented a comprehensive plan to insulate the American economy from the rest of the world. A State Department statistical analysis concluded that conversion to self-sufficiency was possible, but at the cost of "ten years of depression and governmental appropriations of $500,000,000. annually." It is uncertain whether Hoover ever read this document, but he did not believe that America's social stability could endure a long strain. The American people "are nearing the end of their patience," he told the cabinet in late November 1932.[108]

Despite continual emphasis on world recovery, pressing domestic crisis at times forced Hoover, and to a lesser extent Stimson, to ignore foreign problems. In late December 1931, they "agreed," Stimson recorded, that the "first" priority was shoring up the domestic banking structure.[109] Such isolation was only temporary. After Hoover put through the Reconstruction Finance Corporation (RFC) and the Glass-Steagall Act, he again focused on disarmament and debt relief as the avenues to prosperity and stability.

Such recovery was essential to combat the mushrooming political opposition that threatened to defeat Hoover in November. Sensitive to the mildest criticism, the president endured constant ridicule, even revilement. He increasingly measured foreign policies according to their impact on voters. His reelection was "necessary for the country," he insisted to Stimson. Hoover's failure with voters was part of his greater failure to shape public opinion, as he had done so successfully from 1917 to 1928. Unable to lead public opinion, he became its victim, tensely waiting reaction to each heavy-handed announcement. Hoover's inability to generate trust and support was especially ironic in light of his conviction that confidence was the essential ingredient to prosperity.

In 1932–33 these dilemmas and difficulties shaped the plot of what Stimson called the "Greek tragedy" of world affairs.[110] The theatre for this performance was a series of conferences at Geneva, Lausanne, and London.[111] The Geneva Disarmament Conference opened in February 1932 and dragged on for more than a year as the powers failed to reconcile French needs for security with German demands for arms equality. Hoover had always insisted that disarmament was a prerequisite to war debt relief. Ignoring this condition, at the Lausanne conclave of June–July 1932 the Allies virtually canceled reparations subject to America doing the same with war debts. This defied Washington's long-standing policy against any linkage of the two sets of debts. As chances for war debt collection faded, Hoover tried to trade this depreciating asset for increased farm exports, a return to gold, or disarmament. In preparation for the 1933 London Economic Conference, he linked these economic, political, and military issues in hopes for a comprehensive solution to the international depression, instability, and tension. The transcendent question remained the pace and nature of change in an increasingly unstable world.

Politics, Debts, and Disarmament

After six years of preparation, the Geneva Disarmament Conference met at an unhappy time for peace. During its tenure Japan bombarded Shanghai, the Nazis assumed power, and the Depression got worse. Since the Europeans had not resolved their underlying political differences, the Americans were not optimistic. Although Stimson was the nominal chief of the delegation, he remained in Washington for most of the negotiations. The main United States representatives were Hugh Gibson, veteran Hoover assistant and disarmament expert, and Norman Davis, undersecretary of state for Woodrow Wilson and troubleshooter for the Republicans.

The chief issue before the conference was Germany's demand for equal treatment in arms limitation. This meant either fulfilling the Allied pledge of 1919 to disarm down to Germany's level or allowing Germany to rearm. The Americans and British urged the first thesis, pointing at France, the most heavily armed military power. France demanded a guarantee of security before it disarmed and pointed back at the Anglo-Saxons' large navies. This touched the basic issue of whether Versailles treaty revision or enforcement could better prevent renewed German aggression. Norman Davis told André Tardieu, French premier, that France needed "moral and not military strength"—what Borah termed peace resting on contentment rather than force.[112]

The conference quickly stalemated. France reacted angrily, stepping up gold withdrawals from America and expanding its quota import system. Yet France suffered budget and balance-of-payments difficulties and shuddered at the thought of being left alone with Germany. In mid-March 1932, Paris signaled a desire to break the impasse. Davis urged Washington officials to increase United States involvement in the conference. Hoover and Stimson could afford to redirect attention to Europe since the Far Eastern crisis had cooled, and Congress had passed the RFC and the Glass-Steagall Act. Herbert Feis, State Department economic adviser, warned that these domestic banking measures were unable to restore prosperity without renewed European stability and American exports. On April 5, Hoover announced that the secretary of state would go to Geneva.[113]

Stimson was determined to get France and Germany talking about their underlying political differences and to line up Europe's support against further Japanese aggression. In the latter effort he sidetracked British resistance by appealing to the dominions. "It was like talking to your own country," he enthused after conferences with New Zealand and South African officials.[114] Worried about a Japanese attack, the Russian delegate appealed to America for cooperation.

Davis, who claimed to have written the 1920 memorandum on which Bainbridge Colby based the nonrecognition policy, replied that if Russia wanted to "play the game," it must first "get rid" of the Third International.[115]

Stimson was far more sympathetic with Germany's problems. Germany did not expect France to disarm down to its low level, Chancellor Brüning stressed. It would settle for some French disarmament, recognition of Berlin's theoretical right to arms equality, and small adjustments in the military restrictions. Pleased with Brüning's apparent moderation, Stimson and MacDonald believed that such Versailles revision and French disarmament would satisfy Germany's grievances. The Americans and British hoped this constituted a solid basis for Franco-German agreement.

However, since such direct talks had to await the upcoming French elections, Stimson decided to return to the United States. He was careful to conserve America's prestige or moral power by rationing intervention. "The spectacle of the American Secretary of State hanging around during these ... delays," he feared, "will ... diminish the influence of our country."[116] Despite Stimson's hopes, however, Franco-German differences kept the conference stalled.

Meanwhile, domestic politics and political debts complicated disarmament. "The situation in Geneva has touched bottom," Davis warned Washington at the end of May 1932. Hoover wanted to break the stalemate with a dramatic disarmament initiative, as Hughes had done in 1921. Worried about the Far East, Stimson and the navy chiefs opposed this sacrifice. Hoover was also looking for a way to bolster domestic confidence and his own election chances. "A sensational speech on disarmament," coupled with dramatic naval savings, he told the cabinet, "might give new hope ... to ... the world."[117] Such psychological improvement would soon translate into economics. Stimson agreed with this analysis, but "doubt[ed] ... whether this Conference could be dramatized" sufficiently. Nor did he want to reduce the navy.[118] The president went ahead with his plan, hoping to win voters and defuse resentment over the Lausanne meeting on reparations and war debts.

European and congressional obstinance crippled the administration's war debt policy. In the fall of 1931, Hoover and Stimson told the British and French first to reduce reparations and armaments. Then the United States would respond with war debt relief. As the British ambassador put it, this amounted to "Open your mouth and shut your eyes and see what I will give you."[119] In December 1931, Congress refused to resurrect the WWFDC and rejected the idea of war debt relief. At Lausanne, the Allies nearly eliminated reparations, a step the administration feared would overstrengthen Germany and accelerate revision. Trapped, Hoover advised the Allies to disarm. Perhaps then Congress would relent on war debts. Without such disarmament, Hoover warned, "Heaven help the British and French when they come to America about their debts next December."[120]

The interplay of disarmament, debt, and domestic political factors meant that once again American leaders shaped policy with the intent of influencing public opinion. Counting on a dramatic response to his disarmament plan, Hoover worried that hostile newspapers would leak "antagonistic publicity." As with the debt moratorium announcement, these fears propelled the president to act with insufficient notice to other powers. Predictably, the British foreign secretary was "extremely upset."[121] Hoover's manifesto fit the pattern of deus ex machina diplomacy, in which America momentarily descended from an aloof position and pointed Europe down the road to salvation.[122]

Hoover's June 22 plan was a bolt out of the blue. He proposed an abolition of offensive weapons such as tanks and bombers and proportionate reduction of all defensive land, air, and naval forces. This answered Germany's demand for Allied disarmament while assuaging French fears of future attack. Realizing that Gallic cooperation was essential to disarmament, Hoover also proposed leaving defense fortifications intact. Because the Hoover plan sacrificed United States naval strength, other nations initially found it difficult to oppose. Although all the Geneva delegates genuflected before the proposal, Grandi of Italy was the "real star of the day," Gibson reported. Mussolini claimed naval parity with France, but could not afford to match French expenditures. In a speech to the conference, Grandi quoted Hoover's plan point by point and after each dramatically declared: "Italy accepts." This met "uproarious applause which we have never heard at a League meeting," Gibson cabled. Such enthusiasm doubtless reflected genuine longing for disarmament; but when the clapping ceased, great power maneuvering resumed. Italy, Germany, and Russia remained the only major powers to accept Hoover's plan. Irked by the president's precipitous action, Britain and France insisted on diluting the scheme. At Stimson's urging, Hoover backed off, and the United States agreed on July 23 to a weakened plan that adjourned the conference for six months. Germany and Russia denounced this retreat. The German government, now under Chancellor Franz von Papen, made future participation conditional on acceptance of Germany's theoretical right to arms equality.[123]

This was the first important German-American split on disarmament since the war, and it signaled growing divergence between the two powers. Brüning's gamble to contain extremist pressures with foreign policy successes failed. In early June 1932, President Paul von Hindenburg had replaced Brüning with Papen, an archconservative Catholic Centrist. Hindenburg acted on influence from army officers and other conservatives impatient with Brüning's moderation and distrustful of the chancellor's ties with the Social Democrats. A military attaché in Washington in 1915, Papen had been under indictment for plotting to destroy a canal. Hindenburg's appointment of a man who could be arrested if he visited America testified to Germany's reduced concern for friendship with a county no longer the source of loans and inspiration and committed to only slow, moderate revision.[124]

"I can't understand it!" Stimson groaned. After Brüning's fall, America and the other Western powers felt less compelled to appease Berlin in order to bolster moderate government. Publication in May 1932 of Stresemann's private correspondence revealed his broad revisionist ambitions, further disillusioning Westerners. State Department analysts feared that Papen's ascendancy signaled the transition to a Hohenzollern monarch, a Nazi takeover, or both.[125]

Yet the aristocratic chancellor was not Hitler, and he, too, needed foreign policy success to stave off the Nazis. At Lausanne, Papen reaped Brüning's harvest when the Allies agreed to slash reparations. Yet this was not the total cancellation Germans wanted, and when Papen returned to Berlin he was pelted with rotten eggs and denounced by the Nazis.[126] This experience only reinforced his demands for equal armament rights.

Even as Germany's demands accelerated after June 1932, American enthusiasm for such change decelerated. "The old Prussian spirit is coming up," Stimson believed, "and we have a new very dangerous sore spot in the world." The secretary still sought a middle way between revolutionary upheaval and the sterile rigidity that could prove equally explosive. It was sometimes "necessary to modify a treaty in the interests of justice and fairness," he lectured the Italian ambassador, but such change "should be made not by violence or by threats or by breaking the treaty, but by consultation."[127] However, as Germany and Japan proved unwilling or unable to wait for change by consultation, Stimson became increasingly concerned with the sanctity of treaties. His reaction to upheaval fit the pattern established in 1919, when Woodrow Wilson backed off from a balanced version of Article 10 because he feared uncontrolled change.

European and Asian problems intertwined, since hope for French support in the Far East hardened American opposition to German rearmament. The British also wanted to control revision, but were more willing to appease Japan and Germany. "The Americans have been the devils of the piece," growled Stanley Baldwin in September 1932—"turning away from the League, from the Guarantee, collaring the gold."[128] Despite such complaints, Stimson urged Western solidarity to "prevent Germany and Japan from lining up together at Geneva with disastrous consequences to the future of [the] peace treaties." (He and Hoover rebuffed offers of cooperation from Soviet Russia, however.) Worried about the elections, Hoover feared that Stimson's opposition to Berlin would alienate German-American votes. The secretary had his way on this matter, but the president stopped him from moving beyond moral condemnation of Japan.[129] Stimson searched for a way out of the dilemma imposed by Hoover's restrictions, French security demands, and the German-Japanese challenges.

On August 8, 1932, the secretary tackled these problems in a major policy address delivered to the Council on Foreign Relations, which had become a major forum for government and private leaders. Stimson had two interrelated goals: to rally Europe around the Kellogg-Briand Pact as the basis for condemning Japanese aggression and to bolster Europe's security by promising consultation on American neutrality policy in the event of war. He emphasized that the Peace Pact made war illegal and neutrality obsolete. Thus, "consultation between the signatories of the Pact ... becomes inevitable." In other words, if an aggressor broke the peace, the United States would consult with Europe and probably restrict its neutrality rights so as not to interfere with the enforcement of sanctions. Stimson predicted that the United States, which had fathered the pact and invoked it during the Russo-Chinese and Manchurian crises, would continue to organize public opinion. Stimson's strategy was to create precedents for future consultation so as to reassure Europe while avoiding the "trouble in the Senate" that would accompany a formal treaty.[130]

In other words, he tried to assimilate consultation to the pattern of United States informal diplomacy. Consonant with Republican policy since 1921, Stimson committed America to little. He *predicted* that consultation would occur; he did not promise. He invoked the principles of "independence of judgment" and "flexibility of action." He did not say that America would fight an aggressor.[131] This ambiguity was an attempt to bridge the differences between the martial secretary of state and the pacifistic president. The speech also tackled the dilemma of how the United States could exercise power in the world and yet retain its freedom of action. Finally, Stimson's focus on peace rather than peaceful change reflected his increased concern for the status quo.

Because of America's growing resistance to change, the French ambassador and Stimson "had quite a love-feast," the secretary recorded.[132] Correspondingly, relations with Germany hardened. If Berlin's demand for arms equality wrecked disarmament, Castle warned, American reactions would "be very bitterly anti-German." "After all, the Treaty of Versailles ... [is] still in effect," he reminded the Germans. In July, Stimson scolded the Germans for their impatience with peaceful change. "I underst[and] Germany's unwillingness" to be content with Versailles, he told Berlin's ambassador, but it was necessary" to have "a gradual rather than an abrupt transition."[133] Relations with Rome also cooled as Mussolini, disgusted with Geneva's failure and fired by his own revisionist ambitions, dropped Grandi and supported Germany. Stimson warned Il Duce: "I am not inclined ... [to let] Germany go any faster than we had intended."[134] Completing the diplomatic realignment, the Soviet Union now found value in Versailles. Russia favored "maintenance of the *status quo*," explained Karl Radek in a *Pravda* article, since "no peaceful revision is to be hoped for at present."[135]

The Lausanne Conference and the World
Economic Conference

Despite their consensus against wholesale treaty change, America and its former allies differed on financial revision. Since 1919, they had quarreled over the relationship of war debts to reparations. Officially Washington denied any connection, but tacitly it admitted a loose one. Washington always insisted, however, that the Allies bear the political burden of the unpopular debts. In 1924, 1928–29, and 1931–32, Americans indicated that they might reduce war debts, but only after the Allies cut reparations. In the 1920s, Washington gave the Allies the economic benefit of partial cancellation by slashing interest. The Allies reaped little political benefit, however, since Washington emphasized publicly that it was collecting the principal in full.

The Lausanne Conference of June–July 1932 and the Allies' unwillingness to pay the December 1932 installment were closing acts in the debt scenario. Germany needed the economic and political benefits of cancellation. The British believed that cancellation would revive trade and stabilize Europe. London officials also feared that if Germany refused to pay, Britain would be stuck with large payments to America. France wanted to keep the burden on Germany, but feared alienation from Britain. Italy wanted total cancellation of both sets of debts. A European decision on reparations required parallel action by America on war debts. In debt, security, disarmament, and other matters, Europe could no longer act independent of America, as it had before 1914. Trapped between Congress and Europe, Hoover refused to go to Lausanne. Stimson and Lamont begged the Allies not to cancel reparations completely or link them with war debts.

The Europeans spurned this advice, fulfilling Washington's nightmare of a debtors' coalition. In effect, the Allies at Lausanne canceled reparations, but, as a sop to France and America, provided for payment of $750 million sometime in the future. In return, France won England's promise to consult. France tried to magnify this Pact of Confidence into a security arrangement; Britain tried to minimize it by inviting Germany and Italy to join. In a "Gentleman's Agreement," the Allies made reparation cancellation conditional on war debt cancellation. This was "a Hell of a thing," Hoover exploded; "they are trying to 'gang' us."[136] Despite such defiance, the Allies still hoped that America would forgive the war debts, thus sparing them the onus of default. They waited expectantly for the U.S. November elections.

Despite his agonizing effort, Hoover suffered an electoral defeat matched only by his victory four years earlier. He kept fifty-nine electoral votes, little more than one-eighth Franklin D. Roosevelt's total. "Well, it's all over," Lou Hoover sighed on election night.[137] For Herbert Hoover, however, the campaign was not over. He still pursued the genie of public approval and confidence. The president reacted to criticism, Stimson noted in late November, "as if we were still in the campaign."[138] And in fact Hoover had just begun the campaign to win for himself and his administration the approval of history—the public opinion of the future.[139]

The worsening crisis aggravated Hoover's personal depression. Between Hoover's defeat and Roosevelt's inauguration, Hitler assumed power, Allies defaulted, the world economy sagged, and numerous United States banks collapsed.[140]

In this desperate hour Hoover's answer was not self-sufficiency, but a revitalized world economy and foreign trade. "The important thing is to stabilize foreign currencies," the president asserted, echoing his 1922 analysis. He understood that America could no longer deal with each problem separately so as to secure optimal benefits in each area. Hoover sought a comprehensive solution and urged congressional leaders to endorse what Stimson termed a bipartisan "interlocking directorate" to negotiate "in the Disarmament Conference, the Debt Conference and the Economic Conference."[141] He hoped this strategy would commit Roosevelt to an internationalist course and block the national self-sufficiency approach of Raymond Moley and Rexford Tugwell.

Despite his rhetoric about self-sufficiency, Hoover appointed Edmund Day and John Williams delegates to the preparatory commission for the world economic conference. These economists worked from the assumption that America's "vital welfare is at stake in the current world depression." They emphasized the importance of "London's return to gold."[142] Hoover endorsed FRBNY studies demonstrating that American farm prices moved in direct relation to the British pound. As the pound declined, so did U.S. commodity prices. "In attempting to reverse the downward movement of prices," the FRBNY concluded, "measures of an international character will, on the whole, be more effective than purely domestic measures." The United States could not isolate its economy from Europe.[143] Yet how could Hoover persuade the British to give up the benefits of a managed currency and imperial preference?

In the London Economic Conference negotiations, the British refused to return to gold without comprehensive financial reforms, most of which harked back to the 1922 Genoa proposals. Germany focused on private debt relief and expanded markets. France shared America's monetary conservatism, but angered the United States with its discriminatory tariff. And so it went—or rather, the London Conference went nowhere. The basis for international cooperation—too thin in the 1920s—had evaporated. The major powers, including the United States under Roosevelt, each preferred self-centered approaches, which destroyed Hoover's dream of concerted recovery.[144]

Clinging to this dream during his last months in office, Hoover tried to head off the chaotic consequences of a war debt default. Many others also disliked the drastic solutions of default or cancellation. A poll of local chambers of commerce yielded an 18-to-1 margin favoring war debt relief but a 40-to-1 ratio opposed to cancellation.[145] Harvey Bundy, Stimson's assistant, warned of the "very serious [weakening] throughout the world [of] the will of all debtors to pay their debts." Following default, Thomas Lamont warned Stimson, "probably we would see Germany eagerly grasping at private default."[146] Property relationships at home and abroad were inseparable, yet Congress was opposed to war debt relief, which could prevent default.[147] Hoover desperately courted farm support by offering Britain debt concessions in return for expanded purchase of United States agricultural products. London officials refused, since war debts were nearly dead already, and such purchases conflicted with the imperial preference system. At the last moment, Britain, mindful of its worldwide creditor position, paid the December 15, 1932 installment under protest. France, Italy, and most other war debtors defaulted.[148]

The Rise of Hitler

At the close of 1932, the crises of disarmament and German politics also came to a climax. On December 11, the Western powers acknowledged Germany's "equality of [armament] rights in a system which would provide security for all nations." This vague statement settled little, but still amounted to a German victory. Papen did not benefit from this concession, however, since General Kurt von Schleicher had replaced him in November. Schleicher's government marked a further shift to the right, and American officials worried over German extremism. Strong Communist showing in the November 6 election convinced Sackett that Germany needed "a strong centralized more or less military Government."[149] American officials feared that a Nazi takeover, like a Communist one, meant upheaval: treaty repudiation, as Hitler and Hermann Göring promised; social revolution, as Otto Strasser urged, monarchical restoration, as reactionaries wanted; or private loan default, as Nationalist ally Alfred Hugenberg recommended.

Adolf Hitler, taking office on January 30, 1933, tried to soothe such fears. Schacht, the Führer's financial adviser, assured Sackett that "American business in Germany had nothing to fear." The German ambassador—presumably with a straight face—informed Castle that "Hitler had almost a pacifist mentality." Hitler told Norman Davis that Germany preferred international disarmament to rearmament. His nation would honor private debts to the best of its ability. When the Führer then excitedly demanded treaty revision, Davis tried to calm him by pointing to Germany's past success at working "quietly" for moderate change.[150] Although wary, most U.S. officials were not aghast at Hitler's regime. State Department analysts compared the Nazis and the Italian Fascists, with whom the United States had worked so closely.[151] Later, Americans grew disgusted with Hitler's anti-Semitism, bilateral trading, and loan repudiation.[152] But in January–March 1933, Americans believed they could work with Hitler who, Davis hoped, would "withstand the radical leaders in his own Party."[153] Such accommodation contrasted with Hoover's and Stimson's continued nonrecognition of the Soviet Union.

Davis's evaluation of Hitler symbolized American policy's continuity from 1919 to 1933. As economic adviser at Versailles, Davis watched Woodrow Wilson sacrifice flexibility in the League of Nations Covenant for stability in Europe. In 1919, Wilson and Hoover supported right-wing forces in Russia and Rumania to counter the Bolsheviks. After the war, Americans favored reactionaries in Bulgaria, Mussolini in Italy, and the moderate right in Germany. Similarly, the United States pressed Europe to undergo the deflationary rigors of returning to gold and paying war debts. American policy stemmed not from love of right-wing dictatorships or deflation, but from fear of chaos. The search for order led Americans in 1919 to support Social Democrats and in 1933 to hope that Hitler was the solution. This summed up the constancy in American policy and the change in the world.

Throughout the 1919–33 period, Americans hoped that prosperity and peaceful change would contain revolutionary upheaval. With stability secured, United States traders, investors, and poets could expand frontiers while reshaping the world in the American image. Washington tried to build a world order conducive to this process. Yet it wanted also to protect America's preeminent world position, freedom of action, and political and economic safety. American policy surmounted these dilemmas in the sunny 1920s, but it foundered in the Depression.

Hard times sharpened the difficulties of the previous decade while dulling policy tools. The American formula of security and stability through disarmament, prosperity and peaceful change broke down. France demanded guarantee of the Versailles order before it would disarm. Germany aggravated French insecurity by pressing for rapid treaty revision. Impatient with the impasse, Italy supported Germany's bid for extensive change. Disturbed by this growing militance, the United States became more attached to the status quo. Russia, too, found new value in the Versailles order, even though it remained an outcast. British leaders divided on the Versailles issue, but agreed on the necessity of wholesale financial reform. After September 1931, London's independent sterling bloc and agitation for political debt cancellation challenged the American and French-dominated financial order. Hoover and Stimson tried to break this logjam by rekindling confidence, trading war debtors for disarmament, and pushing for peaceful treaty revision.

Yet political paralysis at home and nervous intransigence in Europe defeated their efforts. The Depression stripped the administration of its financial tools, congressional support, and moral power. Economic experts and unofficial diplomats lost credibility and effectiveness. Hoover's experiment with decentralized voluntarism, coordinated by publicity, failed as the laboratory suffered a series of explosions. In Europe, the Americanist dream faded; parliamentary governments collapsed; international conferences proved futile; and the willingness to wait and compromise evaporated. As in 1919, America's reformist middle road led nowhere in a world torn between revolution and rigidity.

These economic, cultural, political, and military strands made a rope that pulled down the international system. The intriguing, unanswerable question is whether the American-shaped world order could have secured long-term stability or was merely a deceptive lull in the chaos unleashed by the Great War.

Conclusion

Although it is impossible to determine definitively whether the postwar order could have achieved lasting stability, it is equally impossible to avoid evaluating that international system. Despite its flaws, the American policy of peaceful change and economic reconstruction displayed flashes of imagination and insight. Leaders such as Charles E. Hughes, Herbert Hoover, and Owen Young were creative in fashioning the tools of economic, unofficial diplomacy. They used these implements with a sophisticated understanding of the limits and the abuses of power. American leaders carefully packaged and advertised their policies to win public acceptance. Their economic, unofficial approach was aided by the growth of American business and cultural influence in Europe, influence that in turn was nurtured by the diplomacy's success. Yet U.S. policy and the system it fostered suffered from fatal flaws: the dependence on prosperity supported by private loans, the elusiveness of moral power, and the ease of separating technological change from the more liberal elements of Americanization, the unequal distribution of economic costs and benefits, the limits to American intervention, and the dilemma of seeking stabilizing change in a revolutionary era. These faults certainly weakened the postwar order, and perhaps destroyed it.

And yet as one catalogs these problems, one cannot escape the thought that historians too easily and too neatly ascribe causes to cataclysmic events that we can understand only imperfectly. A convincing indictment of Republican foreign policy requires counterfactual proof that different policies would have avoided the catastrophes of the 1930s and 1940s. This of course is impossible. Moreover, the frustrations of the post-1945 era highlight America's difficulty in solving global problems even when it committed resources with little restraint. The post–World War II experience also demonstrates how long-term prosperity (coupled with German division and American intervention) could promote European peace and integration. The failure to achieve such lasting prosperity in the 1920s is, at least in part, attributable to American policies and miscalculations. Yet a more fundamental cause of the 1930s depression may lie in that decade's position in the long-range Kondratieff cycle, which, since the start of the industrial era, has periodically devastated the international economy.[1] This is not to dismiss American responsibility for the problems of 1919–33; rather, it is to place those disappointments in the perspective of human fallibility and policy limitation. Failure and miscalculation are, after all, the most frequent outcome of human endeavor.

Despite the difficulty in satisfactorily evaluating Republican foreign policy from 1919 to 1933, certain aspects of the period stand out: America's predominant power, the caution with which policymakers exercised that strength, and the problems that plagued the American policy of peaceful change and economic reconstruction. America's preeminence— its industrial strength, commercial aggressiveness, financial leverage, military potential, naval might, and cultural appeal—was a fact that permeated Europe. This was "our century," concluded Edwin L. James after spending the 1920s as chief *New York Times* reporter in Europe. America's economic supremacy produced "enormous political influence.... There is no country where the power of the dollar has not reached. There is no capital which does not take the United States into consideration at almost every turn.... Isolation is a myth. We are not isolated and cannot be isolated. The United States is ever present."[2] "No final settlement of any major international issue can be reached," concluded British Foreign Office experts, "without the approval of the United States of America."[3] As a Belgian put it, "We have to live under the rule of the 'Pax Americana.' "[4] Such preeminence often generated resentment. Bertrand Russell observed: "The dislike of America which has grown up in England is due to the fact that world empire has now passed from Lombard Street to Wall Street. The British Navy ... is still nominally ours, but we dare not employ it in any way displeasing to Washington."[5] Like many Europeans, Russell linked America's economic and political power with its cultural influence. America had developed an "industrial philosophy ... of life" and was leading the Old World in that direction, since "whether we like it or not ... [the American way] is obviously more suited to the modern world than that of most Europeans."[6] As Russell observed, Europeans looked to the Yankees for assistance and relief, for answers to the dilemmas of the machine age and mass society. That America became a metaphor for the modernization forces transforming Europe underscored the nation's central position. Whether Europeans reviled America or respected it—and many did both—they saw in that secular city on the hill the image of their own societies' future.

With this cultural, economic, and political influence the United States—both intentionally and unintentionally—shaped European developments. Europe did not enjoy America's luxury in being able to measure and control its transatlantic ties. Thus the United States, for example, molded issues to suit its economic, unofficial diplomacy. Americans promoted the worldwide Kellogg-Briand Pact to reduce chances of military conflict, while they aggressively penetrated foreign markets. Countries like Germany, of course, succeeded in entangling America more than it wished or expected. Nevertheless, the European nations were outclassed by America and depended upon it. America's preeminent power restricted European options. As a British financier put it, "No country is independent except the United States, which secures independence through its dominion over all others."[7]

Americans were proud of their dominion. In the Great War, Calvin Coolidge recalled, the United States massed "the greatest power . . . on earth." A decade later, the Vermonter declared that America had worldwide concerns: "Our interests all over the earth are such that a conflict anywhere would be enormously to our disadvantage."[8] Benjamin Strong believed that "our influence in central bank circles . . . is almost predominant."[9]

Yet most American leaders also perceived the dangers of overweening power. Coolidge explained that America practiced in its "political relationship with the rest of the world . . . restraint and assistance," abstaining from "intervention which was unsought or . . . would be ineffective."[10] Hoover acknowledged that America's "colossal power overshadows scores of freedom-loving nations."[11] Paul Cravath, a New York lawyer and former Wilson administration adviser, was relieved that the Washington Naval Conference scotched plans for U.S. naval superiority. We "are saved from the fearful temptations that are involved in having the biggest navy in the world. God knows what would not be the dangers of our being in that position."[12] Strong, who pushed for New York's financial preeminence, backed off when an aide urged that the Federal Reserve System fulfill its "manifest destiny" by formally regulating world banking, questioning "whether we had the wisdom and experience to enable us to successfully fulfill the role."[13] Such caution was partially a product of the checks and balances that prevented the Federal Reserve, the president, the cabinet, Congress, or the private sector from completley dominating policymaking. But the sense of limit also reflected realistic skepticism of the efficacy and benefits of wholesale American intervention.

Despite the magnitude of American power and the restraint with which leaders exercised it, severe problems plagued Americn policy toward Europe. In the 1920s, policymakers banked on long-term prosperity. They trusted that economic growth would lubricate treaty revision, end bolshevism's appeal, ease the political debts' burden, and enable European recovery without significant American sacrifice. Such confidence expressed Progressive trust in scientific, economic reform. Thus, in 1927 Federal Reserve officers saw "no reason why this progressive amelioration should not go on.... We should have no recurrence of the old-time, prolonged depressions ... like those of thirty and fifty years ago; especially if we have as astute and clearsighted a banking policy as we have had in the last few years."[14]

Contrary to expectations, Federal Reserve and government authorities were unable to fine-tune the economy after 1927. Why the Depression was so long and so severe is still hotly debated. But most agree that the 1928–30 sharp cutback in U.S. foreign lending throttled a world economy already suffering from the deflationary impact of raw material glut, stagnant demand, and declining prices.[15] To regulate the vital capital flow, Americans insistently trusted the marketplace, the collective wisdom of individual investors. The mechanism of the invisible hand failed, however, when faced with the stock market boom and crash. With the Depression, America's economic, political, and cultural influence in Europe—its prestige—dwindled. One flaw that undermined the postwar order was its reliance on prosperity dependent on marketplace control of capital flows.

With the global economy in tatters, Hoover sometimes talked about national self-sufficiency. But instead of introducing a comprehensive plan for transformation to an isolated economy, he continually returned to the dream of rebuilding the world economy as the basis for American prosperity. Domestic and international prosperity seemed nearly inseparable, although of course the president gave America's welfare first priority. In his foreign policy Hoover expected, like every other national leader, that the dividends from international action would exceed the costs.

In the 1920s, this focus on American benefits had weakened the international economy by sticking Europe with most of the adjustment burdens. Thus, the United States pressured Europe to return to the gold standard, balance budgets, and fund the political debts—policies that deflated the European economies while limiting opportunities for European economic expansion. It is debatable whether Europe's competitive disadvantage would have allowed large sales to the United States even without the high tariff. Yet the duties did hurt.[16] Washington pursued an aggressive export drive in the traditional European markets of South

America, the Far East, and the Near East. Simultaneously, New York bankers opposed British efforts to liberalize the world monetary system with the gold exchange standard, foreign loan regulation, and redistribution of gold. American cultural influence had a mixed economic impact on Europe. The tourist and expatriate exodus and art purchases helped balance European payments. Yet Hollywood films stimulated European demand for American products. Similarly, films and tourists projected upon Europe an image of consumption, while American financiers and government officials pressed on Europeans the virtues of work and saving. Certainly the Old World's adoption of modern production techniques helped boost its output. America might have helped Europe find outlets for this production had it not opposed Russia's bid for large-scale credits or Germany's and Britain's efforts through the Schacht and Kindersley plans to finance global development through surplus American and French capital. Americans structured the world economy the way they did not from ignorance, but from confidence that continued world prosperity afforded both U.S. benefits and European stability.

Expectation of future prosperity and eagerness for immediate profits led to a further problem, the entanglements arising from a policy of nonentanglement. The United States stayed clear of military commitment to the frontiers of France or any other European nation. Americans designed the Dawes Plan as a pragmatic, versatile machine that would either produce reparations or demonstrate the impossibility of doing so. As Parker Gilbert put it, the plan contained "the seeds of growth and the flexibility that should make it feasible to keep pace with changing conditions."[17] Yet the bankers' greed, their reliance on marketplace loan control, and the Germans' wish to snare an economic commitment from American and British investors all transformed the plan into an inflexible device that required constant infusions of foreign capital to prevent a collapse. By 1931, America's huge private investments, its war debt credits, and its domestic banking structure all were hostage to the squabble over reparations and war debts.

This transformation of the Dawes Plan underlined the difficulties of the peaceful change policy. Peaceful change was the United States' answer to the dilemma of rigidity and revolution, its solution to the Versailles issue, which plagued Europe for twenty years after 1919. Successful change gave Americans a lucrative stake in the new order, making them less receptive to further adjustments. Americans favored the moderate Versailles revision of 1924–31—the Dawes Plan, the Locarno Pact, the Young Plan, Rhineland evacuation, the Hoover Moratorium, and the attempted Polish corridor adjustment—but balked at Germany's bid for rearmament and more rapid change. A basic question is whether Germany, under whatever government, would have remained content with slow, moderate Versailles revision. Gustav Stresemann, Heinrich Brüning, and other supposedly moderate Weimar leaders did hope to restore German preeminence in Europe.[18] Most American leaders thought such resurgence was inevitable, and not dangerous to their interests so long as Germany adhered to open-door, pacific principles. They envisioned a loose economic, political, and cultural partnership with a largely satisfied, bourgeois-dominated, liberal trade-oriented Germany. And perhaps continued prosperity would have allowed such a nation to evolve.[19]

But the Depression generated pressure for faster change than America and the Allies would accept. This pointed up another dilemma of the peaceful change policy: when upheaval threatened, Americans sought stability in right-wing forces and the status quo. Such was the pattern of American response to Russia in 1919, Italy in 1922, Bulgaria in 1923, and Germany throughout the 1919–33 period. The policy of peaceful treaty revision was part of America's continuing struggle in the twentieth century to outflank revolution and reaction with reform. As the 1919–33 period demonstrated, however, this was a difficult policy to implement in a revolutionary century.

Caught in the riptide of success and failure, most leaders of 1919–33 lacked such long-range perspective. Reinhold Niebuhr, philosopher, theologian, and commentator on American-European relations, offered a perceptive contemporary analysis. As the "wealthiest [nation] in the world," America had "become the real empire of modern civilization." He explained that "our power is derived from our engineering ability," from tapping the resources of a virgin continent and the world around it. Yet Americans were "awkward imperialists," trying unsuccessfully to manage their wealth and the world with the same economic, informal methods which had created their riches. This limited, awkward dominion aggravated world instability. Yet Niebuhr was optimistic that if the United States avoided one fatal error, eventually "a world community" would emerge from the American empire. America had only to "prevent the wedding of economic and military power ... since the more our economic power is supported by military strength, the more we shall be inclined to solve our problems by intransigence and defiance of world opinion, and the more shall we multiply animosities against us."[20]

The Depression swept away the chance for a world community. After World War II, Americans again tried to stabilize the world economic and political system. Once more Yankee culture washed over Europe. After 1945, however, Americans largely abandoned the restraint urged by Niebuhr and honored by 1919–33 leaders. The United States's post-1945 dominion was less awkward than its earlier incarnation, but it was no more permanent.

Notes

Introduction

1. In 1954, William Appleman Williams broke this pattern with the publication of "The Legend of Isolationism in the 1920s" (*Science and Society* 18[1954]:1–20). Williams argued that those who labeled the decade "isolationist" focused too narrowly on American refusal to join the League of Nations or participate in European politics. Much more important, he claimed, was the global expansion of American business. The United States was not isolated from Europe, but intimately involved with the Continent through private loans, booming trade, and multiplying investments. Williams stitched the 1920s into the fabric of his open-door interpretation of twentieth-century American history (*The Tragedy of American Diplomacy* [New York, 1962]). This interpretation stressed that regardless of tactical shifts, such as the decision whether or not to join the League of Nations, the broad strategy of American foreign policy was to secure an open door or equal opportunity for American business. Such economic expansion, Williams emphasized, was believed by policymakers to be essential to the health of American society. Williams's thesis made considerable impact, particularly among the younger diplomatic historians studying with him and Fred Harvey Harrington at the University of Wisconsin.

Yet not until the 1960s and 1970s did historians begin to analyze American diplomacy of the 1919–33 period systematically. Ironically, it was only after the deaths in the early 1960s of Herbert C. Hoover and Owen D. Young, two leading figures of the post–World War I years, that historians began to resurrect their reputations and that of their era. One factor in the resurgent interest was that their freshly opened private papers, as well as those of Benjamin Strong, Alanson Houghton, Thomas Lamont, and others, became a new frontier both for graduate students seeking dissertation topics and for older scholars exploring a relatively neglected period. Witnessing foreign and economic policy failures in their own time, historians were more sympathetic about the travails of the 1919–33 years. European scholars, particularly German, contributed significant studies based on sources from both sides of the Atlantic.

269

Among the most important of these newer studies were overview essays in the Williams tradition by Robert Freeman Smith ("Republican Policy and the Pax Americana, 1921–1932," in William Appleman Williams, ed., *From Colony to Empire* [New York, 1972], 254–92, and "American Foreign Relations, 1920–42," in Barton J. Bernstein, ed., *Towards a New Past* [New York, 1968], 232–62). In the same school was Carl P. Parrini's book, which pointed to the continuity between the Woodrow Wilson and Warren Harding administrations (*Heir to Empire* [Pittsburgh, 1969]). Joan Hoff Wilson questioned the primacy placed by the Williams school on economic motivation in American foreign policy. Emphasizing the divisions among businessmen and other leaders, she stressed the importance of bureaucratic inertia and squabbling in the shaping of foreign policy (*American Business and Foreign Policy, 1920–33* [Lexington, Ky., 1971]; *Ideology and Economics: U.S. Relations with the Soviet Union, 1918–1933* [Columbia, Mo., 1974]). Melvyn P. Leffler followed a similar analysis with studies that stressed the often conflicting imperatives that shaped American policy toward Europe, particularly France ("Political Isolationism, Economic Expansionism, or Diplomatic Realism: American Policy toward Western Europe, 1921–1933," *Perspectives in American History* 8 (1974): 413–61, and *The Elusive Quest: America's Pursuit of European Stability and French Security* [Chapel Hill, N.C., 1979]). Also using a bureaucratic model approach, Michael J. Hogan's work focused on the cooperative, corporative aspects of Anglo-American relations (*Informal Entente: The Private Structure of Cooperation in Anglo-American Economic Diplomacy, 1918–1928* [Columbia Mo., 1977]). Drawing on a wealth of European and American sources, Werner Link stressed, like Williams, the capitalist imperative that powered American economic and political involvement with Germany. Link also emphasized the American policy of peaceful change (*Die amerikanische Stabilisierungspolitik in Deutschland 1921–32* (Düsseldorf, 1970]). Stephen A. Schuker contributed a monograph that focused on French acceptance of the Dawes Plan, yet tried to answer the broader question of why France was unable to enforce the Versailles treaty (*The End of French Predominance in Europe: The Financial Crisis of 1924 and the Adoption of the Dawes Plan* [Chapel Hill, 1976]). A book of essays edited by K. Paul Jones examined the mixed success of American diplomats stationed in Europe (*U.S. Diplomats in Europe, 1919–1942* [Santa Barbara, 1981]). A critique of the Williams thesis and much of the ensuing literature can be found in John Braeman, "The New Left and American Foreign Policy during the Age of Normalcy: A Re-examination," *Business History Review* 57 (Spring 1983):73–104. These studies are only the most significant published works of a secondary literature that amounts to hundreds of books, articles, and unpublished dissertations that have appeared since 1965. See the Bibliography for a listing of this literature.

2. Frederick Lewis Allen, *Only Yesterday* (New York, 1931).

3. John Winthrop, "A Model of Christian Charity," in Perry Miller and Thomas H. Johnson, eds., *The Puritans*, (New York, 1938), 198–99.

4. *New York Times*, February 7, 1930, 20.

5. Hans Joachim, "Romane aus Amerika," *Neue Rundschau*, 41, part 2 (1930):398.

1. The Flawed Peace, 1919–1921

1. Paul Fussell, *The Great War and Modern Memory* (New York, 1975).

2. Isaiah Bowman to Hamilton Fish Armstrong, January 29, 1923, Records

of Meetings (hereafter RM), vol. 1, Council on Foreign Relations (hereafter CFR) Papers, New York City; italics in original.

3. N. Gordon Levin, *Woodrow Wilson and World Politics* (New York, 1968), 54–82.

4. Quoted in Dorothy Ann Pettit, "A Cruel Wind: America Experiences Pandemic Influenza, 1918–1920: A Social History" (Ph.D. dissertation, University of New Hampshire, 1976), 185. *See also* ibid., 182–200; Alfred W. Crosby, Jr., *Epidemic and Peace, 1918* (Westport, Conn., 1976), 171–200.

5. Charles Homer Haskins, "The New Boundaries of Germany," in Edward House and Charles Seymour, eds., *What Really Happened at Paris* (New York, 1921), 37–66; Daniel M. Smith, *The Great Departure* (New York, 1965), 154–57.

6. Robert Howard Lord, "Poland," in House and Seymour, *What Really Happened*, 67–68.

7. Ibid., 67–86; Department of State, *Foreign Relations of the United States Paris Peace Conference* (hereafter *FRUS PPC*) (Washington, 1947) 12:205–10; Smith, *Great Departure*, 162.

8. Ronald Pruessen, "John Foster Dulles and Reparations at the Paris Peace Conference, 1919: Early Patterns of a Life," *Pespectives in American History* (1974):381–410; Thomas W. Lamont, "Reparations," in House and Seymour, *What Really Happened*, 259–90; Robert E. Bunselmeyer, *The Cost of the War 1914–19* (Hamden, Conn., 1975), 75–184; Philip Mason Burnett, *Reparations at the Paris Peace Conference* (2 vols.; New York, 1965). The $5 billion is from Sally Marks, "The Myths of Reparations," *Central European History* 11 (September 1978):231–55.

9. Joseph Rothschild, *East Central Europe between the Two World Wars* (Seattle, 1974), 323–25.

10. House and Seymour, *What Really Happened*, 453.

11. Rothschild, *East Central Europe*, 155.

12. Dragan R. Zivojinovic, *America, Italy and the Birth of Yugoslavia* (Boulder, Colo., 1972), 159–305.

13. Quoted in David Hunter Miller, *The Drafting of the Covenant* (2 vols., New York, 1928) 1:42; italics in original. *See also* Ray Stannard Baker, *Woodrow Wilson and World Settlement* (3 vols., Garden City, N.Y. 1922) 1:246–47; Herbert Hoover, *The Ordeal of Woodrow Wilson* (New York, 1958), 182.

14. Miller, *Drafting of the Covenant*, 2:70; italics added. *See also* Thomas J. Knock, "Woodrow Wilson and the Origins of the League of Nations" (Ph.D. dissertation, Princeton University, 1982), 257, 285–87, 319, 330–31; Arthur C. Walworth, *America's Moment, 1918: American Diplomacy at the End of World War I* (New York,1977), 132; Peter Raffo, "The Anglo-American Preliminary Negotiations for a League of Nations" *Journal of Contemporary History* 9 (1974): especially 161, 164, 171.

15. Miller, *Drafting of the Covenant*, 2:71.

16. Ibid. 1:70–71; 2:146; House and Seymour, *What Really Happened*, 505; Lincoln P. Bloomfield, *Evolution or Revolution?* (Cambridge, 1957), 29; F. P. Walters, *A History of the League of Nations* (London, 1952), 718.

17. Baker, *Woodrow Wilson* 1:219.

18. Miller, *Drafting of the Covenant* 1:202.

19. Ibid., 1:202–3; Lord Robert Cecil, *A Great Experiment* (New York, 1941), 96–97.

20. Miller, *Drafting of the Covenant* 1:203.

21. Bloomfield, *Evolution or Revolution?* 43–58.

22. Edith Bolling Wilson, *My Memoir* (New York, 1938), 239.

23. Warren F. Kuehl, *Seeking World Order* (Nashville, 1969); Wolfgang J. Helbich, "American Liberals in the League of Nations Controversy," *Public Opinion Quarterly* 31 (1968):568–96.

24. Hoover, *Ordeal of Woodrow Wilson*, 248, 183–84, 266–68.

25. Robert Bacon and James Brown Scott, eds., *Men and Policies: Addresses by Elihu Root* (Cambridge, Mass., 1925), 266; Philip C. Jessup, *Elihu Root* (2 vols.; New York, 1938) 2:392–94; J. P. Morgan to Thomas W. Lamont, March 14, 1919, Dwight W. Morrow papers, Amherst College Library.

26. John A. Garraty, *Henry Cabot Lodge* (New York, 1953), 364–66; Jessup, *Root*, 2:389–90, 394, 402–4; Randolph C. Downes, *The Rise of Warren Gamaliel Harding, 1865–1920* (Columbus, 1970), 331–44; Henry L. Stimson and McGeorge Bundy, *On Active Service in Peace and War* (New York, 1948), 102–4.

27. David J. Danelski and Joseph S. Tulchin, eds., *The Autobiographical Notes of Charles Evans Hughes* (Cambridge, Mass., 1973), 210–12.

28. Miller, *Drafting of the Covenant* 1:382–84; Merlo J. Pusey, *Charles Evans Hughes* (2 vols.; New York, 1951) 1:395–99.

29. Ralph A. Stone, "The Irreconcilables' Alternative to the League of Nations," *Mid-America* 49 (July 1967):163–73, and *The Irreconcilables* (New York, 1970), 178–82; Robert James Maddox, *William E. Borah and American Foreign Policy* (Baton Rouge, La., 1969), 60–64.

30. Jessup, *Root*, 2:406–12; Garraty, *Lodge*, 375–90. For a view of Lodge as partisan, *see* David Mervin, "Henry Cabot Lodge and the League of Nations," *Journal of American Studies* 4 (February 1971):201–14; for Lodge as statesman, *see* James E. Hewes, Jr., "Henry Cabot Lodge and the League of Nations," *Proceedings of the American Philosophical Society* 114 (August 1970):245–55.

31. Wesley M. Bagby, *The Road to Normalcy* (Baltimore, 1962), 134–46; John Chalmers Vinson, *Referendum for Isolation* (Athens, Ohio, 1961), 110–20.

32. Quoted in Downes, *Rise of Harding*, 319, 330. On another occasion Harding urged that "the Bolshevik beast [be] slain" (ibid., 321).

33. Ibid., 321.

34. Quoted in ibid., 566–67.

35. Quoted in Gary Dean Best, *The Politics of American Individualism: Herbert Hoover in Transition, 1918–1921* (Westport, Conn., 1975), 138, 123.

36. Thomas W. Lamont to Harding, August 3, 1920, file 97-9, Thomas W. Lamont papers, Baker Library, Harvard Business School; Lamont to Dwight Morrow, July 22, 1920, file 113–14, ibid.; Downes, *Rise of Harding*, 571.

37. Quoted in Downes, *Rise of Harding*, 574–77.

38. Quoted in Best, *Politics of American Individualism*, 139. *See also* ibid., 130–40; Downes, *Rise of Harding*, 598–95.

39. Quoted in Downes, *Rise of Harding*, 594.

40. Levin, *Woodrow Wilson*, 22.

41. Memorandum of Davis and Lamont to Wilson, May 15, 1919, in Baker, *Woodrow Wilson*, 3:352–54.

42. Quoted in Robert H. Van Meter, "The United States and European Recovery, 1918–23: A Study of Public Policy and Private Finance" (Ph.D. dissertation, University of Wisconsin, 1971), 61.

43. Quoted in Bunselmeyer, *Cost of the War*, 101–2; italics added.
44. Ibid., 173.
45. Baker, *Woodrow Wilson*, 3:336–43.
46. Wilson to Lloyd George, May 5, 1919, in ibid., 334–46.
47. Quoted in Van Meter, "United States and European Recovery," 80–85.
48. Leffingwell to Davis, May 7, 1919 in Baker, *Woodrow Wilson*, 3:373.
49. Ibid., 373–76; Paul B. Abrahams, "American Bankers and the Economic Tactics of Peace: 1919," *Journal of American History* 56 (December 1969):573; Van Meter, "United States and European Recovery," 34–38.
50. Van Meter, "United States and European Recovery," 41–43.
51. Quoted in ibid., 153–54.
52. Quoted in Abrahams, "American Bankers," 578. *See also* ibid., 576–78; Parrini, *Heir to Empire*, 79–82.
53. Parrini, *Heir to Empire*, 82–100.
54. Lester V. Chandler, *Benjamin Strong, Central Banker* (Washington, 1958), 144–45; Benjamin D. Rhodes, "Reassessing 'Uncle Shylock': The United States and the French War Debt, 1917–29," *Journal of American History* 55 (March 1969): 787–803; Melvyn P. Leffler, "The Origins of Republican War Debt Policy, 1921–23; A Case Study in the Applicability of the Open Door Interpretation," *Journal of American History* 49 (December 1972):585–601; Wilson, *American Business*, 123–56.
55. Quoted in Van Meter, "United States and European Recovery," 69.
56. Parrini, *Heir to Empire*, 15–39.
57. Hogan, *Informal Entente*, 20–37.
58. Quoted in Van Meter, "United States and European Recovery," 69.
59. Ibid., 255. For British resentment, see Dan P. Silverman, *Reconstructing Europe after the Great War* (Cambridge, Mass., 1982), 148.
60. Quoted in, Van Meter, "United States and European Recovery," 257.
61. Quoted in ibid., 130.
62. Quoted in ibid., 74. For other examples of Americans' concern that Europeans work hard, *see* Suda Lorena Bane and Ralph Haswell Lutz, eds., *Organization of American Relief in Europe, 1918–1919* (Stanford, 1943), 542; *FRUS PPC*, 10:462; Leo Eugene Chavez, "Herbert Hoover and Food Relief: An Application of American Ideology" (Ph.D. dissertation, University of Michigan, 1976), 255–56, 263.
63. Quoted in Chavez, "Hoover and Food Relief," 58–59.
64. Many Republicans, including Lodge, supported the treaty. See Lloyd E. Ambrosius, "Wilson, the Republicans, and French Security after World War I," *Journal of American History* 49(1972):341–52.
65. Melvin Roy Strausburgh, "Great Britain and the Diplomacy of Reparation: 1919–21" (Ph.D. dissertation, Case Western Reserve, 1974), especially 479–87.
66. Quoted in Van Meter, "United States and European Recovery," 80.
67. Ibid. *See* chaps. 2, 3.
68. Quoted in Van Meter, "United States and European Recovery," 231–34; Parrini, *Heir to Empire*, 148.
69. Quoted in Daniel M. Smith, *Aftermath of War* (Philadelphia, 1970), 47. On the oil controversy, *see* Parrini, *Heir to Empire* 159–61; John A. DeNovo, "The Movement for an Aggressive American Oil Policy Abroad, 1918–20,"

American Historical Review 71 (1956):854–76; Hogan, *Informal Entente*, 159–85.

70. Quoted in Smith, *Aftermath of War*, 51–53.

71. Quoted in ibid., 51.

72. Quoted in Van Meter, "United States and European Recovery," 231.

73. Quoted in ibid., 243.

74. Ibid., 243–45.

75. U.S. Bureau of the Census, *Historical Statistics of the United States, Colonial Times to the Present* (Washington, 1960), 550.

76. *See* chap. 6.

77. Quoted in Herbert Hoover, *An American Epic* (3 vols.; Chicago, 1961) 2:30.

78. Francis Miller and Helen Hill, *The Giant of the Western World* (New York, 1930), 101.

79. John Maynard Keynes applauded Hoover as "the only man who emerged from the ordeal of Paris with an enhanced reputation" (*The Economic Consequences of the Peace* [New York, 1919], 257). For a general account of Hoover's activities and impact in the immediate postwar years, *see* Best, *Politics of American Individualism.*

80. "Central Europe" here refers to Europe west of the Soviet Union and east of Germany, Italy, and Switzerland.

81. John Pershing to Hoover, December 12, 1918, in Bane and Lutz, *Organization of American Relief*, 85. *See also* Chavez, "Hoover and Food Relief," 96–102.

82. Hoover to Wilson, November 7, 1918, Bane and Lutz, *Organization of American Relief*, 32–33. *See also* memorandum by Hoover, November 15, 1918, ibid., 50; Chavez, "Hoover and Food Relief," 74–75.

83. Quoted in Harold H. Fisher, *The Famine in Soviet Russia, 1919–1923* (New York, 1927), 57.

84. Quoted in John M. Thompson, *Russia, Bolshevism, and the Versailles Peace* (Princeton, 1966), 222.

85. Quoted in Chavez, "Hoover and Food Relief," 78; memorandum by Hoover, November 15, 1918, in Bane and Lutz, *Organization of American Relief*, 53; Thompson, *Russia, Bolshevism*, 258.

86. Hoover to Wilson, March 28, 1919, in Fisher, *Famine in Soviet Russia*, 13.

87. Walter Johnson, ed. *Turbulent Era* (Boston, 1952) 1:385.

88. Herbert Hoover, *The Memoirs of Herbert Hoover* (3 vols.; New York, 1952) 1:333; Baker, *Woodrow Wilson*, 3:324; Gary Dean Best, "Food Relief as Price Support: Hoover and American Pork, January–March 1919," *Agricultural History* 45 (April 1971):79–84; Chavez, "Hoover and Food Relief," 132, 140–46.

89. Hoover to Julius Barnes, May 7, 1919, in Bane and Lutz, *Organization of American Relief*, 470.

90. Louis John Nigro, Jr., "Propaganda, Politics, and the New Diplomacy: The Impact of Wilsonian Propaganda on Politics and Public Opinion in Italy, 1917–19" (Ph.D. dissertation, Vanderbilt University, 1978).

91. Hoover to William Grove, February 3, 1919, in Bane and Lutz, *Organization of American Relief*, 228; Hoover, *Memoirs*, 1:321.

92. Hoover to Wilson, June 6, 1919, in Bane and Lutz, *Organization of*

American Relief, 541–42. *See also* Hoover to heads of missions, April 26, 1919, ibid., 426.

93. Hoover quoted in Thomas Herbert Dressler, "The Foreign Policies of American Individualism: Herbert Hoover, Reluctant Internationalist" (Ph.D. dissertation, Brown University, 1973), 23; Rickard quoted in Chavez, "Hoover and Food Relief," 283.

94. Hoover to Wilson, January 1, 1919, in Suda Lorena Bane and Ralph Haswell Lutz, eds., *The Blockade of Germany after the Armistice 1918–1919* (Stanford, 1942), 24–25. Wilson jotted down: "To these conclusions I entirely agree."

95. James A. Logan to Hoover, March 6, 1919, in ibid., 188.

96. Klaus Schwabe, *Deutsche Revolution and Wilson-Frieden* (Düsseldorf, 1971), 364; Bane and Lutz, *Blockade of Germany*, 138.

97. Bane and Lutz, *Blockade of Germany*, 208–9; Schwabe, *Deutsche Revolution*, 354–79.

98. Hoover, *Ordeal of Woodrow Wilson*, 170–72. Under the Brussels agreement Germany bought $282 million of food, of which the United States supplied $158 million, Britain $76 million, and other nations $48 million. Frank M. Surface and Raymond L. Bland, *American Food in the World War and Reconstruction Period* (Stanford, 1931), 197.

99. Schwabe, *Deutsche Revolution*, 376; Surface and Bland, *American Food*, 194–95.

100. Hoover, *American Epic*, 3:89–92.

101. Schwabe, *Deutsche Revolution*, 373–79.

102. Logan to Hoover, March 6, 1919, in Bane and Lutz, *Blockade of Germany*, 188.

103. Schwabe, *Deutsche Revolution*, 377.

104. Hoover to Wilson, April 11, 1919, in Bane and Lutz, *Organization of American Relief*, 399–401.

105. T. T. C. Gregory, "Stemming the Red Tide," *The World's Work* (in 3 parts, vols. 41–42, April–June, 1921), part 1:608.

106. Ibid.; Hoover, *American Epic*, 2:372–75; Donald R. Van Petten, "The European Technical Adviser and Post-war Austria, 1919–1923" (Ph.D. dissertation, Stanford University, 1943), 280–82; Chavez, "Hoover and Food Relief," 6.

107. Zivojinovic, *Birth of Yugoslavia*, 217–39.

108. William Causey to T. T. C. Gregory, February 23, 1919 in Bane and Lutz, *Organization of American Relief*, 290; ibid., 315–20; Hoover, *American Epic*, 2:417–19.

109. Zivojinovic, *Birth of Yugoslavia*, 217–99.

110. William G. Atwood to Hoover, June 19, 1919, in Bane and Lutz, *Organization of American Relief*, 555–57; Harold H. Fisher, *America and the New Poland* (New York, 1928), 196–200; Hoover, *American Epic*, 2:420–22; Gregory, "Stemming the Red Tide," part 2:98–99.

111. Fisher, *America and New Poland*, 197–200; Hoover, *American Epic*, 2:388; Gregory, "Stemming the Red Tide," part 2:98–99; Goodyear to Atwood, June 22, 1919; Gregory to Logan, June 24, 1919, both in Bane and Lutz, *Organization of American Relief*, 564–66; memorandum by John Simpson, January 17, 1919, ibid., 203–4.

112. Hoover to Wilson, January 25, 1919, in Bane and Lutz, *Organization of American Relief*, 212.

113. Hoover to Heinz, January 26, 1919, ibid., 216; Hoover to Gregory, February 2, 1919, ibid., 224.

114. J. W. McIntosh to Hoover, January 16, 1919, ibid., 180.

115. Hoover to Heinz, February 28, 1919, ibid., 310–11.

116. Hoover to Goodyear, May 2, 1919; Hoover to prime minister of Serbia, May 2, 1919; minutes of Supreme Economic Council, April 28, 1919, all in ibid., 453–57.

117. Hoover to Goodyear, May 2, 1919, ibid., 454.

118. Fisher, *America and New Poland*, 206–7.

119. Causey to Atwood, May 6, 1919, in Bane and Lutz, *Organization of American Relief*, 465.

120. "Report of the Coal Commission for the territory included in the former empire of Austria-Hungary and Poland, by Anson C. Goodyear," September 10, 1919, ibid., 686.

121. Hoover to Goodyear, May 16, 1919, ibid., 488; "Report of the Coal Commission," ibid., 703.

122. Hoover memorandum on the economic situation of Europe, July 3, 1919, ibid., 591. *See also* Chavez, "Hoover and Food Relief," 263.

123. Quoted in "Report of the Coal Commission," in Bane and Lutz, *Organization of American Relief*, 694.

124. Ibid., 706–7.

125. *See* chap. 5.

126. "Report of the Coal Commission," in Bane and Lutz, *Organization of American Relief*, 703; Causey to Atwood, July 20, 1919, ibid., 643–44.

127. Hoover to ARA, in Bane and Lutz, *Organization of American Relief*, 623–26.

128. Surface and Bland, *American Food*, 144–45. Of the total $212.4 million received by the ARAECF during 1919–23, private U.S. contributions totaled $32.5 million; Hoover added $25.1 million from "surplus" funds of the U.S. Grain Corporation; the ARA earned $28.7 million from exchange remittances, food drafts, and bulk sales; the British government contributed $18.2 million, central European governments $14.7 million, and the Soviet government $11.5 million.

129. Hoover to Wilson, June 24, 1919; Wilson to Hoover, June 25, 1919, in Bane and Lutz, *Organization of American Relief*, 570–71; Hoover to Beneš, July 11, 1919, ibid., 610–11.

130. Alvin B. Barber, *Report of European Technical Advisers' Mission to Poland, 1919–19233* (New York, 1923), 6–7.

131. Quoted in Van Petten, "European Technical Adviser," 359.

132. Barber, *Report*, 7–8; Van Petten, "European Technical Adviser," 321; Gary Dean Best, "Herbert Hoover's Technical Mission to Yugoslavia, 1919–20," *Annals of Iowa* 42 (Fall 1974):449; for Logan, numerous letters in Box 1, Ferdinand Eberstadt Papers, Mudd Library, Princeton University.

133. William Causey to J. E. Otis, quoted in Van Petten, "European Technical Adviser," 319.

134. Ibid., 280–82, 686–87.

135. Barber, *Report*, 7.

136. Ibid., 18–20, 36–40; Van Petten, "European Technical Adviser," 358–65, 583–90.

137. Van Petten, "European Technical Adviser," 447–54.

138. Ibid., 374–80; Best, "Hoover's Technical Mission to Yugoslavia," 453–56.

139. Barber, *Report*, 25, 30.

140. Ibid., 41–42; Best, "Hoover's Technical Mission to Yugoslavia," 456–57.

141. Causey to Logan, November 10, 1919, in Van Petten, "European Technical Adviser," 812; Causey to Cox, October 6, 1922, ibid., 515.

142. Quoted in ibid., 428.

143. Barber, *Report*, 34–35.

144. *FRUS 1920* (Washington, 1936), 3:417–21.

145. Barber, *Report*, 40, 66.

146. Vernon Kellogg to Hoover, January 6, 1919, quoted in Hoover, *American Epic* 3:64.

147. Quoted in ibid., 65.

148. Ibid., 65; Vernon Kellogg, "Paderewski, Pilsudski, and Poland," *The World's Work* 38 (May 1919):111–12; Hoover, *Memoirs* 1:357; *FRUS PPC* (Washington, 1942) 2:427–29, 12:365–67; Piotr S. Wandycz, *The United States and Poland* (Cambridge, 1980), 127–30.

149. Admiral Huse of *Pittsburgh* to Daniels, October 5, 1920; Daniels to Huse, October 5, 1920, both enclosed in Daniels to Colby, October 5, 1920, 760c.61/372, General Records of the Department of State, Record Group 59, National Archives, Washington (hereafter NARG 59). For background, *see FRUS 1920* 3:395–96, 404; Daniels to Colby, August 28, 1920, 760c.61/267; Kasimierz Lubomirski to Colby, September 14, 1920, 760c.61/311, both in NARG 59.

150. Quoted in William Appleman Williams, *American Russian Relations, 1781–1947* (New York, 1952), 173.

151. Hoover to Wilson, March 28, 1919, in Fisher, *Famine in Soviet Russia*, 12–13.

152. Quoted in Hoover, *Ordeal of Woodrow Wilson*, 119.

153. Fisher, *Famine in Soviet Russia*, 16–17; Thompson, *Russia, Bolshevism*, 232–33, 249–60; Benjamin M. Weissman, *Herbert Hoover and Famine Relief to Soviet Russia, 1921–1923* (Stanford, 1974), 30–34.

154. Thompson, *Russia, Bolshevism*, 247, 253, 255–56.

155. Ibid., 262–67; Fisher, *Famine in Soviet Russia*, 23–24.

156. Weissman, *Hoover and Famine Relief to Soviet Russia*, 36–37; Surface and Bland, *American Food*, 240–43.

157. Colby to Camillo Avezzano, August 10, 1920, *FRUS 1920* 3:463–68.

158. Harold B. Whitman, ed. *Charles Seymour: Letters from the Paris Peace Conference* (New Haven, 1965), 185; George W. Hopkins, "The Politics of Food; the United States and Soviet Hungary March–August, 1919," *Mid-America* 55 (October 1973):247.

159. Quoted in Thompson, *Russia, Bolshevism*, 204–05; *see also* Hopkins, "Politics of Food," 250–51.

160. Hoover, *Ordeal of Woodrow Wilson*, 136.

161. Hoover, *American Epic*, 3:120–21.

162. Rothschild, *East Central Europe*, 140–49; Rudolf L. Tokes, *Bela Kun*

and the Hungarian Soviet Republic (New York, 1967), 123–36; Sherman David Spector, *Rumania at the Paris Peace Conference* (New York, 1962), 131–58.

163. *FRUS PPC*, 11:259.

164. Quoted in Arno J. Mayer, *Politics and Diplomacy of Peacemaking* (New York, 1967), 828–32.

165. *FRUS PPC* 11:260; Hopkins, "Politics of Food," 262–63.

166. *FRUS PPC* 11:314–22.

167. Mayer, *Politics and Diplomacy of Peacemaking*, 833–34, 840.

168. Rothschild, *East Central Europe*, 145–50; Tokes, *Bela Kun*, 175–206.

169. Quoted in Tokes, *Bela Kun*, 203.

170. Rothschild, *East Central Europe*, 150; Hopkins, "Politics of Food," 267.

171. Gregory, "Stemming the Red Tide," part 3:155–61; Hopkins, "Politics of Food," 264–66.

172. The declaration did not mention Böhm specifically, lest the plot's failure further damage Western prestige in Hungary.

173. Quoted in Tokes, *Bela Kun*, 203; Hopkins, "Politics of Food," 266. On the eve of Kun's overthrow, Gregory lacked the food or funds to make good on the promise of immediate relief. He negotiated a $1 million food sale to Kun's government, received payment in hard currency, purchased food from private dealers and delivered it only after Kun fell. Gregory, "Stemming the Red Tide," part 3:162–63.

174. Gregory, "Stemming the Red Tide," part 1:609.

175. Quoted in Mayer, *Politics and Diplomacy of Peacemaking*, 850; Spector, *Rumania*, 159–96.

176. Hopkins, "Politics of Food," 268; Surface and Bland, *American Food*, 236.

2. The Domestic Roots of Republican Foreign Policy

1. Quoted in Downes, *Rise of Harding*, 490. *See also* Robert Clinton Hilderbrand, "Power and the People: Executive Management of Public Opinion in Foreign Affairs, 1869–1921" (Ph.D. dissertation, University of Iowa, 1977), 505–17.

2. Josephine Young Case and Everett Needham Case, *Owen D. Young and American Enterprise* (Boston, 1982); Ida Tarbell, *Owen D. Young* (New York, 1932).

3. Robert K. Murray, *The Politics of Normalcy* (New York, 1973), 1; Bureau of the Census, *Historical Statistics*, 682–83.

4. Kurt Wimer and Sarah Wimer, "The Harding Administration, the League of Nations and the Separate Peace Treaty," *Review of Politics* 29(January 1967): 14–16; Best, *Politics of American Individualism*, 148–52; Danelski and Tulchin, eds., *Hughes*, 212–13; Thomas N. Guinsburg, *The Pursuit of Isolationism in the United States Senate from Versailles to Pearl Harbor* (New York, 1982), 53–55.

5. Robert K. Murray, *The Harding Era* (Minneapolis, 1969), 194. For an introduction to Hughes *see* Pusey, *Hughes*; Betty Glad, *Charles Evans Hughes and the Illusions of Innocence* (Urbana, 1966); Danelski and Tulchin, eds., *Hughes*; Nelson Eugene Woodard, "Postwar Reconstruction and International Order: A Study of the Diplomacy of Charles Evans Hughes, 1921–25" (Ph.D. dissertation,

University of Wisconsin, 1970); Charles E. Hughes, *The Pathway of Peace* (New York, 1925).

6. Danelski and Tulchin, eds., *Hughes*, 75–118; Glad, *Hughes*, 59–62.

7. Quoted in Peter Henry Buckingham, "Diplomatic and Economic Normalcy: America's Open Door Peace with the Former Central Powers 1921–29" (Ph.D. dissertation, Washington State University, 1980), 8. Danelski and Tulchin, eds., *Hughes*,: 119–185; Pusey, *Hughes* 2: 132–366; Glad, *Hughes*, 63–81.

8. Quoted in Dieter Bruno Gescher, *Die Vereinigten Staaten von Nordamerika und die Reparationen, 1920–1924* (Bonn, 1956), 213.

9. Hughes, "Deal Only with Upright States," *Nation's Business* 10 (June 5, 1922):11.

10. For Genoa and Dawes conferences, see Chap. 3–4; for Lausanne, *see* FRUS 1923, 2:879–1040.

11. Quoted in Pusey, *Hughes* 2:437.

12. Ibid., 423–25; Glad, *Hughes*, 142–48.

13. Quoted in Woodard, "Postwar Reconstruction," 2.

14. Quoted in Pusey, *Hughes*, 2:579.

15. Quoted in Danelski and Tulchin, eds., *Hughes*, 258.

16. Quoted in Buckingham, "Diplomatic and Economic Normalcy," 176; Woodard, "Postwar Reconstruction," 13.

17. Quoted in Pusey, *Hughes* 1:397.

18. Quoted in Glad, *Hughes*, 178.

19. Quoted in ibid., 317.

20. William R. Castle, Jr. diary entry, November 20, 1922, transmitted in Castle to Alanson B. Houghton, December 30, 1922, Alanson B. Houghton Papers, Corning, N.Y. Senatory Henry Cabot Lodge endorsed administration policy "to use our great influence and power" in world affairs. Quoted in John M. Carroll, "Henry Cabot Lodge's Contributors to the Shaping of Republican European Diplomacy, 1920–1924," *Capitol Studies* 3 (Fall 1975):156.

21. Mitchell interview with Charles Evans Hughes, November 11, 1941, Houghton Papers.

22. Hoover, *Memoirs* 2:36; Best, *Politics of American Individualism* 166–68. The best general biography of Hoover is Joan Hoff Wilson, *Herbert Hoover, Forgotten Progressive* (Boston, 1975). *See also* Joseph H. Davis, "Herbert Hoover, 1874–1964:Another Appraisal," *The South Atlantic Quarterly* 68 (Summer 1969):295–318; David Burner, *Herbert Hoover: A Public Life* (New York, 1979).

23. Best, *Politics of American Individualism*, 54–118; Craig Lloyd, *Aggressive Introvert: Herbert Hoover and Public Relations Management, 1912–1932* (Columbus, 1972), 109–11.

24. Quoted in Murray, *Politics of Normalcy*, 25.

25. Quoted in ibid., 33.

26. Joseph Brandes, *Herbert Hoover and Economic Diplomacy: Department of Commerce Policy, 1921–28* (Pittsburgh, 1962); Wilson, *Hoover*, 79–121.

27. Quoted in Wilson, *Hoover*, 79.

28. Murray, *Politics of Normalcy*, 32–33.

29. Quoted in Wilson, *Hoover*, 122.

30. American Bankers Association, *Journal* 13 (January 1921):462–63.

31. Hoover to Harding, January 4, 1922, Commerce Personal File (hereafter CPF), Herbert Hoover Papers, Herbert Hoover Presidential Library, West Branch, Iowa.

32. Hoover to Benjamin Strong, August 30, 1921, sent only in draft form, CPF, Hoover Papers; *see also* Hoover to Harding, January 23, 1922, ibid.

33. Quoted in Lloyd, *Aggressive Introvert*, 70.

34. Quoted in ibid., 45.

35. Quoted in ibid., 45, 107; Wilson, *Hoover*, 57–61, 81–83, 139–42.

36. Gabriel Kolko, *The Triumph of Conservatism* (New York, 1963), 217–54.

37. Chandler, *Strong.* On the foreign policy of the FRBNY, see Frank Costigliola, "The Politics of Financial Stabilization: American Reconstruction Policy in Europe, 1924–30" (Ph.D. dissertation, Cornell University, 1973).

38. Sir Henry Strakosch to Basil Blackett, October 17, 1925, T176/25B Otto Niemeyer Papers, Public Record Office, London (hereafter PRO).

39. Wilson, *American Business*, 23–30.

40. Tarbell, *Young*; Frank Costigliola, "The United States and the Reconstruction of Germany in the 1920s," *Business History Review* 50 (Winter 1976):477–502, and "The Other Side of Isolationism: The Establishment of the First World Bank, 1929–30," *Journal of American History* 59 (December 1972):602–20.

41. Owen D. Young to Joseph Tumulty, October 6, 1925, Owen D. Young Papers, Van Hornesville, N.Y.

42. *First General Conference of the International General Electric Company and Associated Companies* (no pub., no date, but conference held at Briarcliff Manor, N.Y., October 25–29, 1920), 13.

43. Owen Young speech, November 5, 1921, Young Papers; Case and Case, *Owen D. Young*, 173–91. For an account which emphasizes Anglo-American cooperation, *see* Hogan, *Informal Entente* 105–58.

44. Bullard told the story to Young, who passed it along to the GE Conference. *First General Conference*, 17–18. For the general impact of the Fourteen Points in Europe, *see* Victor S. Mamatey, *The United States and East Central Europe, 1914–1918: A Study of Wilsonian Diplomacy and Propaganda* (Princeton, 1957), 189–219.

45. Walter Lippmann, *Public Opinion* (New York, 1965), 133.

46. Young speech, November 5, 1921, Young Papers.

47. Young speech, January 6, 1926, Young Papers.

48. *See* chap. 4.

49. *See* Lamont's discussion of interview with Hughes in letter to J. P. Morgan, October 6, 1922, file 108–13, Lamont Papers.

50. Chap. 4.

51. *See* Robert Dominic Accinelli, "The United States and the World Court, 1920–27" (Ph.D. dissertation, University of California at Berkeley, 1968).

52. Carroll, "Lodge's Contributions," 157.

53. As Senator Henry Cabot Lodge put it, America "has never been isolated, never can be isolated, and has no desire to be isolated ("Foreign Relations of the United States, 1921–24," *Foreign Affairs* 2 [1924]:538). *See also* Michael James Conwell, "Opinion Maker and Foreign Policy: The Concept of America's Role in World Affairs, the 1920s" (Ph.D. dissertation, Michigan State University, 1977), 171–72; Homer E. Socolofsky, *Arthur Capper* (Lawrence, Kans., 1962), 134–64.

54. Carroll, "Lodge's Contributions," 159–62; Marian C. McKenna, *Borah* (Ann Arbor, 1961), 217–18; John Chalmers Vinson, *William E. Borah and the*

Outlawry of War (Athens, Ohio, 1957), 78–94; Howard A. Dewitt, "The 'New' Harding and American Foreign Policy: Warren G. Harding, Hiram W. Johnson, and Pragmatic Diplomacy," *Ohio History* 86 (Spring 1977), 96-114.

55. Quoted in Barbara McKay Shaver, "American Policy and European Collective Security, 1921–1925" (Ph.D. dissertation, University of Colorado, 1972), 45.

56. U.S. Department of Census, *Historical Statistics*, 537.

57. A representative account of the national debate on economic self-sufficiency appeared in the American Academy of Political and Social Science's *Annals. See* especially the following issues: "The International Trade Situation" 94 (March 1921); "The Place of the United States in a World Organization for the Maintenance of Peace," 96 (July 1921); "The Revival of American Business," 97 (September 1921); "America and the Rehabilitation of Europe," 102 (July 1922); "Western Europe and the United States," 104 (November 1922); "America's Relation to the European Situation," 108 (July 1923); "America and the Post-War European Situation," 114 (July 1924). After mid-1924 debate fell off until the turbulence of the early 1930s crippled foreign trade.

58. Treasury Department, *Annual Report 1923* (Washington, 1924), 2.

59. William S. Culbertson, "America's Interest in the Rehabilitation of Europe," *Annals* (America and the Rehabilitation of Europe) 102 (July 1922):61.

60. *See* Wilson, *Hoover*, 65–67, 170–71; Leffler, "Political Isolationism," 428–29, 458–59; Braeman, "New Left and American Foreign Policy," 73–104.

61. Frank W. Taussig, *The Tariff History of the United States* (New York, 1964) 55–57; John D. Hicks, *Republican Ascendancy 1921–1933* (New York, 1960).

62. Department of Commerce, *Annual Report 1926* (Washington, 1926), 97; Treasure Department, *Annual Report 1921* (Washington, 1922), 42–43.

63. "Democratic Platform of 1928," in Arthur M. Schlesinger, Jr., ed. *History of U.S. Political Parties* (New York, 1973), vol. 3, 1916.

64. Department of Commerce, *Statistical Abstract of the United States 1930,* (Washington, 1930), 465.

65. Will Payne, "Income Tax Dividends," *Saturday Evening Post* 196 (September 1, 1923):122. Payne quotes Hoover. *See also* Wilson, *Hoover*, 65–67, 170–71, passim. In part Hoover aimed such talk at "European businessmen and economists," who "overestimate[d] our dependency upon Europe" and so failed to do the belt-tightening prerequisite to American aid. Herbert Hoover, "A Year of Cooperation," *Nation's Business* 10 (June 5, 1922):13.

66. Department of Commerce, *Annual Report 1928* (Washington, 1928), 93–94; *Annual Report 1926*, 29–30; *Annual Report 1927* (Washington, 1927), xxi. Other business, political, and intellectual leaders agreed. *See*, for example, Silas Strawn, "Can Germany Pay and Not Work?" *Nation's Business* 10 (June 5, 1922):21; Dwight W. Morrow, "How Europe's Plight Affects Us," ibid., 22–23; Francis H. Sisson, "What May We Expect?" ibid., 23; Treasury Department, *Annual Report 1921* (Washington, 1922), 42; *Annual Report 1922* (Washington, 1923), 2; Henry H. Morse and Walter F. Wyman, "The Part of Direct Exporting in the Future of American Industry," *Annals* ("The International Trade Situation") 94 (March 1921):54–59; O. K. Davis, "The National Foreign Trade Council," ibid., 118; George M. Reynolds, "Capital: Shall We Export It or Use It for American Business?" *Annals* ("The Revival of American Business") 97 (September 1921): 1–2; Senator Thomas Sterling, "Foreword," *Annals* ("America and

the Rehabilitation of Europe") 102 (July 1922):40; Pierpont B. Noyes, "America's Cooperation Indispensable to International Security," ibid., 53; Samuel M. Vauclain, "Is American Prosperity Dependent Upon the Rehabilitation of Europe?" ibid., 54–55; G. B. Roorbach, "Europe and the Development of American Foreign Trade," ibid., 70–71; Silas H. Strawn, "America's Cooperation a Prerequisite to European Rehabilitation," ibid., 180–82; Edward A. Filene, "Is American Cooperation Necessary for European Rehabilitation?" ibid., 188; Ernest Minor Patterson, "Western Europe and the United States," *Annals* ("Western Europe and the United States") 104 (November 1922):8; Emil Kiss, "Reconstruction in Europe and the United States," *Annals* ("America's Relation to the European Situation") 108 (July 1923):109; Stephen P. Duggan, "Adapting Our Foreign Policy to World Facts," *Annals* ("American and the Post-War European Situation") 114 (July 1924):108; Harry T. Collings, "Foreign Trade and Increased Foreign Wealth," *Annals* ("Scientific Distribution") 115 (September 1924):241–47; Conwell, "Opinion Makers and Foreign Policy," 112–22. Some who acknowledged that the U.S. could, if necessary, survive without foreign markets or a rehabilitated Europe feared consequences other than economic depression. Fred I. Kent linked foreign trade with the quality of life: "In order that we may grow, ourselves, and increase our understanding of all those things which go to make for beauty and real happiness in the world, we must exchange our resources and the products of our constructive genius with those of the men of other nations. ... Trade ... serves to make life worthwhile" ("The Interdependence of America and Europe," *Annals* ("America and the Rehabilitation of Europe") 102 [July 1922]:170. Culbertson warned that America had "an interest far deeper than economic gain in seeing Europe pull through." At stake was "the white man's" leadership of the globe. Culbertson, "America's Interest in the Rehabilitation of Europe," ibid., 63.

67. Treasury Department, *Annual Report 1923*, 2. In 1922 Mellon affirmed that "business in this country can not progress indefinitely without its foreign markets" (*Annual Report 1922*, 2).

68. H. R. Enslow, "Trends in Agricultural Exports," *Annals* ("Agriculture") 142 (March 1929); 86.

69. Department of Commerce, *Annual Report 1923* (Washington, 1923), 2.

70. Ibid., 15. Europe remained the number one customer throughout the decade. In 1928 Klein noted that Europe's ability to purchase farm products was "a major factor in our prosperity." Department of Commerce, *Annual Report 1928*, xxvii.

71. Department of Commerce, *Annual Report 1926* 47; W. J. Spellman, "A Balanced Agricultural Output in the United States," *Annals* ("The Agricultural Situation in the United States") 117 (January 1925):292; L. C. Gray, "A Domestic Market for American Farm Products," ibid., 156–64. Gray, a Department of Agriculture economist, calculated that the United States could not consume all her bread grains for "another decade at least." Exports of tobacco and cotton would be necessary "for a much longer period."

72. For Hoover's hopes see Dressler, "Foreign Policies of American Individualism" 57. For the practical problems *see* W. E. Grimes, "Diversification of Agriculture: Its Limitations and Advantages," *Annals* ("Agriculture") 142 (March 1929):221.

73. Enslow, "Trends in Agricultural Exports," 86.

74. George H. Mayer, *The Republican Party 1854–1966* (New York, 1967), 385–86.

75. [William R. Castle, Jr.], "Two Years of American Foreign Policy," *Foreign Affairs* 1 (March 15, 1923):18. Harding also attributed the defeat to farm discontent. See Murray, *Harding Era*, 320.

76. *Literary Digest* 81 (June 28, 1924):6.

77. *Statistical Abstract of the United States 1930*, 474, 491.

78. Department of Commerce, *Annual Report 1926*, 29; *1923*, 9; *1927*, xxi; William C. Redfield, "The Spirit of Our Foreign Relations," *Annals* ("America's Relation to the European Situation") 108 (July 1923):197–98.

79. Frank Robert Chalk, "The United States and the International Struggle for Rubber, 1914–1941," (Ph.D. dissertation, University of Wisconsin, 1970), 44–162; Brandes, *Herbert Hoover*, 84–128.

80. Quoted in Dressler, "Foreign Policies of American Individualism," 78.

81. *Department of Commerce, Annual Report 1926*, 35.

82. U.S. Department of Census, *Historical Statistics*, 537.

83. Charles Beard, "The American Invasion of Europe," *Harper's Magazine* 158 (March 1929):470–79; Cleona Lewis, *America's Stake in International Investments* (Washington, 1938), 606. Of this total, $4.6 billion was in Europe.

84. Coolidge address, November 11, 1928, printed in *Commercial and Financial Chronicle* 128-2 (November 17, 1928):2759–61.

85. Whitney H. Shepardson, *Early History of the Council on Foreign Relations* (Stamford, Conn., 1960), 1–16; Harold Jefferson Coolidge and Robert Howard Lord, *Archibald Cary Coolidge, Life and Letters* (Boston, 1932), 307–8; Herbert Heaton, *A Scholar in Action: Edwin F. Gay* (Cambridge, Mass., 1952), 204; Hamilton Fish Armstrong, *Peace and Counterpeace* (New York, 1971), 181–97.

86. Hamilton Fish Armstrong to Frank Lowden, November 25, 1922, RM 1, CFR Papers. *See also* Laurence H. Shoup and William Minter, *Imperial Brain Trust* (New York, 1977), 11–26; Robert F. Byrnes, *Awakening American Education to the World: The Role of Archibald Cary Coolidge, 1866–1928* (Notre Dame, 1982), 183–85, 190–202.

87. Others among the first members were Owen Young, Walter Lippmann, Otto Kahn, Hugh Gibson, John Foster Dulles, Joseph P. Cotton, David F. Houston, Dwight Morrow, Russell Leffingwell, Paul Warburg, George Wickersham, Norman Davis, Paul Cravath, and Raymond Fosdick.

88. Armstrong to Lowden, November 25, 1922, RM 1, CFR Papers.

89. Armstrong to Charles E. Hughes, January 31, 1923; Hughes to Armstrong, March 6, 1923, RM 1, CFR Papers.

90. The council published the secretaries' speeches in *Foreign Affairs*. See Hughes, "Recent Questions and Negotiations," *Foreign Affairs* 2 (Special Supplement, December 1923):i–xxii; Frank B. Kellogg, "Some Foreign Policies of the United States," *Foreign Affairs* 4 (Special Supplement, January 1926):i–xvii; Henry L. Stimson, "The Pact of Paris: Three Years of Development," *Foreign Affairs* 11 (Special Supplement, 1932):i–ix.

91. Ramsay MacDonald's address, October 1, 1929, copy in RM 2, CFR Papers; Walter Mallory to Isaiah Bowman, October 1, 1929, ibid.

92. Armstrong to Dwight Morrow, October 16, 1922, Morrow Papers; Armstrong to Hughes, January 31, 1923, RM 1, CFR Papers.

93. William R. Grace to CFR members, February 17, 1922, RM1, CFR Papers.

94. Armstrong to Lowden, November 25, 1922, RM 1, CFR Papers.

95. Armstrong to Russell C. Leffingwell, January 18, 1923, RM 1, CFR Papers; Armstrong to Paul Warburg, January 22, 1923, ibid.; Armstrong to Lowden, November 25, 1922, ibid.

96. Paul Warburg to Armstrong, August 22, 1928, RM 2, CFR Papers; Walter H. Mallory to Bowman, January 15, 1929, ibid. The council maintained a reference libary and staff for members as well as "a much wider public." Armstrong to Morrow, December 10, 1924, Morrow Papers.

97. Shepardson to Morrow, December 28, 1922, Morrow Papers.

98. A persistent theme of CFR study groups and meetings was that for economic and cultural reasons, "the American people are vitally concerned in the welfare of the peoples of Europe." Report of Study Group 3, January 1923, Records of Groups (hearafter RG) 1, CFR Papers; January 11, 1921 meeting, RM I, ibid.

99. A. C. Coolidge to Armstrong, May 13, 1924, quoted in Coolidge and Lord, *Coolidge, Life and Letters*, 318; Armstrong, *Peace and Counterpeace*, 182.

100. *Foreign Affairs* 1 (September 15, 1922):2; Coolidge and Lord, *Coolidge, Life and Letters*, 312–13; A. C. Coolidge to Morrow, September 15, 1922, Morrow Papers.

101. Coolidge and Lord, *Coolidge, Life and Letters*, 312–13.

102. Quoted in ibid., 356.

103. F. A. Golder to Coolidge, December 11, 1922, quoted in ibid., 315. Golder managed to secure Lenin's annotated copy, which he passed on to Coolidge. After one year subscribers numbered more than 5,000; after five years, more than 10,000. Ibid., 316.

104. Quoted in ibid., 318.

105. Paul U. Kellogg, *Ten Years of the Foreign Policy Association* (New York, 1929), 7; Helbich, "American Liberals," 568–69.

106. Kellogg, *Foreign Policy Association*, 10; Helbich, "American Liberals," 574–75.

107. Helbich, "American Liberals," 592–93.

108. Kellogg, *Foreign Policy Association*, 12–15.

109. Ibid., 2.

110. Ibid., 14–15.

111. James McDonald to Morrow, March 28, 1922, Morrow Papers. Like the council, the FPA rallied support on specific issues such as the World Court. *See*, for example, McDonald to Morrow, May 20, 1925, ibid.

112. *Round-Table Conferences of the Institute of Politics. First Session 1921* (New Haven, 1923), ix–xii, 431–38. At the close of the 1921 session Elihu Root praised speakers for having "struck the imagination of the American press.... The substance of your words has been carried to the remotest part of this great country, published in a thousand journals, commented upon in thousands of editorials." Ibid., 440. *See also* Byrnes, *Awakening American Education*, 185–90.

113. *Round-Table Conferences. First Session 1921*, v–viii, 7–12, 439–49.

114. Ibid., 3.

115. Ibid., 7–11.

116. Other important ones included the World Peace Foundation, the Carnegie

Endowment for International Peace, and the Committee of One Hundred on Foreign Relations of the National Civic Federation. *See* Elihu Root speech to National Civic Federation, in Bacon and Scott, eds., *Men and Policies*, 489–97; Selig Adler, *The Isolationist Impulse* (New York, 1957), 121–22.

117. Walter Lippmann, *The Phantom Public* (New York, 1925), 197.

118. Ibid., 155.

119. *See*, for example, *Round-Table Conferences. First Session 1921*, 15; Lippmann, *Public Opinion*, 224; Hughes, "Upright States," 11.

120. Lippmann, *Phantom Public*, 144–45, passim.

121. Elihu Root, "A Requisite for the Success of Popular Diplomacy," *Foreign Affairs* 1 (September 15, 1922); *Round Table Conferences. First Session 1921*, 439–49.

122. Armstrong, *Peace and Counterpeace*, 197.

123. Stuart Ewen, *Captains of Consciousness* (New York, 1976), 62.

124. Edward L. Bernays, *Propaganda* (New York, 1928), 19.

125. Ibid., 48, 50, 101.

126. Lippmann, *Public Opinion*, 158.

127. Quoted in Nigro, "Propaganda, Politics, and the New Diplomacy," 215–16, 249. For CPI movie propaganda during World War I, *see* Emily S. Rosenberg, *Spreading the American Dream: American Economic and Cultural Expansion, 1890–1945* (New York, 1982), 79–81.

128. *Fortune* advertisement, 1 (February 1930):125; *New York Times*, November 9, 1930, sec. 2:12.

129. Quoted in Downes, *Rise of Harding*, 463.

130. Quoted in Frank Presbrey, *The History and Development of Advertising* (Garden City, N.Y., 1929), 620.

3. The Frustration of American Policy, 1921–1923

1. Hughes to Harvey, May 11, 1921, 763.72119/1135A, General Records of the Department of State, NARG 59, Washington, D.C.

2. Wimer and Wimer, "Harding Administration," 15–17; Danelski and Tulchin, eds., *Hughes*, 225–26; Sally Marks and Denis Dulude, "German-American Relations, 1918–1921," *Mid-America* 53 (October 1971):221; David H. Jennings, "President Harding and International Organization," *Ohio History* 75 (Summer 1966):155.

3. Hoover to Hughes, April 6, 1921, 711.62119/107, NARG 59. *See also* Hoover to Hughes, April 9, 1921, enclosing memorandum by John Foster Dulles, April 7, 1921, 711.62119/4, NARG 59.

4. Van Meter, "United States and European Recovery," 285–88.

5. The extent of General Eelctric's prewar German relations is apparent in Anson W. Burchard to Owen D. Young and other GE officers, August 28, 1920, Young Papers.

6. Link, *Die amerikanische Stabilisierungspolitik*, 75 and passim.

7. Quoted in ibid., 90.

8. Among them were the executive secretary of the American Chamber of Commerce in Berlin, the head of the Berlin branch of Mergenthaler Linotype Corporation, and the head of National Cash Register's German subsidiary. *See*

James L. Colwell, "The American Experience in Berlin during the Weimar Republic" (Ph.D. dissertation, Yale University, 1961), 56, 258.

9. Ibid., 21.

10. Ibid., 191.

11. J. Anton de Haas, "The Present Outlook for United States' Trade with Germany," *Annals* ("The International Trade Situation") 94 (March 1921):85; Link, *Die amerikanische Stabilisierungspolitik*, 60–72; for the speculation, Carl-Ludwig Holtfrerich, *Die deutsche Inflation, 1914–1923* (Berlin, 1980), 279–93.

12. One of the most important prewar economic bonds allied GE and the Allgemeine Elektrizitaets Gesellschaft. The two giants traded patents and divided markets on a worldwide basis. In August 1920, representatives of the two firms met in Switzerland and agreed to renew ties upon signature of a formal peace. This industrial alliance was of far more than corporate significance, for the chief officers of the German firm (Walther Rathenau and Felix Deutsch) and the American (Owen Young and Gerard Swope) played crucial roles in international economic and political affairs of the 1920s. *See* n. 5 above, and chap. 5 below.

13. Marks and Dulude, "German-American Relations," 219–20; see also ibid., 211–26.

14. Ibid., 221–22; Pusey, *Hughes*, 1:441–42; Wimer and Wimer, "Harding Administration," 17–18; Danelski and Tulchin, eds., *Hughes*, 225–27.

15. Quoted in Link, *Die amerikanische Stabilisierungspolitik*, 97.

16. Quoted in ibid., 100. For the German-American negotiations *see FRUS, 1921,* 1:1–24; Marks and Dulude, "German-American Relations," 222–24; Wimer and Wimer, "Harding Administration," 18; Link, *Die amerikanische Stabilisierungspolitik*, 91–97; Buckingham, "Diplomatic and Economic Normalcy," 19–43.

17. Carroll, "Lodge's Contributions," 157; Maddox, *Borah*, 122; Nan K. Lowerre, "Warren G. Harding and American Foreign Affairs, 1915–23" (Ph.D. dissertation, Stanford University, 1968), 136.

18. Quoted in Wimer and Wimer, "Harding Administration," 23.

19. Quoted in Buckingham, "Diplomatic and Economic Normalcy," 64.

20. William Borah, "The Ghost of Versailles at the Conference," *The Nation* 113 (November 9, 1921):525.

21. Quoted in Charles Leonard Hoag, *Preface to Preparedness: The Washington Disarmament Conference and Public Opinion* (Washington, 1941), 82.

22. Quoted in Roberta Allbert Dayer, "The British War Debts to the United States and the Anglo-Japanese Alliance, 1920–23," *Pacific Historical Review* 45 (November 1976):577.

23. On the U.S. and the Anglo-Japanese alliance, *see* ibid, 569–95; Ira Klein, "Whitehall, Washington and the Anglo-Japanese Alliance," *Pacific Historical Review* 41 (1972), 460–83; Ian Nish, *Alliance in Decline: A Study in Anglo-Japanese Relations, 1908–23* (London, 1972), chaps. 18–22; Clarence B. Davis, "The Defensive Diplomacy of British Imperialism in the Far East, 1915–22: Japan and United States as Partners and Rivals" (Ph.D. dissertation, University of Wisconsin, 1972); Howard L. English, "Great Britain and the Problem of Imperial Defense: The Far East, 1919–23" (Ph.D. dissertation, Fordham University, 1971); Maynard J. Toll, Jr., "Australia in the Evolution of the British Commonwealth, 1919–39: The Impact of the International Environment" (Ph.D. dissertation, Johns Hopkins, 1970), 79–108; Neville K. Meaney, "The American Attitude towards the British Empire 1919–22: A Study in the Diplomatic Relations of the

English-Speaking Nations" (Ph.D. dissertation, Duke University, 1958), 330–407; William Roger Louis, *British Strategy in the Far East, 1919–1939* (Oxford, 1971), 40–108; M. G. Fry, "The North Atlantic Triangle and the Abrogation of the Anglo-Japanese Alliance," *Journal of Modern History*, 39 (March 1967):46–64.

24. Quoted in Louis, *British Strategy in the Far East*, 26–27; *see also* Davis, "Defensive Diplomacy of British Imperialism," 479–81.

25. Russell Wayne Anderson, "The Abandonment of British Naval Supremacy, 1919–20" (Ph.D. dissertation, University of Kentucky, 1974), especially 167; James H. Mannock, "Anglo-American Relations, 1921–28" (Ph.D. dissertation, Princeton University, 1962), 1–64.

26. Quoted in Louis, *British Strategy in the Far East*, 54.

27. Ibid., 46–47, 54.

28. Quoted in ibid., 54–55.

29. Quoted in ibid., 58.

30. Dayer, "British War Debts," 569–95.

31. Ibid., 580; Louis, *British Strategy in the Far East*, 61; Davis, "Defensive Diplomacy of British Imperialism," 448; Roger Dingman, *Power in the Pacific* (Chicago, 1976), 160–77.

32. Quoted in Louis, *British Strategy in the Far East*, 75. See also Philip G. Wigley, *Canada and the Transition to Commonwealth* (London, 1977), 134–41.

33. Quoted in ibid., 65; *see also* English, "Great Britain," 140–41.

34. The first statement quoted in English, "Great Britain," 80; the second quoted in Louis, *British Strategy in the Far East*, 70. New Zealand prime minister William Massey agreed with Hughes. See ibid., 71–72.

35. Ibid., 71.

36. *Documents on British Foreign Policy*, 1st ser. 14:271–76; *see* also English, "Great Britain," 126, 276.

37. Louis, *British Strategy in the Far East*, 79–84. For a contrary view, *see* Dayer, "British War Debts."

38. Maddox, *Borah*, 86–96; Thomas H. Buckley, *The United States and the Washington Conference, 1921–22* (Knoxville, 1970), 11–12; John Chalmers Vinson, *The Parchment Peace* (Athens, Ga., 1955), 78–96; Dingman, *Power in the Pacific*, 143–45.

39. Quoted in Lowerre, "Warren G. Harding," 99.

40. Danelski and Tulchin, eds., *Hughes*, 240; Pusey, *Hughes*, 2:454–55; Hoag, *Preface to Preparedness*, 73–123.

41. Hoag, *Preface to Preparedness*, 73.

42. Quoted in Van Meter, "United States and European Recovery," 297, 299. *See also* ibid., 296–302; Thomas Lamont to Hughes, July 25, 1921, file 99-4, Lamont Papers; Hoag, *Preface to Preparedness*, 73–79, 112; *Nation's Business* 9 (October 5, 1921):7.

43. Danelski and Tulchin, eds., *Hughes*, 241–42.

44. Pusey, *Hughes*, 2:456–57; Davis, "Defensive Diplomacy of British Imperialism," 489–90.

45. Quoted in Louis, *British Strategy in the Far East*, 85.

46. Quoted in ibid., 88.

47. Ibid., 88–90; Davis, "Defensive Diplomacy of British Imperialism," 498.

48. Quoted in Davis, "Defensive Diplomacy of British Imperialism," 503;

see also ibid., 501–5; Louis, *British Strategy in the Far East*, 92–93; Pusey, *Hughes*, 2:458.

49. Hoag, *Preface to Preparedness*, 89–123. Hoag mistakes the shadow for the substance by failing to perceive his own evidence that the administration molded and used public opinion rather than meekly follow it.

50. Quoted in ibid., 113–14.

51. Quoted in ibid., 126; Hoover, *Memoirs* 2:179. *See also New York Times*, November 2, 1921, 2.

52. Quoted in Hoag, *Preface to Preparedness*, 132–36.

53. Davis, "Defensive Diplomacy of British Imperialism," 527–45.

54. Quoted in ibid., 530.

55. Carroll, "Lodge's Contributions," especially 164–65; Buckley, *Washington Conference*, 45–46.

56. Ibid., 47–57; Ernest Andrade, "The United States Navy and the Washington Conference," *The Historian* 31 (May 1969):345–52; Pusey, *Hughes*, 2:464.

57. *New York Times*, November 12, 1921, 2.

58. Mark Sullivan, *The Great Adventure at Washington* (New York, 1922), 18–19. *See also* ibid., 1–31; Buckley, *Washington Conference*, 63–74; Harold Sprout and Margaret Sprout, *Toward a New Order of Sea Power* (Princeton, 1946), 153–57; Pusey, *Hughes* 2:466–73; Dingman, *Power in the Pacific*, 196–98.

59. Quoted in Pusey, *Hughes* 2:473; on the conference and French and British public opinion, *see* Donald S. Birn, "Open Diplomacy at the Washington Conference of 1921–22: The British and French Experience," *Comparative Studies in Society and History* 12 (July 1970):297–319.

60. Quoted in Buckley, *Washington Conference*, 74.

61. Ibid., 86–89, 104–13; Sprout and Sprout, *New Order of Sea Power*, 161–70; Leffler, *Elusive Quest*, 33–39; Louis, *British Strategy in the Far East*, 102; Stephen Roskill, *Hankey, Man of Secrets* (London, 1972), 2:248; Mannock, "Anglo-American Relations," 22–24; Dingman, *Power in the Pacific*, 199–214.

62. Buckley, *Washington Conference*, 110–19; Dingman, *Power in the Pacific*, 207–9; Louis, *British Strategy in the Far East*, 99–103; Birn, "Washington Conference," 312–16; Sprout and Sprout, *New Order of Sea Power*, 190–216; Leo Winston Hindsley, "In Search of an Ally: French Attitudes toward America" (Ph.D. dissertation, Michigan State University, 1980), 102–18. The conference set a 10,000-ton limit on cruisers, larger than existing vessels, and so pointed the direction of future naval competition.

63. Buckley, *Washington Conference*, 89, 95–96, 102–3, 127–56; Davis, "Defensive Diplomacy of British Imperialism," 588–641; Pusey, *Hughes* 2:491–500.

64. Guinsburg, *Pursuit of Isolationism*, 55–78; Buckley, *Washington Conference*, 172–84; Vinson, *Parchment Peace*, 196–212; Maddox, *Borah*, 107–17; Hoag, *Preface to Preparedness*, 143–60; *Literary Digest* 73 (April 8, 1922):12–13; Dewitt, " 'New' Harding," 111–13.

65. Quoted in Van Meter, "United States and European Recovery," 295–96.

66. Quoted in Jennings, "Harding," 160.

67. Quoted in Buckley, *Washington Conference*, 172.

68. "Regarding Defacto Recognition of Russia," Foreign Policy Association pamphlet no. 12 (June 1922). For other liberal opinion *see* Anne Vincent Mei-

burger, *Efforts of Raymond Robins toward the Recognition of Soviet Russia and the Outlawry of War, 1917–33* (Washington, 1958); "Minutes of Group Meeting on Russia," January 24, 1924, RG 1, CFR. On the controversy over Russian policy in the business community *see* Wilson, *Ideology and Economics.*

69. David Glen Singer, "The United States Confronts the Soviet Union, 1919–33: The Rise and Fall of the Policy of Nonrecognition" (Ph.D. dissertation), Loyola University, 1973), 20; Wilson, *Ideology and Economics,* 14–48; Pusey, *Hughes,* 2:526–28.

70. Williams, *American Russian Relations,* 181–85, 205. The American ambassador to London advised that "our logical method of *escape*" from recognition was to insist on complete cessation of Soviet propaganda in the U.S. Alanson B. Houghton to Kellogg, November 11, 1926, Houghton Papers; emphasis added.

71. Quoted in Weissman, *Hoover and Famine Relief,* 44–45.

72. Quoted in Fisher, *Famine in Soviet Russia,* 52–53. Fisher was a member of the ARA team in Russia. *See also* Wilson, *Ideology and Politics,* 23–25.

73. For the text of the "treaty," *see* Fisher, *Famine in Soviet Russia,* 507–10. At first, Hoover wanted extraterritorial privileges like those the ARA enjoyed in Poland and Austria. Hoover "must be slapped publicly before the whole world," Lenin raged. With the talks at an impasse, a telegram from the ARA representative suggested "concessions," since "very radical changes in Soviet government anticipated." Hoover accepted this advice, and the August 20 "treaty" granted ARA personnel not extraterritorial rights, but those of accredited diplomats. *See* Weissman, *Hoover and Famine Relief,* 54, 59 for the quotations and 53–59 for the story.

74. Hoover, *American Epic* 3:446–48; Weissman, *Hoover and Famine Relief,* 71–72, 104–7.

75. Lloyd, *Aggressive Introvert,* 54.

76. Fisher, *Famine in Soviet Russia,* 139; Hoover, *American Epic,* 3:44.

77. Fisher, *Famine in Soviet Russia,* 140–41; Weissman, *Hoover and Famine Relief,* 70.

78. For the financial accounting *see* Hoover, *American Epic* 3:451.

79. Quoted in Weissman, *Hoover and Famine Relief,* 93.

80. Ibid., 98–100; Fisher, *Famine in Soviet Russia,* 149–54; *FRUS 1921* 2:823–24.

81. Quoted in Weissman, *Hoover and Famine Relief,* 89. *See also* ibid., 88.

82. *Department of Commerce 1923* (Washington, 1923), 24–25; Weissman, *Hoover and Famine Relief,* 90, 192; *FRUS 1921* 2:825–27.

83. Quoted in Weissman, *Hoover and Famine Relief,* 124; italics in original. For Stalin and Trotsky, *see* ibid, 124–26.

84. Memorandum by Archibald Cary Coolidge of conversation with Chicherin, quoted in Coolidge and Lord, *Coolidge, Life and Letters,* 280; *see also* Weissman, *Hoover and Famine Relief,* 129–30, 137; Fisher, *Famine in Soviet Russia,* 397.

85. Quoted in Fisher, *Famine in Soviet Russia,* 397.

86. Weissman, *Hoover and Famine Relief,* 130; Fisher, *Famine in Soviet Russia,* 373.

87. Weissman, *Hoover and Famine Relief,* 81–88, 119–21; Fisher, *Famine in Soviet Russia,* 367–69, 405–26.

88. Ibid., 206; Haskell quoted in Weissman, *Hoover and Famine Relief,* 116, 118.

89. Anna Louise Strong to Sydney Strong, April 13, 1923, Box 3, Anna Louise Strong Papers, University of Washington Library; Weissman, *Hoover and Famine Relief*, 53.

90. Fisher, *Famine in Soviet Russia*, 217, 227–28, 294–97, 383. *See also* Frank A. Golder and Lincoln Hutchinson, *On the Trail of the Russian Famine* (Stanford, 1927).

91. Coolidge quoted in William Bentinck-Smith, *Building a Great Library: The Coolidge Years at Harvard* (Cambridge, Mass., 1976), 126; Anna Louise Strong to Sydney Strong, December 31, 1921; January 31, 1921, Box 3, Anna Louise Strong Papers. *See also* Byrnes, *American Education*, 122.

92. Quoted in Weissman, *Hoover and Famine Relief*, 164–65.

93. Ibid., 166–178; Fisher, *Famine in Soviet Russia*, 369–71.

94. Hoover to Hughes, December 6, 1921, Box 137, Commerce Official File (hereafter COF), Hoover Papers.

95. *New York Times*, July 23, 1923, 1; Frederic Lewis Propas, "The State Department, Bureaucratic Politics and Soviet-American Relations, 1918–1938" (Ph.D. dissertation, University of California, Los Angeles, 1982). Kelley's work is a major subject of this dissertation. The intelligence agent was Hugh S. Martin. See pp. 78–81.

96. On State Department interest in Communist activities in Austria, *see* file 863.00B/, especially Joseph Grew to Washburn, February 18, 1925, 863.00B/37; Washburn to F. B. Kellogg, July 29, 1927, 863.00B/57, all NARG 59; for interest in the Communist situation in Bulgaria, *see* Hughes to Charles Wilson, July 25, 1923, 874.00B/7a; Allen Dulles to William Phillips, June 8, 1922, 874.00B/4; Evan E. Young to Hughes, February 7, 1924, 874.00B/17, all in ibid.

97. Propas, "State Department," 57–58. *See* 811.00B/ NARG 59 for extensive files on American Communists and radicals; on radical immigrants, *see* Robert D. Schulzinger, *The Making of the Diplomatic Mind* (Middletown, Conn., 1975), 63.

98. For the quotations, Homer Brett to Frank B. Kellogg, May 5, 1926, 841.5045/147, NARG 59; Henry Fletcher to Kellogg, May 13, 1926, Box 12, Henry Fletcher Papers, Library of Congress. *See also* F.A. Sterling to Kellogg, May 8, 1926, 841.5045/155; Courtland Christian to Kellogg, May 15, 1926, 841.5045/167, both in NARG 59.

99. Hemingway in *Toronto Daily Star*, May 13, 1922, 7; John D. Bell, *Peasants in Power* (Princeton, 1977), 154–207; Nissan Oren, *Revolution Administered: Agrarianism and Communism in Bulgaria* (Baltimore, 1973), 9–11; Hugh Seton-Watson, *Eastern Europe between the Wars, 1918–41* (New York, 1967), 242–44.

100. Charles Wilson to Colby, September 8, 1920, 760c.61/350, NARG 59. For a similar despatch to Hughes, *see* Wilson to Hughes, May 19, 1922, quoted in A.W. Dulles to William Phillips, June 8, 1922, 874.00B/4, ibid.

101. Charles Wilson to Colby, August 25, 1920, 760c.61/313; A.W. Dulles to William Phillips, June 8, 1922, 874.00B/4, ibid. Dulles remained skeptical that the Communists would actually take over in Bulgaria.

102. Herschel V. Johnson to Hughes, June 14, 1923, 874.00/228; Johnson to Hughes, June 13, 1923, 874.00/226, ibid.; Bell, *Peasants in Power*, 208–41; Seston-Watson, *Eastern Europe*, 244–46; Oren, *Agrarianism and Communism*, 11–12.

103. Charles Wilson to Hughes, August 16, 1924, 874.00B/26, NARG 59;

see also Wilson to Hughes, August 14, 1924, 874.00B/25; Wilson to Hughes, September 1, 1924, 874.00B/29; Wilson to Kellogg, May 4, 1925, 874.00B/55 Wilson to Kellogg, April 21, 1925, 874.00B/39, all in ibid.

104. Kellogg memorandum of conversation with Bulgarian minister, March 19, 1925, 874.00/272-1/2, ibid.

105. William R. Castle to Fred M. Dearing, March 4, 1922, 860c.51/215A; Dearing to Henry Fletcher, February 5, 1922, 860c.51/213, both in ibid. Loan negotiations went forward until the French vetoed the purchase. AFW to Castle, June 30, 1922, 860c.51/246, ibid.

106. Quoted in Nigro, "Propaganda, Politics, and the New Diplomacy" 171, 116, 247, 242. It is not known whether or not Mussolini took the money.

107. Ibid., 11, 208, 216.

108. Quoted in Louis A. DeSanti, "U.S. Relations with Italy under Mussolini, 1922–41: A Study Based on Records of the Department of State and Documents from the Captured Files of Mussolini" (Ph.D. dissertation, Columbia University, 1951), 42. *See also* ibid., 36. For Italy's postwar problems, *see* Adrian Lyttelton, *The Seizure of Power, Fascism in Italy, 1919–1929* (London, 1973), 30–41; Charles S. Maier, *Recasting Bourgeois Europe* (Princeton, 1975), 109–34; 305–50.

109. *New York Times*, October 31, 1922, 5.

110. Quoted in DeSanti, "U.S. Relations with Italy," 42.

111. Quoted in ibid., 36–48. *See also* Wayne Laylon Jordan, "America's Mussolini: The United States and Italy, 1919–36" (Ph.D. dissertation, University of Virginia, 1972) 51, 73; John P. Diggins, *Mussolini and Fascism: The View from America* (Princeton, 1972), 27–28, 265; Benito Mussolini, *My Autobiography* (New York, 1938).

112. Quoted in DeSanti, "U.S. Relations with Italy," 38.

113. Quoted in ibid., 60–62. *See also* 40–42. A State Department dispatch mentions the letter, but historians have not found any copy in the Mussolini, Harding, or State Department files. *See* ibid.; Diggins, *Mussolini and Fascism*, 262–63.

114. Stimson and Bundy, *Peace and War*, 269; memorandum by State Department legal adviser, November 29, 1932, 711.654/62, NARG 59. For a view that emphasizes Mussolini's bombastic rhetoric, *see* Carl James Francese, "United States Policy toward Italy on Arms Limitation and War Debts, 1929–33" (Ph.D. dissertation, University of Houston, 1982).

115. Quoted in *Literary Digest* 77 (June 9, 1923):72; *see also* the rest of the article "Why Mussolini Charms the American Business Man."

116. Quoted in *The Nation* 66 (April 18, 1923):459.

117. Kent to Seward Prosser, April 3, 1923; April 14, 1923, May 8, 1923; Prosser to Kent, May 18, 1923, all in Frederick Kent Papers, Mudd Library, Princeton University. Kent feared danger to Mussolini from "women of good standing but no real character" (letter to Prosser, April 14, 1923, ibid.). For Mussolini's efforts to woo U.S. business, *see* John Morris Berutti, "Italo-American Diplomatic Relations, 1922–28" (Ph.D. dissertation, Stanford University, 1960), 21–22. For a description of American business in Italy, *see* chap. 5 below.

118. For Morgan and Company activities in Italy, *see* the numerous letters in the Lamont Papers, especially Lamont to Dwight Morrow, May 23, 1923, file 113-14; Lamont to Russell Leffingwell, April 20, 1925, file 103-11; Lamont to Giovanni Fummi, December 11, 1925, file 190-17; Lamont's memorandum of

conversation with Mussolini, April 15, 1930, file 191-1; Lamont's memorandum of interview with Mussolini, April 16, 1937, file 191-13; DeSanti, "U.S. Relations with Italy," 100. The direct investment figure is for 1929. *See* Diggins, *Mussolini and Fascism*, 149.

119. Hoover to Calvin Coolidge, February 7, 1924, Box 169, COF, Hoover Papers.

120. Kent to Prosser, April 14, 1923, Kent Papers; Lamont to Leffingwell, April 20, 1925, file 103-11, Lamont Papers; speech by Elihu Root, December 14, 1926, RM 1, CFR Papers; Diggins, *Mussolini and Fascism*, 21, 156–61.

121. Will Rogers, *Letters of a Self-Made Diplomat to His President* (New York, 1926), 142.

122. For discussion of Mussolini as media event, *see* Diggins, *Mussolini and Fascism*, 22–57.

123. Rogers, *Letters of a Self-Made Diplomat*, 128, 145.

124. For a brilliant analysis, *see* Diggins, *Mussolini and Fascism*, 68–73. A typical newspaper interview entitled "Mussolini—Italy's Man of Tomorrow" argued that the dictator's achievements proved what "discipline, and organization, guided by an indomitable will, personal fearlessness, powerful intellect, profound learning, straight thinking, direct action can do." *New York Times*, November 5, 1922, sec. 9, 1.

125. Board of Governors of the Federal Reserve System, *Banking and Monetary Statistics* (Washington, 1943), 681.

126. Parrini, *Heir to Empire*, 101–37; Clyde Phelps, *The Foreign Expansion of American Banks* (New York, 1927). The key journal for following the expansion of New York's short-term money market was the *Acceptance Bulletin*. Before 1914, when Britain suffered a balance-of-payments deficit, the Bank of England would raise interest rates and so attract funds from abroad. The boast ran that a 10 percent rate would draw gold from the moon.

127. A. C. Pigou, *Aspects of British Economic History, 1918–25* (London, 1971), 148; Susan Howson, *Domestic Monetary Management in Britain, 1919–38* (London, 1975), 9–63; D. E. Moggridge, *British Monetary Policy, 1924–31: The Norman Conquest of $4.86* (Cambridge, 1972), 37–97.

128. John Maynard Keynes, *A Tract on Monetary Reform* (London, 1971; first printed in 1923), 138–39.

129. Otto Niemeyer to Montagu Norman, June 23, 1923, T176/13, Niemeyer Papers. *See also* Niemeyer to Norman, November 20, 1923, T176/5, ibid.; R. G. Hawtrey, "Monetary Policy (October 1923)," October 31, 1923, T176/5, ibid.

130. Norman to Niemeyer, November 20, 1923, T176/5, Niemeyer Papers.

131. For a picture of Norman's policies, *see* Andrew Boyle, *Montagu Norman* (London, 1967); Sir Henry Clay, *Lord Norman* (London, 1957); Chandler, *Strong*; Strong-Norman correspondence in Strong Papers; Émile Moreau, *Souvenirs d'un gouverneur de la Banque de France* (Paris, 1954). For a study that emphasizes the cooperative aspect while minimizing the competitive side of Britain's co-opting policy, *see* Hogan, *Informal Entente*.

132. Memorandum by Federation of British Industry, "The Trade Depression," October 12, 1921, T172/1315 British Treasury Records, Miscellaneous Files, PRO.

133. Quoted in Dayer, "British War Debts," 584.

134. Debts figures changed throughout the 1920s and early 1930s as nations reduced and funded them. The $33 billion reparations figure was lower than

previous Allied demands. The Allies reduced it further under the Dawes and Young plans of 1924 and 1929. In 1932 the present value of the German debt was $25.6 billion and war debts owed to the U.S., Britain, and France (the chief creditors) amounted roughly to $27 billion present value. *See* Harold G. Moulton and Leo Pasvolsky, *War Debts and World Prosperity* (Washington, 1932), 488. For amounts owed to Britain at the time of the Armistice, *see* ibid., 426.

135. Memorandum by British Treasury, quoted in David Felix, *Walther Rathenau and the Weimar Republic* (Baltimore, 1971), 110.

136. Silverman, *Reconstructing Europe*, 147–60; Hermann-Josef Rupieper, *The Cuno Government and Reparations 1922–1923"* (The Hague, 1979), 78–84.

137. Address by Walter Lippmann before the Foreign Policy Association, February 1922, FPA pamphlet no. 6, 2.

138. For discussion of French policy and historians' analysis of it, *see* Jon Jacobson, "The Strategies of French Foreign Policy after World War I," *Journal of Modern History* 55 (1983):78–95; Jon Jacobson, "Is There a New International History of the 1920s?" *American Historical Review* 88 (June 1983):617–45; Jay L. Kaplan, "The Internationalist Alternative: Economic and Ideological Aspects of French Security Policy, 1919–25," presented before Conference on European Security in the Locarno Era, Mars Hill, N.C., October 16–18, 1975, and "France's Road to Genoa: Strategic, Economic and Ideological Factors in French Foreign Policy, 1921–22" (Ph.D. dissertation, Columbia University, 1974); Maier, *Recasting Bourgeois Europe*, 208.

139. Kaplan essay and dissertation cited above; Maier, *Recasting Bourgeois Europe*, 229–420; Rupieper, *Cuno Government and Reparations*, 78–96. For war debt statistics, *see* Moulton and Pasvolsky, *War Debts*, 430–31.

140. Maier, *Recasting Bourgeois Europe*, especially 353–55.

141. Ibid., 210–11, 244, 300, 383–84, 444–46; Felix, *Rathenau*, 8–24.

142. Quoted in Hermann-Josef Rupieper, "Politics and Economics: The Cuno Government and Reparations, 1922–1923" (Ph.D. dissertation, Stanford University, 1974), 20.

143. See Colwell, "American Experience in Berlin," and chap. 6 below.

144. For the effects of the inflation, *see* Rupieper, "Politics and Economics," 106–12, 122–25, 332–66; Maier, *Recasting Bourgeois Europe*, 358–63. For the diplomacy and consequences of the Ruhr occupation, *see* ibid., 356–86; Kenneth Paul Jones, "Stresemann and the Diplomacy of the Ruhr Crisis, 1923–24" (Ph.D. dissertation, University of Wisconsin, 1970); Donald Bishop Saunders, "Stresemann vs. Poincaré: The Conduct of Germany's Western Policy during Stresemann's Chancellorship, August–November 1923" (Ph.D. dissertation, University of North Carolina, 1975); Henry A. Turner, Jr., *Stresemann and the Politics of the Weimar Republic* (Princeton, 1963), 144–53.

145. Commercial attaché Walter S. Tower to Julius Klein, August 24, 1922, transmitted to Hoover, September 11, 1922, file 601.2 United Kingdom, Records of the Bureau of Foreign and Domestic Commerce, NARG 151.

146. For a case study, *see* Frank Costigliola, "American Foreign Policy in the 'Nutcracker': United States Relation with Poland in the 1920s," *Pacific Historical Review* 48 (February 1979):85–105.

147. Hoover, "Memorandum," January 4, 1922, Box 91, COF, Hoover Papers.

148. For a study that focuses on the tactical disagreements among business

and political leaders rather than on their overall consensus, *see* Leffler, *Elusive Quest.*

149. Hoover speech, reported in *New York Times,* October 17, 1922, 14; *see also* Hoover's speech at Owen Young dinner, December 11, 1924, Box 75, CPF, Hoover Papers.

150. Strong to Andrew Mellon, May 27, 1924, files of the Federal Reserve Bank of New York (hereafter FRBNY); Chandler, *Strong,* 190–94 and passim.

151. Draft of unsent letter, Hoover to Strong, August 30, 1921, Box 284, COF, Hoover Papers.

152. Speech by Roland Boyden, unofficial U.S. representative, copy in *International Financial Conference Brussels 1920* vol. 3, League of Nations Archives, Geneva.

153. Speech by John Foster Dulles, "America's Part in an Economic Conference," January 19, 1922, John Foster Dulles Papers, Mudd Library, Princeton University. This was a common theme. *See,* for example, speech by Garrard B. Winston, October 26, 1926, Box 267, Records of the Department of the Treasury, Secretary's File, NARG 56; Strong's testimony in W. Randolph Burgess, ed., *Interpretations of Federal Reserve Policy* (New York, 1930), 287; speech by Julius Klein, May 13, 1925, in family possession (Baltimore, Md.).

154. Lewis Einstein to Hughes, February 16, 1923, 800.51/460, NARG 59.

155. Strong to Mellon, May 27, 1924, FRBNY files. For similar expressions, *see* Lamont to Charles A. Kittle, November 24, 1922, file 80-16, Lamont Papers; memorandum by Lamont, "The Allied Debt to the United States Government" (no date, but evidence indicates November 1922), file 80-17, ibid.

156. Strong to Mellon, May 27, 1924, FRBNY files. A leader of these critics was influential Yale economist Irving Fisher. See his *Stabilizing the Dollar* (New York, 1920).

157. Quotation from Lamont, "The Allied Debt to the United States Government," file 80-17, Lamont Papers; *see also* Strong to Mellon, May 27, 1924, FRBNY files. For competition between the gold dollar and paper pound, *see* Parrini, *Heir to Empire,* 115–37; *Acceptance Bulletin*; Frank Costigliola, "Anglo-American Financial Rivalry in the 1920s," *Journal of Economic History* 37 (December 1977):911–34.

158. For the Commerce perspective, *see* Hoover, *Memoirs,* 2:85–91; Grosvenor Jones to Hoover, April 1, 1922, Box 76, COF, Hoover Papers; for Treasury, S. Parker Gilbert to Mellon, June 11, 1921, Box 261, NARG 56; Gilbert to Strong, May 21, 1921, May 28, 1921, June 11, 1921, all in Strong Papers; for State, Hughes to Hoover, December 7, 1921, 811.51/3042a, NARG 59; Hughes to Mellon, December 7, 1921, ibid.; for Strong, Strong to Gilbert, May 23, 1921, Strong Papers; Strong to Hughes, April 14, 1922, 800.51/316, NARG 59; for Strong and Lamont, Lamont to N. Dean Jay, June 3, 1922, file 112-18, Lamont Papers. For the controversy between bankers and manufacturers on whether to tie loans to purchase of U.S. goods, *see* memorandum by A. N. Young of conversation with O. K. Davis of the National Foreign Trade Council, May 16, 1922, 800.51/481; A. N. Young to Hughes, March 29, 1922, 800.51/482, both in NARG 59. For secondary accounts of loan policy, *see* Parrini, *Heir to Empire,* 184–211; Leffler, *Elusive Quest,* 58–64; Chandler, *Strong,* 265–66; Brandes, *Herbert Hoover,* 151–213. *See also* a long history Herbert Feis prepared for the State Department, January 22, 1932, 800.51/655-1/2, NARG 59.

159. Hoover, *Memoirs,* 2:85–88.

160. In terms of 1926 value dollars, exports to Europe declined from $3.75 billion in 1919 to $2.15 billion in 1921 and the total trade surplus declined from $2.88 billion in 1919 to $.72 billion in 1922. U.S. Bureau of Census, *Historical Statistics*, 550, 552.

161. National Foreign Trade Council, *Official Report of the 1921 Convention* (New York, 1921), vii. *See also* Parrini, *Heir to Empire*, 233–35; Wilson, *American Business*, 65–86.

162. In 1920–21 the quantity of imported wheat jumped elevenfold over 1919–20 (*Statistical Abstract of the United States 1923* [Washington, 1924], 214). Butter, cheese, and egg imports doubled from 1919 to 1921; ibid., 464. For the breakdown of business sentiment, *see* Parrini, *Heir to Empire*, 234; Wilson, *American Business*, 65–86.

163. For the Emergency Tariff Act, *see* Murray, *Harding Era*, 206–7; Parrini, *Heir to Empire*, 226; Leffler, *Elusive Quest*, 43–44; for WFC funding *see* Murray, *Harding Era*, 208–11.

164. Leffler, *Elusive Quest*, 45–53; Parrini, *Heir to Empire*, 229–35.

165. Buckingham, "Diplomatic and Economic Normalcy," 222–54; Link, *Die amerikanische Stabilisierungspolitik* 324–37; Parrini, *Heir to Empire*, 235–44; Hoover to Hughes, December 19, 1924, Box 136, COF, Hoover Papers. Despite criticism by contemporaries and historians, the 1922 Fordney-McCumber tariff was lower than previous Republican tariffs and levied lower duties on manufactured goods than the tariff of 1909 (Murray, *Harding Era*, 279). Some of the individual rates that raised the overall level of the tariff were irrelevant. For instance, before 1922 the United States imported virtually no sewing machines or cash registers, and continued to outsell competitors in foreign markets throughout the 1920s. Yet the 1922 tariff imposed duties on these items of 25 and 30 percent (M. E. Falkus, "United States Economic Policy and the 'Dollar Gap' of the 1920s," *Economic History Review*, 2d ser., 24 [1971]:614). As Hoover never tired of explaining, an increasing percentage of U.S. imports came in duty free. Hoover expected that Europe would close its dollar gap with such invisible balance items as tourist expenditures, immigrant remittances, and U.S. investments (Hoover speech, quoted in *New York Times*, October 17, 1922, 14). Recent economic analysis suggests that even with much lower tariff rates, the U.S. would not have imported significantly more from Europe (Falkus, "United States Economic Policy," 599–623).

166. Quoted in Woodard, "Postwar Reconstruction," 14.

167. Ibid., 218–26; Leffler, *Elusive Quest*, 51–53; Parrini, *Heir to Empire*, 244–47.

168. For a perceptive discussion of such political schizophrenia, *see* Walter Lippman, "Democracy, Foreign Policy and the Split Personality of the Modern Statesman," *Annals* ("America and the Rehabilitation of Europe") 102 (July 1922):190–93.

169. *See*, for example, Paul M. Warburg to Norman Davis (not sent), November 17, 1919, Box 10, Paul M. Warburg Papers Sterling Library, Yale University; Learned Hand to Warburg, May 5, 1921, ibid.; Lamont to H. deW. Fuller, December 29, 1921, file 80-15, Lamont Papers; Chandler, *Strong*, 284–85; Maddox, *Borah*, 126–28.

170. Van Meter, "United States and European Recovery," 367; Leffler, "Republican War Debt Policy," 597; Lamont to J. P. Morgan (quoting Hughes's

views), October 6, 1922, file 108-13, Lamont Papers; Henry L. Stimson to Owen D. Young, April 8, 1929, 462.00R296/2773, NARG 59.

171. Department of State, Bureau of Public Affairs, "Foreign Indebtedness to U.S." *GIST* (May 1975), par. 6.

172. Moulton and Pasvolsky, *War Debts*, 71–80; Leffler, "Republican War Debt Policy," 591–96.

173. Leffler, "Republican War Debt Policy," 596–97; Lowerre, "Warren G. Harding," 149–50; Van Meter, "United States and European Recovery," 368. Strong favored lower payments than Hoover or Mellon, but his reaction to the WWFDC legislation expressed the rough consensus: "I have never favored an outright declaration of forgiveness of the debts, nor in fact of a policy of forgiveness without consideration in return. But the duties imposed upon this commission are so impossible of accomplishment as to make its efforts futile" (Strong to Russell Leffingwell, June 1, 1922, 640.1 Strong Papers).

174. Lamont to H. deW. Fuller, December 29, 1921, file 80–15, Lamont Papers; *see also* Hoover to Harding, January 4, 1922, Box 91, COF, Hoover Papers; Hoover speech in Toledo, quoted in *New York Times*, October 17, 1922, 14; Rhodes, "Hoover and War Debts," 130–34; Child to Hughes, October 24, 1922, 462.00R296/5, NARG 59.

175. Speech by Julius Barnes, quoted in *Commercial and Financial Chronicle* 115 (October 28, 1922):1883–84.

176. Maier, *Recasting Bourgeois Europe*, 286–87; Leffler, *Elusive Quest*, 66–67.

177. *New York Times*, August 2, 1922, 1, 4; August 3, 1922, 1, 6. For background, *see* Dayer, "British War Debts," 588–89; *Documents on British Foreign Policy* 1st ser., 19:625–26; Silverman, *Reconstructing Europe*, 178–79; John Carroll, "America Reacts to the Balfour Plan: The Debate over War Debt Cancellation," *Research Studies* 41 (June 1973):107–17; James Logan to Leland Harrison, August 18, 1922, copy in Box 9, Henry Fletcher Papers; Logan to Hughes, September 7, 1922, ibid.; Lamont to Morgan, October 6, 1922, file 108-13, Lamont Papers; *New York Times*, August 3, 1922, 6. The Balfour Note frustrated the desire of some officials, especially in the Treasury Department, to "get together" with London on the debts issue. *See* Gilbert to Mellon, February 4, 1923, Box 262, NARG 56; Lamont to E. C. Grenfell, September 27, 1922, file 111-14, Lamont Papers.

178. *New York Times*, August 3, 1922, 6; October 17, 1922, 1, 4; Christian A. Herter to Arthur Switzer [*sic*], October 26, 1922, CPF, Hoover Papers; Lamont to E. C. Grenfell, October 19, 1922, file 111-14, Lamont Papers.

179. Immediately after the conversation, Lamont put Hughes's remarks "into direct quotation" in a letter to Morgan. Lamont to Morgan, October 6, 1922, file 108-13, Lamont Papers. *See also* Hughes to Child, October 18, 1922, 462.00R296/1, NARG 59.

180. Memorandum by William R. Castle of conversation with Hughes, August 1, 1922, copy in Houghton Papers.

181. Lamont to Morgan, October 6, 1922, file 108-13, Lamont papers.

182. Hughes to Child, October 18, 1922, 462.00R296/1, NARG 59. *See also* Castle diary, November 21, 1922, copy in Houghton Papers; Harding to Hughes, November 9, 1922, 462.00R296/8, NARG 59.

183. Quoted in Pusey, *Hughes* 2:579. *See also* R. W. Boyden to Hughes,

November 28, 1922, copy in Box 9, Fletcher Papers; memorandum by Hoover, February 4, 1923, Box 29, CPF, Hoover Papers.

184. For background to Hughes's speech, *see* John M. Carroll, "Making of the Dawes Plan, 1919–1924" (Ph.D. dissertation, University of Kentucky, 1972); 116–20; Pusey, *Hughes* 2:581–82. On the Ruhr occupation, *see* Denise Artaud, "A propos de l'occupation de la Ruhr," *Revue d'histoire modererne et contemporaine* 17 (January–March 1970):1–21; Royal J. Schmidt, *Versailles and the Ruhr: Seedbed of World War II* (The Hague, 1968).

185. *FRUS 1923* (Washington, 1938), 56. *See also* ibid., 61–62. On America's Rhine army, *see* Keith L. Nelson, *Victors Divided: America and the Allies in Germany, 1918–1923* (Berkeley, 1975); Jolyon Pitt Girard, "Bridge on the Rhine: American Diplomacy and the Rhineland, 1919–23" (Ph.D. dissertation, University of Maryland, 1973); John Curtis Rasmussen, Jr., "The American Forces in Germany and Civil Affairs, July 1919–January 1923" (Ph.D. dissertation, University of Georgia, 1972).

186. Chancellor of the Exchequer Winston Churchill agreed. *See* statement by Churchill and Walter Runciman in House of Commons, December 10, 1924, copy in F.O.371/9683, PRO. In 1923, most of the cabinet opposed repudiation. *See* Keith Middlemas and John Barnes, *Baldwin* (London, 1969), 144–47.

187. Middlemas and Barnes, *Baldwin*, 131, 138.

188. Lamont to E. C. Grenfell, February 20, 1922, file 111-13, Lamont Papers; September 27, 1922; October 19, 1922; October 24, 1922, all in file 111-14, ibid; Lamont, "The Allied Debt to the United States Government" (copy sent to administration in Washington); Grenfell to Lamont, November 28, 1922 file 111-15; Lamont to Morgan, October 6, 1922, file 108-13; Lamont to Grenfell, January 26, 1923, file 111-15, all in ibid.

189. *See* accounts in Lamont to Grenfell, October 19, 1922, file 111-14; Grenfell to Lamont, November 28, 1922, file 111-15, both in ibid.

J. P. Morgan partners had other means to influence government. Tom Cochran reported a conversation with irreconcilable Senator Medill McCormick: "Under proper conditions such as you and I might subscribe for [,] McCormick is for the cancellation of the European debt and he follows our line of thought in most things, I think. His present problem is to raise $300,000. to elect a Republican senate in the fall.... I told him he ought to be able to find 25 men in New York to give $5000. apiece, which is what he wants in New York City, and I would furnish him with a list of names where to go" (Cochran to Morrow, July 25, 1922, Cochran File, Morrow Papers. *See also* speech by Julius Barnes, quoted in *Commercial and Financial Chronicle* 115 (October 28, 1922):1883–84.

190. Hoover to Mellon, January 6, 1923, Box 367, COF, Hoover Papers; Hoover, "Memorandum," February 4, 1923, Box 29, CPF, ibid. Strong was less confident than Hoover in Britain's capacity to pay and urged "flexibility" by linking payments to the exchange rate between the pound and dollar. Strong to Gilbert, October 20, 1922, Strong Papers.

191. *Congressional Record*, 67th Congress, 4th sess., December 28, 1922, 982.

192. Quoted in Middlemas and Barnes, *Baldwin*, 139.

193. Moulton and Pasvolsky, *War Debts*, 83–86, 91–93.

194. Quoted in Middlemas and Barnes, *Baldwin*, 139; *see also* ibid., 141–47; quoted in Mannock, "Anglo-American Relations" 143; Clay, *Lord Norman*, 76–

77; Dayer, "British War Debts," 592–93. For a study that minimizes British resentment of the debt settlement, *see* Hogan, *Informal Entente*, 38–56.

195. For the congressional debate, *see* Van Meter, "United States and European Recovery," 381–86; Dewitt, "Harding," 111.

196. Carl Bergmann, *Der Weg der Reparationen* (Frankfurt, 1926), 403.

197. For documentation on Genoa, *see Documents on British Foreign Policy 1919–39*, 1st ser., 19 (London, 1974); *FRUS 1922* (Washington, 1938), 2:770–818. For secondary accounts, *see* Silverman, *Reconstructing Europe*, 258–69; Parrini, *Heir to Empire*, 154–71; Felix, *Rathenau*, 127–46; Abdul Khair Siddique, "The International Monetary and Economic Conference of the Inter-war Period" (Ph.D. dissertation, Yale University, 1970), 79–116.

198. R. G. Hawtrey, "The Genoa Currency Proposals," February 4, 1925, T172/1499B, PRO; *Documents on British Foreign Policy*, 1st ser. 19:703–23; Clay, *Lord Norman*, 137–39; Boyle, *Montagu Norman*, 128, 141–44; Stephen V. O. Clarke, "The Reconstruction of the International Monetary System: The Attempts of 1922 and 1933," Princeton Studies in International Finance no. 33 (Princeton, 1973), 12–14; Dean E. Traynor, *International Monetary and Financial Conferences in the Interwar Period* (Washington, 1949), 67–87; for the significance of the gold exchange standard, *see* chap. 4.

199. Maier, *Recasting Bourgeois Europe*, 282–85; Kaplan, "French Foreign Policy."

200. Quoted in Kurt Rosenbaum, *Community of Fate: German-Soviet Diplomatic Relations, 1922–1928* (Syracuse, 1965), 28. On early German-Russian cooperation, *see* F. L. Carsten, *The Reichswehr and Politics 1918–1933* (Oxford, 1966), 135–39; Felix, *Rathenau*, 133–37; Edward H. Carr, *The Bolshevik Revolution* (New York, 1961), 3:339–72.

201. Teddy J. Uldricks, "Changing Soviet Perspectives on National Security in the 1920s," presented at Mars Hill Conference on European Security in the Locarno Era, October 17, 1975, especially 7–14; Teddy J. Uldricks, *Diplomacy and Ideology: The Origins of Soviet Foreign Relations, 1917–1930* (London, 1979), 73; Evgeny Chossudovsky, "Genoa Revisited: Russia and Co-existence," *Foreign Affairs* (April 1972):556–65; Carr, *Bolshevik Revolution*, 3:339–82.

202. Quoted in Carr, *Bolshevik Revolution*, 3:341.

203. *DBFP*, 1st ser., 19:913.

204. Parrini, *Heir to Empire*, 152–65; speech by John Foster Dulles, "America's Part in an Economic Conference," January 19, 1922, Dulles Papers; *FRUS 1922* 1:393.

205. Clarke, "International Monetary System," 14–15.

206. *FRUS 1922* 1:393; Hoover to Harding, January 23, 1922, Box 21, CPF, Hoover Papers; *see also* Castle to Houghton, May 11, 1922, Houghton Papers; Lamont to Grenfell, February 20, 1922, file 111-13, Lamont Papers.

207. Hoover to Harding, January 23, 1922, Box 21, CPF, Hoover Papers; Lamont to Grenfell, February 20, 1922, file 111-13, Lamont papers.

208. John M. Carroll, "The Paris Bankers' Conference of 1922 and America's Design for a Peaceful Europe," *International Review of History and Political Science* 10 (August 1973):45; Maier, *Recasting Bourgeois Europe*, 286–87.

209. Quotation from Logan to Leland Harrison, May 5, 1922, copy in Box 9, Fletcher Papers. *See also* Logan to Harrison, April 28, 1922, Box 8, Fletcher Papers; Houghton to Castle, June 19, 1922, Houghton Papers; Richard Washburn Child, *A Diplomat Looks at Europe* (New York, 1925), 38. Castle summed

it up: "Personally I do not like it, although I have no particular feeling against Germany for having negotiated it" (to Houghton, April 22, 1922, Houghton Papers).

210. Child to Harding, May 22, 1922; italics added. For Harding's agreement, *see* Harding to Child, June 17, 1922, both quoted in Lowerre, "Warren G. Harding," 140.

211. Minutes of meeting, February 17, 1922, RM 1, CFR Papers.

4. *Building the New Order, 1924–1926*

1. *See* chaps. 5 and 6.

2. Henry Fletcher to Charles Evans Hughes, January 13, 1925, Box 12, Fletcher Papers.

3. For Causey's work, *see* Van Petten, "European Technical Adviser," and chap. 1 above. For an account of Austrian internal affairs, *see* Charles A. Gulick, *Austria from Habsburg to Hitler* (Berkeley, 1948), vol. 1.

4. Clay, *Lord Norman*, 179–80; memorandum by Central European Department, April 5, 1923, F.O.371/8540, PRO; Lord Salter, *Memoirs of a Public Servant* (London, 1961), 178; Hogan, *Informal Entente*, 60–65; Parrini, *Heir to Empire*, 129.

5. For the details, *see* League of Nations, *The Reconstruction of Austria, General Survey and Principal Documents* (Geneva, 1926); William F. LaForge, "The Financial Reconstruction of Austria by the League of Nations" (Ph.D. dissertation, University of North Carolina, 1954); Van Meter, "United States and European Recovery," 415–25. For comment on the high interest rate, *see* Arthur Salter to Alfred Zimmerman, May 11, 1923, Box S/109, League of Nations Archives, United Nations Library, Geneva; Salter to Pierre Quesnay, May 9, 1923, Box S/116, ibid.

6. N. Dean Jay to Morrow, February 2, 1923, Morrow Papers; Morrow to Raymond B. Fosdick, May 15, 1923, ibid; Lamont to Grenfell, March 10, 1923, file 82-18, Lamont Papers; Parrini, *Heir to Empire*, 55–57.

7. Van Petten, "European Technical Adviser," 550–53; Department of State, *Foreign Relations of the United States 1922* (Washington, 1938) 1:613–22. Since the Allies had subordinated Austria's reparations to relief payments, this postponed reparations as well.

8. Lamont to Hughes, February 8, 1923, file 82-18, Lamont Papers. *See also* Lamont to Hughes, April 27, 1923; April 24, 1923 and enclosure, both in ibid.

9. Lamont to Hughes, October 3, 1922, file 82-17, Lamont Papers; Lamont to Hughes, January 26, 1923 and enclosed memorandum "A"; Hughes to Lamont, April 26, 1923, both in file 82-18, ibid.

10. Bruce Barton to Morrow, May 24, 1923, Morrow Papers; Fred Kent to Seward Prosser, May 23, 1923, Fred I. Kent Papers, Princeton University Library; *New York Times*, June 11, 1923, 1, 7. Morgan and Company's advertising dovetailed with the efforts of Arthur Salter, Morrow's wartime associte and head of the League Financial Committee. *See* Salter to Edwin Gay, March 19, 1923; Salter to Morrow, March 31, 1923, both in Box S/116, League of Nations.

11. *New York Times*, June 12, 1923, 1.

12. Kent to Prosser, June 11, 1923, Kent Papers; Kent to Prosser, June 23,

1923, ibid.; N. S. Jay to Morrow, February 2, 1923, Morrow Papers; W. H. Booth to Salter, February 29, 1924, Box R/390, League of Nations; Salter to Booth, March 13, 1924, ibid.

13. For the quotation, James Logan to Benjamin Strong, December 28, 1923, Strong Papers. *See also* Boyle, *Montagu Norman*, 147.

14. Memorandum by E. Felkin, November 23, 1923, Box S/113, League of Nations; Salter to Sir Basil Blackett, June 6, 1923, Box S/115, ibid.

15. Kent to Prosser, June 11, 1923, Kent Papers; Charles Whigham to Lamont, February 3, 1925, file 83-1, Lamont Papers.

16. *New York Times*, June 27, 1926, sec. 8, 12.

17. Department of State, *FRUS 1923* 2:52–53; Werner Link, *Die amerikanische Stabilisierungspolitik*, 172–73; and "Die Ruhrbesetzung und die wirtschaftlichen Interessen der USA," *Vierteljahrsheft für Zeitgeschichte* 17 (October 1969):373–74.

18. Link, *Die amerikanische Stabilisierungspolitik*, 175.

19. Unsigned, undated (but probably July 1923) memorandum, file 046 Ruhr General 1923, Records of the Department of Commerce, Bureau of Foreign and Domestic Commerce, NARG 151; Hoover press release, October 19, 1923, Box 74, COF, Hoover Papers; Link, "Die Ruhrbesetzung," 379.

20. Alanson B. Houghton to William R. Castle, February 12, 1923, Houghton Papers; Castle to Houghton, March 17, 1923, ibid.; Roland Boyden to Hallowell, February 16, 1923, copy in Young Papers; Link, "Die Ruhrbesetzung," 379–81.

21. Notes of Council on Foreign Relations group discussion, February 21, 1923, Morrow Papers.

22. For Hughes's diplomacy, *see* for example *FRUS 1923* 2:66; for Dulles's negotiations, *see* memoranda by John Foster Dulles, July 5, 10, 12, 15, 17, 21, 25, 1923; September 17, 1923, Dulles Papers; Rupieper, "Politics and Economics," 314–31. For Kent's, *see* Hughes to Kent, February 8, 1923, file 800.51/457A, General Records of the Department of State, NARG 59; Kent to Seward Prosser, May 3, 1923, Kent Papers; Kent to Prosser, May 28, 1923, ibid.; Rupieper, "Politics and Economics," 279–85.

23. Houghton to Hughes, March 6, 1923, Houghton Papers; William R. Castle Diary, November 2, 1923, quoted in Gescher, *Vereinigten staaten*, 199–200. For the interaction of France's financial crisis and foreign policy, *see* Schuker, *End of French Predominance*, especially 89–104.

24. Logan to Hughes, June 8, 1923, copy in Box 10, Fletcher Papers; *FRUS 1923* 2:67.

25. Alanson B. Houghton diary, September 22, 1923, Houghton Papers. *See also* entries for October 15, 1923; December 7, 1923, ibid.; Houghton to Hughes, October 7, 1923, ibid.

26. Houghton diary, September 23, 1923, ibid. For further detail see Costigliola, "Reconstruction of Germany," 480–83.

27. Houghton diary, September 23, 1923, Houghton Papers.

28. For Coolidge's opinion, *see* Otto Wiedfeldt to Auswärtiges Amt (Foreign Office), December 7, 1923, Microfilm Role No. T120/1490, Captured German Records, National Archives, Washington; for Castle's, *see* Castle diary, November 18, 1922, copy in Houghton Papers; for Houghton's, *see* Houghton Diary, June 23, 1922, ibid.

29. Houghton to Hughes, October 7, 1923, Houghton Papers; Houghton to

Castle, December 3, 1923, ibid. Castle agreed. Castle to Houghton, November 2, 1923, ibid. *See also* Carsten, *Reichswehr and Politics*, 116–43.

30. Maier, *Recasting Bourgeois Europe* 355–420; Jones, "Stresemann and Diplomacy," Saunders, "Stresemann vs. Poincaré."

31. Leffler, *Elusive Quest*, 88–89.

32. Martin Wolfe, *The French Franc between the Wars* (New York, 1951), 33–35; Eleanor Lansing Dulles, *The French Franc, 1914–28* (New York, 1929), 170–72; Schuker, *End of French Predominance*, 171–73; Stuart M. Crocker interview with James Logan, April 26, 1925, Young Papers; Lamont to Morgan, Harjes & Cie., October 30, 1923, file 176-8, Lamont Papers; J. P. Morgan to Morgan and Company, November 2, 1923, ibid.; Logan to Hughes, November 30, 1923, Box 10, Fletcher Papers; Logan to Hughes, December 3, 1923; December 6, 1923, Box 11, ibid.

33. Lamont to Grenfell, June 18, 1929, file 91-10, Lamont Papers; Bascom N. Timmins, *Portrait of an American: Charles G. Dawes* (New York, 1953). Morrow suggested to Hughes the nomination of Young. *See* Harold Nicolson, *Dwight Morrow* (New York, 1935), 273; Young to Herrick, May 23, 1924, Young Papers; Crocker interview with Logan, April 25, 1925, ibid. On Young's background and business dealings, *see* chaps. 2 and 5; Case and Case, *Owen D. Young*, 3–271.

34. Owen D. Young speech, December 11, 1924, Young Papers.

35. Charles G. Dawes, *A Journal of Reparations* (London, 1939), 213, 63. Houghton said that the report "must be shrieked from the housetops and megaphoned to all the world" (to Hughes, January 8, 1924, Houghton Papers). *See also* Castle to Houghton, November 2, 1923, ibid.; Castle to Houghton, January 16, 1924, ibid.; Hoover speech, December 11, 1924, Box 75, COF, Hoover Papers.

36. Dawes speech, Janaury 14, 1924, copy in Young Papers.

37. Memorandum by Crocker, December 29, 1923, ibid. *See* Alan Goldsmith to Christian A. Herter, January 28, 1924, copy in Leonard Ayres Papers, Library of Congress. From a thirty-year perspective, Young recalled: "The chief burden was to find something which would seem to hurt Germany so that the public would be placated, but would at the same time allow Germany a chance to pay the charges levied against her" (Mildred Adams Kenyon interview with Young, July 28–29, 1955, copy in possession of Everett N. Case, Van Hornesville, N.Y.).

38. Paraphrase of Young's remarks in Rufus C. Dawes, *The Dawes Plan in the Making* (Indianapolis, 1925), 34.

39. Houghton's paraphrase of Young's remarks, Houghton diary, January 11, 1924, Houghton Papers. *See also* Kent to Douglas Miller, April 1, 1924, 046 peace treaty reparations, RG 151. In ensuing months, the committee, largely under Young's direction, fleshed out the scheme. British delegate Josiah Stamp did the technical work in drafting the plan. Germany would pay an ascending scale of annuities that would reach the "standard" level of 2.5 billion gold marks (roughly $625 million). A "prosperity clause" required the payment of even higher sums as Germany's production rose. A gold-value clause provided for adjustment of the nominal amount of payments in the event of a drastic change in world prices. In keeping with the American drive to roll back state enterprise, the plan denationalized German railroads and recommended establishment of a private company in which private interests, the German government, and a foreign director would share control. Industry and the railroads contributed to internal

collection of reparations through special bonds. An American agent general oversaw the reparations machinery and the German economy. Visiting Germany eighteen months later, Strong commented, "The extensive character of these controls in Germany is really unbelievable" (memorandum, July 22, 1925, Strong papers). For a technical description of the Dawes Plan, *see* Moulton and Pasvolsky, *War Debts*, 161–74.

40. Young speech, June 25, 1925, Young Papers; Crocker interview with Jean Parmentier, May 15, 1925, ibid.; Goldsmith to Herter, February 4, 1924, Ayres Papers; Walter S. Tower to Henry M. Robinson, March 26, 1924, Young Papers; Basil Miles, "Memorandum for the Members of the Committee on Economic Restoration, November 7, 1924, ibid.; Henry M. Robinson, "American Banking and World Rehabilitation," June 25, 1925, ibid.

41. Memorandum by Young of trip to Berlin, February 3, 1924, Young Papers.

42. Wiedfeldt to German Foreign Office, June 14, 1924, T120/1491, National Archives; Crocker interview with Tower, May 4, 1925, Young Papers; Goldsmith to Herter, February 4, 1924, Ayres Papers; memorandum by Russell Leffingwell, April 18, 1924, file 176-8, Lamont Papers; Morrow to Lamont, July 24, 1924, 176–19, ibid.; Morgan, Harjes to Morgan and Company, August 20, 1924, 177–2, ibid. For Mellon's opinion, Strong to Pierre Jay, April 23, 1924, Strong Papers; Houghton to Castle, April 6, 1924, Houghton Papers. Schuker, *French Predominance*, 195.

43. Houghton to Castle, April 6, 1924, Houghton Papers.

44. Strong to Pierre Jay, April 23, 1924, Strong Papers.

45. Quoted in Houghton to Hughes, February 19, 1924, Houghton Papers. *See also* "Summary of Part One of the Report of the First Committee of Experts at Paris" (by Young), copy in Box 75, CPF, Hoover Papers; Morrow to Young, February 28, 1924, file 176-2, Lamont Papers; Case and Case, *Owen D. Young*, 282–93.

46. Young speech in Cincinnati, January 6, 1926, Young Papers.

47. Dawes speech, January 14, 1924, ibid.; Dawes, *Journal*, 6, 183–86, 207. The technical experts complained that they were systematiclly ignored. See Goldsmith-Herter correspondence in Ayres Papers.

48. Young speech, December 11, 1924, Young Papers.

49. For a description of Young's superb negotiating talents, *see* Goldsmith to Herter, January 28, 1924, Ayres Papers.

50. Walter S. Tower to Julius Klein, February 1, 1924, 046.21 peace treaty reparations, NARG 151; Schuker, *End of French Predominance*, 89–104.

51. Costigliola, "Reconstruction of Germany," 490.

52. Wiedfeldt to German Foreign Office, June 14, 1924, Reel T120/1490, NA. American expert Karl von Schubert agreed (to Wiedfeldt, June 19, 1924, ibid.).

53. Quoted in Schuker, *End of French Predominance*, 267.

54. Quoted in ibid., 231.

55. Ibid., 17.

56. Ibid., 296–97, *passim*.

57. Quoted in William A. Williams, "The Legend of Isolationism in the 1920s," in William A. Williams, ed., *History as a Way of Learning* (New York, 1973), 132.

58. Leffingwell, "The Dawes Report," April 18, 1924, file 176-8, Lamont

Papers. For further analysis *see* Leffingwell's memoranda, May 5, 1924, file 176-9, ibid.; July 1, 1924, file 176-11, ibid.

59. William Phillips to Logan, April 10, 1924, 462.00R296/275a; Hoover press release, April 10, 1924, box 75, COF, Hoover Papers; Houghton diary, April 2, 1924, Houghton Papers. The Dawes Plan's popularity among German-American voters paid off in November. *See* Castle to Hoover, October 2, 1928, William R. Castle, Jr. Papers, Herbert Hoover Presidential Library, West Branch, Iowa.

60. *FRUS 1924* (Washington, 1939), 2:14–15.

61. As journalist Mark Sullivan remarked, Dawes was "the author of the plan for the increase of the European market for farm products by the stabilization of Europe" (*Literary Digest* 8 [June 28, 1924]:6).

62. Kent to Houghton, April 11, 1924, Houghton Papers; Houghton diary, April 26, 1924, ibid.; Kent, "America and the Dawes Plan," National Foreign Trade Council, *Official Report of the 1924 Convention* (New York, 1924), 373–86.

63. *Literary Digest*, 81 (April 19, 1924):5–8; (April 26, 1924):10–12; (May 17, 1924):11–12, 20–21; (June 28, 1924):5–8; *Literary Digest* 82 (August 9, 1924):5–7, (August 30, 1924):5–8; (September 13, 1924):10–12; (September 27, 1924):12–13; *Literary Digest* 83 (October 25, 1924):16.

64. Morrow, Cochran, and Leffingwell to Lamont, July 23, 1924, file 176-18, Lamont Papers; Hoover speech, December 11, 1924, Box 75, CPF, Hoover Papers; Young speech, June 19, 1924, Young Papers; Hughes speech, July 21, 1924, Box 173, Charles Evans Hughes Papers, Library of Congress; Morrow to Gates McGarrah, November 25, 1924, Morrow Papers; Schuker, *End of French Predominance*, 249–56, 388–90.

65. Morrow to Hughes, July 12, 1924, file 176-13, Lamont Papers.

66. Morgan, Morrow, and Leffingwell to Lamont, July 18, 1924, file 176-16, Lamont Papers.

67. Leffingwell to Lamont, July 9, 1924, file 176-12, ibid.

68. Recounted in Lamont to Morrow, July 11, 1924, ibid.

69. Under the new arrangement, the Reparations Commission could declare Germany in default only with the unanimous consent of its members. The membership now included an American "Citizen Member" who, though officially independent of his government, enjoyed full voting rights. If the Reparations Commission could not reach a unanimous decision, the issue went to the Dawes Plan Arbitration Commission, dominated by its American chairman. In effect, the real power shifted from the Reparations Commission to the Dawes Plan machinery headed by the American agent general, whom Strong dubbed the "King" of the plan. Strong to Pierre Jay, April 23, 1924, Strong Papers; Young to James H. Perkins, January 6, 195, Young Papers; T. N. Perkins to Young, October 2, 1925, ibid. For hourly coverage of the London Conference, *see* boxes 176 and 177 in the Lamont Papers. For secondary accounts, *see* Schuker, *End of French Predominance*, 295–382; Link, *Die amerikanische Stabilisierungspolitik*, 296–306; Leffler, *Elusive Quest*, 105–11.

70. Kellogg to Lamont, August 20, 1924, file 177-2, Lamont Papers; Lamont to J. .P Morgan, August 25, 1924, file 177-6, ibid.

71. Crocker interview with Rufus Dawes, May 13, 1925, Young Papers; Schuker, *End of French Predominance*, 239, 292, 324–25, 343, 386.

72. Gilbert to Morrow, November 26, 194, Morrow Papers. *See also* Leffingwell to Lamont, July 22, 1924, file 176-18, Lamont Papers.

73. Lamont to J. P. Morgan and Co., August 19, 1924, file 177-2, Lamont Papers; Pusey, *Hughes*, 2:587–93; David Bryn-Jones, *Frank B. Kellogg: A Biography* (New York, 1937), 144–55; Donald McCoy, *Calvin Coolidge: The Quiet President* (New York, 1967), 192.

74. Schuker, *End of French Predominance*, 284–89; Link, *Die amerikanische Stabilisierungspolitik*, 315–16.

75. Wiedfeldt to German Foreign Office, August 27, 1924, T120/1490, National Archives. *See also* Lamont to J. P. Morgan and Co., August 22, 1924, file 177-4, Lamont Papers; Leffingwell to Lamont, August 15, 1924, file 176-27, ibid.; Logan to Hoover, September 5, 1924, Box 250, COF Hoover Papers; Crocker interview with Logan, May 15, 1925, Young Papers, K. Paul Jones, "Discordant Collaboration: Choosing an Agent General for Reparations," *Diplomatic History* 1 (Spring 1977):119–39.

76. "Dawes Plan" (Beerits Memorandum), 25–27, Box 172, Hughes Papers.

77. Houghton diary, August 20, 1924, Houghton Papers.

78. *FRUS 1924* 2:32.

79. Leffingwell to Lamont, August 19, 1924, file 177-2, Lamont Papers; Leffingwell to Lamont, August 15, 1924, file 176-27, ibid. For other bankers' ambitions, *see* Logan to Hoover, September 5, 1924, Box 250, COF, Hoover Papers; Schuker, *End of French Predominance*, 309,

80. Lamont to Morgan, Grenfell Co., May 22, 1924, file 176-10, Lamont Papers; Otto Niemeyer to Howard Smith, June 5, 1924, F.O. 371/9908, PRO.

81. Roland W. Boyden, "The Dawes Report," *Foreign Affairs* 2 (June 1924):590; Kent to Houghton, April 11, 1924, Houghton Papers; Edwin W. Kemmerer to Leonard Ayres, May 7, 1924, Edwin W. Kemmerer Papers, Mudd Library, Princeton University; National City Bank of New York, *Economic Conditions, Government Finance, United States Securities* (June 1924), 87.

82. Board of Governors of the Federal Reserve System, *Banking and Monetary Statistics* (Washington, 1943), 440.

83. Lamont to Jeremiah Smith, May 22, 1924, through British legation in Budapest, F.O.371/9908, PRO. *See also* Lamont to Morgan, Grenfell Co., May 22, 1924, file 176-10, Lamont Papers.

84. Morgan partners to J. P. Morgan, October 4, 1924, file 177-23, Lamont Papers. *See also* Morgan to Morgan and Co., October 3, 1924, file 177-22 ibid.

85. Lamont to Morgan and Co., September 1, 1924, file 177-9, ibid.; C. Barclay to Foreign Office, August 15, 1924, F.O.371/9909, PRO: *New York Times*, June 26, 1924, 17; July 4, 1924, 18; September 5, 1924, 26.

86. Morrow and Whitney to Morgan, Lamont, and Anderson, October 7, 1924, file 177-26, Lamont Papers; Herman Harjes to Lamont, September 9, 1924, file 177-13, ibid.; Cochran to Morgan, Grenfell Co., October 9, 1924, file 178-1, ibid.

87. Morrow to Hughes, September 18, 1924, quoted in Morrow to Morgan and Lamont, September 20, 1924, file 177-13, Lamont Papers. For detail on the final loan negotiations, *see* Stephen V. O. Clarke, *Central Bank Cooperation 1924–31* (New York, 1967), 67–70.

88. Hughes to Morrow, September 19, 1924, quoted in Morrow to Morgan and Lamont, September 20, 1924, file 177-13, Lamont Papers.

89. Morrow to Morgan and Lamont, September 20, 1924, ibid.

90. George Whitney to Morgan, October 14, 1924, file 178-6, ibid; Lamont to J. P. Morgan and Co., October 14, 1924, ibid.

91. Consul Maynard B. Barnes to Kellogg, December 19, 1925, 862.51/2165, RG 59; *Commercial and Financial Chronicle* 119 (October 18, 1924):1771.

92. Lloyd C. Gardner, Walter LaFeber, and Thomas J. McCormick, *Creation of the American Empire* (Chicago, 1973), 361.

93. Houghton diary, November 26, 1924, Houghton Papers; December 4, 1924, ibid.; Young speech, December 11, 1924, Young Papers.

94. Arthur N. Young speech, August 24, 1924, copy in Young Papers.

95. Memorandum by Arthur N. Young, "German Loans," August 7, 1925, 862.51/2045, NARG 59.

96. Mellon to Kellogg, November 3, 1925, 862.51/2104, ibid.

97. Memorandum by Grosvenor Jones (prepared at request of Julius Klein), rough draft, no date (but internal evidence suggests mid-1925), COF Hoover Papers.

98. Hoover to Henry M. Robinson, October 23, 1925, CPF, Hoover Papers.

99. Young speech, June 25, 1925, Young Papers.

100. Strong to Pierre Jay, April 23, 1924, Strong Papers.

101. *Literary Digest* 85 (May 16, 1925):5. For Coolidge's approval, *see* Coolidge to Houghton, May 8, 1925, Reel 53, Microfilm Edition, Calvin Coolidge Papers, Library of Congress. For the Locarno negotiations, *see* Jon Jacobson, *Locarno Diplomacy: Germany and the West 1925–29* (Princeton, 1972), 3–67; F. G. Stambrook, " 'Das Kind'—Lord D'Abernon and the Origins of the Locarno Pact," *Central European History* 1 (1968):233–63. Houghton originally suggested to the Germans the idea of a pact guaranteeing the western borders. *See* Houghton diary, December 4–30, 1922, Houghton Papers.

102. Houghton's speech to Pilgrim Society, London, May 4, 1925, Houghton Papers. The British and Germans greeted this pronouncement warmly, but the French reaction was cool. Austen Chamberlain to Esme Howard, April 27, 1925, F. O. 371/10639, PRO (repeating Chamberlain's conversation with Houghton); A. von Maltzan to Houghton, May 13, 1925, Houghton Papers; Stresemann to Houghton, June 2, 1925, ibid.; Harjes to Lamont, May 8, 1925, file 113-3, Lamont Papers.

103. Barnes to Kellogg, December 19, 1925, 862.51/2165, NARG 59.

104. Coolidge speech, July 3, 1925, reported in *New York Times*, July 4, 1925, 4.

105. Strong to Pierre Jay, August 31, 1925, Strong Papers; Strong's memorandum of discussion at Reichsbank luncheon, July 11, 1925, ibid.; Strong's memorandum of conversation with Schacht, November 14, 1925, ibid. Morrow also put financial pressure on Germany. *See* Morrow to Lamont, July 11, 1925, file 113-14, Lamont papers.

106. Chamberlain to Esme Howard (regarding conversation with Houghton), April 27, 1925, F.O.371/10639, PRO.

107. Houghton to Coolidge, August 19, 1925, Houghton Papers; Castle to Houghton, November 3, 1925, ibid.; *see also* Houghton to Castle, November 3, 1925, ibid.

108. Parrini, *Heir to Empire*, 112–18; R. S. Sayers, *The Bank of England 1891–1944* (3 vols.; Cambridge, 1976) 1:163–73. On Norman's struggle to dominate the Austrian central bank, *see* memorandum by de Bordes (Zimmerman's assistant in Vienna), "The Dispute between the Bank of England and the

Austrian National Bank," January 17, 1925, S/113, League of Nations; Zimmerman to Salter, September 9, 1925, S/109, ibid.

109. Sayers, *Bank of England*, 1:174–76; Hjalmar Schacht, *My First Seventy-Six Years* (London, 1955), 194–205; Link, *Die amerikanische Stabilisierungspolitik*, 224–28.

110. Quoted in ibid., 227. Norman made the sterling link a condition of financial aid (ibid., 237).

111. Quoted in Clarke, *Central Bank Cooperation*, 59; emphasis in original.

112. Stuart M. Crocker to Gerard Swope, January 26, 1924, Stuart M. Crocker Papers, Library of Congress.

113. Edwin W. Kemmerer to Hughes, June 24, 1924, 462.00R296/386, NARG 59; Logan to Hughes, March 14, 1924, 462.00R296/213, ibid.

114. Schuker, *End of French Predominance*, 114.

115. Paul M. Warburg to Young, March 21, 1924, copy in Strong Papers. *See also* Warburg to Young, March 14, 1924, Young Papers; Young to Warburg, March 14 or 15, 1924, ibid.; *Federal Reserve Bulletin* 10 (June 1924):60–61; Arthur N. Young to Hughes, June 9, 1924, 462.00R296/386, NARG 59. For British resentment of American ambitions, *see* (London) *Financial Times*, May 16, 21, 1924, copy in 462.00R296/356, ibid.

116. A. N. Young to Hughes, April 14, 1924, 462.00R296/285½; Kemmerer to Hughes, June 24, 1924, 462.00R296/386, NARG 59; Dawes, *Journal*, 170–72.

117. Strong to Mellon, May 27, 1924, file c261.1 Bank of England, FRBNY Files; Strong to Norman, July 9, 1924; November 4, 1924, both in Strong Papers.

118. Schacht to Warburg, May 31, 1924, copy in Strong Papers; Clarke, *Central Bank Cooperation*, 66; Link, *Die amerikanische Stabilisierungspolitik*, 236–39.

119. British financiers feared that the world's adoption of the simple gold standard advocated by America rather than the gold exchange standard would lead to a competitive scramble for gold reserves. This would bid up the price (and hence the commodity purchasing power) of the yellow metal; in other words, world prices would decline as the purchasing power of gold increased. A drop in world prices would depress economic activity in general. But the impact would be especially bad for England by frustrating efforts to make British exports more competitive by reducing domestic prices relative to world prices. *See* 120 below.

120. R. G. Hawtrey, "The Genoa Currency Proposals," February 4, 1925, file T172/1499B, Chancellor of the Exchequer's Office: Miscellaneous Papers, PRO; *Documents on British Foreign Policy* (hereafter *DBFP*), 1st ser. 19:703–23; Josiah Stamp to Owen Young, March 31, 1925, Young Papers; Niemeyer to Churchill, March 20, 1925, T172/1499B, PRO. As Niemeyer explained, Genoa was "a plan by which gold will be economised if there is a scarcity, or an excess equally divided among the [central] banks; if there is a surplus."

121. Sayers, *Bank of England*, 1:163–67; Clay, *Lord Norman*, 179–86; Boyle, *Montagu Norman*, 143–48.

122. Committee on Finance and Industry (Macmillian Committee), *Minutes of Evidence* (London, 1931), paragraphs 6085, 6094; "Mr. Churchill's Exercise," January 29, 1925, T172/1499B, PRO.

123. Strong to Mellon, May 27, 1924, FRBNY Files; Strong to Pierre Jay, April 23, 1924, Strong Papers; Strong to Norman, June 3, 1924, July 9, 1924, November 4, 1924, all in ibid.; Clarke, *Central Bank Cooperation*, 76.

124. Strong to Norman, March 25, 1925, T172/1500A, PRO; Norman to Strong, April 15, 1925, Strong Papers; Strong to Norman, April 27, 1925, ibid.; Norman to Strong, May 11, 1925, ibid. For the details, *see* Costigliola, "Financial Stabilization," 199–201.

125. Memorandum by Strong of conversation with Norman, July 22, 1925, Strong Papers.

126. Norman to Niemeyer, December 4, 1924, T172/1500A, PRO; Norman to Cecil Lubbock, January 6, 1925, T172/1500A, PRO; Burgess, ed., *Federal Reserve Policy*, 266–68; Chandler, *Strong*, 308–9.

127. Quoted in Young to Josiah Stamp, March 3, 1925, Young Papers.

128. Niemeyer to Norman, December 8, 1924, T172/1500A, PRO. See also "Mr. Churchill's Exercise," January 29, 1925, T172/1499B, ibid. Memorandum by McDougal, February 23, 1926, T172/1534, PRO; Department of Commerce, *Statistical Abstract of the United States 1928*, 462–67. During the 1920s, the dominions struck up direct financial and political ties with New York and Washington. *See* W. H. Clegg to Strong, February 4, 1925; H. T. Armitage to Strong, December 5, 1927, FRBNY Files. The cumulative effect of such developments, noted one Foreign Office American expert, was "to entice the Dominions away from Britain" (minute by Geoffrey Thompson, December 1, 1928, on memorandum by Leopold S. Amery, "Anglo-American Relations," November 26, 1928, Cabinet 24/199, PRO).

129. Churchill's statement is quoted in M. P. A. Hankey, "The One-Power Standard," November 27, 1928, Cabinet 24/199, PRO.

130. Kemmerer conducted most of the investigation. *See* Edwin W. Kemmerer and Gerard Vissering, *Report on the Resumption of Gold Payments by the Union of South Africa* (Pretoria, 1925), iii, paragraphs 2071, 3300–3306, 1332, 1259, 1262, 2072, 2061, 4331–32. South Africans appreciated Kemmerer's racial argument. "One difficulty with paper money with natives ... is that the money which they carry becomes very insanitary; whereas metallic money does not to any great extent become insanitary. With the metal there is said to be an acid reaction that kills the disease germs" (par. 1181).

131. W. H. Clegg, "Currency," *The Monthly Journal of the Johannesburg Chamber of Commerce* (March 1925):16.

132. This quotation is from a State Department memorandum explaining why the British disliked Kemmerer. Memorandum by Arthur N. Young, July 14, 1926, 860c.51A/4, NARG 59.

133. Gerhard De Kock, *The South African Reserve Bank 1920–25* (Pretoria, 1954), 76–77. Strong was "very glad" about this. Strong to Kemmerer, March 24, 1925, Kemmerer Papers.

134. Governor general of Australia to L. S. Amery, January 8, 1925, file T160/463, Treasury, Finance Files, PRO; Amery to governor general, January 22, 1925, ibid. Memorandum, February 20, 1925, ibid.; L. F. Giblin, *The Growth of a Central Bank* (Melburne, 1951), 11; Kemmerer and Vissering, *Report*, par. 468, 1472.

135. For details of Churchill's trenchant but ineffective criticism of Norman's and Niemeyer's domestic policy, *see* Costigliola, "Financial Stabilization," 211–16, 383–85.

136. "Mr. Churchill's Exercise," January 29, 1925, T172/1499B, PRO, also printed in Moggridge, *British Monetary Policy*, 260–62. Moggridge dismisses Churchill's "Exercise" as not a statement of belief, but merely a device to elicit

from his advisers strong arguments in favor of an immediate return to gold. Moggridge's evidence for this assertion is shaky. He relies on memoir accounts of Churchill's "style of decision making" that deal not with the 1920s, but with the World War II years. Furthermore, the observers cited by Moggridge explain that Churchill tested his technical advisers most severely when he intuitively opposed their recommendations (66); Arthur Salter, *Slave of the Lamp: A Public Servant's Notebook* (London, 1967), 248–50; Frederick Leith-Ross, *Money Talks* (London, 1968), 118; P. J. Grigg, *Prejudice and Judgement* (London, 1948), 175–76; J. Wheeler-Bennett, *Action This Day: Working with Churchill* (London, 1968), 27–28, 185–87, 191–92, 233; Harold Macmillan, *Winds of Change* (London, 1966), 204–5. Most important, "Mr. Churchill's Exercise" is not an aberration in the chancellor's files, but rather only one of several memoranda that fundamentally questioned the deflationary gold standard policies of Norman and Niemeyer. *See* Churchill to Niemeyer, February 22, 1925, T172/1499B, PRO and the Niemeyer-Churchill exchange in April–May 1927, especially Churchill to Niemeyer, April 20, 1927, T175/11 Richard Hopkins Papers, PRO. Sayers, *Bank of England*, 1:134, simply accepts Moggridge's thesis. Hogan, *Informal Entente*, 71–76, does not cite Moggridge, but discounts the sincerity of Churchill's challenge. Hogan misses the context of Churchill's persistent criticism and the dominions' defection from the pound. He confuses Niemeyer's and Norman's arguments to Churchill, which understated conflicts with the United States, with their beliefs revealed in other letters and memoranda that betrayed suspicion and resentment of American dominance. For corroboration of my view, *see* Martin Gilbert, *Winston S. Churchill* (Boston, 1977), 5, 92–100. *See also* the controversy in the London *Times*, March 17, 1969, 25; March 27, 1969, 27. Churchill could not translate his criticisms into policy alternatives because of his weak political position and ignorance of theoretical economics. *See* Costigliola, "Financial Stabilization," 215–16, 239.

137. As late as March 16, 1925, Niemeyer questioned the wisdom of borrowing more from Britain's creditor, the U.S. (to Norman, March 16, 1925, T172/1500A, PRO). Yet in discussion with Churchill, whom he wanted to convince, Niemeyer withheld misgivings that he expressed to Norman, who was already committed to gold. Similarly, Norman voiced doubts to Strong that he withheld from his British associates. The effect of this was to distort the perception of options facing British leaders. For the response to Churchill, *see* Niemeyer's commentary on Churchill's "Exercise," February 2, 1925, T172/1499B, PRO; Norman's commentary, February 2, 1925, ibid.; both printed in Moggridge, *British Monetary Policy*, 267–72.

138. Niemeyer to Churchill, "The Gold Export Prohibition," February 2, 1925, T175/9 Hopkins Papers, PRO; Niemeyer to Churchill, March 1925, T176/5 Niemeyer Papers, PRO. *See also* Norman's commentary, February 2, 1925, T172/1499B, ibid.

139. Winston Churchill speech, May 4, 1925, "The Gold Standard Bill," copy in T172/1520, PRO.

140. Churchill and Norman were soon bombarded with complaints that London's financial stringency made the dominions financially dependent on New York and so threatened Britain's trade. Board of Trade Sydney Chapman to Niemeyer, June 24, 1925, T176/17, Niemeyer Papers; Robert Horne to Churchill, mid-1925, ibid.; Niemeyer to Churchill, July 21, 1925, ibid.; Niemeyer to Churchill

(no date, but internal evidence indicates early July 1925), ibid.; Clay, *Lord Norman*, 220; Clarke, *Central Bank Cooperation*, 99, 102.

141. Committee on Finance and Industry, *Minutes of Evidence*, paragraphs 3360–63, 3466–67, 7622, 7633–35.

142. For the quotation, Norman to Niemeyer, March 21, 1925, T172/1499B. For the effects of gold standard monetary policy on Britain's economy, see Moggridge, *British Monetary Policy*, 98–158; Howson, *Domestic Monetary Management*, 30–63.

143. Garrard B. Winston, "American War Debt Policy," June 1928, Box 220, Records of the Department of the Treasury, Country File, NARG 39.

144. Assistant Secretary of State Leland Harrison, "Memorandum of Conversation with Mr. Herbert Hoover," November 20, 1924, Leland Harrison Papers, Library of Congress; Arthur N. Young, "Financial Pressure on Debtor Governments," May 29, 1925, ibid.; Hughes to American Embassy, Paris, November 11, 1924, 462.00R296/694a, NARG 59; Whitehouse to Hughes, November 12, 1924, 462.00R296/695, ibid.; Hughes to Logan and Herrick, December 31, 1924, 462.00R296/807b, ibid.

145. Harrison, memorandum of conversation with Hoover, November 20, 1924, Leland Harrison Papers; Hoover to Hughes, November 20, 1924, 851.51/499, NARG 59.

146. L. Harrison to Kellogg, April 10, 1925, Harrison Papers; Mellon to Calvin Coolidge, February 10, 1926, quoted in Garrard Winston to Strong, February 12, 1926, Strong Papers.

147. Lamont to Herman Harjes, January 8, 1925, file 113-3, Lamont Papers. Harjes acted as a conduit to the French government, as did E.C. Grenfell with the British government and Giovanni Fummi with the Italian.

148. Moulton and Pasvolsky, *War Debts*, especially 82–108.

149. Mitchell Ira Serota, "The Effect of the War Debt Question upon French Internal Politics and Diplomacy, 1924–1926" (Ph.D. dissertation, University of Chicago, 1976), 95–96.

150. Ibid., 91, 135–39.

151. Ibid., 101–2.

152. Robert E. Olds to Kellogg, September 7, 1925, transmitted by Kellogg to Hoover, September 17, 1925, Box 369, COF, Hoover Papers; memorandum by Hoover, September 29, 1925, Box 20, CPF, ibid.

153. Hoover memorandum, September 30, 1925, Box 20, CPF, Hoover Papers; *see also* Hoover memorandum, September 23, 1925, ibid.

154. Winston, "American War Debt Policy," June 1928, Box 220, RG 39; Hoover, "Conclusion," (no date, but October 1 or 2, 1925), Box 20, CPF, Hoover Papers; Serota, "War Debt Question," 141–45; Leffler, *Elusive Quest*, 130–38; Benjamin Rhodes, "Reassessing 'Uncle Shylock': The United States and the French War Debt, 1917–1929," *Journal of American History* 55 (March 1969):795–98.

155. Lamont to Giovanni Fummi, June 9, 1925, July 9, 1925, August 18, 1925, file 190-16, Lamont Papers.

156. Henry Fletcher diary, December 20, 1925, Box 1, Fletcher Papers.

157. Quoted in DeSanti, "U.S. Relations with Italy," 91.

158. Castle to Houghton, November 12, 1925, Houghton Papers. For Hoover's agreement, *see* Lamont to Morrow, October 29, 1925, Morrow Papers.

159. Quoted in DeSanti, "U.S. Relations with Italy," 93; unsigned, undated memorandum, November 3, 1925, Box 372, COF, Hoover Papers.

160. Lamont to Morrow, October 29, 1925, Morrow Papers.

161. Castle to Houghton, November 12, 1925, Houghton Papers. *See also* Houghton to Castle, November 23, 1925, ibid.

162. Mellon to Coolidge, February 10, 1926, quoted in Winston to Strong, February 12, 1926, Strong Papers.

163. Moulton and Pasvolsky, *War Debts*, 96–96, 101; Benjamin Rhodes, "The United States and the War Debt Question" (Ph.D. dissertation, University of Colorado, 1965), 201–9.

164. Herbert Feis, *Diplomacy of the Dollar 1919–32* (New York, 1950), 25. For details on the loans *see* chap. 5.

165. Moulton and Pasvolskyk, *War Debts*, 87, 97; Leffler, *Elusive Quest*, 140–42; Rhodes, "Reassessing 'Uncle Shylock,' " 799. *See also* Ellen Wolf Schrecker, "The French Debt to the United States, 1917–1929" (Ph.D. dissertation, Harvard University, 1973).

166. Quoted in Serota, "War Debt Question," 218; *see also* 224. Bérenger's other considerations were regaining American friendship and reestablishing French credit.

167. Strong to Garrard Winston, August 6, 1926, Strong Papers. On the Franco-British debt, *see* Churchill's public letter to Caillaux, quoted in Carl M. Frasure, *British Policy on War Debts and Reparations* (Philadelphia, 1940), 62; Churchill's memorandum of conversation with Ambassador de Fleurian, July 21, 1925, T172/1504, PRO. For British industry's long-running anxiety, Federation of British Industries to Churchill, February 25, 1925, enclosed in F. A. Sterling to Hughes, March 9, 1925, 800.51W89/111, NARG 59.

168. *See*, for example, *Literary Digest* 90 (July 31, 1926):5–7.

169. Churchill to Austen Chamberlain, September 1, 1925, T172/1498, PRO.

170. Castle to F. A. Sterling, March 26, 1926, Castle Papers.

171. Garrard Winston conversation with John Balfour, transmitted by Henry Chilton to William Tyrrell, November 17, 1926, F.O. 371/11198, PRO.

172. Minute by R. L. Craigie, August 7, 1926; minute by Robert Vansittart, August 9, 1926, F.O. 371/11197; Craigie memorandum of conversation with Niemeyer, October 11, 1926, F.O. 371/11198, PRO.

173. Rhodes, "Reassessing 'Uncle Shylock,' " 801.

174. *See* for example, *New York Times*, July 20, 1926, 2; July 21, 1926, 2; July 23, 1926, 1; July 24, 1926, 1; July 25, 1926, 1; July 26, 1926, 6; July 28, 1926, 1; July 29, 1926, 4; August 16, 1926, 1.

175. Ibid., August 3, 1926, 23. For a general discussion of the impact of U.S. tourism, *see* chap. 6.

176. *New York Times*, July 24, 1926, 2.

177. Memorandum by Stresemann, "The Central Problem of European Understanding," October 7, 1926, Eric Sutton, ed., *Gustav Stresemann* (New York, 1937), 3:39–40. For evidence of such cooperation in iron and steel, see Maier, *Recasting Bourgeois Europe*, 516–44.

178. Hoover to Kellogg, July 28, 1926, enclosed in Leland Harrison to American Diplomatic Officers, August 3, 1926, Leland Harrison Papers.

179. Strong to George Harrison, May 15, 1926, Strong Papers; Lamont and Harjes to Morgan and Co., May 8, 1926, file 172-30, Lamont Papers; Leffingwell

to Lamont, May 7, 1926, file 172-29, ibid.; Eberstadt diary, May 20, 1926; June 27, 1926, Box 1, Eberstadt Papers; Chandler, *Strong*, 361–62.

180. Maier, *Recasting Bourgeois Europe*, 502–3. However, the traditional political spectrum did not explain the division in France between employees and producers, who had lost least in the inflation, and savers, who had suffered the most and wanted the franc to increase in value.

181. Chandler, *Strong*, 366.

182. Winston to Coolidge, August 9, 1926, 800.51W89 France/397, RG 59.

183. For the quotation, Strong to George Harrison, July 24, 1926, FRBNY Files; Moreau, *Souvenirs*, 58–67.

184. *See* Gilbert to Winston, October 18, 1925, Strong Papers, and Chap. 3.

185. Strong to Mellon, August 10, 1926, Strong Papers. *See also* Strong to George Harrison, July 26, 1926, FRBNY Files; Strong to Winston, August 3, 1926, Strong Papers; Strong to Winston, August 30, 1926, ibid.

186. For Mellon's reaction, *see* Strong to George Harrison, August 3, 1926, ibid.; for Coolidge's, Coolidge to Winston, August 11, 1926, Box 62, RG 39.

187. McCoy, *Coolidge*, 165–72, 320.

188. Shepard Morgan to Strong, January 15, 1926, Strong Papers, for German ambitions toward France and Poland. *See also* Jacobson, *Locarno Diplomacy*, 84–85; Manfred J. Enssle, "Germany and Belgium, 1919–29: A Study of German Foreign Policy" (Ph.D. dissertation, University of Colorado, 1970); Costigliola, "American Foreign Policy," 96.

189. Sutton, *Stresemann*, 2:415–17; Moreau, *Souvenirs*, 77–78; Ferdinand Eberstadt diary, July 8, 1926; July 11, 1926; Ferdinand Eberstadt to Clarence Dillon, November 3, 1926; November 4, 1926, all in Box 1, Eberstadt Papers; Morrow, Dean Jay, and Carter to Leffingwell, August 30, 1926, Morrow Papers; Lamont and Harjes to Morgan and Co., May 10, 1926, file 172-30, Lamont Papers; Lamont to Clarence Dillon, May 14, 1926, enclosed in Lamont to Harjes, May 14, 1925, file 173–15; ibid.; Lamont to Morgan, Harjes et Cie., May 17, 1926, file 173-16, ibid.; Morgan, Harjes et Cie. to Lamont, May 17, 1926, ibid.

190. Lamont to Morgan, Harjes et Cie., May 21, 1926, file 173-17, Lamont Papers.

191. Robert Warren memorandum of Strong's conversation with Pierre Quesnay, August 24, 1926, Strong Papers; Moreau, *Souvenirs*, 82.

192. Sutton, *Stresemann*, 3:17–26; Jacobson, *Locarno Diplomacy*, 84–90; Link, *Die amerikanische Stabilisierungspolitik*, 401–3; Eckhard Wandel, *Die Bedeutung der Vereinigten Staaten von Amerika für das deutsche Reparationsproblem* (Tuebingen, 1971), 43–77. *See* Costigliola, "Financial Stabilization," 280–99, for details of Thoiry and subsequent negotiations.

193. DeWitt Clinton Poole to Kellogg, October 2, 1926, 751.62/64, RG 59. *See also* memorandum by Hans Dieckhoff of conversation with Castle, October 5, 1926, T120/1491, National Archieves; memorandum by Arthur N. Young, October 11, 1926, 462.00R2962/66½, RG 59; Poole to Kellogg, September 21, 1926, 751.62.51, ibid.

194. Niemeyer to Foreign Office, October 1, 1926, F.O.371/11330, PRO; Albert Dufour-Feronce of London embassy to Stresemann, September 25, 1926, file Sonderband: Mobilisierung der Obligationen, Auswärtiges Amt, Politisches Archiv, Bonn, Germany (hereafter AA, Bonn); Stresemann to German Embassy in London, September 27, 1926, ibid.; memorandum by Orme G. Sargent of conversation with Niemeyer, October 9, 1926, F.O.371/11331.

195. Stresemann to London Embassy, October 1926 (no day), Mobilisierung der Obligationen, AA, Bonn; Gilbert to Norman, October 1, 1926, copy in Houghton Papers; Gilbert to Morrow and Leffingwell, October 8, 1926, Box 220, RG 39; D'Abernon to Chamberlain, October 7, 1926, F.O.371/11331; D'Abernon to Chamberlain, September 30, 1926, F.O.371/11250, PRO. Despite his concern for revision, Stresemann would not consider any policy "that would bring us into direct opposition to America." Stresemann to embassies in Europe, October 26, 1926, Mobilisierung der Obligationen, AA, Bonn; *see also* Schubert's memorandum of conversation with Poole, Octrober 11, 1926, ibid.

196. Moreau, *Souvenirs*, 111; Jacobson, *Locarno Diplomacy*, 104–13; Sheldon Whitehouse to Kellogg, October 7, 1926, copy in Box 220, RG 39.

197. Gilbert to Morrow and Leffingwell, October 8, 1926, Box 220, RG 39. Gilbert asked the bankers to pass this telegram along to Mellon.

198. Kellogg to Jacob Gould Schurman, October 29, 1926, 462.00R2962/66a; memorandum by Dorsey Richardson of conversation with Swedish minister, November 29, 1926, 462.00R2962/71, RG 59; Moreau, *Souvenirs*, 141–42; 150–51.

199. Moreau, *Souvenirs*, 79–80; Sheldon Whitehouse to Kellogg, October 7, 1926, copy in Box 220, RG 39.

200. Moreau, *Souvenirs*, 112.

201. Americans and British competed to blame each other for the collapse. See Costigliola, "Financial Stabilization," 295–99.

202. Dulles, *French Franc*, 405–44.

203. Lamont to Strong, January 17, 1927, file 132-3, Lamont Papers. *See also* Moreau, *Souvenirs*, 213, 218.

204. Mellon quotation in Lamont to Morrow, May 12, 1927, Morrow Papers.

5. The Factory on a Hill: American Business Relations with Europe in the 1920s

1. Quoted in Ludwell Denny, *America Conquers Britain* (New York, 1930), 405–6. Despite its hyperbolic title, this is a solidly researched work.

2. Young speech, July 30, 1930, Young Papers. *See also* Case and Case, *Owen D. Young.*

3. Department of Commerce, *Commerce Yearbook 1931* (Washington, 1931), 2:723; U.S. Bureau of Census, *Historical Statistics*, 537.

4. On the tariff, see Leffler, *Elusive Quest*, 80, 169–73; *Statistical Abstract of the United States 1933*, 408, 411. Even U.S. exports to Britain fit this pattern. Manufactured goods as a percentage of total sales to Britain rose from 22 percent in 1913 to 34 percent in 1928. In world exports of machinery, Americans sold 86 percent as much as the British in 1913 and 149 percent in 1926. Department of Commerce, Bureau of Foreign and Domestic Commerce, *The United Kingdom: An Industrial, Commercial and Financial Handbook*, Trade Promotion ser. no. 94 (Washington, 1930): 789, 221.

5. Committee on Industry and Trade, Survey of Textile Industries (London, 1928), 74. *See also* Lynn Ramsay Edminster, "Anglo-America Trade Rivalry as a Source of International Friction," January 14, 1931, in RG 2, CFR; Michael D. Goldberg, "Anglo-American Economic Competition, 1920–1930," *Economy*

and History 16 (1973): 33. For the trade theory, see Louis T. Wells, *The Product Life Cycle and International Trade* (Boston, 1972).

6. Committee on Industry and Trade, *Final Report* [Balfour Report] (London, 1929), 297. For a definition of *rationalization, see* 156.

7. Link, *Die amerikanische Stabilisierungspolitik*, 356–81.

8. Committee on Industry and Trade, *Final Report*, 26–27; L. S. Amery, *The Empire in the New Era* (London, 1928), 6–12; memorandum by Winston Churchill, March 8, 1927, T172/1530, PRO; Denny, *America Conquers Britain*, 91–123; Ronald S. Russell, *Imperial Preference* (London, 1947), 24–25.

9. In both these industries, America in the 1920s increased its production and export lead over Britain. *See* Department of Commerce, *Commerce Yearbook 1928* (Washington, 1928) 2:716; *Statistical Abstract of the United States 1933*, 470–71; Bureau of Foreign and Domestic Commerce, *The United Kingdom*, 228.

10. Chalk, "International Struggle for Rubber," 28–31.

11. Quoted in P. L. Palmerston, chief, Commerce Department Rubber Division, to Stokes, August 3, 1925, Box 371, COF, Hoover Papers; L. S. Amery to Winston Churchill, October 19, 1925, T172/1486, PRO; Hogan, *Informal Entente*, 192; Chalk, "International Struggle for Rubber," 33.

12. Chalk, "International Struggle for Rubber," 50–99; Hogan, *Informal Entente*, 193–97.

13. Alanson B. Houghton to Owen Young, February 13, 1926, Houghton Papers; *See also* Houghton to Kellogg, February 1, 1926, ibid.; Houghton to John Dwight, December 18, 1925, ibid.

14. Houghton to Kellogg, November 9, 1925, ibid. The rubber companies also attempted negotiatins with the British. *See* Bernard Baruch to Churchill, November 2, 1925, T172/1486, PRO.

15. Hoover to Kellogg, November 28, 1925, Box 279, COF, Hoover Papers.

16. Hoover quotation in Leland Harrison to Kellogg, August 4, 1926, 862.51D481/31, NARG 59. Kellogg feared that if the administration permitted financing of the potash monopoly, Congress would attack with "legislation . . . to control such loans." Memorandum by Kellogg, January 22, 1926, 862.51D481/6, NARG 59. This would open the door to congressional rather than executive loan control. Mellon did not originally favor the ban on this type of loan. *See* Arthur N. Young to Kellogg, March 6, 1926, 862.51 D481/5, NARG 59.

17. "Statement by Secretary Hoover before the House Committee on Interstate and Foreign Commerce investigating foreign government control and monopolies of raw material imports to the US," January 6, 1926, copy in Houghton Papers.

18. Ibid.; Chalk, "International Struggle for Rubber," 108; Hogan, *Informal Entente*, 204; Brandes, *Herbert Hoover*, 95–128.

19. Quoted in Chalk, "International Struggle for Rubber," 109.

20. Houghton to Kellogg, February 1, 1926, Houghton Papers.

21. Quoted in Hogan, *Informal Entente*, 201.

22. Chalk, "International Struggle for Rubber," 112, 123–24. Others whispered that during his years as engineer and businessman, Hoover himself had arranged monopolies, including "a corner of the ruby market." Reported in Percy Blair to Castle, January 6, 1926, Castle Papers.

23. Quoted in Hogan, *Informal Entente*, 198. *See also* Amery to Churchill, October 19, 1925, T172/1486, PRO; Hoover to Houghton, May 1, 1926, Houghton Papers.

24. Castle to Houghton, January 7, 1926, Houghton Papers; Castle to Fred A. Sterling, March 18, 1926, Castle Papers; Houghton to John Dwight, January 5, 1926, Houghton Papers.

25. Denny, *America Conquers Britain*, 208; Brandes, *Herbert Hoover*, 95–105. Two days before Congress defeated this measure (the Newton bill), the British announced their intention to dismantle the Stevenson Plan. Ibid., 101.

26. Hogan, *Informal Entente*, 206.

27. John Foster Dulles, "Our Foreign Loan Policy," *Foreign Affairs* 4 (October 1926):41.

28. Brandes, *Herbert Hoover*, 101; Hogan, *Informal Entente*, 207.

29. "The Power of International Finance Discussed by John Foster Dulles and Morris Hillquit," FPA pamphlet no. 51 (May 1928):9, 14, 16. *See also* Dulles speech, April 29, 1929, copy in Young Papers.

30. Robert R. Kuczynski, *Bankers' Profits from German Loans* (Washington, 1932), 141; Holtfrerich, *Die deutsche Inflation*, 279–93.

31. In 1929, the American portfolio of loans to Europe amounted to $3.05 billion. Of this total $964.4 million was to Germany, $334.6 million to France, $315 million to Italy, and $143 million to Britain. These amounts were smaller than the original issues because of repayment and repatriation to Europe of loans issued in the U.S. Lewis, *International Investments*, 652.

32. Dillon, Read to Kellogg, June 7, 1926, 862.51 V58/1; Harold P. Stokes to Leland Harrison, June 17, 1926, 862.51 V58/2, both in NARG 59, for the steel trust loan. For the story of German loan flood, see the extensive file 862.51, ibid.

33. Joseph Wood Krutch, "Berlin Goes American," *The Nation*, 126 (May 16, 1928):564–65; Colwell, "The American Experience in Berlin"; John Henry Zammito, "Art and Action in the Metropolis: The Berlin Avant-Garde, 1900–1930" (Ph.D. dissertation, University of California at Berkeley, 1978), 475–76; Eberstadt diary, February 26, 1926, Box 1, Eberstadt Papers.

34. For the priority issue, *see* chaps. 4 and 7.

35. Kuczynski, *Bankers' Profits*, 141.

36. Ibid., 129; Morgan and Company partners to J. P. Morgan, October 2, 1924; J. P. Morgan to partners, October 3, 1924, files 177-21, 177–22, Lamont Papers.

37. Thomas S. Lamont to Thomas W. Lamont, May 5, 1927, file 96-13, Lamont Papers.

38. Kuczynski, *Bankers' Profits*, 42.

39. Memorandum by Castle of conversation with de Haas of German Embassy, April 20, 1926, 862.51/226, NARG 59. The nine most important American banks in Germany, ranked in order of business, were: Harris Forbes, Lee Higginson, Dillon Read, National City Bank, First National Bank of Boston, Brown Brothers, Equitable Trust, Guaranty Trust, and Chase National Bank of New York. *See* "American Banks in Germany," September 3, 1928, in Jacob Gould Schurman Papers, Cornell University.

40. Thomas W. Lamont speech, May 2, 1927, copy in Box 50, CPF, Hoover Papers; *New York Times*, May 33, 1927, 3; Costigliola, "Financial Rivalry," 929.

41. Henry Fletcher to Kellogg, April 20, 1927, copy in Box 13, Fletcher Papers.

42. John B. Stetson to Kellogg, May 10, 1926, 860c.51/567, NARG 59; the

Polish diplomat quoted in Neal Pease, "Poland, the United States and the Stabilization of Europe, 1924–1933" (Ph.D. dissertation, Yale University, 1982), 90.

43. Lamont to Dwight Morrow, May 5, 1922, file 113-14, Lamont Papers.

44. Lamont to J. P. Morgan, March 3, 1925, file 108-14, ibid.

45. Lamont to Morrow, May 23, 1923, file 113-14, ibid.; Lamont to Vivian Smith, August 1, 1923, file 111-15, ibid.

46. Fletcher to Kellogg, April 20, 1927, Box 13, Fletcher Papers; Lamont to Ogden Mills, January 14, 1926, file 190-18, Lamont Papers.

47. R. C. Leffingwell to Morrow, April 13, 1926, Morrow Papers. Such support could yield profits. National City Bank president Charles Mitchell determined that the bond market underestimated Italy's credit. He had his bank buy "a block of bonds," then issued a press statement that his trip to Italy had convinced him of that country's excellent future prospects. Italian bonds jumped 2 1/2 points. Mitchell to Fletcher, October 14, 1927, Box 14, Fletcher Papers.

48. Morrow to David Reed, February 8, 1926, Morrow Papers.

49. *See*, for example, Lamont's remarks at the Foreign Policy Association luncheon, January 23, 1926, file 190-18, Lamont Papers.

50. Lamont to Giovanni Fummi, November 14, 1926, file 190-22, ibid. Edgar Sisson was the publicist.

51. *See* for example, Lamont to Herbert Bayard Swope of *The World*, August 23, 1928, file 190-25, ibid.

52. Lamont to Fummi, May 29, 1930, file 191-1, ibid.

53. Fletcher to Kellogg, April 22, 1926, Box 12, Fletcher Papers; Fletcher to Kellogg, May 13, 1926, ibid.; Strong to George L. Harrison, May 29, 1926, Strong Papers. Like Fletcher, Castle believed that although Il Duce's bombastic "stunts and speeches" were harmful, Mussolini was too sensible "to start out on any fantastic adventure." Castle to Fletcher, June 15, 1926, Box 13, Fletcher Papers; Fletcher to Castle, May 13, 1926, Box 12, ibid.

54. Castle to Fletcher, June 15, 1926, Box 13, *ibid.*

55. Lamont memorandum of conversation with Mussolini, April 15, 1930, file 191-1, Lamont Papers. The relationship deteriorated rapidly with Mussolini's adventure in Ethiopia. *See* Lamont to Fummi, June 6, 1935, file 191-4 ibid.; Leffingwell to Lamont, July 12, 1935, ibid.; Lamont's memorandum of talk with Mussolini, August 1935, ibid.

56. As "financial dictator" with power of the budget, Smith was probably the most powerful. James Logan to Strong, December 28, 1923, Strong Papers. On his activities, *see* file 864.51A/, NARG 59; Commissioner-general of the League of Nations for Hungary, *Final Report 1926* (Geneva, 1926); *New York Times*, June 27, 1926, sec. 8, 12; June 28, 1926, 16. For Gilbert, see Chaps. 4 and 7 and agent general for reparations, *Reports* (1925–30). For Dewey, file 860c.51A/, NARG 59; Costigliola, "American Foreign Policy," 85–105; Pease, "Stabilization of Europe," 234–38.

57. *See* Robert N. Seidel, "American Reformers Abroad: The Kemmerer Missions in South America, 1923–31," *Journal of Economic History* 32 (June 1972):520–45.

58. Kemmerer speech to Bond Club, no date (internal evidence indicates 1928), file xxi-A a-6, Kemmerer Papers. *See also* Kemmerer, "Economic Advisory Work for Governments," *The American Economic Review* 17 (March 1927):1–12; Seidel, "Kemmerer Missions," 544–45.

59. *See* notes 56–58. Gilbert had far more influence with Mellon and FRBNY officials than did Dewey. To many Europeans unfamiliar with U.S. distinctions between "official" and "unofficial," these advisers seemed simply representatives of the most powerful nation in the world.

60. Seidel, "Kemmerer Missions," 521.

61. Quotation by E. Dana Durand in *Annals* (America and the Rehabilitation of Europe) 102 (July 1922):39. Durand was food adviser to the Polish Government until 1921, then chief of the Commerce Department's Eastern Europe Division. In 1927 he took a leave of absence from Commerce to help Dewey set up the Warsaw adviser office.

62. Mira Wilkins, *The Maturing of Multinational Enterprise: American Business Abroad from 1914 to 1970* (Cambridge, Mass., 1974), 31.

63. Ibid., 3–32, 55, 155, Parrini, *Heir to Empire*, 133–36. Charles Kindleberger points out that book value usually underestimates real or market value of investments ("Origins of U.S. Direct Investment in France," *Business History Review* 48 [1974]:407–8).

64. Wilkins, *Multinational Enterprise*, 71, 130; Frank A. Southard, Jr., *American Industry in Europe* (Boston, 1931), 52–53; Louis P. Cassimatis, "Greek-American Relations, 1917–1929" (Ph.D. dissertation, Kent State University, 1978), 294–319. On this and other Greek construction projects, Ulen shut out its British competitors.

65. Wilkins, *Multinational Enterprise*, 84, 60–91; Southard, *American Industry*, 17–122.

66. Ibid., 109–110.

67. *Fortune* advertisement, 1 (February 1930):125.

68. *New York Times*, November 9, 1930, 2:12.

69. Wilkins, *Multinational Enterprise*, 79; Link, *Die amerikanische Stabilisierungspolitik*, 369; speech by William S. Daugherty, March 7, 1928, RG 1, CFR Papers; Gerard Colby Zilg, *Du Pont behind the Nylon Curtain* (Englewood Cliffs, N.J., 1974), 303–4.

70. George Sweet Gibb and Evelyn H. Knowlton, *History of Standard Oil (New Jersey). The Resurgent Years, 1911–1927* (New York, 1956), 2:278–90; Stephen G. Rabe, "Anglo-American Rivalry for Venezuelan Oil, 1919–1929," *Mid-America* 58 (April–July 1976):97–100.

71. Ibid., 103; Hogan, *Informal Entente*, 172–75, 183–84.

72. Quoted in Hogan, *Informal Entente*, 183. *See also* ibid., 169–85; William Stivers, *Supremacy and Oil. Iraq, Turkey, and the Anglo-American World Order, 1918–1930* (Ithaca, 1982), 128–32; Wilson, *American Business*, 192–95; Gibb and Knowlton, *Standard Oil*, 2:291–308; Rosenberg, *Spreading the American Dream*, 128–32.

73. Rabe, "Venezuelan Oil," 108–9; Harold F. Williamson, Ralph L. Andreano, Arnold R. Daum, and Gilbert C. Klose, *The American Petroleum Industry: The Age of Energy 1899–1959* (Evanston, 1963), 522.

74. Quoted in Wilkins, *Multinational Enterprise*, 111. *See also* ibid., 109–112, 167–68. For British resistance to American penetration of utilities in India, *see* ibid., 134.

75. Ibid., 112–13.

76. For the origins of RCA, *see* Bernard Baruch to Owen Young, January 5, 1929, V. 23, Bernard Baruch Papers, Firestone Library, Princeton, N.J.; Erik Barnouw, *A Tower in Babel: A History of Broadcasting in the United States*

(New York, 1966), vol. 1, especially 59–73; David Loth, *Swope of GE* (New York, 1958), 99–101; Wilkins, *Multinational Enterprise*, 70–72.

77. For the domestic communications trust, *see* Thomas Lamont diary, February 3, 1929, Lamont Papers; for the foreign group, Young to Felix Pole (not sent) November 29, 1929, Young Papers; Case and Case, *Owen D. Young*, 417–33.

78. Ibid., 361–82.

79. Southard, *American Industry*, 23.

80. Owen Young speech, July 26, 1922, Young Papers; *First General Conference of the International General Electric Company and Associated Companies* (no publisher, no date), 1.

81. The conference was at Briarcliff Manor, N.Y. October 25–29, 1920. *See* ibid., 22–23, 261–63, 312–14, and passim.

82. For the 1920 negotiations, *see* Anson W. Burchard to Young and other GE officers, August 28, 1920, Young Papers. For the contract, *see* "Agreement between AEG and General Electric," January 2, 1922, Young Papers.

83. U.S. Senate, Subcommittee of the Committee on Interstate Commerce. Hearings on S. 4301: A Bill to Prevent the Unauthorized Landing of Submarine Cables, 66th Cong., 3d sess. (Washington, 1921), 87. *See also* Burchard to Young, May 17, 1919, Young Papers.

84. Hogan, *Informal Entente*, 105–28.

85. U.S. Senate, Committee on Interstate Commerce, Hearings on S.6: A Bill to Provide for the Regulation of the Transmission of Intelligence by Wire or Wireless, 71st Cong., 1st sess. (Washington, 1930), 217–21.

86. *First General Conference of the International General Electric Company*, p. 19.

87. Quoted in Case and Case, *Owen D. Young*, 241. *See also* ibid., 237–42; Young to Hoover, October 29, 1921, Box 90, CPF, Hoover Papers. Hogan recognizes that Americans had the dominant voice in the consortium, but with no cited evidence asserts that Young's victory was "paper concessions to conventional nationalist dogma like the Monroe Doctrine" *Informal Entente*, 143, 158. Certainly Young thought the superior position of RCA and the U.S. was real and worth hard negotiation.

88. Denny, *America Conquers Britain*, 383.

89. Hogan, *Informal Entente*, 146–53; Case and Case, *Owen D. Young*, 242–43. For RCA's installation of radio communication with Poland, *see* file 860c.74/, NARG 59 for 1919–22; for Russia, *see* text below.

90. Young speech, July 14, 1929, Young Papers.

91. Young to Gerard Swope, March 14, 1929, ibid.

92. Hermann Bücher to Young, March 21, 1929, ibid.; Young to Swope, March 24, 1929, ibid.; Southard, *American Industry*, 17–32; Wilkins, *Mulinational Enterprise*, 65–69: Link, *Die amerikanische Stabilisierungspolitik*, 371–73.

93. Anthony C. Sutton, *Western Technology and Soviet Economic Development, 1917–1930* (Stanford, 1968), 1:6, 197–98.

94. Wilkins, *Multinational Enterprise*, 67.

95. Young to Felix Pole (not sent), November 29, 1929, Young Papers; Southard, *American Industry*, 6.

96. Federal Trade Commission, *Supply of Electrical Equipment and Competitive Conditions* (Washington, 1928), 145.

97. *Statistical Abstract of the United States 1931*, 405, 564.

98. Alfred E. Kahn, *Great Britain in the World Economy* (New York, 1946), 112; Wilkins, *Multinational Enterprise*, 75; Mira Wilkins and Frank Ernest Hill, *American Business Abroad. Ford on Six Continents* (Detroit, 1964), 356–57, 377–78.

99. Ibid., 434–35. General Motors also assembled in Europe. *See* Alfred P. Sloan, *My Years with General Motors* (New York, 1964), 321.

100. U.S. Bureau of Foreign and Domestic Commerce, *United Kingdom*, 228.

101. Wilkins and Hill, *Ford on Six Continents*, 111, 138.

102. Ibid., 155; Link, *Die amerikanische Stabilisierungspolitik*, 377–79; Southard, *American Industry*, 164. For Britain's benefit from the tariff on autos, *see* Committee on Industry and Trade, *Final Report*, 276.

103. Wilkins and Hill, *Ford on Six Continents*, 145–56.

104. Sloan, *General Motors*, 320–27; Wilkins, *Multinational Enterprise*, 73; Southard, *American Industry*, 72–75. Southard lists the purchase price as $30 million; Link, *Die amerikanische Stabilisierungspolitik*, 379, as 155 million marks, or $39 million.

105. Southard, *American Industry*, 76–79; Wilkins and Hill, *Ford on Six Continents*, 194–96. Reportedly, American investors snapped up 90 percent of the English stock (Southard, *American Industry*, 77). As part of an industrial entente, the German chemical trust I. G. Farben took a 15 percent interest in the German Ford subsidiary (Wilkins and Hill, *Ford on Six Continents*, 196).

106. Wilkins and Hill, *Ford on Six Continents*, 185–207, 232–5; Southard, *American Industry*, 77; Wilkins, *Multinational Enterprise*, 72–73.

107. Wilkins, *Multinational Enterprise*, 75; L. T. Steele, "Driving Wedge for the Global Client," *Printers' Ink, Advertising Today/Yesterday/Tomorrow* (New York, 1963), 208.

108. Domeratzky, "American Industry Abroad," 570; Julius Klein, *Frontiers of Trade* (New York, 1929), 169–71; Department of Commerce, "American Branch Factories Abroad," Senate Doc. no. 258, 71st Cong., 3d sess. (January 1931). Brandes sees Commerce policy as unambiguously against branch plants (*Herbert Hoover*, 163–69).

109. Edouard Herriot, *The United States of Europe* (New York, 1930), 3–4. *See also* ibid., 49–56.

110. Denny, *America Conquers Britain*, 94–100; *see also* note 8 above.

111. Felix Deutsch to Owen Young, September 20, 1929, Young Papers.

112. Domeratzky, "American Industry Abroad," 570.

113. Department of Commerce, "Branch Plants Abroad," 22; Southard, *American Industry*, 176–86.

114. Wilkins, *Multinational Enterprise*, 55; Lewis, *International Investments*, 558.

115. Link, *Die amerikanische Stabilisierungspolitik*, 379–81.

116. Southard, *American Industry*, 189; John H. Dunning, *American Investment in British Manufacturing* (London, 1958), 46; Miller and Hill, *Giant of the Western World*, 171–80; *World Trade* 1 (October 1929):31; Henry S. Dennison speech, May 17, 1927, RG 1, CFR Papers; Charles S. Maier, "Between Taylorism and Technocracy: European Ideologies and the Vision of Industrial Productivity in the 1920s," *Journal of Contemporary History* 5 (1970):54.

117. Maier, "Between Taylorism and Technocracy," 27–61; Robert A. Brady, "The Meaning of Rationalization: An Analysis of the Literature," *Quarterly*

Journal of Economis 46 (May 1932):526–40; Southard, *American Industry*, 189–90; Miller and Hill, *Giant of the Western World*, 180–94.

118. Quoted in Peter G. Filene, ed., *Americans and the Soviet Experiment, 1917–33* (Cambridge, Mass., 1967), 125.

119. *See* Henry Ford and Samuel Crowther, *My Life and Work* (Garden City, N.Y., 1923); Owen Young speech to National Industrial Conference Board, May 20, 1926, Young Papers; Houghton speech at Queens College, England, May 10, 1928, Houghton Papers. On Ford's image, *see* David Lewis, *The Public Image of Henry Ford* (Detroit, 1976), 113–234.

120. Quoted in Lewis, *Henry Ford*, 219.

121. Julius Barnes speech in *Proceedings of the Fourteenth Annual National Foreign Trade Convention*, 10.

122. Southard, *American Industry*, 153–55. This policy encouraged open shops in highly unionized countries. Other American manufacturers, however, paid prevailing wages and accepted union shops.

123. Sigismund Heryng to John B. Stetson, transmitted in J. Webb Benton to Frank B. Kellogg, July 18, 1929, 711.60c/9, NARG 59.

124. Lewis, *Henry Ford*, 215; Peter Berg, *Deutschland und Amerika, 1918–1929: Über das deutsche Amerikabild der zwanziger Jahre* (Lübeck and Hamburg, 1963), 100–3.

125. Berg, *Deutschland und Amerika*, 104–5; Maier, "Between Taylorism and Technocracy," 55–59.

126. André Siegfried, *America Comes of Age* (New York, 1927), 349, 51. For an excellent study of French resistance to American mass culture, *See* David Strauss, *Menace in the West: The Rise of French Anti-Americanism in Modern Times* (Westport, Conn., 1978), especially 175–84. On British resistance to Americanization, *see* David Allen Richards, "The Abortive Entente: The American Popular Mind and the Idea of Anglo-American Cooperation to Keep the Peace 1921–1931" (Ph.D. dissertation, Florida State University, 1976), 221. One American company with factories dispersed through Europe explained: "With the exception of Germany, all the other countries seem to have difficulty in understanding production processes. In England they don't like it because it is different from what they have done before. In France, their individualism creates the desire to do things differently than asked, and they are prone to jump from one thing to another. In Italy they work under supervision, but have a tendency to break away from routine whenever possible. In Germany, they like to be told what to do and will follow directions explicitly" (Quoted in Southard, *American Industry*, 152).

127. Henry Dubreuil, *Robots or Men? A French Workman's Experience in American Industry* (New York, 1930), 246, passim. Other European labor leaders were highly suspicious of Fordism, especially in its capitalist context. *See* Department of Commerce, "American Branch Factories Abroad," 23.

128. Siegfried, *America Comes of Age*, 347, 349.

129. Maurice Hindus, "Henry Ford Conquers Russia," *The Outlook* 146 (June 29, 1927):280. Hindus described a village wedding procession in which the bride-and-groom cart was pulled by a Fordson tractor rather than the traditional horse. For the second quotation, *see Nation's Business* 18 (April 1930):266. On *Fordizatsia*, see Filene, *Americans and the Soviet Experiment*, 124–29; Wilson, *Ideology and Economics*, 9–11; Floyd James Fithian, "Soviet-American

Economic Relations, 1918–1933" (Ph.D. dissertation, University of Nebraska, 1964), 307; *New York Times*, February 17, 1928, 7.

130. Quoted in Fithian, "Soviet-American Economic Relations," 219. *See also New York Times*, February 6, 1931, 1, 12.

131. Quoted in Dorothy Thompson, *The New Russia* (New York, 1928), 168. *See also* ibid., 160–67; Wilson, *Ideology and Economics*, 12–13; Fithian, "Soviet-American Economic Relations," 220.

132. Filene, *Americans and the Soviet Experiment*, 124–25; *New York Times*, February 17, 1928, 7.

133. *New York Times*, January 29, 1928, sec. 3, 8.

134. Robert F. Kelley to Robert Olds, February 10, 1928, 711.61/130-1/2, NARG 59.

135. Wilson, *Ideology and Economics*, 30–40; Sutton, *Soviet Economic Development*, 1:296–99; Feis, *Diplomacy of the Dollar*, 46–48.

136. Fithian, "Soviet-American Economic Relations," 139–45, 196–97; Wilson, *Ideology and Economics*, 40–48; James K. Libbey, *Alexander Gumberg and Soviet-American Relations, 1917–33* (Lexington, Ky., 1977), 118–64.

137. Young speech, July 30, 1930, Young Papers. *See also* Young to Henry L. Stimson, August 7, 1930, 861.6463/47, NARG 59; Ford, "Why I Am Helping Russian Industry," *Nation's Business* 18 (June 1930):20–23; Fithian, "Soviet-American Economic Relations," 324–25. Of course, many businessmen refused to trade with Russia, and divisions among businessmen as well as political leaders complicated the issue of political recognition of the Soviet regime.

138. Walter A. Rukeyser, "Do Our Engineers in Russia Damage America?" *Scribner's Magazine* 90 (November 1931):524.

139. Helen C. Wilson and Elsie R. Mitchell, "A Light-Running Utopia," *Asia* 28 (December 1928):955–56. Ruth Kennell and Milly Bennett, "American Immigrants in Russia," *American Mercury* 25 (April 1932):464, 468; Peter G. Filene, ed., *American Views of Soviet Russia* (Homewood, Ill., 1968); 90; Theodore M. Knappen, "The Apogee of Strange Partnerships—Soviet Socialists and American Capitalists," *Magazine of Wall Street* 43 (January 26, 1929):592; Anna Louise Strong to Sydney Strong, July 20, 1923, Box 3, Anna Louise Strong Papers. *See also* Hugh Cooper, "Observations of Present Day Russia," *Annals* ("Some Aspects of the Present International Situation") 138 (July 1928):118; Edward Angly, "Thomas Campbell: Master Farmer," *Forum* 86 (July 1931):21–22.

140. "The Possibilities of Russia," *Commercial and Financial Chronicle* 120 (March 7, 1925):1139. Kennell and Bennett, "American Immigrants in Russia," 465; Rukeyser, "Engineers in Russia," 523; emphasis in original. *See also* Hindus, "Ford Conquers Russia," 280–81.

141. Paraphrased in Alexander Gumberg to Reeve Schley, December 12, 1928, Alexander Gumberg Papers, State Historical Society of Wisconsin, Madison.

142. Memorandum of conversation between Dewitt Clinton Poole and Gilbert, transmitted by Jacob Gould Schurman to Kellogg, July 7, 1926, 462.00 R296/1464, NARG 59. Stalin's analysis of the Dawes Plan was cruder, but essentially followed Gilbert's: "Germany must squeeze out pennies for Europe from the Russian markets." This plan did not, Stalin warned, consider Russian aspirations: "We are not at all inclined to convert Russia into an agrarian country.... We, ourselves, shall manufacture machines and other means of production" (in December 25, 1924 issue of *Rote Fahne*, transmitted by Schurman to Hughes, January 6, 1925, 462.00 R296/1227, NARG 59).

143. Alexander Gumberg to Reeve Schley and Frank Callahan, January 6, 1928, Gumberg Papers; Young speech, July 30, 1930, Young Papers.

144. Department of Commerce, *Commerce Yearbook 1928* 2:556; *Commerce Yearbook 1931* (Washington, 1931) 2:275; Fithian, "Soviet-American Economic Relations," 180, 214.

145. *New York Times*, November 1, 1967, 26; Charles E. Sorenson, *My Forty Years with Ford* (New York, 1956), 197.

146. Sutton, *Soviet Economic Development* 1:117; *New York Times*, November 1, 1967, 26.

147. Ibid.; Sutton, *Soviet Economic Development* 1:117.

148. Ibid., 1:227; Anna Louise Strong, *I Change Worlds* (Garden City. N.Y., 1937), 157. Americans established a total of 25–30 agricultural communes. *See* Sutton, *Soviet Economic Development* 1:126–32.

149. Quoted in Strong, *I Change Worlds*, 161–62. On Shatov *see* also William Henry Chamberlain, "Missionaries of American Technique in Russia," *Asia* 32 (July–August 1932):422–23; *New York Times*, November 1, 1967, 26.

150. For the quotation, Ruthe Kennell to Mellie Calvert, April 29, 1923, in microfilm "IWW Kuzbas in Kemerara, USSR, 1921–23," Edwin W. Hopkinson Papers, University of Washington Library. *See also* Sam Shipman to Edwin Hopkinson, July 14, 1926, ibid.; testimony by Ida Aho, November 15, 1928, transmitted by Consul James R. Wilkinson to secretary of state, November 19, 1928, General Records of the Department of State, Microcopy reel 316/110, frames 793–801; William Thomas Smith, "The Kuzbas Colony in Soviet Russia 1921–1926" (Ph.D. dissertation, University of Miami, 1977); *The Nation* 116 (January 23, 1923):7–9; 116 (May 2, 1923):511–12; 117 (August 8, 1923):145–46; 119 (November 26, 1924):566–67; 128 (February 6, 1929):170–72; R. E. Kennell, "The New Innocents Abroad," *American Mercury* 17 (May 1929):10–18; Wilson and Mitchell, "A Light-Running Utopia," 955–62, 1034–38; Sutton, *Soviet Economic Development* 1:48–50.

151. Anna Louise Strong to Sydney Strong, June 8, 1926, Box 4, Anna Louise Strong Papers.

152. *The Nation* 15 (December 27, 1922):713–14; Sutton, *Soviet Economic Development* 1:227–29.

153. The gap between American companies' small Eastern Hemisphere crude oil resources and large refined oil markets underscored the importance of Russian crude. In 1929, Soviet production amounted to one-third the world total, and it was often available at below market rates. In 1919, Jersey Standard bought Russian oil properties at bargain prices from foreign investors and the short-lived Azerbaijan government. Although the Soviets in 1920 took over the oil-producing region and confiscated foreign holdings, Standard of Jersey gambled on the regime's fall and bought up more foreign claims. In the next decade, Jersey Standard agonized over whether to boycott the Bolshevik expropriators or profit from cheap Russian crude. President Walter Teagle feared that if the Russians got away with confiscation, it would set a bad example for other "irresponsible governments." Jersey Standard's dilemma symbolized the quandary of overall U.S. Russian policy. The Soviets defeated Western boycotts by offering crude at low prices and playing up to companies like Standard Oil of New York that had not had Russian investments. In 1929, Jersey Standard finally decided it could not profitably serve its world markets without Russian crude. By this time even the U.S. Shipping Board had purchased Soviet oil. In the late twenties and early

thirties, Jersey Standard and the other major Western companies struggled to limit Soviet exports that contributed to the growing oil glut (Gibb and Knowlton, _Standard Oil_ 2:328–58; Singer, "The United States Confronts the Soviet Union," 36–54; Wilson, _Ideology and Economics_, 164–68; Henrietta M. Larson, Evelyn H. Knowlton, and Charles S. Popple, _Standard Oil_ [New York, 1971] 3:305–12).

154. Sutton, _Soviet Economic Development_ 1:16–44.

155. Ibid., 94–96. On American investment in Lena Goldfields, _see_ Castle to Schurman, January 26, 1926, Schurman Papers. In the late twenties, the Soviets pressured out this and other concessions, such as Averell Harriman's manganese mining operation, and substituted technical assistance agreements. These contracts purchased technology and equipment without giving up operating control to foreigners. For the Harriman concession, _see_ W. Averell Harriman, _America and Russia in a Changing World_ (Garden City, N.Y., 1971), 2–7; Sutton, _Soviet Economic Development_, 1:86–91; Wilson, _Ideology and Economics_, 158–60; Wilkins, _Multinational Enterprise_, 107–8. The protrade Russian-American Chamber of Commerce claimed that in 1926–27 the ninety-seven concessions in the Soviet Union earned a net profit of 85.5 percent on total capital. _See_ "Concessions," published by American-Russian Chamber of Commerce, copy in Gumberg Papers.

156. Quoted in Fithian, "Soviet-American Economic Relations," 263.

157. Clark Minor and Owen Young to Amtorg, October 9, 1928, copy in Gumberg Papers. Other accounts give the amount as $26 million. _See_ Fithian, "Soviet-American Economic Relations," 277–304; Sutton, _Soviet Economic Development_ 1:186–98.

158. James Harbord to David Sarnoff, June 7, 1927, copy in Young Papers; Harbord to Henry L. Stimson, April 22, 1929, ibid.; Sutton, _Soviet Economic Development_ 1:250–52.

159. Young speech, July 30, 1930, Young Papers.

160. For the first quotation, Ford, "Why I Am Helping Russian Industry," 22; the second is quoted in Wilkins and Hill, _Ford on Six Continents_, 217. These authors relate that Ford expected the Soviets eventually would "go under" (ibid., 211–12).

161. Wilkins and Hill, _Ford on Six Continents_, 209–15; Fithian, "Soviet-American Economic Relations," 307–19; Sorenson, _My Forty Years with Ford_, 202–3.

162. Ibid., 195–207; Wilkins and Hill, _Ford on Six Continents_, 218–24; Fithian, "Soviet-American Economic Relations," 326–31; Wilson, _Ideology and Economics_, 162.

163. Quoted in Wilkins and Hill, _Ford on Six Continents_, 221. Despite Henry Ford's initial enthusiasm, the Depression reduced Russia's foreign exchange earnings and willingness to purchase Ford vehicles. The cost-plus contract raised vehicle prices as Ford's total production fell. At the end of the four-year contract period, the Russians bought slightly more than half the stipulated 72,000 units. Company officials calculated a net loss on the contract of $578,000. However, this did not figure in an almost $3 million sale of outmoded Model A production equipment that Ford otherwise would have sold as scrap metal. Nor did the loss include advantages of lower unit cost to overall Ford output because of sales to Russia (ibid., 223–25; Fithian, "Soviet-American Economic Relations," 336–46; Wilson, _Ideology and Economics_, 162).

164. Quoted in Anna Louise Strong to Middleton (no first name), June 13, 1929, Box 4, Anna Louise Strong Papers.

165. Fithian, "Soviet-American Economic Relations," 222. Figures vary, especially because of problems defining "American" and the Americans who went to Russia as tourists and then looked for work. See Lewis S. Feuer, "American Travelers to the Soviet Union, 1917–1932: The Formation of a Component of New Deal Ideology," *American Quarterly* 14 (Summer 1962):142; Chamberlain, "Missionaries of American Technique," 426. For Cooper, *see* ibid.; Fithian, "Soviet-American Economic Relations," 265–74; Libbey, *Gumberg*, 152. Autobiographies of these engineers form a whole genre of memoir. The place to begin is Feuer, "American Travelers to the Soviet Union," 136–44; then John Scott, *Behind the Urals* (Cambridge, Mass., 1942); John D. Littlepage, *In Search of Soviet Gold* (New York, 1927); Walter A. Rukeyser, *Working for the Soviets* (New York, 1932).

166. Angly, "Thomas Campbell," 22; Feuer, "American Travelers to the Soviet Union," 143; Cooper, "Observations of Present Day Russia," 118.

167. Quoted in Kennell and Bennett, "American Immigrants in Russia," 465.

168. A.J. Freyn, "Am American Engineer Looks at the Five Year Plan," *New Republic* 66 (May 6, 1931):318–19; Littlepage, *In Search of Soviet Gold*, 308; Strong, *I Change Worlds*, 323–24; Fithian, "Soviet-American Economic Relations," 249.

169. Scott, *Behind the Urals*, 86–87; Chamberlain, "Missionaries of American Technique," 462.

170. Quoted in *New York Times*, November 1, 1967, 26.

171. The ratio of American industrial productivity per man hour to real weekly industrial wages was as follows: 1914—2.30; 1919—2.10;1923—2.69;1925—2.88; 1929—3.12. Source: Bureau of the Census, *Historical Statistics of the United States, 1789–1945* (Washington, 1949), 67, 71–72, 236.

172. See chap. 4.

173. Basil Miles, "Memorandum for the Members of the Committee on Economic Restorations," November 7, 1924, copy in Young Papers.

174. Young speech, June 25, 1925, Young Papers; Robinson speech, June 25, 1925, ibid.; Gilbert speech, June 25, 1925, Box 74, CPF, Hoover Papers.

175. *New York Times*, June 24, 1925, 1, 6; June 27, 1925, 1.

176. See chap. 7.

6. The Americanization of Europe in the 1920s

1. For historical perspective on Americanization, *see* Otto Basler, "Amerikanismus. Geschichte des Schlagwortes," *Deutsche Rundschau* 224 (August 1930):142–46. For Germany, *see* Theodor Lüddecke, "Amerikanismus als Schlagwort und als Tatsache," ibid., 221 (March 1930):214–21; Moritz J. Bonn, *Die Kultur der Vereinigten Staaten von America* (Berlin, 1930), 7 and passim; Heinrich Müller, "Die Amerikanisierung Europas," *Allgemeine Rundschau* 18 (October 1920):510–11; Fritz Behn, "Amerikanismus in Deutschland," *Süddeutsche Monatshefte* 27 (June 1929):672–74; Richard Müller-Freienfels, " 'Amerikanismus' und europäische Kultur," *Der deutsche Gedanke* 4 (1927):30–35; Adolf Halfeld, *Amerika und der Amerikanismus: Krit-*

ische Betrachtungen eines Deutschen und Europäers (Jena, 1927); Jakob Overmans, "Amerikanisierung des Geistes," *Stimmen der Zeit* 118 (1929), 161–73; Paul Rohrbach, "Was heisst Amerikanismus?" *Deutsche Monatshefte 5* (1929): part 2:467–70; Berg, *Deutschland und Amerika,* 132–44; Earl R. Beck, *Germany Rediscovers America* (Tallahassee, 1968), 234–64 and passim; John Willett, *Art and Politics in the Weimar Period* (New York, 1978), 98–99. For France *see* Marcel Braunschvig, *La vie américaine* (Paris, 1931), 359; René Guénon, *Orient et Occident* (Paris, 1924), 22; Lucien Romier, *L'homme nouveau: Esquisse des consequences du progrès* (Paris, 1929), 139; René Jeanne, "L'invasion cinematographique américaine," *Revue des Deux Mondes* (February 15, 1930):857–84; Strauss, *Menace in the West,* 199–204 and passim. For Switzerland, *see* Heinze K. Meier, *Friendship under Stress: U.S.–Swiss Relations 1900–1950* (Bern, 1970), 6–26; for Poland, Alexander Skrzynski, "American and Polish Democracy," speech at Williamsburg Institute of Politics, July 1925, copy in Brown University Rockefeller Library; for Finland, Alfred J. Pearson to Frank B. Kellogg, September 30, 1926, 711.60d/a, General Records of the Department of State, NARG 59. For contemporary overview, *see* Edgar A. Mowrer, *This American World* (New York, 1928); Miller and Hill, *Giant of the Western World;* William Bullitt, *It's Not Done* (New York, 1926), 370; Antonio Gramsci, "Americanism and Fordism," *Selections from the Prison Notebooks* (New York, 1971), 279–318. For studies of cultural relations, *see* Rosenberg, *Spreading the American Dream;* Frank A. Ninkovich, *The Diplomacy of Ideas: United States Foreign Policy and Cultural Relations, 1938–1950* (New York, 1981). Lenin on his deathbed reputedly instructed his followers to "Americanize yourselves" ("Inquiry among European Writers into the Spirit of America," *transition,* no. 13 [1928]:248).

2. Mitchell interview with Hughes, November 11, 1941, copy in Houghton Papers; Castle diary, November 20, 1922, copy in Castle to Alanson B. Houghton, December 30, 1922, Houghton Papers.

3. Quoted in Alfred E. Cornebise, *Typhus and Doughboys: The American Polish Typhus Relief Expedition, 1919–1921* (Newark, Del., 1982), 66.

4. Yves-Henri Nouailhat, *Les Américains à Nantes et Saint-Nazaire, 1917–1919* (Paris, 1972), 191–92; Frank Freidel, *Over There* (Boston, 1964), 67–69; George Creel, *How We Advertised America* (New York, 1972), 238–39; James R. Mock and Cedric Larson, *Words That Won the War* (Princeton, 1939), 248–62.

5. Quoted in Nouailhat, *Les Américains,* 193–94; Freidel, *Over There,* 72–73, 78.

6. Quoted in Nouailhat, *Les Américains,* 195.

7. Willett, *Art and Politics,* 33, 89–90. *See also* note 47, below.

8. Nouaihat, *Les Américains,* 186, 196–97; Michael Fanning, ed., *France and Sherwood Anderson: Paris Notebook, 1921* (Baton Rouge, 1976), 51; *New York Times,* June 25, 1919, 16; June 26, 1919, 8.

9. Bernard Ragner, "The Permanent A.E.F.," *Saturday Evening Post* 212 (November 11, 1939):28.

10. Nouailhat, *Les Américains,* 211, 236; Elizabeth Brett White, *American Opinion of France* (New York, 1927), 285.

11. Nouailhat, *Les Américains,* 201–3; Freidel, *Over There,* 363–64; *New York Times,* May 13, 1919, 12.

12. For 1917–19 complaints, *see* Nouailhat, *Les Américains,* 204–15.

13. *New York Times,* May 31, 1919, 12; June 11, 1919, 14; Alfred E.

Cornebise, *The AMAROC News: The Daily Newspaper of the American Force in Germany, 1919–1923* (Carbondale, Ill., 1981), 21, 214–15.

14. Rasmussen, "American Forces in Germany," 58, 134–41; Cornebise, *AMAROC News*, 7, 29, 113–14, 181–85. Like the French, some Germans worried that their "girls were being ruined by American soldiers" (ibid., 186).

15. Rasmussen, "American Forces in Germany," 41, 44, 116, 168–84, 212–13, 225, 227. *See also* Lüddecke, "Amerikanismus," 221; Beck, *Germany Rediscovers America*, 14–16; Nelson, *Victors Divided*, 33–34, 50–51; Harry A. Franck, "Through Germany on Foot, Part II: Coblenz under the Stars and Stripes," *Harper's Magazine* 139 (August 1919):311–25; White, *American Opinion of France*, 285; Nouailhat, *Les Américains*, 212, Cornebise, *AMAROC News*, 240.

16. Eugen Diesel, *Die deutsche Wandlung* (Stuttgart/Berlin, 1931), 49. *See also* Halfeld, *Americka und der Amerikanismus*, x; Beck, *Germany Rediscovers America*, 11.

17. A. M. Dike, *Special Report of the Commissioner of the American Committee for Devastated France* (Paris, 1921), 32.

18. André Tardieu, *Devant l'Obstacle* (Paris, 1927), 199; *see also* 197–212.

19. Dike, *Special Report*, 57, for the quotation; *see also* 30–38. In Greece the American Red Cross trained the first women paramedics. *See* Cassimatis, "Greek-American Relations," 197–99.

20. *New York Times*, June 25, 1919, 16.

21. Joan Fultz Kontos, *Red Cross, Black Eagle: A Biography of Albania's American School* (New York, 1981), 154, for the quotation. See also ibid., passim; Rose Wilder Lane, "What the Albanians Think of America," *Travel* 48 (February 1927):25, 52; Charles F. Bove with Dana Lee Thomas, *A Paris Surgeon's Story* (Boston, 1956). Arthur P. Young, *Books for Sammies* (Pittsburgh, 1981), 76–77, tells of the Paris Library School operated until 1929 by the American Library Association.

22. Quoted in Cornebise, *Typhus and Doughboys*, 145.

23. Quoted in Cornebise, *AMAROC News*, 22. *See also* ibid., 122. 192.

24. Warren Irving Susman, "Pilgrimage to Paris: The Backgrounds of American Expatriation, 1920–1934" (Ph.D. dissertation, University of Wisconsin, 1957), 176; F. W. Ogilvie, *The Tourist Movement* (London, 1933), 210–18.

25. *Literary Digest* 94 (September 3, 1927):12; ibid., 90 (September 11, 1926):86; ibid., 97 (June 30, 1928):48–50.

26. Alanson B. Houghton diary, January 29, 1925, Houghton Papers.

27. *New York Times*, July 29, 1926, 4; *Literary Digest*, 90 (August 14, 1926):12–13.

28. Literary Digest 90 (August 14, 1926):12–13; *New York Times*, July 28, 1926; August 1, 1926, 22; Maurice Muret, "L'opinion américaine et la France," *Revue de Paris* (March 1, 1927):25.

29. Ogilvie, *Tourist Movement*, 218.

30. Alfred M. Brace, ed., *Americans in France: A Directory* (Paris, 1929); Susman, "Pilgrimage to Paris," 163–67; Ragner, "Permanent A.E.F.," 31, 36.

31. Colwell, "American Experience in Berlin," 22–23, 62–68, 75–87.

32. Matthew Josephson's foreword to Hugh Ford, ed., *The Left Bank Revisited: Selections from the Paris Tribune, 1917–1934* (University Park, Pa., 1972), xix. *See also* John W. Aldridge, "Afterthoughts on the 20's," *Commentary* 56 (November 1973):37–41; Noel Riley Fitch, *Sylvia Beach and the Lost Generation* (New York, 1983), 162–300.

33. Geoffrey Wolff, *Black Sun: The Brief Transit and Violent Eclipse of*

Harry Crosby (New York, 1976), 94, 107–8, 238–41; Caresse Crosby, *The Passionate Years* (New York, 1953), 208–9.

34. Wolff, *Black Sun*, 119–30; Susman, "Pilgrimage to Paris," 125–26, 276; Case and Case, *Owen D. Young* 302; Eberstadt diary, February 12, 1926, Box1, Eberstadt Papers.

35. Alan Howard Levy, "The Unintegrated Personality: American Music and the Muses of Europe, 1865–1930," (Ph.D. dissertation, University of Wisconsin at Madison, 1979), 78–81, 104–11; Léonie Rosenstiel, *Nadia Boulanger* (New York, 1982), 140–41, 153, 161–62.

36. Levy, "American Music," 43–45

37. Harold Loeb, "Foreign Exchange," *Broom* 2 (May 1922):176. *See also* Harold Loeb, "Broom: 1921–1923," *Broom* 5 (August 1923):55, and *The Way It Was* (New York, 1959); *Secession*, no. 2 (July 1922):33; Frederick J. Hoffman, Charles Allen, and Carolyn F. Ulrich, *The Little Magazines* (Princeton, 1946), 93–107.

38. Susman, "Pilgrimage to Paris," 205.

39. Quoted in David E. Shi, *Matthew Josephson, Bourgeois Bohemian* (New Haven, 1981), 58; emphasis in original.

40. Levy, "American Music," 95–100; Noel Stock, *The Life of Ezra Pound* (New York, 1970), 262–63.

41. Calvin Tomkins, *Living Well Is the Best Revenge* (New York, 1971), 131–48.

42. Hemingway appeared in translation sooner than most expatriates. In Italy a short story surfaced in 1925; in Germany *The Sun Also Rises* came out in 1928; in France by that year he was widely read. Anne Marie Springer, "The American Novel in Germany: A Study of the Critical Reception of Eight American Novelists between the Two World Wars" (Ph.D. dissertation, University of Pennsylvania, 1959), 135; Roger Asselineau, "French Reaction to Hemingway's Works between the Two World Wars," in Asselineau, ed., *The Literary Reputation of Hemingway in Europe* (New York, 1965), 51–57; Ernest S. Falbo, "Carlo Linati: Hemingway's First Italian Critic and Translator," *Fitzgerald/Hemingway Annual 1975*, 295; Wayne E. Kvam, *Hemingway in Germany* (Athens, Ohio, 1973), 5. For Hemingway's work and thrift ethics, *see* Scott Donaldson, *By Force of Will: The Life and Art of Ernest Hemingway* (New York, 1977), 91, 21–33; Richard P. Sugg, "Hemingway, Money, and *The Sun Also Rises*," *Fitzgerald/Hemingway Annual 1972*, 257; Ernest Hemingway, *The Sun Also Rises* (New York, 1926, 1954), 148.

43. Anna Louise Strong to Syndey Strong, July 14, 1926, Box 4, Anna Louise Strong Papers.

44. Malcolm Cowley, *Exile's Return* (New York, 1951), 62–63.

45. Walter Lowenfels in "Why Do American Live in Europe?" 108.

46. Andrew Turnbull, ed., *The Letters of F. Scott Fitzgerald* (New York, 1963), 326.

47. Levy, "American Music," 104–33; Claude McKay, *A Long Way from Home* (New York, 1937), 311; Walter White, "The Color Line in Europe," *Annals* 140 (November 1928):331–36; Basil Woon, *The Paris That's Not in the Guide Books* (New York, 1926), 174–82; Susman, "Pilgrimage to Paris," 218–27.

48. Springer, "American Novel in Germany," 100; Cowley, *Exile's Return*, 291.

49. Quoted in Springer, "American Novel in Germany," 42, and in Asseli-

neau, "French Reaction to Hemingway," 59, 58. *See also* Falbo, "Hemingway's First Italian Critic," 297, 302.

50. Quoted in Springer, "American Novel in Germany," 150. *See also* Kvam, *Hemingway in Germany*, 5–7.

51. O. R. Geyer, "Winning Foreign Film Markets," *Scientific American* 125 (August 20, 1921):132, 140; Rachael Low, *The History of the British Film 1918–1929* (London, 1971), 76–77; Rosenberg, *Spreading the American Dream*, 79–81.

52. William Victor Strauss, "Foreign Distribution of American Motion Pictures," *Harvard Business Review* 8 (April 1930):309. Of course not all American films were popular among all foreign audiences. Generally American movies were appreciated more in large cities than in the hinterland. *See* Paul Monaco, *Cinema & Society: France and Germany During the Twenties* (New York, 1976), 72–74; Charles Pomaret, *L'Amerique à la Conquête de l'Europe*, (Paris, 1931), 100–7; Jeanne, "L'invasion cinematographique américaine," 857–67. Robert Sklar, *Movie-Made America: A Cultural History of American Movies* (New York, 1972), 217. Apparently the Russians also loved American movies, when they could get to see them. *See* Walter A. Rukeyser, "I Work for Russia," *The Nation* 132 (June 17, 1931):653.

53. Willett, *Art and Politics*, 142.

54. Strauss, *Menace in the West*, 147.

55. Strauss, "Foreign Distribution of American Motion Pictures," 307–8; Raymond Moley, *The Hays Office* (New York, 1945), 169; Edward G. Lowry, "Trade Follows the Film," *Saturday Evening Post* 198 (November 7, 1925):12–13; John Eugene Harley, *World-Wide Influences of the Cinema* (Los Angeles, 1940), 27–28; Low, *British Film*, 79.

56. Lowry, "Trade Follows the Film," 12–13, 151; Walter Wanger, "120,000 American Ambassadors," *Foreign Affairs* 18 (October, 1939):50–51; Charles Merz, "When the Movies Go Abroad," *Harper's Monthly Magazine* 152 (January, 1926):162.

57. Hays quoted in Merz, "When the Movies Go Abroad," 162; Klein, quoted in Harley, *World-Wide Influences of the Cinema*, 245. *See also* Peter Odegard, *The American Public Mind* (New York, 1930), 208; Klein, *Frontiers of Trade*, 88–89; Lowry, "Trade Follows the Film," 13; Rosenberg, *Spreading the American Dream*, 99–103.

58. Clement Vautel in *Cyrano*, quoted in *Living Age* 336 (July 1929):382. See also Odegard, *American Public Mind*, 209; Jeanne, "L'invasion cinematographique," 877–84.

59. Quoted in Strauss, *Menace in the West*, 148.

60. Pomaret, *L'Amerique à la conquête de l'Europe*, 190.

61. Quoted in Harley, *World-Wide Influences of the Cinema*, 248–49. *See also* ibid., 32; Thelma Gutsche, *The History and Social Significance of Motion Pictures in South Africa, 1895–1940* (Cape Town, 1972), 166, 177–79; Low, *British Film*, 95–96; Lowry, "Trade Follows the Film," 12–13; George Bernard Shaw, *The Political Madhouse in America and Nearer Home* (London, 1933), 20.

62. Quoted in Lowry, "Trade Follows the Film," 12–13. Germans voiced similar concerns. *See* Monaco, *Cinema & Society*, 71; Strauss, "Foreign Distribution of American Motion Pictures," 310. For Italian concern, *see* Heinz Reiske, *Die USA in den Berichten italienischer Reisender* (Meisenheim am Glan, 1971), 120.

63. In 1928, the market share of American films in Britain was 81 percent,

in Germany 47 percent, in France 63 percent, in Italy 79 percent, in Australia 82 percent, and New Zealand 90 percent. *See* Strauss, "Foreign Distribution of American Motion Pictures," 311.

64. Sklar, *Movie-Made America*, 219–21; Jack C. Ellis, *A History of Film* (Englewood Cliffs, N.J., 1979), 109–10; Low, *British Film*, 91–106; Moley, *Hays Office*, 172–73; Monaco, *Cinema & Society*, 28; Siegfried Krakauer, *From Caligari to Hitler* (Princeton, 1947), 134; Lewis Jacobs, *The Rise of the American Film* (New York, 1939), 302–25.

65. *FRUS 1928*, 2:844–49, 918–23; *FRUS 1929* 2:1006–23; Moley, *Hays Office*, 171–76.

66. Sklar, *Movie-Made America*, 222–23; René Jeanne, "La France et le film parlant," *Revue des Deux Mondes*, (June 1, 1931), 536.

67. Quoted in Zammito, "The Berlin Avant-Garde," 510.

68. Anna Louise Strong to Tracy Strong, April 17, 1923, Box 3, Anna Louise Strong Papers. *See Also* references in note 1, above.

69. Jean-Paul Sartre, *Situations III* (Paris, 1949), 122.

70. Siegfried, *America Comes of Age*, 347.

71. Krutch, "Berlin Goes American," 564–65.

72. Ibid.; Zammito, "The Berlin Avant-Garde," 475–76; Ferdinand Eberstadt diary, March 12, 1926, Eberstadt Papers.

73. *Ford-Betriebe und Ford-Methoden* (Munich/Berlin, 1925), 29. *See also* Basler, "Amerikanismus," 145–46; Lüddecke, "Amerikanismus," 214–21; Halfeld, *Amerika und der Amerikanismus*, 25–37; Müller, "Die Amerikanisierung Europas," 510–11; Rohrbach, "Was heisst Amerikanismus?" 467–70; Rainer Hanns Tolzmann, "Objective Architecture: American Influences in the Development of Modern German Architecture" (Ph.D. dissertation, University of Michigan, 1975), 19–52; Berg, *Amerika und Deutschland*, 132–53; Beck, *Germany Rediscovers America*, 95–102, 233–46.

74. Willett, *Art and Politics*, especially 10–11, 82, 111–12, 224–25; Tolzmann, "Objective Architecture," 252–56; Peter Gay, *Weimar Culture* (New York, 1968); Walter Laqueur, *Weimar: A Cultural History* (New York, 1974), 162–73.

75. Tolzman, "Objective Architecture," 251–53.

76. Quoted in Zammito, "The Berlin Avant-Garde," 476.

77. Quoted in ibid., 492 (emphasis in original).

78. Quoted in ibid., 607.

79. Quoted in ibid., 350.

80. Frank B. Kellogg to Myron T. Herrick, June 30, 1927, 811.79651 L 64/107, NARG 59.

81. Herrick to Kellogg, May 10, 1927, 811.79651 N92/1, NARG 59; Kellogg to Herrick, May 10, 1927, ibid.; Laney, *Paris Herald*, 212–16; Kenneth S. Davis, *The Hero Charles A. Lindbergh and the American Dream* (Garden City, N.Y., 1959), 161, 165–67.

82. Herrick to Kellogg, June 30, 1927, 811.79651 L64/1, NARG 59. *See also* Kellogg to Herrick, June 30, 1927, 811.79651 L64/107, ibid. T. Bentley Mott, *Myron T. Herrick, Friend of France* (Garden City, 1930), 352.

83. Davis, *The Hero Charles A. Lindbergh*, 215; Mott, *Herrick*, 347–48.

84. Coolidge to Lindbergh, May 21, 1927, 811.79651 L64/8c, NARG 59; Coolidge to Gaston Doumergue, May 21, 1927, 811.79651 L64/8a, ibid.; Herrick

to Kellogg, May 28, 1927, 811.79651 L64/40, ibid.; Davis, *The Hero Charles A. Lindbergh*, 215.

85. Sheldon Whitehouse to Kellogg, June 2, 1927, 800.51W89 France/495–1/2, NARG 59.

86. Whitehouse to Kellogg, June 3, 1927, 651.5531/27, NARG 59. A tariff truce was reached a few months later. *See* Leffler, *Elusive Quest*, 169–70.

87. James Dunn to Gibson, May 24, 1927, 811.79651 L64/15, NARG 59; Dunn to Kellogg, June 1, 1927, 811.79651 L64/76, ibid.; Sterling to Kellogg, June 6, 1927, 841.000/1047, ibid.; Sterling to Kellogg, June 3, 1927, 811.79651 L64/55, ibid.; Davis, *The Hero Charles A. Lindbergh*, 221.

88. Sterling to Kellogg, June 6, 1927, 841.00/1047, NARG 59; Report of military attaché Major Robert G. Richardson, May 25, 1927, 811.79651 L64/-, ibid. Henry Fletcher boasted that the flight had done more "to help the prestige of the United States than winning a war" (Fletcher to William Castle, May 27, 1927, Box 13, Fletcher Papers).

89. The long quotation is a translation of the address of the Speaker of the Hungarian House of Commons, enclosed in George A. Gordon to Kellogg, June 2, 1927, 811.79651 L64/97, NARG 59. The others are from *ibid.*; W.S. Culbertson to Kellogg, May 25, 1927, L64/80; Wesley Frost to Kellogg, May 31, 1927, L64/85; Belgian Ambassador to Kellogg, May 24, 1927, L64/32; Mussolini to Fletcher, May 22, 1927, L64/-; Gaston Doumergue to Coolidge, May 30, 1927, L64/52, all in NARG 59. Alfred Einstein, "Lindbergh Cantata," in *New York Times* February 2, 1930, sec. 8, 8; Kim H. Kowalke, "Der Lindbergh-Flug: Kurt Weill's Musical Tribute to Lindbergh," *Missouri Historical Society Bulletin*, 33 (April 1977):193–96. For the American reaction to the flight, *see* John W. Ward, "The Meaning of Lindbergh's Flight," *American Quarterly* 10 (Spring 1953):3–16.

90. Self-declared anarchists and draft evaders, Sacco and Vanzetti were declared guilty in 1921 of murdering a factory paymaster and guard during a robbery in South Braintree, Mass. Recent evidence indicates that Sacco may have been guilty of the crime, but probably Vanzetti was not. The judge allowed the prosecuting attorney to exploit the unpopularity of the defendant's political beliefs. In a series of appeals and investigations, the case dragged on until the August 23, 1927 execution.

91. Wesley Frost (Marseilles) to Kellogg, August 10, 1926, 311.6521 Sal/304; for the incidents, American minister (Copehagen) to Kellogg, August 9, 1927, 311.6521 Sal/730; Sheldon Whitehouse (Paris) to Kellogg, August 8, 1927, 311.6521 Sal/587; American minister (Lisbon) to Hughes, November 1, 1921, 311.6521 Sal/66; W.R. Castle to John Wigmore, August 4, 1927, 311.6521 Sal/518; undated department memorandum, 311.6521 Sal/-; C. C. Spamer (Amsterdam) to Kellogg, September 19, 1927, 311.6521 Sal/919, all in NARG 59; Samuel Putnam, *Paris Was Our Mistress* (Carbondale, Ill., 1947), 116–17.

92. Ravndal (Zurich) to Kellogg, June 23, 1926, 311.6521 Sal/258, NARG 59. *See also* Richard M. Tobin (Hague) to Kellogg, August 11, 1927, 311.6521 Sal/743; Schurman (Berlin) to Kellogg, August 23, 1927, 311.6521 Sal/746; Schurman to Kellogg, August 24, 1927, 311.6521 Sal/821; American minister (Madrid) to Hughes, November 12, 1921, 311.6521 Sal/88; Dodge (Copenhagen) to Kellogg, August 9, 1927, 311.6521 Sal/610, all in NARG 59.

93. American minister (Madrid) to Hughes, November 12, 1921, 311.6521 Sal/88, NARG 59.

94. Castle to Hughes, October 14, 1921, 311.6521 Sal/157; Hughes to all diplomatic missions, written by Castle November 10, 1921, 311.6521 Sal/53a; Fred

M. Dearing to Kellogg, May 28, 1926, 311.6521 Sal/248; Castle to Robert Dalton, July 1, 1926, 311.6521 Sal/284, all in NARG 59.

95. D. C. Poole to Kellogg, December 14, 1927, 311.6521 Sal/955; Schurman to Kellogg, August 13, 1927, 311.6521 Sal/791; Castle to Schurman, September 2, 1927, 311.6521 Sal/791; Washburn (Vienna) to Kellogg, September 21, 1927, 311.6521 Sal/896; Carr to Washburn, September 22, 1927, 311.6521 Sal/896, all in NARG 59.

96. Washburn to Kellogg, August 24, 1927, 311.6521 Sal/826, NARG 59.

97. Whitehouse to Kellogg, August 17, 1928, 311.6521 Sal/706; James G. Bailey (Christiana, Norway) to Hughes, November 2, 1921, 311.6521 Sal/67; Dodge (Copenhagen) to Kellogg, January 14, 1927, 311.6521 Sal/372; Dodge to Kellogg, January 27, 1927, 311.6521 Sal/374; Frost (Marseille) to Kellogg, November 20, 1926, 311.6521 Sal/354; Frost to Kellogg, January 20, 1927, 311.6521 Sal/373; John B. Stetson (Warsaw) to Kellogg, August 9, 1927, 311.6521 Sal/792, all in NARG 59. For a list of prominent European protesters *see Literary Digest* 94 (September 3, 1927):7.

98. William C. Burdett to Kellogg, August 26, 1927, 311.6521 Sal/844, NARG 59.

99. Mussolini to Fletcher, transmitted to Kellogg, July 24, 1927, 311.6521 Sal/556, NARG 59.

100. Emphasis added. Article in *Kristeligt Dagblad*, transmitted in Dodge to Kellogg, September 1, 1927, 311.6521 Sal/868, NARG 59. *See also* Leon Ellis (Bern) to Kellogg, July 22, 1927, 311.6521 Sal/692; Stetson to Kellogg, August 9, 1927, 311.6521 Sal/792, both in NARG 59. The American consul in Brussels observed that the Sacco-Vanzetti case "lined up all the respectable classes to a realization that the United States is the center of the world defense against radicalism" (William C. Burdett to Kellogg, October 11, 1927, 811.43 American Legion/-, NARG 59).

7. The Limits of the American Order, 1927–1929

1. Quoted in Beth Irwin Lewis, *Georg Grosz* (Madison, 1971), 29; Zammito, "The Berlin Avant-Garde," 816; italics added.

2. Ogden Mills speech before the Economic Club of New York, March 6, 1930, Box 267, NARG 56.

3. For two key expressions of the belief that America had already sacrificed enough for Europe, see Coolidge Armistice Day speech, reported in *New York Times*, November 12, 1928, 2; Strong to Owen D. Young, August 20, 1928, Strong Papers.

4. Quoted in Miller and Hill, *Giant of the Western World*, 258. *See also* William Allen White, *A Puritan in Babylon* (New York, 1938), 410.

5. *New York Times*, November 12, 1928, 2.

6. For the background in Anglo-American relations, *see* Raymond G. O'-Connor, *Perilous Equilibrium: The United States and the London Naval Conference of 1930* (Lawrence, Kans., 1962), 1–17; Mannock, "Anglo-American Relations"; Stephen Roskill, *Naval Policy between the Wars: The Period of Anglo-American Antagonism, 1919–29,* (New York, 1968), 331–466; Gerald E. Wheeler, *Prelude to Pearl Harbor* (Columbia, 1963), 131–39. On the connection between commercial and naval rivalry, *see* Christina E. Newton, "Anglo-American Relations and Bureaucratic Tensions, 1927–1930" (Ph.D. dissertation, Uni-

versity of Illinois, 1975), 122. For an account focusing on the cooperative aspects, *see* Hogan, *Informal Entente.*

7. W. N. Medlicott, Douglas Dakin, and M. E. Lambert, eds., *DBFP*, ser. IA, 5:883–84.

8. Craigie memorandum in ibid., 860–62, italics in original. *See also* ibid., 777; Churchill speech, April 15, 1929, T172/1523, PRO; L. S. Amery, "Anglo-American Relations," November 26, 1928, C.P. 367 (28), PRO. *See also* Newton, "Anglo-American Relations," 122–24; David Carlton, "Great Britain and the Coolidge Naval Disarmament Conference of 1927," *Political Science Quarterly* 83 (December 1968):590–91.

9. Carlton, "Naval Disarmament Conference", 590; *DBFP*, ser. IA, 5:861–66; for the quotation, ibid., 888.

10. F.O. quotation from minute by Geoffrey Thompson, December 1, 1928, on memorandum by Amery, "Anglo-American Relations," November 26, 1928, A8217/39/45 F.O.371/12813, Documents of the Foreign Office, RG 371, PRO; Craigie's minute on same document, December 3, 1928; Wiliam Foster Trimble, "The United States Navy and the Geneva Conference for the Limitation of Naval Armament, 1927" (Ph.D. dissertation, University of Colorado, 1974), 55–57; Amery, *The Empire in the New Era*, 11.

11. Craigie in *DBFP*, ser. IA, 5:866, 871; Churchill in ibid., 883–84; Hankey in Carlton, "Naval Disarmament Conference," 578, and Newton, "Anglo-American Relations," 20. Another official commented: "The potential power and influence of the United States are so immense that it is important to . . . if possible mould them nearer to our hearts' desire and make a good world citizen of them" (R. I. Campbell minute on report of Esme Howard, September 9, 1926, A3954/3954/45, F.O. 371/11198, PRO). See also Trimble, "Geneva Conference," 212–13.

12. Coolidge in *Commercial and Financial Chronicle*, November 17, 1928, 127-2, 2760; Hilary Jones quoted in Trimble, "Geneva Conference," 345.

13. Quoted in Hoag, *Preface to Preparedness*, 148.

14. Kellogg to Henry Fletcher, March 1, 1926, Box 12, Fletcher Papers; *see also* Kellogg to Houghton, December 20, 1925; Houghton to Kellogg, December 22, 1925, both paraphrased in Houghton's compilation of the telegrams on disarmament issue, February 27, 1926 (hereafter Houghton compilation), Houghton Papers; O'Connor, *Perilous Equilibrium*, 14–15.

15. Kellogg to Houghton, January 2, 1926; Castle to Houghton, January 7, 1926; Houghton to Castle, December 7, 1925, all in Houghton compilation, Houghton Papers.

16. Trimble, "Geneva Conference," 92; Leffler, *Elusive Quest*, 159–61; Robert H. Ferrell, *Peace in Their Time* (New York, 1969), 50.

17. Trimble, "Geneva Conference," 106–7.

18. Quoted in Newton, "Anglo-American Relations," 32. *See also* ibid., 12–37; Trimble, "Geneva Conference," 225; O'Connor, *Perilous Equilibrium*, 15–19; Roskill, *Naval Policy between the Wars*, 1:498–516; Carlton, "Naval Disarmament Conference," 573–98; Robert W. Dubay, "The Geneva Naval Conference of 1927: A Study of Battleship Diplomacy," *Southern Quarterly* 8 (January 1970):177–99.

19. Quoted in Trimble, "Geneva Conference," 323; *see also* 340.

20. Hugh Gibson to William R. Castle, September 30, 1928, 500.A15 Franco-

British/132½, NARG 59. Chamberlain quoted in Trimble, "Geneva Conference," 354.

21. Trimble, "Geneva Conference," 396. As Houghton, the ambassador to London, put it, the naval bill "gives us a definite status," demonstrating that America was serious about parity (Houghton to Castle, January 31, 1928, Houghton Papers).

22. Gibson to Castle, September 30, 1928, 500.A15 Franco-British/132½, NARG 59; Coolidge to Kellogg, August 3, 1928, 500.A15 Franco-British/6½, ibid.; Kellogg to Coolidge, August 4, 1928, 500.A15 Franco-British/10½, ibid.; Houghton to Kellogg, September 12, 1928, 500.A15 Franco-British/41, ibid.; Ray Atherton to Kellogg, August 31, 1928, 500.A15 Franco-British/38, ibid.; David Carlton, "The Anglo-French Compromise on Arms Limitations, 1928," *Journal of British Studies* 8 (May 1969):11–62; Ferrell, *Peace in Their Time*, 209.

23. The two main articles of the Kellogg-Briand Pact read:
Art. I The High Contracting Parties solemnly declare in the names of their respective peoples that they condemn recourse to war for the solution of international controversies, and renounce it as an instrument of national policy in their relations with one another.
Art. II The High Contracting Parties agree that the settlement or solution of all disputes or conflicts of whatever nature or of whatever origin they may be, which may arise among them, shall never be sought except by pacific means. [*FRUS 1928*, 1:153–56]

24. For the president's evaluation, see Coolidge speech, November 11, 1928, printed in *Commercial and Financial Chronicle* 27-2 (November 17, 1928):2760.

25. Charles DeBenedetti, "The American Peace Movement and the State Department in the Era of Locarno," in Solomon Wank, ed., *Doves and Diplomats* (Westport, Conn., 1978), 202–16; Harold Josephson, *James T. Shotwell and the Rise of Internationalism in America* (Rutherford, N.J., 1975), 116–55; Ferrell, *Peace in Their Time*, 13–37.

26. Ferrell, *Peace in Their Time*, 66–127; Stephen John Kneeshaw, "The Kellogg-Briand Pact: The American Reaction" (Ph.D. dissertation, University of Colorado, 1971), 5–23; John E. Stoner, *S. O. Levinson and the Pact of Paris* (Chicago, 1942), 67–80.

27. *FRUS 1927*, 2:619; Howard H. Quint and Robert H. Ferrell, eds., *The Talkative President: The Off-the-Record Press Conferences of Calvin Coolidge* (Amherst, 1964), 214–15.

28. Quoted in Ferrell, *Peace in Their Time*, 139; *see also* 138–43. Borah was not the only one to come up with the multilateral idea. *See also* Drew Pearson and Constantine Brown, *The American Diplomatic Game* (Garden City, N.Y., 1935), 26–38; Vinson, 122–75.

29. Ferrell, *Peace in Their Time*, 144–69.

30. Stresemann to Kellogg through Schurman, April 13, 1928, 711.6212 Anti-War/14 (italics added); Robert Bennett Dockhorn, "The Wilhelmstrasse and the Search for a New Diplomatic Order 1926–30" (Ph.D. dissertation, University of Wisconsin, 1972), 174; on Hungary see *FRUS 1928* 1:217–19.

31. Dockhorn, "Wilhelmstrasse," 174–92; Kellogg to American Embassy, Berlin, April 23, 1928, 711.6212 Anti-War/15, NARG 59; Ferrell, *Peace in Their Time*, 144–220; *DBFP*, ser. IA, 5:635–38, 648.

32. Poole to Kellogg, October 23, 1928, 762.00/40, NARG 59.

33. Walter Lippmann, "The Political Equivalent of War," *Atlantic Monthly* 142 (August 1928):181–87. For similar discussions by others, *see* Charles E. Hughes, "Pan-American Peace," *Yale Review* 18 (June 1929):646–48; Kneeshaw, "Kellogg Briand Pact," 64, 405 (for William Borah); 406 (for Salmon O. Levinson).

34. Castle to David Reed, December 19, 1928, Box 3, Castle Papers; Kellogg to American Embassy in Berlin, April 23, 1928, 711.6212 Anti-War/15, NARG 59. *See also* Houghton to Sarah Cleghorn, September 17, 1928, Houghton Papers; Ferrell, *Peace in Their Time*, 156. Castle was satisfied that the pact enabled the United States to square the circle: "We had taken the position of leadership in world matters, without in the slightest degree involving ourselves in either League or European political questions" (Castle to Reed, December 19, 1928, Castle Papers).

35. White, *Puritan in Babylon*, 410.

36. Loucheur paraphrased in S. Pinkney Tuck to Frank B. Kellog, September 26, 1925, copy in Box 91, CPF, Hoover Papers.

37. For the Brussels meeting, see Parrini, *Heir to Empire*, 142–47.

38. Arthur N. Young memorandum of conversation with T. W. Page, December 18, 1926, file 550.M1/59, NARG 59. *See also* A. N. Young, "Reasons for American Participation in the Economic Conference," January 8, 1927, 550.M1/62; memorandum by Wallace McClure, December 22, 1926, 550.M1/61; A. N. Young to William R. Castle, May 25, 1927, 550.M1/343; Hoover to Kellogg, January 28, 1927, 550.M1/55, all in NARG 59.

39. Hoover to Chester H. Rowell, January 20, 1927, Box 51, CPF, Hoover Papers. Henry M. Robinson chaired the United States delegation; members were Norman Davis, John W. O'Leary, Alonzo Taylor, and Julius Klein. *See* State Department memorandum, March 16, 1927, 550.M1/132; A. N. Young to Kellogg, April 14, 1927, 550.M1/231, both in NARG 59; Henry M. Robinson, "Some Lessons from the Economic Conference," *Foreign Affairs* 6 (October 1927):16.

40. For negotiations leading up to the conference, see file IB, Band 1, Sonderreferat/Wirtschaft, AA, Bonn; Tuck to Kellogg, September 26, 1925, Box 51, CPF, Hoover Papers; F. A. Sterling to Kellogg, January 23, 1926, 550.M1/7; Robert F. Skinner to Kellogg, April 26, 1926, 550.M1/16; memorandum by Wallace McClure of Conversation with Dr. Alfred Zimmern, October 24, 1926, 550.M1/29; memorandum by McClure, December 9, 1926, 550.M1/4; memorandum by McClure, "Benefits Likely to Be Derived from Participation by the United States," December 22, 1926, 550.M1/61; A. N. Young memorandum of conversation with Thomas Walker Page, December 18, 1926, 550.M1/59; Myron Herrick to Kellogg, April 1, 1927, 550.M1/197; Leland Harrison to Herbert Hoover, January 17, 1927, 550.M1/42; Houghton to Kellogg, February 21, 1927, 550.M1/94, all in NARG 59; Leland Harrison to Kellogg, March 14, 1927, Box 20, Harrison Papers.

41. A. N. Young to William R. Castle, May 25, 1927, 550.M1/343, NARG 59. Echoing Hoover, Davis defended America's balance-of-payments policy by emphasizing tourist expenditures, triangular trade, and foreign investments as means that pumped dollars into the world economy. A. N. Young to Kellogg, June 1, 1927, 550.M1/336, NARG 59.

42. Alonzo Taylor to Hoover, June 28, 1927, Box 84, CPF, Hoover Papers. Boyden's close cooperation with other American delegates was no accident. Owen Young, chairman of the International Chamber's American Section, cleared Boy-

den's appointment with Kellogg. *See* O. D. Young to Kellogg, January 27, 1927, 550.M1/54, NARG 59.

43. Quoted in A. N. Young to Kellogg, June 1, 1927, 550.M1/336, NARG 59.

44. Memorandum by McClure, December 17, 1926, 550.M1/191; December 22, 1926, 550.M1/61, both NARG 59; Leffler, *Elusive Quest*, 167–71.

45. A. N. Young to W. R. Castle, May 25, 1927, 550.M1/343, NARG 59. *See also* A. N. Young to Kellogg, May 20, 1927, 550.M1/280; Norman Davis to Kellogg, May 23, 1927, 550.M1/314; A. N. Young to Kellogg, June 1, 1927, 550.M1/330, all in NARG 59; Robinson, "Economic Conference," 18.

46. Davis to Kellogg, May 23, 1927, with enclosure, 550.M1/314; A. N. Young to Kellogg, May 26, 1927 with enclosure, 550.M1/313, both in NARG 59; Robinson, "Economic Conference," 18.

47. A. N. Young to Kellogg, May 3, 1927, 550.M1/256, NARG 59.

48. Quoted in A. N. Young to Kellogg, May 26, 1927, 550.M1/313, NARG 59. *See also* memorandum by E. Dana Durand, "Resolutions of the Economic Conference in regard to 'Industry,' " transmitted by A. N. Young to Kellogg, May 26, 1927, 550.M1/311, NARG 59. For further discussion of the rationalization movement, *see* chap. 5.

49. A. N. Young to Kellogg, May 25, 1927, 550.M1/343, NARG 59.

50. Georg Schwarzenberger, *Die internationalen Banken für Zahlungsausgleich and Agrarkredite* (Berlin, 1932).

51. Richard B. Day, *Leon Trotsky and the Politics of Economic Isolation* (Cambridge, Mass., 1973), 151–52, 167, 173–74; Stephen F. Cohen, *Bukharin and the Bolshevik Revolution* (New York, 1973), 289–95; Alexander Erlich, *The Soviet Industrialization Debate, 1924–1928* (Cambridge, Mass., 1960), 25–28, 141.

52. *New York Times*, May 15, 1927, sec. 9, 4; Isaac Deutscher, *The Prophet Unarmed: Trotsky 1921–1929* (New York, 1959), 289; for the Bolshevik return to gold *see* John Parke Young, ed., *European Currency and Finance* (Washington, 1925), 251–69.

53. Littauer of the Polish Foreign Ministry made a memorandum of his conversation with Rosenblatt of the Soviet delegation to Geneva. In Warsaw the Foreign Ministry passed a copy to the American minister, who then translated and transmitted it to Washington (John B. Stetson to Kellogg, May 13, 1927, 760c.61/556, NARG 59).

54. Klein to Hoover, May 19, 1927, Box 90, COF, Hoover Papers; *New York Times*, May 8, 1927, see 1, 21.

55. Littauer memorandum, transmitted by Stetson to Kellogg, May 13, 1927, 760c.61/556, NARG 59.

56. Reported in Cavendish-Bentinck to Austen Chamberlain, May 23, 1927, N2390/9/38, F.O. 371/12581, PRO.

57. Davis to Kellogg, May 23, 1927, 550.M1/314, NARG 59.

58. Quoted in Day, *Trotsky*, 181. *See also* ibid., 173–80; Robert C. Tucker, *Stalin as Revolutionary 1879–1929* (New York, 1973), 368–420; Edward H. Carr and R. W. Davies, *Foundations of a Planned Economy, 1926–1929* (New York, 1969), 1:299–305; Erlich, *Soviet Industrialization Debate*, 171–72; Cohen, *Bukharin*, 289–90, 295; Adam B. Ulam, *Expansion and Coexistence* (New York, 1968), 164–66; Jane De Gras, ed., *Soviet Documents on Foreign Policy* (New York, 1952), 2:202–14.

59. U.S. Bureau of the Census, *Historical Statistics*, 550.

60. Stetson to Kellogg, November 19, 1928, 811.503160c/6, NARG 59. *See also* Costigliola, "American Foreign Policy," 85–105.

61. John Foster Dulles speech to International Chamber of Commerce, April 29, 1929, copy in Young Papers.

62. Russell C. Leffingwell to Thomas W. Lamont, July 20, 1927, file 103-12, Lamont Papers.

63. Leffingwell to Lamont, October 22, 1928, file 103-13, Lamont Papers.

64. Hoover speech, quoted in *New York Times*, October 17, 1922, 14; Rhodes, "Hoover and the War Debts," 130–34; Calvin Coolidge speech, November 11, 1928, in *Commercial and Financial Chronicle*, 128-2 (November 17, 1928):2759–61; R. L. Craigie to S. D. Waley, December 7, 1928, A8451/39/45, F.O.371/12813, PRO.

65. Craigie to Waley, December 7, 1928, A8451/39/45, F.O.371/12813, PRO; W. N. Medlicott, et al., ed., *DBFP*, ser. IA, 5:832–34, 861, 864–65.

66. See Costigliola, "United States and Poland"; Chandler, *Strong*, 390–422; Richard Hemmig Meyer, *Bankers' Diplomacy: Monetary Stabilization in the Twenties* (New York, 1970).

67. Jacobson, *Locarno Diplomacy*, 187–207, 220–22, 239–41, 316–18.

68. Eliot Wadsworth to Hoover, February 14, 1925, Box 376, COF, Hoover Papers; *see also* chap. 4.

69. Jacob Gould Schurman to Kellogg, July 24, 1926, 862.51P95/22; Gilbert to Strong and Mellon, transmitted through Schurman to Kellogg, April 19, 1926, 862.00/2257; Gilbert to Strong and Mellon, transmitted through Schurman to Kellogg, March 5, 1926, 862.51/2222, all in NARG 59. For a picture of the loan sales compaign by a leading banking firm in Germany, see Ferdinand Eberstadt to Clarence Dillon, October 31, 1926, Box 1, Eberstadt Papers; Eberstadt to Dillon, November 20, 1926, ibid., and other letters in this collection. For discussion of the priority issue with regard to state and municipal loans, *see* Strong to Gilbert, September 24, 1927, Strong Papers; memorandum by John Foster Dulles, January 10, 1927, copy in 862.51P95/37, NARG 59. The 1924 Dawes loan was the only private loan that enjoyed undisputed priority over reparations transfers.

70. S. Parker Gilbert to German finance minister, September 20, 1926, copy in 862.51P95/9; *see also* D. C. Poole to Kellogg, September 22, 1926, 862.51P95/39, both in NARG 59.

71. Memorandum by John Foster Dulles, January 10, 1927, 862.51P95/37, NARG 59.

72. Ray O. Hall to Julius Klein, "Misrepresentation in German Loan Prospectuses," January 20, 1927, file 640 Germany, Records of the Bureau of Foreign and Domestic Commerce, NARG 151; Castle to Kellogg, February 4, 1926, 862.51/2178; Arthur N. Young to Castle, May 14, 1927, 862.51B32/29, both in NARG 59. The administration also met frustration in the attempt to ban French loans until Paris ratified the war debt agreement. Americans bought French bonds issued in other investment markets. *See* memorandum by Leland Harrison of conversation between Kellogg and Fred Kent, March 17, 1927, Box 20, Harrison Papers; A. N. Young memorandum, "Foreign Loan Policy," March 21, 1927, 800.51/560, NARG 59; Leffler, *Elusive Quest*, 173–77. The British encountered similar problems with loan control. *See* Norman to Niemeyer, February

21, 1927; Norman to Hopkins, February 4, 1928; Fisher to Norman, September 28, 1928, all in file T175/4, Richard Hopkins Papers, PRO.

73. For the quotation, *see* Pierre Jay to Benjamin Strong, June 22, 1927, Box 1, Pierre Jay Papers, Sterling Library (Yale University); Gilbert to George L. Harrison, transmitted by Ogden Mills to Castle, September 24, 1927, 862.51/2504; Castle to Schurman, September 26, 1927; Castle memorandum of conversation with Dr. Kiep, September 29, 1927, both in 862.51/2508, NARG 59; Eberstadt diary, August 23, 1927, Box 1, Eberstadt Papers.

74. Gilbert to Strong, November 14, 1927; Strong to Gilbert, November 22, 1927, both transmitted by Strong to Kellogg, November 22, 1927, 862.51/2544, NARG 59; Strong to Gilbert, September 24, 1927, Strong Papers; Schurman to Kellogg, October 28, 1927, 862.51/2535; Gilbert to Strong, September 21–22, 1927, 862.51P95/41, Castle to Gilbert, September 22, 1927, 862.51P95/42, all in NARG 59.

75. Yet Strong believed it was "utterly impossible and dangerous for the FRBNY or bankers to regulate loans." Attempts to do so would antagonize bankers and invite congressional interference (Strong to George Harrison, July 21, 1927, file 0798, FRBNY Files).

76. Strong to Gilbert, November 11, 1927; Strong to Gilbert, November 22, 1927; Gilbert to Strong, November 14, 1927, all transmitted by Strong to Kellogg, November 22, 1927, 862.51/2544; *see also* Strong to Kellogg, October 22, 1927, 862.51/2519, both in NARG 59.

77. For Strong's biography, see Chandler, *Strong*; for Norman *see* Clay, *Lord Norman*; Boyle, *Montagu Norman*; for Moreau, *see* Moreau, *Souvenirs*; for Schacht, *see* Helmut Mueller, *Die Zentralbank—eine Nebenregierung Reichsbankpräsident Hjalmar Schacht as Politiker der Weimarer Republik* (Opladen, Germany, 1973); Amos E. Simpson, *Hjalmar Schacht in Perspective* (The Hague, 1969); Schacht, *My First Seventy-Six Years*.

78. Clarke, *Central Bank Cooperation*, 115–17; Moreau, *Souvenirs*, May 13, 16, 18, 1927.

79. For the quotation, *see* memorandum by Harry A. Siepmann of conversation with Bank of France secretary Pierre Quesnay, June 1–3, 1927, T176/29, Niemeyer Papers; *see also* Frederick Leith Ross to Churchill, June 13, 1927, ibid. For the financial background, see Clarke, *Central Bank Cooperation*, 116–20; Sayers, *Bank of England* 3:101–7.

80. Norman's "Notes" for July 3–9, 1927, reproduced in Sayers, *Bank of England* 3:96–100. For the rivalry over Poland, *see* Costigliola, "The United States and Poland," 98–104.

81. Strong to Pierre Jay, August 4, 1927; Strong to Jay, November 10, 1927; Strong to Jay, July 21, 1927, all in Strong Papers; Strong to Émile Moreau, August 10, 1927, FRBNY Files.

82. Quoted in Clarke, *Central Bank Cooperation*, 127. *See also* ibid., 124–26; Elmus Wicker, *Federal Reserve Monetary Policy, 1917–33* (New York, 1966), 110–16; Charles S. Hamlin diary, July 25, 27, 1927; September 6, 1927, Charles Hamlin Papers, Library of Congress.

83. U.S. Bureau of Census, *Historical Statistics*, 564, 660; Board of Governors of the Federal Reserve System, *Banking and Monetary Statistics* (Washington, 1943), 537.

84. Strong to Bachmann, November 18, 1927, C261 Suisse, FRBNY Files; Strong to Pierre Jay, March 26, 1928, Strong Papers; Strong to Walter W. Stewart,

August 3, 1928, FRBNY Files; Strong to Owen Young, August 17, 1928, Strong Papers; W. Randolph Burgess, "The Money Market in 1928," *The Review of Economic Statistics* 11 (February 1929):24.

85. Clarke, *Central Bank Cooperation*, 131–34.

86. Ingvar Svennilson, *Growth and Stagnation in the European Economy* (Geneva, 1954), 234. During the same four-year period, U.S. wholesale prices fell 12 percent, but America did not start off with an overvalued currency.

87. Churchill to Niemeyer, April 20, 1927, T175/11, Hopkins Papers; memorandum, by R. G. Hawtrey, "Recent Price Movements," March 1, 1927, Hawtrey memorandum, July 12, 1928, both in T176/16, Niemeyer Papers. Snowden quoted in Moreau, *Souvenirs*, October 22, 1927, 411; Sayers, *Bank of England* 1:347; (no author), *The International Gold Problem* (London, 1931); Memorandum by Ivy Lee to Thomas Lamont, "The World Crisis as Viewed Abroad Especially in England," September 30, 1930, 103–7 Lamont Papers.

88. For Anglo-American controversy on these issues, *see* Strong to George Harrison, July 6, 1928, Strong Papers; Strong to Norman, August 30, 1927, ibid.; Strong to George Harrison, December 24, 1927, FRBNY Files; Strong to Norman, March 27, 1928, Strong Papers; Strong to George Harrison, July 8, 1928, ibid.; memorandum of conversation between Strong and Arthur Salter, May 25, 1928, ibid.; memorandum by George Harrison of conversation with Salter, February 26, 1929, FRBNY Files; Churchill speech, June 27, 1927, copy in T172/1522, PRO. For the loan question, *see* Arthur Salter to Niemeyer, April 14, 1927; Dwight Morrow to Salter, September 2, 1927; Norman to Salter, September 6 and 8, 1927, all in Box 123, League of Nations Archives, United Nations Library, Geneva.

89. Sayers, *Bank of England*, 1:331–46.

90. Strong to Owen Young, July 14, 1927, C798, FRBNY Files.

91. Memorandum by O. Ernest Moore of conversation between Strong and Salter, May 25, 1928, Strong Papers.

92. For the quotation, Jeremiah Smith to George L. Harrison, August 28, 1930, C798, FRBNY Files. Strong described the controversy with the board in a long letter to Owen Young, March 6, 1927, Young Papers. For the price stabilization controversy, see Chandler, *Strong*, 189, 199–204, 245–46, 355–56; Burgess, ed., *Interpretations*; Lawrence E. Clark, *Central Banking under the Federal Reserve System* (New York, 1935); Irving Fisher, *Stable Money: A History of the Movement* (New York, 1934).

93. Strong to Owen Young, June 11, 1928, FRBNY Files.

94. O. Ernest Moore memorandum of conversation between Strong and Salter, May 25, 1928, Strong Papers; Strong to George Harrison, July 6, 1928, ibid.; Jeremiah Smith to George E. Roberts, July 23, 1930, FRBNY Files.

95. Costigliola, "Financial Rivalry," 931-32; Wicker, *Monetary Policy*, 116–23, 129; Lester V. Chandler, *American Monetary Policy, 1928–41* (New York, 1971), 42–46.

96. Clarke, *Central Bank Cooperation*, 147–50.

97. *See* note 66.

98. Chandler, *Strong*, 390–459.

99. Ibid., 471-73.

100. Owen Young to Gilbert, November 12, 1928; Owen Young to Gilbert, November 19, 1928, Young Papers. This left the way clear for deputy-governor George Harrison, who never matched Strong's national or international influence.

101. Leffingwell to Lamont, October 22, 1928, file 101-13, Lamont Papers.

102. For the quotation see Gilbert to Pierre Jay, September 17, 1926, Young Papers. For Gilbert's role in communications between Mellon and Europeans, see Moreau, Souvenirs, passim; Gilbert to Andrew Mellon, June 22, 1929, Box 879, Presidential Papers, Hoover Papers; for his ties with State Department officials, see for example, memorandum by Castle of conversation with Gilbert, January 3, 1928, 462.00R296/2189, NARG 59; Gilbert to Castle ("Dear Bill"), December 3, 1927, Castle Papers; Gilbert to Alanson B. Houghton, May 25, 1927, Houghton Papers; Houghton to Gilbert, September 6, 1928, ibid.; Gilbert to Winston Churchill, copy enclosed in Gilbert to Houghton, July 7, 1928, ibid. In a dispute between Gilbert and Ambassador Schurman, Kellogg and Castle sided with the former (Kellogg to Schurman, April 11, 1927, Schurman Papers). For an indication of how Gilbert helped American businessmen in Germany, see Eberstadt diary, April 9, 1926, Box 1, Eberstadt Papers.

103. Gilbert to Leon Fraser, March 9, 1929, Young Papers.

104. Wilson quoted in State Department memorandum, April 15, 1929, 462.00R296/2784, NARG 59; Stimson to Owen Young, April 15, 1929, printed in Department of State, Foreign Relations of the United States 1929 (Washington, 1943) 2:1061.

105. Kuczynski, Bankers' Profit, 141.

106. See chaps. 3–5; Costigliola, "First World Bank," 612–13.

107. See text below.

108. Poole to Kellogg, December 30, 1927, 462.00R.00R296/2111, NARG 59. See also Schurman to Kellogg, October 11, 1928, 462.00R296/2404; Poole to Kellogg, October 23, 1928, 762.00/40, both in ibid.

109. Quoted in Jacobson, Locarno Diplomacy, 193–94.

110. Ibid., 42.

111. Houghton to Gilbert, September 6, 1928, Houghton Papers; Henry L. Stimson memorandum of conversation with German Ambassador von Prittwitz, May 9, 1929, 462.00R296/2865; Karl von Schubert memorandum of conversation with Gilbert, February 28, 1928, frame E111000, reel 2249, Captured German Documents, NA; Costigliola, "United States and Poland," 96–98. See also chap. 8.

112. See text below; Jacobson, Locarno Diplomacy, 187–235; Carlton "Arms Limitation," 141–62.

113. Schurman to Kellogg, October 11, 1928, 462.00R296/2404, NARG 59; see also Poole to Arthur N. Young, September 21, 1928, 462.00R296/2380½; Schurman to Kellogg, August 21, 1928, 762.00/36, both in ibid.

114. Moreau, Souvenirs, October 15, 1927, 406.

115. Jacobson, Locarno Diplomacy, 157, 160–62; Gilbert's memorandum of conversation with Stresemann, November 13, 1928, copy in Young Papers.

116. Gilbert to Kellogg, Mellon and Coolidge, transmitted through Paris Embassy, October 4, 1928, Box 78, Country File, Records of the Department of the Treasury, NARG 39.

117. A. N. Young to Kellogg, January 2, 1929, 462.00R296/3060, NARG 59; see also A. N. Young to Kellogg October 12, 1928, 462.00R296/2691; A. N. Young to Kellogg, October 26, 1928, 462.00R296/2959; Norman Armour to Kellogg, November 13, 1928, 462.00R296/2465, all in ibid.

118. Gilbert paraphrased in Poole to A. N. Young, October 5, 1928, 462.00R296/2389½, ibid.

119. Gilbert to Houghton, April 20, 1928, Houghton Papers; see also Houghton to Gilbert, September 21, 1928, ibid.; Houghton to Gilbert, April 17, 1928, ibid.; Edwin C. Wilson to Kellogg, June 27, 1927 462.00R296/1897, NARG 59; E. C. Wilson to Stimson, June 3, 1930, 462.00R296 Bank for Interntional Settlements/114, ibid.; Gilbert to Pierre Jay, September 24–25, 1928, copy in Young Papers; memorandum by R. L. Craigie, August 7, 1926, A4144/3895/45, F.O.371/11197, PRO; Craigie memorandum of conversation with Otto Niemeyer, A5046/3895/45, F.O.371/11198, PRO.

120. Quoted in Jacobson, *Locarno Diplomacy*, 204. See also *DBFP*, ser. IA, 5:385–86; Gilbert to Kellogg and Mellon, October 25, 1928, Box 78, NARG 39; Schurman to Kellogg, October 31, 1928, ibid.; Leith-Ross, *Money Talks*, 102–5.

121. The plan first took shape in 1927–28, a prosperous time when it seemed possible to lessen the sting of the political debts. American leaders predicted that expanded trade would soon dwarf these obligations. Mellon apparently planned to retire the United States national debt by 1940, and thereafter forgive the remaining war debts. (This is based on what Craigie termed two "reliable" sources: Esme Howard to Chamberlain, November 17, 1927 and minute by R. L. Craigie, December 1, 1927, A6875/935/45, F.O.371/12053, PRO.) Even Hoover, the administration official who took the hardest line, acknowledged in 1925 that reaching a final settlement "may be a process of trial and error" (Hoover to Owen Young, September 18, 1925, Young Papers). Young and other financiers favored a series of German bond issues that would raise in the world investment markets sufficient money for a lump sum reparations settlement. According to this scenario, the United States would then grant the Allies a generous discount for cash payment of the war debts. The operation would reduce the debt's size and "commercialize" it. Germany could not repudiate bonds held by private investors, financiers believed, without destroying its international credit. Young hoped that the reparation bonds would become "truly international securities," supplementing gold reserves in balance-of-payments corrections. After mid-1928, demand for foreign bonds dropped as the stock boom offered greater profits. Yet Gilbert, Leffingwell, and other financiers expected that the bond market soon would recover sufficiently to float reparation securities. Widespread distribution of these bonds, Gilbert believed, would "guarant[ee] peace" and "consolidat[e] the peaceful reconstruction of Europe" (paraphrsed in Poole to A. N. Young, October 5, 1928, 462.00R296/2389½, NARG 59; Leffingwell to Lamont, October 22, 1928, file 103-13, Lamont Papers; Bernard Baruch to Owen Young, June 11, 1928, Baruch Papers. The "principal market" for the bonds, Gilbert acknowledged, would be America. This would make U.S. investors Germany's principal reparation creditor, a prospect that worried administration officials. When Gilbert outlined the plan to Coolidge in 1927, the president "preserved his usual silence" (paraphrased in Poole to A. N. Young, October 5, 1928, 462.00R296/2389½, NARG 59). A year later, Coolidge warned publicly that unless the Allies reduced armament spending and criticism of the United States they could not expect a continued outflow of American capital. In 1928–30, State and Commerce department officials grew cooler to the idea of American investors sinking huge amounts into reparation bonds, especially since France, the chief beneficiary, was defiant on the disarmament issue. Nevertheless, Arthur Young, Stimson, and Mills favored the commercialization-liquidation scheme as long as United States investors did not have to buy the bulk of the reparation

bonds (A. N. Young to Kellogg, October 26, 1928, 462.00R296/2959; A. N. Young to Kellogg, January 2, 1929, 462.00R296/3060; Stimson to Owen Young, April 8, 1929, 462.00R296/2773, all in NARG 59; Mills to Mellon, April 6, 1929, file G733 C.01, NARG 39; Mills to John Foster Dulles, June 16, 1931, Dulles Papers. Thus, throughout the Young Plan's 1927–30 gestation period, lump sum payment seemed a real, although receding, possibility.

122. Gilbert's memorandum of conversation with Stresemann, November 13, 1928, Young Papers; *see also* Gilbert to Kellogg and Mellon, October 25, 1928, Box 78, NARG 39.

123. Quoted in Jacobson, *Locarno Diplomacy*, 225, 231.

124. Gilbert's memorandum of conversation with Stresemann, November 13, 1928, Young Papers.

125. Young speech at Camp General, July 24, 1929, Young Papers.

126. Jacobson, *Locarno Diplomacy*, 199–224; A. N. Young to Kellogg, October 12, 1928, 462.00R296/2691, NARG 59; A. N. Young to Kellogg, October 26, 1928, 462.00R296/2959, NARG 59.

127. For the first quotation, Charles G. Dawes, *Notes as Vice-President, 1928–1929* (Boston, 1935), 156; for the second, Dawes to Lamont, December 3, 1928, file 91-110, Lamont Papers.

128. F. W. M. Cutcheon, to Thomas Nelson Perkins, December 9, 1928, Young Papers; *see also* Gilbert to Owen Young, December 28, 1928, ibid.; Mellon to Owen Young, December 29, 1928, ibid.; Case and Case, *Owen D. Young*, 421–31.

129. Moreau to Owen Young, J. P. Morgan, and N. D. Jay through Morgan and Company, January 24, 1929, Young Papers; Leon Fraser to Gilbert, January 24, 1929, ibid.; unsigned memorandum, February 7, 1929, ibid.; Owen Young to Gerard Swope, February 13, 1929, ibid.; Case and Case, *Owen D. Young*, 432–35.

130. Owen Young to J. P. Morgan and Co., June 1, 1929, Lamont Papers.

131. Costigliola, "First World Bank," 607–8; Case and Case, *Owen D. Young*, 436–39.

132. Young speech at Camp General, July 24, 1929, Young Papers.

133. Costigliola, "First World Bank," 608. In contrast to the Genoa proposal for central bank cooperation under Bank of England leadership, the BIS assembled the central banks under private American aegis. The BIS refused to become involved in the LNFC gold shortage inquiry and rejected British plans for wholesale creation of credit.

134. Young speech at Camp General, July 24, 1929, Young Papers.

135. J. P. Morgan and Lamont to J. P. Morgan and Co., March 11, 1929, file 178-18, Lamont Papers.

136. Young speech, transmitted by Edwin C. Wilson to Stimson, June 11, 1929, 462.00R296/3000, NARG 59.

137. Young to Kellogg, March 19, 1929, 462.00R296/2771, ibid.

138. Walter W. Stewart, Shepard Morgan, and W. Randolph Burgess to Owen Young, March 2, 1929, Young Papers. An instrument of the powerful industrial countries, the BIS rejected the bid of Poland and other poor nations for "equal facilities for credit": League of Nations, Bank for International Settlements, Extracts from the Minutes of the Tenth Ordinary Session of the Assembly and the Second Committee of the Assembly, September 10, 1929 (League document C.494.M.158.1929.II).

139. Young to Kellogg, March 19, 1929, 462.00R296/2771, NARG 59.

140. Young to Cutcheon, May 5, 1928 (not sent), Young Papers; Jacobson, *Locarno Diplomacy*, 253.

141. "Memorandum by the German Group Dated April 17, 1929," Young Papers; Stuart M. Crocker diary, May 7, 1929, Young Papers; memorandum by Thomas N. Perkins, April 26, 1929, ibid.; memorandum by de Sanchez, March 7, 1929, ibid.; "Memorandum by the Chairman to the Belgian, French, German, British, Italian and Japanese Groups," May 6, 1929, ibid.; Schacht to Young, May 14, 1929, ibid.; *FRUS 1929* 2:1034–36; Jacobson, *Locarno Diplomacy*, 251–58; Leffler, *Elusive Quest*, 205–6; Case and Case, *Owen D. Young*, 440–42.

142. Leffingwell to Lamont, April 5, 1929, file 83-2, Lamont Papers.

143. Lamont to Leffingwell, March 21, 1929, file 103-13, Lamont Papers; de Sanchez to Lamont, June 20, 1929, file 180-16, ibid.; unsigned memorandum, "Preliminary Summary (unofficial) of Experts Report," June 7, 1929, file 179-11, ibid.; Jacobson, *Locarno Diplomacy*, 260.

144. Dulles was satisfied that "Article 248 is certainly pushed far enough into the background that it need give us no practical concern" (to Robert Olds, June 27, 1929, Dulles Papers); *see also* Olds to Dulles, June 11, 1929, ibid.; Ralph Smiley, "The Lausanne Conference, 1932: The Diplomacy of the End of Reparations," (Ph.D. dissertation, Rutgers University, 1971), 58.

145. Crocker diary, April 26, 27, 1929, Young Papers; David Friday to Schacht, April 22, 1929, ibid.; Lamont to J. P. Morgan and Co., April 26, 1929, file 178-23, Lamont Papers; Jacobson, *Locarno Diplomacy*, 263–65; Link, *Die amerikanische Stabilisierungspolitik*, 452–69.

146. Jacobson, *Locarno Diplomacy*, 258–62; Mueller, *Die Zentralbank*, 80–92.

147. Unsigned memorandum, "Preliminary Summary (unofficial) of the Experts Report," June 7, 1929, file 179-11, Lamont Papers.

148. *FRUS 1929*, 2:1036.

149. Henry L. Stimson diary, August 28, 1930, vol. 10, Henry L. Stimson Papers, Sterling Library, Yale University; Kellogg to Hoover, March 6, 1929, 462.00R296/2768, NARG 59.

150. Ogden Mills to Mellon, April 6, 1929, file G 733, NARG 39, Stimson to Owen Young, April 8, 1929, 462.00R296/2773, NARG 59. *See also* Stimson to Young, April 15, 1929, 462.00R296/2787, ibid.

151. Owen Young to Mellon, April 12, 1929, Young Papers; *see also* Young to Stimson, April 11, 1929, 462.00R296/2778, NARG 59; Case and Case, *Owen D. Young*, 444–49. Ironically, the administration criticized Young for undermining the war debt agreements while he himself believed that despite his personal desire to see the debts eliminated, he was laying a more secure basis for their payment. A few months after the conference, Young confided to Everett N. Case, his private assistant, that he "had the feeling at Paris that the Allies really did not want the [war] debts to be cancelled." Rather, those nations preferred to burden Germany by making it pay the debts plus an additional sum. At Paris, Young "concluded" that if the Allies "wanted a reparations settlement based on the principle that these [war] debts were gong to be paid, I might as well let matters proceed along these lines and clinch payments to America, even though the solution did not coincide with my own views" (Everett N. Case memorandum of conversation with Young, October 10, 1929, Young Papers).

152. Undated, unsigned memorandum in file 179-27, Lamont Papers; Lamont to J. P. Morgan, October 10, 1929, file 108-14, ibid.; Lamont to Elihu Root, April 20, 1929, file 179-27, ibid.

153. Stimson to Armour, June 5, 1929, 462.00R296/2950a, NARG 59 (italics added); *FRUS 1929* 2:1070–72; Stimson to Owen Young, May 2, 1929; Mellon to Young, April 16, 1929, both in Young Papers.

154. Stimson to Hoover, June 8, 1929, 462.00R296/2941½, NARG 59; Morgan to Lamont, July 13, 1929, file 180-23, Lamont Papers. *See also* Joseph Cotton to George Harrison, December 18, 1929, George L. Harrison Papers, copy in FRBNY Archives; Costigliola, "First World Bank," 613–18; Owen Young to Ogden Mills, August 14, 1929, Ogden Mills Papers, Library of Congress. The establishment of the BIS demonstrated the effective working agreement between financial and administration leaders. George Harrison, FRBNY governor, emphasized to Joseph Cotton, under secretary of state, the importance "of having somebody from this bank" at the organizing committee to assist "with technical matters if necessary and also . . . to protect ourselves against any hurtful developments." The Hoover administration had forbidden any formal participation in the BIS by FRS officials. Yet, Cotton indicated to Harrison, "we could avoid this difficulty if we should send some inconspicuous man who just might happen to be . . . wherever the conference meets and just be available if necessary" (Harrison memorandum of conversation with Cotton, September 6, 1929, George L. Harrison Papers, copy in FRBNY Archives). Harrison dispatched Burgess, who had helped draft the BIS plan at the Young conference and who was federal reserve agent at the FRBNY. For the separate agreement with Germany, see Ogden Mills, "America's Separate Agreement with Germany," *Proceeding of the Academy of Political Science*, 14 (January 1931):264–70.

155. Snowden to Lamont, August 23, 1929, file 180-33, Lamont Papers.

156. Lamont to J. P. Morgan and Co., July 11, 1929, file 180-22, ibid.; Costigliola, "First World Bank," 615–18; memorandum by Arthur Salter of conversation with prime minister, September 4, 1929, T172/1656, PRO. With Hoover's approval, Gates McGarrah resigned as chairman of the board of the FRBNY and became the first president of the BIS. Leon Fraser, a former Gilbert assistant, became vice-president and Pierre Quesnay left the Bank of France to become general manager. This shut the British and Germans out of the top management. See Costigliola, "First World Bank," 618–19; Leffler, *Elusive Quest*, 215–16.

157. De Sanchez to Lamont, November 28, 1929, file 181-5, Lamont Papers.

158. Lamont to Charles Dawes, July 30, 1929, file 180-26, ibid.

159. Frederick Leith-Ross to James Grigg, August 26, 1929, T172/1694, PRO; Niemeyer to Grigg, August 19, 1929, T176/13 Niemeyer Papers, PRO; Gilbert to Stimson, December 13, 1929, 462.00R296/3478, NARG 59.

160. Jacobson, *Locarno Diplomacy*, 279–349. Gilbert reported Schacht's comment in Karl von Schubert, February 15, 1930, frame E11543, reel T120/2249, Captured German Documents, NA.

161. Leffler, *Elusive Quest*, 215–16.

162. Stimson memorandum of conversation with British Ambassador, August 29, 1929, 462.00R296/3255, NARG 59.

163. Paraphrased in Lamont to J. P. Morgan and Co., July 30, 1929, file 180-226, Lamont Papers.

164. *Literary Digest* 101 (June 15, 1929):5–7.

165. Stimson to Schurman, October 14, 1929, 862.51/2802; State Department

memorandum, March 10, 1930, 462.00R296 Bank for International Settlements/ 64; Cotton to McFadden, March 13, 1930; McFadden to Cotton, March 27, 1930, 462.00R296 Bank for International Settlements/73; Cotton to McFadden, March 31, 1930, 462.00R296 Bank for International Settlements/74, all in NARG 59; Leffingwell to Lamont, March 21, 1930, file 181-8, Lamont Papers.

166. Quoted in Zammito, "The Berlin Avant-Garde," 816.

8. *Depression and Disintegration, 1930–1933*

1. Quoted in Lloyd, *Aggressive Introvert,*" 163. *See also* ibid., 178.

2. For the historians' debate, *see* Kindleberger, *The World in Depression,* especially 291–308; Friedman and Schwartz, *The Great Contraction*; Temin, *Did Monetary Forces Cause the Great Depression?*; Don Roper, review of above, in *Journal of Monetary Economics* 4 (1978):143–47; Heywood Fleisig, *Long-Term Capital Flows and the Great Depression: The Role of the United States, 1927–1933* (New York, 1975), especially 164–170. For the statistics, see U.S. Bureau of Census, *Historical Statistics,* 73, 139; Kindleberger, *The World in Depression,* 172; Joseph S. Davis, *The World between the Wars, 1919-39* (Baltimore, 1975), 189–301; Heywood Fleisig, "The United States and the World Periphery during the Early Years of the Great Depression" (manuscript), 32. These were current prices.

3. Putnam, *Paris Was Our Mistress,* 238–54; Cowley, *Exile's Return,* 284–86; Ford, ed., *Left Bank Revisited,* 303–8.

4. Strauss, *Menace in the West,* 229–45.

5. Tolzmann, "Objective Architecture;" 207, 220–222, 255–56; Laquer, *Weimar,* 254–69; Zammito, "The Berlin Avant-Garde," 868–973.

6. Quoted in Zammito, "The Berlin Avant-Garde," 815.

7. For overviews see David Schoenbaum, *Hitler's Social Revolution* (New York, 1967); Arthur Schweitzer, *Big Business in the Third Reich* (Bloomington, 1964); Robert R. Taylor, *The Word in Stone: The Role of Architecture in the National Socialist Ideology* (Berkeley, 1974).

8. Robert C. Williams, *Russian Art and American Money, 1900–1940* (Cambridge, 1980), 12, 27, 30, 99–100, 163–69.

9. Fish quoted in Fithian, "Soviet-American Economic Relations," 208. *See also* ibid., 203–13; Singer, "The United States Confronts the Soviet Union," 69–76; Wilson, *Ideology and Economics,* 104–6; Robert Paul Browder, *The Origins of Soviet-American Relations* (Princeton, 1953), 33–38.

10. Fithian, "Soviet-American Economic Relations," 203–10; Williams, *Rusisan Art and American Money,* 169.

11. Quoted in Charles C. Bright, "Britain's Search for Security, 1930–36: The Diplomacy of Naval Disarmament and Imperial Defense" (Ph.D. dissertation, Yale University, 1970), 58 (italics in original).

12. Stimson diary, March 30, 1931, Stimson Papers. In a 1924 letter to editor William Allen White, Hoover was more temperate and precise: "I supported the Treaty, although I did not like it.... It was not possible to remedy every ill in the world at one go.... No international agreement is immutable" (quoted in Royal J. Schmidt, "Hoover's Reflections on the Versailes Treaty," in Lawrence E. Gelfand, ed., *Herbert Hoover: The Great War and Its Aftermath, 1914–23* [Iowa City, 1979], 81).

13. Elting E. Morison, *Turmoil and Tradition* (New York, 1966), 249–50; Robert H. Ferrell, *American Diplomacy in the Great Depression* (New York, 1957), 246–47.

14. Quoted in Martin Egan to Thomas Lamont, October 23, 1929, file 98–16, Lamont Papers. Hoover's dislike of public appearances deepened with the Depression. *See* for example the Stimson diary, July 18, 1932, Stimson Papes.

15. Wilson, *Hoover*, 63–72, 122–67; Lloyd, *Aggressive Introvert*, 123–75; Jordan A. Schwarz, "Hoover and Congress: Politics, Personality, and Perspective in the Presidency," in Martin Fausold and George T. Mazuzan, eds., *The Hoover Presidency* (Albany, 1974), 87–100; Ellis W. Hawley, "Herbert Hoover and American Corporatism, 1929–1933," ibid., 102–19; J. Joseph Huthmacher and Warren I. Susman, eds., *Herbert Hoover and the Crisis of American Capitalism* (Cambridge, Mass., 1973); Mark Hatfield, *Herbert Hoover Reassessed* (Washington, 1981), 123–309.

16. Walter Lippmann, "The Peculiar Weakness of Mr. Hoover," *Harper's Magazine* 161 (June 1930):1–7.

17. Stimson diary, July 12, 1932, Stimson Papers.

18. For the controversy, see Wilson, *Hoover*; Leffler, *Elusive Quest*.

19. *New York Times*, October 16, 1928, 18.

20. Brandes, *Herbert Hoover*; Burner, *Hoover*, 183–85.

21. Minute by Geoffrey Thompson, November 13, 1928 on Horace Rumbold (Berlin) to Lord Cushendun, November 9, 1928, A7756/39/45, F.O.371/12812, PRO. The French remark quoted in Strauss, *Menace in the West*, 99. *See also* minute by R. L. Craigie, November 13, 1928, ibid.; Robert Wilburforce to A. Willert, November 23, 1928, A8331/39/45, F.O.371/12812; memo by Esme Howard of conversation with French ambassador to Washington, Paul Claudel, transmitted to Cushendun, November 20, 1928, A8272/39/45, ibid.; memorandum by R. L. Craigie, November 26, 1928, A8078/39/45, ibid.; memorandum by Geoffrey Thompson of conversation with Walter Edge, August 13, 1928, A5631/39/45, ibid.

22. Myers, *Public Writings of Herbert Hoover* 1:377.

23. Ibid., 377, 574–76, 583, 430.

24. Ibid., 2:544. For the London Conference preparations, *see* James Ray Moore, "A History of the World Economic Conference, London, 1933" (Ph.D. dissertation, SUNY at Stony Brook, 1972), especially 1–100.

25. On Stimson's background, *see* Morison, *Turmoil and Tradition*, 3–245. For the the quotations, Stimson diary, May 24, 1932, September 10, 1931, June 18, 1931, June 8, 1931, Stimson Papers; for the working relationship, see ibid., July 11, 1932, December 17, 1932, January 23, 1933, January 24, 1933; for Stimson's opinion of Hoover's leadership, see ibid., October 6, 1930, December 4, 1930, June 18, 1931, November 11, 1932.

26. Stimson diary, May 25, 1931, June 5, 1931, June 13, 1931, Stimson Papers; memorandum of transatlantic telephone conversation between Stimson and Ramsay MacDonald, May 24, 1932, 550.S 1/17, NARG 59.

27. Stimson diary, July 12, 1931; *see also* May 1, 1932, Stimson Papers.

28. Quoted in Morison, *Turmoil and Tradition*, 262.

29. Bridgeman quoted in Newton, "Anglo-American Relations," 175. MacDonald quoted in Morison, *Turmoil and Tradition*, 263. *See also* Newton, 183–90, 209–14. For MacDonald's memorandum of conversations with Hoover,

see Documents on British Foreign Policy, 1919–39 (London, 1946), 2d ser., 1:106–16. *See also* David Marquand, *Ramsay MacDonald* (London, 1977), 508.

30. Quoted in O'Connor, *Perilous Equilibrium*, 24. *See also* ibid., 20–30.

31. Quoted in Newton, "Anglo-American Relations," 205.

32. Hugh Wilson, *Diplomat Between Wars* (New York, 1941), 236–38. *See also* Stimson diary, February 17, 1930, Stimson Papers; Ferrell, *American Diplomacy*, 87–88; O'Connor, *Perilous Equilibrium*, 62–64.

33. O'Connor, *Perilous Equilibrium*, 73–74. *See also* Newton, "Anglo-Americn Relations," 217; Roskill, *Hankey*, 2:508–20.

34. O'Connor, *Perilous Equilibrium*, 76–83. *See also* Wheeler, *Pearl Harbor*, 159–86. O'Connor suggests that Hoover agreed to the increase in Japanese naval power because he valued Tokyo's role in containing Moscow.

35. Stimson diary, March 4, 1930, Stimson Papers; O'Connor, *Perilous Equilibrium*, 89–104; Ferrell, *American Diplomacy*, 94–100; Wilson, *Diplomat Between Wars*, 240–41; Guinsburg, "Senatorial Isolationism," 128–30; John Spyros Salapatas, "America's Response to Collective Security, 1929–36" (Ph.D. dissertation, University of Wisconsin, 1973), 34–53; Leffler, *Elusive Quest*, 222–28; Nicolson, *Morrow*, 355–71. In 1929, worried about the destabilizing impact of Anglo-American naval rivalry, the Council on Foreign Relations commissioned a study. Distributed in the usual way to top business and political leaders, the CFR study recommended parity and cooperation with Britain. The fate of this report demonstrated the growing challenge to elites in the direction of foreign policy. Henrik Shipstead, senator from Minnesota, obtained a copy and inserted it into the Congressional Record as evidence of conspiracy for an Anglo-American alliance (Guinsburg, *Pursuit of Isolationsim*, 138).

36. Quoted in Stimson diary, March 3, 4, 1930, Stimson Papers. *See also* ibid., February 22, 1930, February 28, 1930, March 6, 1930.

37. O'Connor, *Perilous Equilibrium*, 110–11; Ferrell, *American Diplomacy*, 103.

38. Quoted in O'Connor, *Perilous Equilibrium*, 109.

39. Quoted in Wheeler, *Prelude to Pearl Harbor*, 180.

40. Quoted in Wheeler, *Prelude to Pearl Harbor*, 181–82. For the vote, O'Connor, *Perilous Equilibrium*, 117.

41. For the quotation, Joseph Davis, quoted in Richard N. Kottman, "Herbert Hoover and the Smoot-Hawley Tariff: Canada, A Case Study," *Journal of American History* 62 (December 1975):632. *See also* ibid., 609–35. For the controversy in Congress, see Hoover, *Memoirs* 2:291–99; Edgar Eugene Robinson and Vaughn Davis Bornet, *Herbert Hoover: President of the United States* (Stanford, 1975), 110–22; Hicks, *Republican Ascendancy*, 219–23; Taussig, *Tariff History*, 489–526; Jordan A. Schwarz, *The Interregnum of Despair* (Urbana, 1970), 49; Sidney Ratner, *The Tariff in American History* (New York, 1972), 50–54; McKenna, *Borah*, 261–65; Davis, *The World Between the Wars*, 238–41. For the foreign reaction, see Leffler, *Elusive Quest*, 198–99; André Siegfried, "European Reactions to American Tariff Proposals," *Foreign Affairs* (October 1929):13–19; Jefferson Davis Futch, "The United States and the Fall of the Weimar Republic: German-American Relations, 1930–33" (Ph.D. dissertation, Johns Hopkins University, 1962), 49.

42. For the statistics, see U.S. Commerce Department, *Survey of Current Business, Annual Supplement: 1931* (Washington, 1931), 3, 217, 223; League

of Nations, *Statistical Yearbook of the League of Nations 1932/33* (Geneva, 1933), 143–56, 266–68.

43. Memorandum on reparation bonds by Ray Hall, May 13, 1930, 462.00 R296BIS/111, NARG 59; on McFadden's influence, Lamont to Carl Melchior, May 7, 1930, file 181-16, Lamont Papers; copy of House Resolution 364, June 12, 1930, in file 181-10, Lamont Papers; Joseph Cotton to McFadden, March 10, 1930, 462.00R296, BIS/64, NARG 59.

44. H. Merle Cochran to William R. Castle, March 12, 1931, 462.00 R296 BIS Special Reports/8, NARG 59. *See also* Hugh Wilson to Castle, February 19, 1931, 462.00 R296 BIS Special Reports/5, ibid. For State Department efforts to bypass Congress while supporting the Young Plan, *see* Stimson to Jacob G. Schurman, October 14, 1929, 862.51/2802, ibid.

45. Stimson diary, July 16, 1931, Stimson Papers.

46. Cochran to Castle, June 22, 1932, 462.00 R296 BIS Special Reports/57; Cochran to Castle, February 14, 1933, 462.00 R296 BIS Special Reports/90, both in NARG 59.

47. Quoted in Edward W. Bennett, *Germany and the Diplomacy of the Financial Crisis, 1931* (Cambridge, Mass., 1962), 10. On Brüning, *see* Wolfgang Helbich, "Between Stresemann and Hitler: The Foreign Policy of the Brüning Government," *World Politics* 12 (October 1959); Link, *Die amerikanische Stabilisierungspolitik*, 489–522.

48. Bernard Vincent Burke, "American Diplomats and Hitler's Rise to Power, 1930–33: The Mission of Ambassador Sackett" (Ph.D. dissertation, University of Washington, 1966), 106; Bennett, *Financial Crisis*, 10.

49. Lewis, *International Investments*, 395. For background *see* William C. McNeil, "American Money and the German Economy: Economics and Politics on the Eve of the Great Depression," (Ph.D. dissertation, University of California, Berkeley, 1981).

50. Sackett to Stimson, January 21, 1931, 862.51/2991, NARG 57.

51. The liquidity trap refers to businessmen's unwillingness to invest idle funds, no matter how low the interest rate, because of bleak economic prospects.

52. For Schacht and his scheme, *see* "The Schacht Plan," transmitted by Mary Waite to Owen Young, October 15, 1930; Young to Schacht, August 15, 1930; Young to Pierre Jay, March 30, 1930; Stuart M. Crocker to Young, October 9, 1930, all in Young Papers; Bennett, *Financial Crisis*, 18–23; Futch, "Fall of the Weimar Republic," 65–67; "The Young Plan in Relation to World Economy," FPA publication of discussion by Schacht and Dulles, October 1930; Case and Case, *Owen D. Young*, 517. For the Kindersley Plan, see Montagu Norman to BIS, February 2, 1931, transmitted by Cochran to Cotton, February 11, 1931, 462.00 R296 BIS Special Reports/4, NARG 59; Norman to George Harrison, March 3, 1931, copy in Young Papers; McGarrah to Lamont and Gilbert, March 18, 1931, ibid.

53. Bennett, *Financial Crisis*, 18, 20–26.

54. *World* quoted in Klaus Schoenthal, "American Attitudes toward Germany, 1918–1932" (Ph.D. dissertation, Ohio State University, 1959), 258; Stimson diary, January 2, 1931, Stimson Papers; Leffingwell to Lamont, November 13, 1930, file 103-15, Lamont Papers; Gordon quoted in Burke, "Sackett," 112–13; Hoover quoted in Stimson diary, January 31, 1933, Stimson Papers.

55. Messersmith in Futch, "Fall of the Weimar Republic," 224; Sackett to Stimson, January 12, 1932, 462.00R296A 1/150, NARG 59; Stimson quoted in

Burke, "Sackett," 253-54. For State Department comparison of fascism and nazism, *see FRUS* 1932 2:276–78. For worry about Bulgarian communism, see Henry W. Shoemaker to secretary of state, March 30, 1933, 874.00/453, NARG 59.

56. Stimson diary, March 30, 1931; March 29, 1931, Stimson Papers. *See also* Stimson memorandum of conversation with Dino Grandi, July 9, 1931, enclosed in John W. Garrett to Department of State, July 16, 1931, 033.1140 Stimson Henry L./138; Futch, "Fall of the Weimar Republic," 77–78; Michael J. Sullivan, "Franco-American Relations in the Financial Crisis of 1931" (M.A. thesis, Drake University, 1975), 39–54; Norman M. Johnson, "The Austro-German Customs Union Project in German Diplomacy" (Ph.D. dissertation, University of North Carolina 1974); E. Dana Durand, "The Future of Central Europe," *Atlantic Monthly* 125 (June 1920):830–42.

57. Stimson diary, June 18, 1931, Stimson Papers; Clarke, *Central Bank Cooperation*, 185–89; Boyle, *Montagu Norman*, 260–61.

58. Stimson diary, June 2, 1931; June 11, 1931, Stimson Papers; Bennett, *Financial Crisis*, 116–31.

59. The first quotation from Stimson diary, June 5, 1931, Stimson Papers; the second quoted in ibid., June 13, 1931. For the economic theory, see Heywood Fleisig, "Recent Issues in International Trade and Finance and Their Implications for the History of the Interwar Period" (unpublished manuscript, 1979), 2, 5–6.

60. Lamont to Hoover, June 5, 1931, file 98-18, Lamont Papers; memorandum of conversation between Lamont and Hoover, June 5, 1931, ibid.; Herbert Feis to Felix Frankfurter, June 26, 1931, Herbert Feis Papers, Library of Congress; Stimson diary, June 6, 12, 1931, Stimson Papers.

61. Stimson diary, June 22, 1931, Stimson Papers; *Literary Digest* 110 (July 4, 1931):5–7; (July 11, 1931):42–43.

62. Quoted in Bennett, *Financial Crisis*, 169.

63. Sullivan, "Franco-Americn Relations," 102–3; Leffler, *Elusive Quest*, 241.

64. Quotation from Stimson's account of conversation with Claudel, Stimson diary, June 21, 1931, Stimson Papers. For the "voluntary" concession negotiations, see Sullivan, "Franco-American Relations," 117–22; Bennett, *Financial Crisis*, 182–203; file 462.00 R296/NARG 59, for June–July 1931.

65. Memorandum of telephone conversation between Hoover and Lamont, 6:00 P.M. June 29, 1931, file 98-18, Lamont papers; memorandum of telephone conversation between Hoover aand Lamont, June 20, 1931, ibid.; Lamont to Martin Egan, July 9, 1931, file 98-19, ibid.

66. Hoover, *Memoirs*, 3:75; *Literary Digest*, 110 (August 1, 1931);6.

67. Stimson diary, September 30, 1931 (italics added), Stimson Papers; ibid., July 29, 1931.

68. July 8, 1931; July 11, 1931, both in ibid. *See also* Stimson memorandum of conversations with Grandi and Mussolini, July 9, 1931, enclosed in John W. Garrett to Department of State, July 16, 1931, 033.1140 Stimson, Henry L./138.

69. For the quotations, Stimson press conference, September 9, 1931, 033.1140, Stimson, H.L./173, NARG 59. *See also* Sullivan, "Franco-Americans Relations, 128–60; Bennett, *Financial Crisis*, 204–85; *FRUS 1931* 1:256; Harrison memoranda of conversation with Norman, July 14, 1931; with Ogden Mills, July 17, 1931; with Norman, July 21, 1931, George L. Harrison Papers.

70. Stimson press conference, September 9, 1931, 033.1140, Stimson, H.L./ 173, NARG 59; August 27, 1931; Stimson memorandum of conversation with Hoover, July 17, 1931, 462.00R296/4575½ NARG 59. Lamont agreed on the importance of Franco-German reconciliation. *See* Lamont to Hoover, July 27, 1931, file 98-19, Lamont Papers.

71. Stimson memorandum of conversation with Brüning, July 25, 1931, 033.1140, Stimson, Henry L./135½. *See also* Stimson memorandum of conversation with Hindenburg, July 27, 1931, 033.1140, Stimson, H.L./142½. For Stimson's opposition to Norman's plans for wholesale revision, Stimson memorandum of converation with MacDonald and Tyrrell, July 17, 1931, 462.00R296/ 4579¾; Stimson memorandum of conversation with Edge, Marriner, Arthur Henderson, Flandin, and MacDonald, July 17, 1931, 462.00R296/4580½; Stimson to MacDonald, August 7, 1931, 500.A15A4/321½, NARG 59.

72. *New York Times*, July 22, 1931, 1, 16; Bennett, *Financial Crisis*, 244–85; Sullivan, "Franco-American Relations," 128–60; Leffler, *Elusive Quest*, 253–56.

73. Bennett, *Financial Crisis*, 286–91.

74. Stimson diary, July 31, 1931, Stimson Papers; Clarke, *Central Bank Cooperation*, 202–13.

75. Castle and Pierre Boal comments on memorandum by J. F. Carter, August 25, 1931, 841.51/943. *See also* Charles Dawes to Stimson, August 24, 1931, 841.51/1156, both in NARG 59.

76. Harrison memorandum of conversation with Norman, August 23, 1931, file 3115.2, George L. Harrison Papers; Leffingwell to Lamont August 29, 1931, file 103-15, Lamont Papers; Robert Skidelsky, *Politicians and the Slump* (London, 1967), 378–80.

77. Marquand, *MacDonald*, 614–37.

78. Stimson memorandum of conversation with British chargé, September 18, 1931, 800.51 W89 Great Britain/227½; Stimson to MacDonald, September 25, 1931, 800.51 W89, Great Britain/276¼; Stimson to Dawes, September 19, 1931, 841.51/971A, all in NARG 59. For evidence of bankers' speculation against the pound, see James Warburg to Paul Warburg, September 21, 1931, Box 3, James Warburg Papers, John F. Kennedy Presidential Library, Boston, Mass.

79. Harrison memorandum of conversation with Ernest Harvey, September 19, 1931, file 3117.1, George L. Harrison Papers.

80. Memorandum by John F. Carter, October 28, 1931, 841.00/1220, NARG 59.

81. The joint committee included, among others, former dominion secretary L. S. Amery, former chancellor of the exchequer Robert Horne, and prominent industrialist Frederick Williams-Taylor.

82. *Report on Empire Monetary and Financial Policy* (London, October 7, 1931). For the quotations, *see* 22, 9; Skidelsky, *Politicians and the Slump*, 369–70.

83. Edward Savage Crocker (Sweden) to Stimson, November 12, 1931, 841.51/ 1048; Carl A. Fisher (Greece) to Stimson, September 26, 1931, 868.51/1177; Cochran to Castle, May 5, 1932, 462.00 R296 BIS Special Reports/49; F. W. B. Coleman (Denmark) to Stimson, May 20, 1932, 841.51/1098; Ray Atherton (London) to Stimson, October 13, 1931, 811.51/3660; Sackett (Germany) to Stimson, September 23, 1931, 862.51/3206, all in NARAG 59; E. A. Goldenweiser to Ogden Mills, November 29, 1932, Box 10, Mills Papers. For the

imperial preference system, *see* Henry Chalmers to Lynn W. Meekins, July 13, 1932, file no. 441, Imperial Economic Conference, Records of the Bureau of Foreign and Domestic Commerce, NARG 151 (hereafter BFDC, NARG 151); "The Development and Present Extent of British Imperial Preference," enclosed in Perry Stevenson to John R. Minter, April 14, 1937, file 040 United Kingdom, ibid.

84. Paul Knabenshue (Palestine) to Stimson, October 3, 1931, 867N.5/7; Atherton to Stimson, October 25, 1931, 841.00 P.R./203, both in NARG 59; "Comments of Trade on Devaluation of Pound Sterling," October 6, 1931, Box 12, Records of the Department of Commerce, NARG 40.

85. Amery speech reported in F. W. B. Coleman to Stimson, May 20, 1932, 841.51/1098. *See also* American Embassy in London to Stimson, January 30, 1933, 800.51 W89 Great Britain/422, both in NARG 59.

86. For the first quotation, Atherton to Stimson, October 2, 1931, 841.00/1190; for the second, Wilbur Keblinger (Sydney) to Stimson, December 23, 1931, 811.51/3697. *See also* Warrington Dawson (Paris) to Stimson, July 11, 1932, 811.51/3747; Dawes to Stimson, October 2, 1931, 841.51/988; Atherton to Stimson, April 5, 1932, 811.51/3715; Atherton to Stimson, October 13, 1931, 811.51/3660; Robert C. Tredwell (Sydney) to Stimson, September 30, 1931, 811.51/3673; Walter Edge (Paris) to Stimson, December 31, 1931, 851.51/1750, all in NARG 50; Castle to Mills, October 29, 1931, Mills Papers.

87. Lamont to Louis Wiley, November 2, 1931, file 104-29, Lamont Papers; Herbert Feis memorandum, September 21, 1931, 841.51/972½; John F. Carter's comment, October 2, 1931, on Atherton to Stimson, October 2, 1931, 841.00/1190; memorandum by John F. Carter, October 28, 1931, 841.00/1220; memorandum by Herbert Feis, October 9, 1931, 033.00/5111 Laval, Pierre/98-4/8, all in NARG 59. For the Ottawa conference quotations, Chalmers to Meekins relating conversation with Pierre Boal, July 13, 1932, file no. 441, Imperial Economic Conference, BFDC, NARG 151; *American Exporter* 3 (December 1932):9.

88. Stimson memorandum, March 17, 1932, 793.94/4854, NARG 59.

89. Board of Governors of the Federal Reserve System, *Banking and Monetary Statistics* (Washington, 1943), 537; Chandler, *Monetary Policy*, 167–74. On the 1932 run on the dollar *see*, for example, Leon Dominian (Germany) to Stimson, October 27, 1931, 811.51/3688; J. G. South (Portugal) to Stimson, April 18, 1982, 811.51/3720; Ferdinand L. Mayer (Luxemburg) to Stimson, April 16, 1932, 811.51/3722; Edge (France) to Stimson, April 11, 1932, 811.51/3713; Feis to Stimson, February 24, 1932, 851.51/1761, all in NARG 59.

90. Stimson diary, September 29, 1931, Stimson Papers. *See also* ibid., September 12, 1931; Leffler, *Elusive Quest*, 260–61.

91. Memorandum by Feis, October 20, 1931, 033.5111 Laval, Pierre/217, NARG 59; Schwarz, *Interregnum of Despair*, 84–85.

92. Stimson diary, October 12, 1931, Stimson Papers.

93. Ibid., September 30, 1931; October 6, 1931; Leffler, *Elusive Quest*, 261–66; See also Costigliola, 'American Foreign Policy," 85–105. On July 24, 1931, Laval told Stimson: "The underlying problem which could solve everything else was the question of the Polish Corridor. If that could be solved France would have no other real trouble with Germany" (*FRUS 1931* 1:549).

94. Jay Pierrepont Moffat memorandum of conversation between Stimson and Morrow, October 2, 1931, 033.5111 Laval, Pierre/257. *See also* Moffat

memorandum, October 5, 1931, 033.5111 Laval, Pierre/98 1/8, both in NARG 59.

95. Lamont to Leffingwell and Gilbert, March 23, 1931, file 181-20, Lamont Papers. For Kelley, *see* Pease, "Stabilizaiton of Europe," 374.

96. Quoted in Burke, "Sackett," 101.

97. Walter Lippmann to Stimson, November 21, 1931, 760c.6215/565; Paul Warburg to Stimson, October 6, 1931, 760c.6215/546; Stimson to Paul Warburg, October 8, 1931, ibid., all in NARG 59; Stimson diary, October 12, 1931, Stimson Papers; Pease, "Stabilization of Europe," 316–35.

98. Stimson memorandum of conversation with Polish chargé, September 17, 1931, 760c.6215/544. *See also* Stimson's memorandum of conversation with Polish ambassador, May 7, 1931, 763.72119/12463; Stimson memorandum of conversation with Polish ambassador, June 9, 1931, 760c.6215/534, all in NARG 59.

99. Memorandum of conversation between Dr. Curtius and Norman Davis, September 14, 1931, transmitted by Lawrence Richey (Hoover's secretary) to Stimson, October 8, 1931, 462.00R296/5189, ibid.

100. Costigliola, "American Foreign Policy," 98–100; Leffler, *Elusive Quest,* 266.

101. Stimson diary, October 21, 1931, Stimson Papers; Castle memorandum of conversation with Polish ambassador, October 22, 1931, 760c.6215/550, NARG 59.

102. Stimson diary, October 23, 1931, Stimson papers. The day after this conversation Walter Lippmann asserted publicly, "American opinion is substantially convinced . . . that the Corridor is the insuperable obstacle to a European understanding." He noted that Switzerland and other nations thrived without access to the sea and urged that France invoke Article 19 of the Covenant to revise Versailles. Allan Nevins, ed., *Interpretations 1931–1932 by Walter Lippmann* (New York, 1932), 226–28. Stimson again brought up the corridor in conversation with Laval on October 25. *See* Stimson diary of that date, Stimson Papers.

103. Stimson diary, October 23, 1931, Stimson Papers; memorandum by James Warburg, November 11, 1931, Box 3, Warburg Papers. For a somewhat different interpretation, see Leffler, *Elusive Quest,* 265–72.

104. For the interview, *New York Times,* October 24, 1931, sec. 1, 11. For the reaction, *Literary Digest* 111 (November 7, 1931):7; *New York Times,* October 25, 1931, 31, 24; October 26, 1931, 14; December 8, 1931, 6; Stimson diary, October 24, 1931, Stimson Papers; G. B. Stockton to Stimson, November 18, 1931, 763.72119/12494, NARG 59.

105. Stimson diary, November 13, 1931, Stimson Papers.

106. For Hoover comment, October 5, 1931, ibid. For Grandi's, Castle memorandum of conversation with Signor Grandi, November 17, 1931, 033.6511 Grandi, Dino/99. *See also* Castle and Stimson to American Embassy in Rome, November 27, 1931, 033.6511 Grandi, Dino/107; Stimson diary, November 18–21, 1931, Stimson Papers.

107. Schwarz, *Interregnum of Despair;* Robinson and Bornet, *Hoover,* especially 150–227.

108. The first quotation from BBW (no further identification available), "An Economically Independent United States," February 11, 1932, copy in Box 54, Felix Frankfurter Papers, Library of Congress. *See also* Herbert Feis to Felix

152. *See* Arnold Offner, *American Appeasement* (Cambridge, 1969). However, many American businessmen did find business with Hitler profitable. *See* Gabriel Kolko, "American Business and Germany, 1930–1941," *Western Political Quarterly* 15 (December 1962).
153. *FRUS 1933* 2:217.

Conclusion

1. James E. Shuman and Davis Rosenau, *The Kondratieff Wave* (New York, 1972).
2. Edwin L. James, "Our World Power and Moral Influence," *The International Digest* 1 (October 1930):21.
3. Quoted in Bennett, *German Rearmament*, 111.
4. Quoted in *The Nation* 127 (October 17, 1928):408.
5. Bertrand Russell, "The New Life That Is America," *New York Times*, May 22, 1927, sec. 4, 1.
6. Ibid.
7. Statement by J. R. Bellerby in Royal Institute of International Affairs, *The International Gold Problem* (London, 1931), 16.
8. Calvin Coolidge speech, November 11, 1928, quoted in *New York Times*, November 12, 1928, 2.
9. Benjamin Strong to Owen D. Young, July 14, 1927, C798, FRBNY Files.
10. *New York Times*, November 12, 1928, 2.
11. William Starr Myers, ed., *The State Papers and Other Public Writings of Herbert Hoover* (2 vols., New York, 1970), 1:131.
12. Paul Cravath speech, February 17, 1922, RM 1, CFR Papers.
13. Carl Snyder to Benjamin Strong, November 16, 1927; Strong to Snyder, November 21, 1927, both in Strong Papers.
14. Carl Snyder to Benjamin Strong, April 19, 1927, ibid. Strong agreed with Snyder's analysis.
15. For the controversy, *see* Milton Friedman and Anna Jacobsen Schwartz, *The Great Contraction* (Princeton, 1966); Peter Temin, *Did Monetary Forces Cause the Great Depression?* (New York 1976); Kindleberger, *The World in Depression*, especially 291–307. For the impact of the lending cutback, see Fleisig, *The Great Depression*.
16. Falkus, "U.S. Economic Policy," 599–623; Sean Glynn and Alan L. Lougheed, "A Comment on United States Economic Policy and the 'Dollar Gap' of the 1920s," *Economic History Review*, ser. 2, 26 (1973):692–94.
17. S. Parker Gilbert speech, January 12, 1926, RM 1, CFR Papers.
18. *See*, for example, Link, *Die amerikanische Stabilisierungspolitik*; Bennett, *German Rearmament*, 49–51, passim.
19. For a provocative discussion, see David Calleo, *The German Problem Reconsidered* (New York, 1980).
20. Reinhold Niebuhr, "Awkward Imperialists," *Atlantic Monthly* 145 (June 1930):670, 672; Niebuhr, "Perils of American Power," *Atlantic Monthly* 149 (January 1932):95.

Bibliography

Manuscript Collections

Ayres, Leonard P. Papers. Library of Congress, Washington D.C.
Baruch, Bernard. Papers. Mudd Library, Princeton University, Princeton, N. J.
Castle, William R., Jr. Papers. Herbert Hoover Library, West Branch, Iowa.
Council on Foreign Relations. Archives. New York, N. Y.
Crocker, Stuart M. Papers. Library of Congress, Washington, D. C.
Dulles, John Foster. Papers. Mudd Library, Princeton University, Princeton, N. J.
Eberstadt, Ferdinand. Papers. Mudd Library, Princeton University, Princeton, N. J.
Feis, Herbert. Papers. Library of Congress, Washington, D. C.
Fletcher, Henry P. Papers. Library of Congress, Washington, D. C.
Goldenweiser, Emmanuel. Papers. Library of Congress, Washington, D. C.
Gumberg, Alexander. Papers. State Historical Society, Madison, Wis.
Hamlin, Charles S. Papers. Library of Congress, Washington, D. C.
Harrison, George L. Papers. Columbia University Library, New York, N. Y.
Harrison, Leland. Papers. Library of Congress, Washington, D. C.
Hoover, Herbert C. Papers. Herbert Hoover Presidential Library, West Branch, Iowa.
Hopkinson, Edwin W. Papers. University of Washington Library, Seattle, Wash.
Hopkinson, Richard. Papers. Public Record Office, London.
Houghton, Alanson B. Papers. Houghton Estate, Corning, N. Y.
Hughes, Charles Evans. Papers. Library of Congress, Washington, D. C.
Jay, Pierre. Papers. Sterling Library, Yale University, New Haven, Conn.
Kemmerer, Edwin W. Papers. Mudd Library, Princeton University, Princeton, N. J.
Kent, Fred I. Papers. Mudd Library, Princeton University, Princeton, N. J.
Krock, Arthur. Papers. Mudd Library, Princeton University, Princeton, N. J.
Lamont, Thomas W. Papers. Baker Library, Harvard University, Cambridge, Mass.
Mills, Ogden L. Papers. Library of Congress, Washington, D. C.

Morrow, Dwight M. Papers. Amherst College Library, Amherst, Mass.
Niemeyer, Otto E. Papers. Public Record Office, London.
Poole, DeWitt C. Papers. State Historical Society, Madison, Wisc.
Schurman, Jacob Gould. Papers. Olin Library, Cornell University, Ithaca, N. Y.
Strong, Anna Louise. Papers. University of Washington Library, Seattle, Wash.
Strong, Benjamin. Papers. Federal Reserve Bank of New York, New York, N. Y.
Stimson, Henry L. Papers. Sterling Library, New Haven, Conn.
Warburg, James R. Papers. John F. Kennedy Presidential Library, Boston, Mass.
Warburg, Paul M. Papers. Sterling Library, Yale University, New Haven, Conn.
Young, Owen D. Papers. Van Horne House, Van Hornesville, N. Y.

Unpublished Government Documents

Bonn, Germany. Politisches Archiv des Auswärtigen Amtes. Wirtschafts—
Reparationen.
Geneva, Switzerland. United Nations Library. League of Nations Archives.
London, England, Public Record Office:
Cabinet Papers
General Records of the Foreign Office (Record Office Group 371)
Records of the Treasury
Washington, D. C. Federal Reserve Board. Files.
National Archives
Record Group 39, Records of the Bureau of Accounts, Department of the Treasury.
Record Group 40, General Records of the Department of Commerce.
Record Group 56, General Records of the Department of the Treasury.
Record Group 59, General Records of the Department of State.
Record Group 151, Records of the Bureau of Foreign and Domestic Commerce, Department of Commerce.

Published Government Documents

Annual Report of the Agent General for Reparations. 6 vols., Berlin, 1925–30.
Great Britain, Foreign Office. *Documents on British Foreign Policy, 1919–1939.* London, 1946——.
U. S. Department of Commerce. *Annual Report of the Secretary of Commerce, 1922–29.* Washington, D. C., 1922–29.
U. S. Department of State. *Papers Relating to the Foreign Relations of the United States, 1919–1933.* Washington, D. C., 1934–49.
U. S. Department of State. *Papers Relating to the Foreign Relations of the United States: The Paris Peace Conference, 1919.* 13 vols. Washington, D. C., 1942–47.
U. S. Department of the Treasury. *Annual Report of the Secretary of the Treasury, 1921–28.* Washington, D. C., 1921–28.

Articles

Abrahams, Paul B. "American Bankers and the Economic Tactics of Peace: 1919." *Journal of American History* 56 (December 1969): 572–83.

Aldridge, John W. "Afterthoughts on the 20's," *Commentary* 56 (November 1973):37–41.

Ambrosius, Lloyd E. "Wilson, the Republicans, and French Security after World War I." *Journal of American History* 49 (September 1972): 341–52.

Andrade, Ernest, "The United States Navy and the Washington Conference." *The Historian* 31 (May 1969):345–63.

Angly, Edward. "Thomas Campbell: Master Farmer," *Forum* 86 (July 1931): 21–22.

Artaud, Denise. "A propos de l'occupation de la Ruhr," *Révue d'histoire moderne et contemporaine* 17 (January–March 1970):1–21.

Basler, Otto. "Amerikanismus. Geschichte des Schlagwortes." *Deutsche Rundschau*, 224 (August 1930):142–46.

Behn, Fritz. "Amerikanismus in Deutschland." *Süddeutsche Monatshefte* 27 (June 1929):672–74.

Best, Gary Dean. "Food Relief as Price Support: Hoover and American Pork, January–March, 1919." *Agricultural History* 45 (April 1971):79–84.

———. "Herbert Hoover's Technical Mission to Yugoslavia, 1919–20." *Annals of Iowa* 42 (Fall 1974):443–59.

Birn, Donald S. "Open Diplomacy at the Washington Conference of 1921–22: The British and French Experience." *Comparative Studies in Society and History* 12(July 1970):297–319.

Borah, William. "The Ghost of Versailles at the Conference." *The Nation* 113 (November 9, 1921):525–26.

Boyden, Roland. W. "The Dawes Report." *Foreign Affairs* 2 (June 1924):583–97.

Brady, Robert A. "The Meaning of Rationalization: An Analysis of the Literature." *Quarterly Journal of Economics* 46 (May 1932):526–40.

Braeman, John. "The New Left and American Foreign Policy during the Age of Normalcy: A Re-examination." *Business History Review* 57 (Spring 1983):73–104.

Burgess, W. Randolph. "The Money Market in 1928." *Review of Economic Statistics* 11 (February 1929):19–25.

Carlton, David. "The Anglo-French Compromise on Arms Limitations, 1928." *Journal of British Studies* 8 (May 1969):141–62.

———. "Great Britain and the Coolidge Naval Disarmament Conference of 1927." *Political Science Quarterly* 83 (December 1968):573–98.

Carroll, John. "America Reacts to the Balfour Plan: The Debate over War Debt Cancellation." *Research Studies* 41 (June 1973):107–17.

———. "Henry Cabot Lodge's Contributions to the Shaping of Republican European Diplomacy, 1920–24." *Capitol Studies* 3 (Fall 1975):153–65.

———. "The Paris Bankers' Conference of 1922 and America's Design for a Peaceful Europe." *International Review of History and Political Science* 10 (August 1973):39–47.

Chamberlain, William Henry. "Missionaries of American Technique in Russia." *Asia* 32 (July–August 1932):422–23.

Chossudovsky, Evgeny. "Genoa Revisited: Russia and Co-existence." *Foreign Affairs* 50 (April 1972):556–65.

Cooper, Hugh. "Observations of Present-Day Russia." *Annals* 138 (July 1928): 117–19.

Costigliola, Frank. "American Foreign Policy in the 'Nutcracker': The United States and Poland in the 1920s." *Pacific Historical Review* 48 (February 1979): 85–105.

———. "Anglo-American Financial Rivalry in the 1920s." *Journal of Economic History* 37 (December 1977):911–34.

———. "The Other Side of Isolationism: The Establishment of the First World Bank, 1929–1930." *Journal of American History* 59 (December 1972):602–20.

———. "The United States and the Reconstruction of Germany in the 1920s." *Business History Review* 50 (Winter 1976):477–502.

Davis, Joseph H. "Herbert Hoover, 1874–1964: Another Appraisal." *South Atlantic Quarterly* 68 (Summer 1969):295–318.

Dayer, Robert Allbert. "The British War Debts to the United States and the Anglo-Japanese Alliance, 1920–23." *Pacific Historical Review* 45 (November 1976):569–95.

DeBenedetti, Charles. "The American Peace Movement and the State Department in the Era of Locarno." In Solomon Wank, ed. *Doves and Diplomats*. Westport, Conn., 1978), 202–16.

DeNovo, John A. "The Movement for an Aggressive American Oil Policy Abroad, 1918–20," *American Historical Review* 71 (1965):854–76.

Dewitt, Howard A. "The 'New' Harding and American Foreign Policy: Warren G. Harding, Hiram W. Johnson, and Pragmatic Diplomacy." *Ohio History* 86 (Spring 1977): 96–114.

Dubay, Robert W. "The Geneva Naval Conference of 1927: A Study of Battleship Diplomacy." *Southern Quarterly* 8 (January 1970):177–99.

Dulles, John Foster. "Our Foreign Loan Policy." *Foreign Affairs* 4 (October 1926):33–48.

Durand, E. Dana. "The Future of Central Europe." *Atlantic Monthly* 125 (June 1920): 830–42.

Falkus, M. E. "United States Economic Policy and the 'Dollar Gap' of the 1920s." *Economic History Review*, 2d ser., 24 (1971):599–623.

Feuer, Lewis S. "American Travelers to the Soviet Union, 1917–1932: The Formation of a Component of New Deal Ideology." *American Quarterly* 14 (Summer 1962):119–49.

Freienfels-Müller, Richard. " 'Amerikanismus' und europäische Kultur." *Der deutsche Gedanke* 4 (1927):30–35.

Freyn. A. J. "An American Engineer Looks at the Five Year Plan." *New Republic* 66 (May 6, 1931):318–19.

Fry, M. G. "The North Altantic Triangle and the Abrogation of the Anglo-Japanese Alliance." *Journal of Modern History* 39 (March 1967):46–64.

Glynn, Sean, and Alan L. Loughheed. "A Comment on United States Economic Policy and the 'Dollar Gap' of the 1920s." *Economic History Review*, 2d ser., 26 (1973):692–94.

Gramsci, Antonio. "Americanism and Fordism." *Selections from the Prison Notebooks* (New York, 1971):279–318.

Hawley, Ellis. "Herbert Hoover, the Commerce Secretariat, and The Vision of an Associative State, 1921–28." *Journal of American History* 61 (June 1974): 116–40.

Helbich, Wolfgang. "American Liberals in the League of Nations Controversy." *Public Opinion Quarterly* 31 (1968):568–96.

———. "Between Stresemann and Hitler: The Foreign Policy of the Brüning Government." *World Politics* 12 (October 1959):24–44.

Hewes, James E., Jr. "Henry Cabot Lodge and the League of Nations." *Proceedings of the American Philosophical Society* 114 (August 1970):245–55.

Hindus, Maurice. "Henry Ford Conquers Russia." *The Outlook* 146 (June 29, 1927):280–83.

Hogan, Michael J. "The United States and the Problem of International Economic Control." *Pacific Historical Review* 44 (February 1975):84–103.

Hopkins, George W. "The Politics of Food: The United States and Soviet Hungary March–August, 1919." *Mid-America* 55 (October 1973):245–70.

Hughes, Charles E. "Deal Only with Upright States." *Nation's Business* 10 (June 5, 1922):10–11.

———. "Pan-American Peace." *Yale Review* 18 (June 1929):646–68.

———. "Recent Questions and Negotiations." *Foreign Affairs* 2 (December 1923):i–xxii.

Jacobson, Jon. "Is There a New International History of the 1920s?" *American Historical Review* 88 (June 1983):617–45.

———. "The Strategies of French Foreign Policy after World War I." *Journal of Modern History* 55 (March 1983):78–95.

James, Edwin L. "Our World Power and Moral Influence." *International Digest* 1 (October 1930):21–24.

Jennings, David H. "President Harding and International Organization." *Ohio History* 75 (Summer 1966):149–65.

Jones, K. Paul. "Discordant Collaboration:Choosing an Agent General for Reparations." *Diplomatic History* 1 (Spring 1977):119–39.

Kellogg, Frank B. "Some Foreign Policies of the United States." *Foreign Affairs* 4 (January 1926):i–xvii.

Kennell, Ruthe. "The New Innocents Abroad." *American Mercury* 17 (May 1929):10–18.

Kennell, Ruthe, and Milly Bennett. "American Immigrants in Russia," *American Mercury* 25 (April 1932):464–68.

Kindleberger, Charles P. "Origins of U. S. Direct Investment in France." *Business History Review* 48 (1974):382–413.

Klein, Ira. "Whitehall, Washington and the Anglo-Japanese Alliance." *Pacific Historical Review* 41 (1972):460–83.

Knappen, Theodore M. "The Apogee of Strange Partnerships—Soviet Socialists and American Capitalists." *Magazine of Wall Street* 43 (January 26, 1929):592.

Kolko, Gabriel. "American Business and Germany, 1930–1941." *Western Political Quarterly* 15 (December 1962):713–28.

Kottman, Richard N. "Herbert Hoover and the Smoot-Hawley Tariff: Canada, a Case Study." *Journal of American History* 62 (December 1975):609–35.

Kowalke, Kim H. "*Der Lindbergh-Flug*:Kurt Weill's Musical Tribute to Lindbergh." *Missouri Historical Society Bulletin* 33 (April 1977):193–96.

Krutch, Joseph Wood. "Berlin Goes American." *The Nation* 126 (May 16, 1928):564–65.

Leffler, Melvyn P. "American Policy Making and European Stability, 1921–1933." *Pacific Historical Review* 46 (May 1977):207–28.

———. "The Origins of Republican War Debt Policy, 1921–23:A Case Study in the Applicability of the Open Door Interpretation." *Journal of American History* 49 (December 1972):585–601.

———. "Political Isolationism, Economic Expansionism, or Diplomatic Realism:American Policy toward Western Europe, 1921–1933. *Perspectives in American History* 8 (1974):413–61.

Link, Werner. "Die Ruhrbesetzung und die wirtschaftlichen Interessen der USA." *Vierteljahrsheft für Zeitgeschichte* 17 (October 1969):372–82.

Lippmann, Walter. "The Peculiar Weakness of Mr. Hoover." *Harper's Magazine* 161 (June 1930).

———. "The Political Equivalent of War." *Atlantic Monthly* 142 (August 1928):181–87.

Loeb, Harold. "Foreign Exchange." *Broom* 2 (May 1922):176–81.

———. "*Broom*:1921–1923." *Broom* 5 (August 1923):55–58.

Lowry, Edward G. "Trade Follows the Film." *Saturday Evening Post* 198 (November 7, 1925):12–13.

Lüddecke, Theodor. "Amerikanismus als Schlagwort und als Tatsache." *Deutsche Rundschau* 221 (March 1930):214–21.

Maier, Charles S. "Between Taylorism and Technocracy:European Ideologies and the Vision of Industrial Productivity in the 1920s." *Journal of Contemporary History* 5 (1970):27–61.

Marks, Sally, and Denis Dulude. "German-American Relations 1918–1921." *Mid-America* 53 (October 1971):211–26.

Mervin, David. "Henry Cabot Lodge and the League of Nations." *Journal of American Studies* 4 (February 1971):210–14.

Merz, Charles. "When the Movies Go Abroad." *Harper's Monthly Magazine* 152 (January 1926):159–65.

Mills, Ogden. "America's Separate Agreement with Germany." *Proceedings of the Academy of Political Science* 14 (January 1931):54–60.

Müller, Heinrich. "Die Amerikanisierung Europas." *Allgemeine Rundschau* 18 (October 1920):510–11.

Niebuhr, Reinhold. "Awkward Imperialists." *Atlantic Monthly* 145 (June 1930):670–75.

———. "Perils of American Power." *Atlantic Monthly* 149 (January 1932):90–96.

Overmans, Jakob. "Amerikanisierung des Geistes." *Stimmen der Zeit* 188 (1929):161–73.

Pruessen, Ronald. "John Foster Dulles and Reparations at the Paris Peace Conference, 1919:Early Patterns of a Life." *Perspectives in American History* 8 (1974):381–410.

Raffo, Peter. "The Anglo-American Preliminary Negotiations for a League of Nations." *Journal of Contemporary History* 9 (1974):153–76.

Ragner, Bernard. "The Permanent A. E. F." *Saturday Evening Post* 212 (November 11, 1939):28–29.

Rhodes, Benjamin D. "Herbert Hoover and the War Debts, 1919–1933." *Prologue* 6 (Summer 1974):130–44.

———. "Reassessing 'Uncle Shylock':The United States and the French War Debt, 1917–1929." *Journal of American History* 55 (March 1969):787–803.

Robinson, Henry M. "Are American Loans Abroad Safe?" *Foreign Affairs* 5 (October 1926):49–56.
———. "Some Lessons from the Economic Conference." *Foreign Affairs* 6 (October 1927):14–22.
Rohrbach, Paul. "Was heisst Amerikanismus?" *Deutsche Monatshefte* 5 (1929), part 2:467–70.
Root, Elihu. "A Requisite for the Success of Popular Diplomacy." *Foreign Affairs* 1 (September 1922):3–10.
Rukeyser, Walter A. "Do Our Engineers in Russia Damage America?" *Scribner's Magazine* 90 (November 1931):521–24.
———. "I Work for Russia." *The Nation* 132 (June 17, 1931):652–53.
Siegfried, André. "European Reactions to American Tariff Proposals." *Foreign Affairs* (October 1929):13–19.
Smith, Robert Freeman. "American Foreign Relations, 1920–42." In Barton J. Bernstein, ed., *Towards a New Past*. New York, 1968, 232–62.
———. "Republican Policy and the Pax Americana, 1921–1932," In William Appleman Williams, ed., *From Colony to Empire*, New York, 1972, 254–92.
Stambrook, F. G. " 'Das Kind'—Lord D'Abernon and the Origins of the Locarno Pact." *Central European History* 1 (1968):233–63.
Stimson, Henry L. "The Pact of Paris, Three Years of Development." *Foreign Affairs* 11 (Special Supplement, 1932):i–ix.
Stone, Ralph A. "The Irreconcilables' Alternative to the League of Nations." *Mid-America* 49 (July 1967):163–73.
Strauss, William Victor. "Foreign Distribution of American Motion Pictures." *Harvard Business Review* 8 (April 1930):307–15.
Wanger, Walter. "120,000 American Ambassadors." *Foreign Affairs* 18 (October 1939):45–59.
Ward, John W. "The Meaning of Lindbergh's Flight." *American Quarterly* 10 (Spring 1953):3–16.
White, Walter. "The Color Line in Europe." *Annals* 140 (November 1928):331–36.
Williams, William A. "The Legend of Isolationism in the 1920s." In William A. Williams, ed., *History as a Way of Learning*. New York 1973, 117–34.
Wilson, Helen C., and Elsie R. Mitchell. "A Light-Running Utopia." *Asia* 28 (December 1928):955–56.
Wimer, Kurt, and Sarah Wimer. "The Harding Administration, the League of Nations and the Separate Peace Treaty." *Review of Politics* 29 (January 1967):13–24.

Books and Dissertations

Abraham, David. *The Collapse of the Weimar Republic*. Princeton, 1981.
Accinelli, Robert Dominic. "The United States and the World Court, 1920–27." Ph.D. dissertation, University of California at Berkeley, 1968.
Adams, Frederick C. *Economic Diplomacy:The Export-Import Bank and American Foreign Policy, 1934–1939* Columbia, M. May 1976.
Adler, Selig. *The Isolationist Impulse*. New York, 1957.
Allen, Frederick Lewis. *Only Yesterday*. New York, 1931.

Amery, L. S. *The Empire in the New Era* London, 1928.
Anderson, Russell Wayne. "The Abandonment of British Naval Supremacy, 1919–20." (Ph.D. dissertation, University of Kentuky, 1974.
Armstrong, Hamilton Fish. *Peace and Counterpeace*. New York, 1971.
Artaud, Denise. *La question des dettes interalliées et la reconstruction de l'Europe, 1917–1929*. Lille, 1978.
Bagby, Wesley M. *The Road to Normalcy*. Baltimore, 1962.
Baker, Ray Stannard. *Woodrow Wilson and World Settlement*. 3 vols. Garden City, N. Y., 1922.
Bane, Suda Lorena, and Ralph Haswell Lutz, eds. *The Blockade of Germany after the Armistice, 1918–1919*. Stanford, 1942.
———. *Organization of American Relief in Europe, 1918–1919*. Stanford, 1943.
Barber, Alvin B. *Report of European Technical Advisers' Mission to Poland, 1919–1922*. New York, 1923.
Beck, Earl R. *Germany Rediscovers America*. Tallahassee, 1968.
Bell, John D. *Peasants in Power*. Princeton, 1977.
Bennett, Edward W. *German Rearmament and the West, 1932–1933*. Princeton, 1979.
———. *Germany and the Diplomacy of the Financial Crisis, 1931*. Cambridge, Mass., 1962.
Bentinck-Smith, William. *Building a Great Library:The Coolidge Years at Harvard*. Cambridge, Mass., 1976.
Berg, Peter. *Deutschland und Amerika, 1918–1929:Über das deutsche Amerikabild der zwanziger Jahre*. Lübeck and Hamburg, 1963.
Bergmann, Carl. *Der Weg der Reparationen*. Frankfurt, 1926.
Bernays, Edward L. *Propaganda*. New York, 1928.
Bernstein, Barton J. ed. *Towards a New Past*. New York, 1968.
Berutti, John Morris. "Italo-American Diplomatic Relations, 1922–28." Ph.D. dissertation, Stanford University, 1960.
Best, Gary Dean, *The Politics of American Individualism: Herbert Hoover in Transition, 1918–1921*. Westport, Conn., 1975.
Bloomfield, Lincoln P. *Evolution or Revolution?* Cambridge, 1957.
Bonn, Moritz J. *Die Kultur der Vereinigten Staaten von America*. Berlin, 1930.
Bove, Charles F., with Dana Lee Thomas. *A Paris Surgeon's Story*. Boston, 1956.
Boyle, Andrew. *Montagu Norman*. London, 1967.
Brace, Alfred M., ed. *Americans in France:A Directory*. Paris, 1929.
Brandes, Joseph. *Herbert Hoover and Economic Diplomacy* (Pittsburgh, 1962.
Braunschvig, Marcel. *La vie américaine*. Paris, 1931.
Bright, Charles C. "Britain's Search for Security, 1930–36:The Diplomacy of Naval Disarmament and Imperial Defense." Ph.D. dissertation, Yale University, 1970.
Browder, Robert Paul. *The Origins of Soviet-American Relations*. Princeton, 1953.
Brown, William Adams, Jr.. *The International Gold Standard Reinterpreted, 1914–1954*. (2 vols. New York, 1940).
Bryn-Jones, David. *Frank B. Kellogg: A Biography*. New York, 1937.
Buckingham, Peter Henry. "Diplomatic and Economic Normalcy: America's Open Door Peace with the Former Central Powers, 1921–29." Ph.D. dissertation, Washington State University, 1980.

Buckley, Thomas H. *The United States and the Washington Conference, 1921–22.* Knoxville, 1970.

Bullitt, William. *It's Not Done.* New York, 1926.

Bunselmeyer, Robert E. *The Cost of the War, 1914–19.* Hamden, Conn., 1975.

Burgees, W. Randolph, ed. *Interpretations of Federal Reserve Policys.* New York, 1930.

Burke, Bernard Vincent. "American Diplomats and Hitler's Rise to Power, 1930–33: The Mission of Ambassador Sackett." Ph.D. dissertation, University of Washington, 1966.

Burner, David. *Herbert Hoover: A Public Life.* New York, 1979.

Burnett, Philip Mason. *Reparations at the Paris Peace Conference.* 2 vols. New York, 1965.

Byrnes, Robert F. *Awakening American Education to the World: The Role of Archibald Cary Coolidge, 1866–1928.* Notre Dame, 1982.

Calleo, David. *The German Problem Reconsidered.* New York, 1980.

Carr, Edward H., and R. W. Davies,. *Foundations of a Planned Economy, 1926–1929.* New York, 1969.

Carroll, John M. "The Making of the Dawes Plan, 1919–1924." Ph.D. dissertation, University of Kentucky, 1972.

Carsten, F. L. *The Reichswehr and Politics, 1918–33.* Oxford, 1966.

Case, Josephine Young, and Everett Needham Case. *Owen D. Young and American Enterprise.* Boston, 1982.

Cassimatis, Louis P. "Greek-American Relations: 1917–29." Ph.D. dissertation, Kent State University, 1978.

Cecil, Robert. *A Great Experiment.* New York, 1941.

Chalk, Frank Robert. "The United States and the International Struggle for Rubber, 1914–41." Ph.D. dissertation, University of Wisconsin, 1970.

Chandler, Lester V. *American Monetary Policy, 1928–41.* New York, 1971.

———. *Benjamin Strong, Central Banker.* Washington, 1958.

Chappius, Charles William. "Anglo-German Relations 1929–33: A Study of the Role of Great Britain in the Achievement of the Aims of German Foreign Policy." Ph.D. dissertation, University of Notre Dame, 1966.

Chavez, Leo Eugene. "Herbert Hoover and Food Relief: An Application of American Ideology." Ph.D. dissertation, University of Michigan, 1976.

Child, Richard Washburn. *A Diplomat Looks at Europe.* New York, 1925.

Clarke, Stephen V. O. *Central Bank Cooperation, 1924–31.* New York, 1967.

Clay, Henry. *Lord Norman.* London, 1957.

Cohen, Stephen F. *Bukharin and the Bolshevik Revolution.* New York, 1973.

Colwell, James L. "The American Experience in Berlin during the Weimar Republic." Ph.D. dissertation, Yale University, 1961.

Conwell, Michael James. "Opinion Makers and Foreign Policy: The Concept of America's Role in World Affairs, the 1920s." Ph.D. dissertation, Michigan State University, 1977.

Coolidge, Harold Jefferson, and Robert Howard Lord. *Archibald Cary Coolidge, Life and Letters.* Boston, 1932.

Cornebise, Alfred E. *The AMAROC News: The Daily Newspaper of the American Force in Germany, 1919–1923.* Carbondale, Ill., 1981.

———. *Typhus and Doughboys: The American Polish Typhus Relief Expedition, 1919–1921.* Newark, Del., 1982.

Costigliola, Frank. "The Politics of Financial Stabilization: American Reconstruction Policy in Europe, 1924–30." Ph.D. dissertation, Cornell University, 1973.

Coston, Glen Howard. "The American Reaction to the Post–First World War Search of France for Security: 1919–1930: A Periodical and Period Piece Study." Ph.D. dissertation, University of Georgia, 1971.

Cowley, Malcolm *Exile's Return*. New York, 1951.

Creel, George. *How We Advertised America*. New York, 1972.

Crosby, Alfred W., Jr. *Epidemic and Peace, 1918*. Westport, Conn., 1976.

Crosby, Caresse. *The Passionate Years*. New York, 1953.

Danelski, David J., and Joseph S. Tulchin, eds. *The Autobiographical Notes of Charles Evans Hughes*. Cambridge, Mass., 1973.

Davis, Clarence B. "The Defensive Diplomacy of British Imperialism in the Far East, 1915–22: Japan and the United States as Partners and Rivals." Ph.D. dissertation, University of Wisconsin, 1972.

Davis, Joseph S. *The World between the Wars, 1919–39*. Baltimore, 1975.

Davis, Kenneth S. *The Hero Charles A. Lindbergh and the American Dream*. Garden City, N.Y., 1959.

Dawes, Charles G. *A Journal of Reparations*. London, 1939.

———. *Notes as Vice-President, 1928–1929*. Boston, 1935.

Dawes, Rufus C. *The Dawes Plan in the Making*. Indianapolis, 1925.

Day, Richard B. *Leon Trotsky and the Politics of Economic Isolation*. Cambridge, 1973.

De Gras, Jane, ed. *Soviet Documents on Foreign Policy*. New York, 1952.

Denny, Ludwell. *America Conquers Britain*. New York, 1930.

DeSanti, Louis A. "U. S. Relations with Italy under Mussolini, 1922–41: A Study Based on the Records of the Department of State and from the Captured Files of Mussolini." Ph.D. dissertation, Columbia University, 1951.

Deutscher, Isaac. *The Prophet Unarmed: Trotsky, 1921–1929*. New York, 1959.

Diggins, John P. *Mussolini and Fascism: The View from America*. Princeton, 1972.

Dike, A. M. *Special Report of the Commissioner of the American Committee for Devastated France*. Paris, 1921.

Dingman, Roger. *Power in the Pacific*. Chicago, 1976.

Dockhorn, Robert Bennett. "The Wilhelmstrasse and the Search for a New Diplomatic Order, 1926–30." Ph.D. dissertation, University of Wisconsin, 1972.

Donaldson, Scott. *By Force of Will: The Life and Art of Ernest Hemingway*. New York, 1977.

Downes, Randolph C. *The Rise of Warren Gamaliel Harding, 1865–1920*. Columbus, 1970.

Dressler, Thomas Herbert. "The Foreign Policies of American Individualism: Herbert Hoover, Reluctant Internationalist." Ph.D. dissertation, Brown University, 1973.

Dubreuil, Henri. *Robots or Men? A French Workman's Experience in American Industry*. New York, 1930.

Dulles, Eleanor Lansing. *The French Franc, 1914–28*. New York, 1929.

Dunning, John H. *American Investment in British Manufacturing*. London, 1958.

English, Howard L. "Great Britain and the Problem of Imperial Defense: The Far East, 1919–23." Ph.D. dissertation, Fordham University, 1971.

Erlich, Alexander. *The Soviet Industrialization Debate, 1924–1928*. Cambridge, Mass., 1960.

Ewen, Stuart. *Captains of Consciousness*. New York, 1976.

Fanning, Michael, ed. *France and Sherwood Anderson: Paris Notebook, 1921*. Baton Rouge, 1976.

Feis, Herbert. *The Diplomacy of the Dollar, 1919–32*. New York, 1950.

———. *1933 Characters in Crisis*. Boston, 1966.

Ferrell, Robert H. *American Diplomacy in the Great Depression*. New York, 1957.

———. *Peace in Their Time*. New York, 1969.

Filene, Peter G. ed. *American Views of Soviet Russia*. Homewood, Ill., 1968.

First General Conference of the International General Electric Compaany and Associated Companies. Briarcliff Manor, N.Y., N.Y. 1920.

Fisher, Harold H. *America and the New Poland*. New York, 1928.

———. *The Famine in Soviet Russia, 1919–23: The Operations of the American Relief Administration*. New York, 1927.

Fithian, Floyd James. "Soviet-American Economic Relations, 1918–1933." Ph.D. dissertation, University of Nebraska, 1964.

Fleisig, Heywood. *Long-Term Capital Flows and the Great Depression: The Role of the United States, 1927–1933*. New York, 1975.

Ford, Henry, and Samuel Crowther. *My Life and Work*. Garden City, N. Y., 1923.

Ford, Hugh, ed. *The Left Bank Revisited: Selections from the Paris Tribune, 1917–1934*. University Park, Pa. 1972.

Francese, Carl James. "United States Policy toward Italy on Arms Limitation and War Debts, 1929–33." Ph.D. dissertation, University of Houston, 1982.

Frasure, Carl M. *British Policy on War Debts and Reparation*. Philadelphia, 1940.

Frederick, Richard George. "Old Visions and New Dreams: The Old Progressives in the 1920s." Ph.D. dissertation, Pennsylvania State University, 1979.

Freidel, Frank. *Over There*. Boston, 1964.

Friedman, Milton, and Anna Jacobson Schwartz. *The Great Contraction*. Princeton, 1966.

Fussell, Paul. *The Great War and Modern Memory*. New York, 1975.

Futch, Jefferson Davis. "The United States and the Fall of the Weimar Republic: German-American Relations, 1930–33." Ph.D. dissertation, Johns Hopkins University, 1962.

Garraty, John A. *Henry Cabot Lodge*. New York, 1953.

Gatzke, Hans. *Stresemann and the Rearmament of Germany*. Baltimore, 1954.

Gay, Peter. *Weimar Culture*. New York, 1968.

Gelfand, Lawrence E., ed. *Herbert Hoover: The Great War and Its Aftermath*. Iowa City, 1979.

Gescher, Dieter Bruno. *Die Vereinigten Staaten von Nordamerika und die Reparationen, 1920–1924*. Bonn, 1956.

Gilbert, Martin. *Winston S. Churchill*. Boston, 1977.

Girard, Jolyon Pitt. "Bridge on the Rhine: American Diplomacy and the Rhineland, 1919–23." Ph.D. dissertation, University of Maryland, 1973.

Glad, Betty. *Charles Evans Hughes and the Illusions of Innocence*. Urbana, 1966.

Golder, Frank A. and Lincoln Hutchinson. *On the Trail of the Russian Famine*. Stanford, 1927.

Grew, Joseph C. *Turbulent Era: A Diplomatic Record of Forty Years, 1904–45*, ed. Walter Johnson. 2 vols. Boston, 1952.

Grigg, P. J. *Prejudice and Judgement*. London, 1948.

Guénon, René, *Orient et Occident*. Paris, 1924.

Guinsburg, Thomas N. *The Pursuit of Isolationism in the United States Senate: From Versailles to Pearl Harbor*. New York, 1982.

Gulick, Charles A. *Austria from Habsburg to Hitler*. Berkeley, 1948.

Halfeld, Adolf. *Amerika and der Amerikanismus. Kritische Betrachtungen eines Deutschen und Europäers*. Jena, 1927.

Harley, John Eugene. *World-Wide Influences of the Cinema*. Los Angeles, 1940.

Harriman, W. Averell. *America and Russia in a Changing World*. Garden City, N. Y., 1971.

Hatfield, Mark O., ed. *Herbert Hoover Reassessed*. Washington, 1981.

Hawley, Ellis W. *The Great War and the Search for a Modern Order*. New York, 1979.

———. ed. *Herbert Hoover as Secretary of Commerce: Studies in New Era Thought and Practice*. Iowa City, 1981.

Heaton, Herbert. *A Scholar in Action: Edwin F. Gay*. Cambridge, Mass., 1952.

Hemingway, Ernest. *The Sun Also Rises*. New York, 1926.

Herriot, Edouard. *The United States of Europe*. New York, 1930.

Hicks, John D. *Republican Ascendancy, 1921–33*. New York, 1960.

Hilderbrand, Robert Clinton. "Power and the People: Executive Management of Public Opinion in Foreign Affairs, 1869–1921." Ph.D. dissertation, University of Iowa, 1977.

Hindsley, Leo Winston. "In Search of an Ally: French Attitudes toward America." Ph.D. dissertation, Michigan State University, 1980.

Hoag, Charles Leonard. *Preface to Preparedness: The Washington Disarmament Conference and Public Opinion*. Washington, 1941.

Hoffman, Frederick J., Charles Allen, and Carolyn F. Ulrich. *The Little Magazines*. Princeton, 1946.

Hogan, Michael J. *Informal Entente: The Private Structure of Cooperation in Anglo-American Economic Diplomacy, 1918–1928*. Columbia, Mo., 1977.

Holtfrerich, Carl-Ludwig. *Die deutsche Inflation, 1914–1923*. Berlin, 1980.

Hoover, Herbert. *An American Epic*. 3 vols. Chicago, 1961.

———. *The Memoirs of Herbert Hoover*. 3 vols. New York, 1951–52.

———. *The Ordeal of Woodrow Wilson*. New York, 1958.

House, Edward M., and Charles Seymour, eds. *What Really Happened at Paris*. (New York, 1921).

Howson, Susan. *Domestic Monetary Management in Britain, 1919–38*. (London, 1975).

Hughes, Charles E. *The Pathway of Peace*. New York, 1925.

Huthmacher, J. Joseph, and Warren I. Susman, eds. *Herbert Hoover and the Crisis of American Capitalism*. Cambridge, Mass., 1973.

Jacobson, Jon. *Locarno Diplomacy: Germany and the West, 1925–1929* (Princeton, 1972).

Jessup, Philip C. *Elihu Root* 2 vols. New York, 1938.

Johnson, Norman M. "The Austro-German Customs Union Project in German Diplomacy." Ph.D. dissertation, University of North Carolina, 1974.

Jones, Kenneth Paul. "Stresemann and the Diplomacy of the Ruhr Crisis, 1923–24." Ph.D. dissertation, University of Wisconsin, 1970.

Jones, K. Paul, ed. *U. S. Diplomats in Europe, 1919–1941*. (Santa Barbara, 1981).

Jordan, Laylon Wayne, "America's Mussolini: The United States and Italy, 1919–36." Ph.D. dissertation, University of Virginia, 1972.

Josephson, Harold. *James T. Shotwell and the Rise of Internationalism in America.* Rutherford, N. J., 1975.

Kaplan, Jay L. "France's Road to Genoa: Strategic, Economic and Ideological Factors in French Foreign Policy, 1921–22." Ph.D. dissertation, Columbia University, 1974.

Kaufman, Burton I. *Efficiency and Expansion: Foreign Trade Organization in the Wilson Administration, 1913–1921.* Westport, Conn., 1974.

Kellogg, Paul U. *Ten Years of the Foreign Policy Association.* (New York, 1929).

Kemmerer, Edwin W., and Gerard Vissering. *Report on the Resumption of Gold Payments by the Union of South Africa.* (Pretoria, 1925).

Keynes, John Maynard. *The Economic Consequences of the Peace.* New York, 1919.

———. *A Tract on Monetary Reform.* London, 1971.

Kimmich, Christoph M. *Germany and the League of Nations.* Chicago, 1976.

Kindleberger, Charles P. *The World in Depression, 1929–1939.* Berkeley, 1973.

Klein, Julius. *Frontiers of Trade.* New York, 1929.

Kneeshaw, Stephen John. "The Kellogg-Briand Pact: The American Reaction." Ph.D. dissertation, University of Colorado, 1971.

Knock, Thomas J. "Woodrow Wilson and the Origins of the League of Nations." Ph.D. dissertation, Princeton University, 1982.

Kontos, Joan Fultz. *Red Cross, Black Eagle: A Biography of Albania's American School.* New York, 1981.

Krakauer, Siegfried. *From Caligari to Hitler.* Princeton, 1947.

Kuczynski, Robert R. *Bankers' Profit from German Loans.* Washington, 1932.

Kuehl, Warren F. *Seeking World Order.* Nashville, 1969.

Kvam, Wayne E. *Hemingway in Germany.* Athens, Ohio, 1973.

LaForge, William F. "The Financial Reconstruction of Austria by the League of Nations." Ph.D. dissertation, University of North Carolina, 1954.

Laqueur, Walter. *Weimar: A Cultural History.* New York, 1974.

League of Nations. *The Reconstruction of Austria, General Survey and Principal Documents.* Geneva, 1926.

———. *Statistical Yearbook of the League of Nations, 1932–33.* Geneva, 1933.

Leffler, Melvyn P. *The Elusive Quest: America's Pursuit of European Stability and French Security.* Chapel Hill, 1979.

Leith-Ross, Frederick. *Money Talks.* London, 1968.

Levin, N. Gordon. *Woodrow Wilson and World Politics.* New York, 1968.

Levy, Alan Howard. "The Unintegrated Personality: American Music and the Muses of Europe, 1865–1930." Ph.D. dissertation, University of Wisconsin at Madison, 1979.

Lewis, Cleona. *America's Stake in International Investments.* Washington, 1938.

Lewis, David. *The Public Image of Henry Ford.* Detroit, 1976.

Libbey, James K. *Alexander Gumberg and Soviet-American Relations, 1917–33.* Lexington, Ky., 1977.

Link, Arthur S. *Wilson the Diplomatist.* Baltimore, 1957.

Link, Werner. *Die amerikanische Stabilisierungspolitik in Deutschland, 1921–32.* Düsseldorf, 1970.

Lippmann, Walter. *The Phantom Public.* New York, 1925.

———. *Public Opinion.* New York, 1965.

Littlepage, John D. *In Search of Soviet Gold.* New York, 1927.

Lloyd, Craig. *Aggressive Introvert: A Study of Herbert Hoover and Public Relations Management, 1912–32.* Columbus, 1972.

Loeb, Harold. *The Way It Was.* New York, 1959.

Louis, William Roger. *British Strategy in the Far East, 1919–1939.* Oxford, 1971.

Lowerre, Nan K. "Warren G. Harding and American Foreign Affairs, 1915–23." Ph.D. dissertation, Stanford University, 1968.

Macmillan, Harold. *Winds of Change.* London, 1966.

Maddox, Robert James, *William Borah and America Foreign Policy.* Baton Rouge, 1969.

Maier, Charles S. *Recasting Bourgeois Europe.* Princeton, 1975.

Major, Mark Imre. "American-Hungarian Relations: 1918–1944." Ph.D. dissertation, Texas Christian University, 1972.

Malament, Barbara Carol. "British Politics and the Crisis of 1931." Ph.D. dissertation, Yale University, 1969.

Mamatey, Victor S. *The United States and East Central Europe, 1914–1918: A Study of Wilsonian Diplomacy and Propaganda.* Princeton, 1957.

Mannock, James W. "Anglo-American Relations, 1921–38." Ph.D. dissertation, Princeton University, 1962.

Marks, Sally. *The Illusion of Peace.* New York, 1976.

Marquand, David. *Ramsay MacDonald.* London, 1977.

Mayer, Arno J. *Politics and Diplomacy of Peacemaking.* New York, 1967.

McCoy, Donald R. *Calvin Coolidge: The Quiet President.* New York, 1967.

McDougall, Walter A. *France's Rhineland Diplomacy, 1914–24: The Last Bid for a Balance of Power in Europe.* Princeton, 1978.

McKenna, Marian C. *Borah.* Ann Arbor, 1961.

McNeil, William C. "American Money and the German Economy: Economics and Politics on the Eve of the Great Depression." Ph.D. dissertation, University of California, Berkeley, 1981.

Meaney, Neville, K. "The American Attitude towards the British Empire, 1919–22: A Study in the Diplomatic Relations of the English-Speaking Nations." Ph.D. dissertation, Duke University, 1958.

Meiburger, Anne Vincent. *Efforts of Raymond Robins toward the Recognition of Soviet Russia and the Outlawry of War, 1917–33.* Washington, 1958.

Meier, Heinze K. *Friendship under Stress: U. S.–Swiss Relations, 1900–1950.* Bern, 1970.

Meyer, Richard Hemmig. *Bankers' Diplomacy: Monetary Stabilization in the Twenties.* New York, 1970.

Miller, David Hunter. *The Drafting of the Covenant.* 2 vols. New York, 1928.

Miller, Francis, and Helen Hill. *The Giant of the Western World.* New York, 1930.

Mock, James R., and Cedric Larson. *Words That Won the War.* Princeton, 1939.

Moggridge, D. E. *British Monetary Policy, 1924–31: The Norman Conquest of $4.86.* Cambridge, 1972.

———. *The Return to Gold, 1925: The Formulation of Economic Policy and Its Critics.* Cambridge, 1969.

Moley, Raymond. *The Hays Office.* New York, 1945.

Monaco, Paul. *Cinema & Society: France and Germany During the Twenties.* New York, 1976.

Moore, James Ray. "A History of the World Economic Conference, London, 1933." Ph.D. dissertation, SUNY at Stony Brook, 1972.

Moreau, Émile. Souvenirs d'un gouverneur de la Banque de France. Paris, 1954.

Morison, Elting E. Turmoil and Tradition. New York, 1966.

Mott, T. Bentley. Myron T. Herrick, Friend of France. Garden City, N. Y., 1930.

Moulton, Harold G. and Leo Pasvolsky. War Debts and World Prosperity. Washington, 1932.

Mowrer, Edgar A. This American World. New York, 1928.

Murray, Robert K. The Harding Era. Minneapolis, 1969.

———. The Politics of Normalcy. New York, 1973.

Myers, William Starr, ed. The State Papers and Other Public Writings of Herbert Hoover 2 vols. New York, 1970.

Nearing, Scott, and Joseph Freeman. Dollar Diplomacy: A Study in American Imperialism. New York, 1926.

Nelson, Keith L. Victors Divided: America and the Allies in Germany, 1918–1923. Berkeley, 1975.

Nevins, Allan, ed. Interpretations 1931–1932 by Walter Lippmann. New York, 1932.

Newton, Christina. "Anglo-American Relations and Bureaucratic Tensions, 1927–1930." Ph.D. dissertation, University of Illinois, 1975.

Nicolson, Harold. Dwight Morrow. New York, 1935.

Nigro, Louis John, Jr. "Propaganda, Politics, and the New Diplomacy: The Impact of Wilsonian Propaganda on Politics and Public Opinion in Italy, 1917–19." Ph.D. dissertation, Vanderbilt University, 1978.

Nouailhat, Yves-Henri. Les Américains à Nantes et Saint-Nazaire, 1917–1919. Paris, 1972.

O'Connor, Raymond G. Perilous Equilibrium: The United States and the London Naval Conference of 1930. Lawrence, Kans., 1962.

Odegard, Peter. The American Public Mind. New York, 1930.

Offner, Arnold. American Appeasement. Cambridge, 1969.

Ogilvie, F. W. The Tourist Movement. London, 1933.

Oren, Nissan, Revolution Administered: Agrarianism and Communism in Bulgaria. Baltimore, 1973.

Parrini, Carl P. Heir to Empire. Pittsburgh, 1969.

Pearson, Drew, and Constantine Brown. The American Diplomatic Game. Garden City, N. Y., 1935.

Pease, Neal. "Poland, the United States, and the Stabilization of Europe, 1924–1933." Ph.D. dissertation, Yale University, 1982.

Pettit, Dorothy Ann. "A Cruel Wind: America Experiences Pandemic Influenza, 1918–1920: A Social History." Ph.D. dissertation, University of New Hampshire, 1976.

Phelps, Clyde. The Foreign Expansion of American Banks. New York, 1927.

Pomaret, Charles. L'Amérique à la conquête de l' Europe. Paris, 1931.

Propas, Frederic Lewis. "The State Department, Bureaucratic Politics and Soviet-American Relations, 1918–1938." Ph.D. dissertation, University of California, Los Angeles, 1982.

Pusey, Merlo J. Charles Evans Hughes. 2 vols. New York, 1951.

Putnam, Samuel. Paris Was Our Mistress. Carbondale, Ill., 1947.

Quint, Howard H., and Robert H. Ferrell, eds. The Talkative President: The Off-the-Record Press Conferences of Calvin Coolidge. Amherst, 1964.

Rasmussen, John Curtis, Jr., "The American Forces in Germany and Civil Affairs, July 1919–January 1923." Ph.D. dissertation, University of Georgia, 1972.

Reiske, Heinz. *Die USA in den Berichten italienischer Reisender.* Meisenheim am Glan, 1971.

Richards, David Allen. "The Abortive Entente: The American Popular Mind and the Idea of Anglo-American Cooperation to Keep the Peace, 1921–1931." Ph.D. dissertation, Florida State University, 1976.

Robinson, Edgar Eugene, and Vaughn Davis Bornet. *Herbert Hoover: President of the United States.* Stanford, 1975.

Rogers, Will. *Letters of a Self-Made Diplomat to His President.* New York, 1926.

Rosen, Elliot A. *Hoover, Roosevelt and the Brains Trust.* New York, 1977.

Rosenbaum, Kurt. *Community of Fate: German-Soviet Diplomatic Relations, 1922–1928.* Syracuse, 1965.

Rosenberg, Emily S. *Spreading the American Dream: American Economic and Cultural Expansion, 1890–1945.* New York, 1982.

Rosentiel, Léonie. *Nadia Boulanger.* New York, 1982.

Roskill, Stephen. *Hankey, Man of Secrets.* London, 1972.

———. *Naval Policy between the Wars: The Period of Anglo-American Antagonism, 1919–29.* New York, 1968.

Rothschild, Joseph. *East Central Europe between the Two World Wars.* Seattle, 1974.

Royal Institute of International Affairs. *The International Gold Problem.* London, 1931.

Rukeyser, Walter A. *Working for the Soviets.* New York, 1932.

Rupieper, Hermann-Josef. *The Cuno Government and Reparations, 1922–23: Politics and Economics.* The Hague, 1979.

———. "Politics and Economics: The Cuno Government and Reparations, 1922–23. Ph.D. dissertation, Stanford University, 1974.

Salapatas, John Spyros. "America's Response to Collective Security, 1929–36." Ph.D. dissertation, University of Wisconsin, 1973.

Salter, Arthur. *Memoirs of a Public Servant.* London, 1961.

———. *Slave of the Lamp: A Public Servant's Notebook.* London, 1967.

Saunders, Donald Bishop. "Stresemann vs. Poincaré: The Conduct of Germany's Western Policy during Stresemann's Chancellorship, August–November 1923." Ph.D. dissertation, University of North Carolina, 1975.

Sayers, R. S. *The Bank of England, 1891–1944* 3 vols. Cambridge, 1976.

Schacht, Hjalmar. *My First Seventy-Six Years.* London, 1955.

Schmidt, Royal J. *Versailles and the Ruhr: Seedbed of World War II.* The Hague, 1968.

Schoenthal, Klaus. "American Attitudes toward Germany, 1918–1932." Ph.D. dissertation, Ohio State University, 1959.

Schrecker, Ellen Wolf. "The French Debt to the United States, 1917–1929." Ph.D. dissertation, Harvard University, 1973.

Schuker, Stephen A. *The End of French Predominance in Europe: The Financial Crisis of 1924 and the Adoption of the Dawes Plan.* Chapel Hill, 1976.

Schulzinger, Robert D. *The Making of the Diplomatic Mind.* Middletown, Conn., 1975.

Schwabe, Klaus. *Deutsche Revolution und Wilson-Frieden.* Düsseldorf, 1971.

Schwarz, Jordon A. *The Interregnum of Despair.* Urbana, 1970.

Scott, John. *Behind the Urals.* Cambridge, 1942.

Serota, Mitchell Ira. "The Effect of the War Debt Question upon French Internal Politics and Diplomacy, 1924–1926." Ph.D. dissertation, University of Chicago, 1976.

Seton-Watson, Hugh. *Eastern Europe Between the Wars, 1918–41.* New York, 1967.

Seymour, Charles. *Letters from the Paris Peace Conference.* ed Harold B. Whitman. New Haven, 1965.

Shaver, Barbara McKay. "American Policy and European Collective Security, 1921–25." Ph.D. dissertation, University of Colorado, 1972.

Shepardson, Whitney H. *Early History of the Council on Foreign Relations.* Stamford, Conn., 1960.

Shi, David E. *Matthew Josephson, Bourgeois Bohemian.* New Haven, 1981.

Shoup, Laurence H., and William Minter. *Imperial Brain Trust.* New York, 1977.

Shuman, James E., and David Rosenau. *The Kondratieff Wave.* New York, 1972.

Siddique, Abdul Khair. "The International Monetary and Economic Conferences of the Inter-war Period." Ph.D dissertation, Yale University, 1970.

Siegfried, André, *America Comes of Age.* New York, 1927.

Silverman, Dan P. *Reconstructing Europe after the Great War.* Cambridge, Mass., 1982.

Simpson, Amos E. *Hjalmar Schact in Perspective.* The Hague, 1969.

Singer, David Glen. "The United States Confronts the Soviet Union, 1919–33: The Rise and Fall of the Policy of Nonrecognition." Ph.D. dissertation, Loyola University, 1973.

Skidelsky, Robert. *Politicians and the Slump.* London, 1967.

Sklar, Robert. *Movie-Made America: A Cultural History of American Movies.* New York, 1972.

Sloan, Alfred P. *My Years with General Motors* (New York, 1964).

Smiley, Ralph. "The Lausanne Conference of 1932: The Diplomacy of the End of Reparations." Ph.D. dissertation, Rutgers University, 1971.

Smith, Daniel M. *Aftermath of War.* Philadelphia, 1970.

Smith, William Thomas. "The Kuzbas Colony in Soviet Russia, 1921–1926." Ph.D. dissertation, University of Miami, 1977.

Sorenson, Charles E. *My Forty Years with Ford.* New York, 1956.

Southard, Frank A., Jr. *American Industry in Europe.* Boston, 1931.

Spector, Sherman David. *Rumania at the Paris Peace Conference.* New York, 1962.

Springer, Anne Marie. "The American Novelists between the Two World Wars." Ph.D. dissertation, University of Pennsylvania, 1959.

Sprout, Harold, and Margaret Sprout. *Toward a New Order of Sea Power.* Princeton, 1946.

Stimson, Henry L., and McGeorge Bundy. *On Active Service in Peace and War.* New York, 1948.

Stivers, William. *Supremacy and Oil: Iraq, Turkey, and the Anglo-American World Order, 1918–1930.* Ithaca, 1982.

Stock, Noel. *The Life of Ezra Pound.* New York, 1970.

Stone, Ralph A. *The Irreconcilables.* New York, 1970.

Strausburgh, Melvin Roy. "Great Britain and the Diplomacy of Reparation: 1919–21." Ph.D. dissertation, Case Western Reserve, 1974.

Strauss, David. *Menace in the West: The Rise of French Anti-Americanism in Modern Times.* Westport, Conn., 1978.

Striner, Richard Alan, "The Machine as Symbol: 1920–1939." Ph.D. dissertation, University of Maryland, 1982.

Strong, Anna Louise. *I Change Worlds*. Garden City, N.Y., 1937.

Sullivan, Mark. *The Great Adventure at Washington*. New York, 1922.

Sullivan, Michael J. "Franco-American Relations in the Financial Crisis of 1931." M.A. thesis, Drake University, 1975.

Surface, Frank M., and Raymond L. Bland. *American Food in the World War and Reconstruction Period*. Stanford, 1931.

Susman, Warren Irving. "Pilgrimage to Paris: The Backgrounds of American Expatriation, 1920–1934." Ph.D. dissertation, University of Wisconsin, 1957.

Sutton, Anthony C. *Western Technology and Soviet Economic Development, 1917–1930*. Stanford, 1968.

Svennilson, Ingvar. *Growth and Stagnation in the European Economy*. Geneva, 1954.

Tarbell, Ida, *Owen D. Young*. New York, 1932.

Tardieu, André. *Devant l'obstacle*. Paris, 1927.

Temin, Peter. *Did Monetary Forces Cause the Great Depression?* New York, 1976.

Thompson, Dorothy. *The New Russia*. New York, 1928.

Thompson, John M. *Russia, Bolshevism, and the Versailles Peace*. Princeton, 1966.

Timmins, Bascom N. *Portrait of an American: Charles G. Dawes*. New York, 1953.

Tokes, Rudolf L. *Bela Kun and the Hungarian Soviet Republic*. New York, 1967.

Tolzmann, Rainer Hanns. "Objective Architecture. American Influences in the Development of Modern German Architecture." Ph.D. dissertation, University of Michigan, 1975.

Tomkins, Calvin. *Living Well Is the Best Revenge*. New York, 1971.

Trachtenburg, Marc. *Reparation in World Politics: France and European Economic Diplomacy, 1916–1923*. New York, 1980.

Traynor, Dean E. *International Monetary and Financial Conferences in the Interwar Period*. Washington, 1949.

Trice, Cicil W. "America and Weimar Culture, 1919–1933." Ph.D. dissertation, University of Oklahoma, 1979.

Trimble, William Foster. "The United States Navy and the Geneva Conference for the Limitation of Naval Armament, 1927." Ph.D. dissertation, University of Colorado, 1974.

Tucker, Robert C. *Stalin as Revolutionary, 1879–1929*. New York, 1973.

Turner, Henry A., Jr. *Stresemann and the Politics of the Weimar Republic*. Princeton, 1963.

Uldricks, Teddy J. *Diplomacy and Ideology: The Origins of Soviet Foreign Relations, 1918–1930*. London, 1979.

U.S. Department of Commerce, Bureau of Foreign and Domestic Commerce, *The United Kingdom. An Industrial, Commercial and Financial Handbook*, Trade Promotion ser. no. 94. Washington, 1930.

Van Meter, Robert. "The United States and European Recovery, 1918–1923: A Study of Public Policy and Private Finance." Ph.D. dissertation, University of Wisconsin, 1971.

Van Petten, Donald R. "The European Technical Advisor and Post-war Austria 1919–1923." Ph.D. dissertation, Stanford University, 1943.

Vinson, John Chalmers. *The Parchment Peace*. Athens, Ohio, 1955.

——. *William E. Borah and the Outlawry of War*. Athens, Ohio, 1957.

Walters, F. P. *A History of the League of Nations*. London, 1952.

Walworth, Arthur C. *America's Moment, 1918: American Diplomacy at the End of World War I*. New York, 1977.

Wandel, Eckhard. *Die Bedeutung der Vereinigten Staaten von Amerika für das deutsche Reparationsproblem*. Tübingen, 1971.

Wandycz, Piotr S. *The United States and Poland*. Cambridge, 1980.

Weissman, Benjamin M. *Herbert Hoover and Famine Relief to Soviet Russia: 1921–23*. Stanford, 1974.

Wheeler, Gerald E. *Prelude to Pearl Harbor*. Columbia, 1963.

White, Elizabeth Brett. *American Opinion of France*. New York, 1927.

White, William Allen. *A Puritan in Babylon*. New York, 1938.

Wicker, Elmus. *Federal Reserve Monetary Policy, 1917–33*. New York, 1966.

Wilkins, Mira. *The Maturing of Multinational Enterprise: American Business Abroad from 1914 to 1970*. Cambridge, 1974.

Wilkins, Mira, and Frank Ernest Hill. *American Business Abroad: Ford on Six Continents*. Detroit, 1964.

Willett, John. *Art and Politics in the Weimar Period*. New York, 1978.

Williams, Robert C. *Russian Art and American Money, 1900–1940*. Cambridge, 1980.

Williams, William Appleman. *American-Russian Relations, 1781–1947*. New York, 1952.

Wilson, Edith Bolling. *My Memoir*. New York, 1938.

Wilson, Hugh. *Diplomat Between Wars*. New York, 1941.

Wilson, Joan Hoff. *American Business and Foreign Policy, 1920–1933*. Lexington, Ky., 1971.

——. *Herbert Hoover, Forgotten Progressive*. Boston, 1975.

——. *Ideology and Economics: U.S. Relations with the Soviet Union, 1918–1933*. Columbia, Mo., 1974.

Wolfe, Martin. *The French Franc between the Wars*. New York, 1951.

Wolff, Geoffrey. *Black Sun: The Brief Transit and Violent Eclipse of Harry Crosby*. New York, 1976.

Woodard, Eugene. "Postwar Reconstruction and International Order: A Study of the Diplomacy of Charles Evans Hughes, 1921–25." Ph.D. dissertation, University of Wisconsin, 1970.

Woon, Basil. *The Paris That's Not in the Guide Books*. New York, 1926.

Young, Arthur P. *Books for Sammies*. Pittsburgh, 1981.

Young, John Parke, ed. *European Currency and Finance*. Washington, 1925.

Zammito, John Henry, "Art and Action in the Metropolis: The Berlin Avant-Garde, 1900–1930." Ph.D. dissertation, University of California at Berkeley, 1978.

Zilg, Gerard Colby. *Du Pont behind the Nylon Curtain*. Englewood Cliffs, N.J., 1974.

Zivojinovic, Dragan R. *America, Italy, and the Birth of Yugoslavia*. Boulder, 1972.

Index

373

Library of Congress Cataloging in Publication Data

Costigliola, Frank, 1946-
  Awkward dominion

  Bibliography: p.
  Includes index.
  1. Europe—Relations—United States. 2. United States—Relations—Europe.
3. United States—Foreign relations—20th century. 4. Europe—Civilization—
American influences. I. Title.
D1065.U5C58 1984   303.4'8273'04   84-45150
ISBN 0-8014-1679-5

381

DATE DUE

DEMCO 38-297